Called To and From

A Personal Reflection on Life and Leadership in the Mainline American Church at the End of the Twentieth Century

RICHARD L. HAMM

A Project of the Disciples of Christ Historical Society

Copyright © 2025 by Richard L. Hamm

All rights reserved. For permission to reuse content, please contact the Disciples of Christ Historical Society.

Cover Image: © Shutterstock
Cover and interior design: Connie H. C. Wang

Print: 9780827207561
EPUB: 9780827207578
EPDF: 9780827207585

Printed in the United States of America

Table of Contents

Foreword — v

Part I: Where I Came From — 1

Chapter 1: My Own Beginnings — 2

Chapter 2: "I Got to Kansas City on a Friday ... by Saturday I'd Larned a Thing or Two" — 37

Chapter 3: Off to the City of Three Rivers — 51

Chapter 4: The Three States of Tennessee — 64

PART II: The Office of General Minister and President — 79

Chapter 5: A Gathering Storm — 80

Chapter 6: Getting Started — 92

Chapter 7: Challenges and Initiatives — 113

Chapter 8: Controversies and Catastrophes — 175

Chapter 9: Ecumenical and Interfaith Engagements — 186

Chapter 10: My Resignation and Life after GMP — 201

Chapter 11: What I Have Learned — 214

Epilogue — 251

Appendix 1: Formal and Informal Power and Authority — 258

Appendix 2: Some Pertinent Statements and Addresses — 262

Foreword

I am writing this narrative, in part, because the Disciples of Christ Historical Society has demonstrated a desire to understand and record the experiences of former general ministers and presidents, our personal formation, theological convictions, and leadership goals and strategies seen through the lens of our personal reflections. I am writing also because I think it is important for current and future leaders to know what happened before their tenure, both to help them avoid mindlessly or inadvertently repeating history and to help them better understand the ongoing interplay of the church with American culture as a whole. Of course, I also hope there were some seeds planted during my years of leadership that can be appreciated, will yet bear some fruit, and can be further nurtured to that end.

In 1993, I was the first baby boomer to be elected as head of a mainline church. As an early boomer (born in 1947), I thought the decade of the 1990s was going to be the start of a new era for the mainline churches, as a new generation took leadership. But it gradually dawned on me over the course of the next ten years that it was not so much the start of a *new* era as it was the end of an *old* era.

The speed of cultural and technological change had already quickened in the 1950s, and the powerful vision for the world generated by the builder generation (born between 1915 and 1930)—which was largely assumed and further fostered by the silent generation (born between 1930 and 1945)—was already beginning to unravel in the 1960s. That unraveling picked up velocity in the 1970s, 1980s, and 1990s and was reflected in the church as well as in other social institutions and practices. That unraveling continues to this day in the church.

Some speak of this as a time of cultural deconstruction or devolution. Others (most notably Episcopal Bishop Mark Dyer and author Phyllis Tickle) have described it as a church "rummage sale" that happens about every five hundred years. Things that seemed important and even sacrosanct a few decades ago, now (in the early twenty-first century) seem unimportant and even burdensome and are being jettisoned in favor of newly emerging ideas and approaches.

Of course, the world doesn't change from one era to another overnight. I am reminded of when my family moved from Crawfordsville, Indiana, to St. Petersburg, Florida, in 1957. Being nine years old and not having been to Florida before, I thought when one reached the Florida state line, it was palm trees from there all the way down to Key West. What I discovered, of course, is that northern Florida looks very much like southern Georgia, and one must drive quite a way south after crossing the state line before seeing significant numbers of naturally occurring palm trees. The palm tree population gradually increases as the yellow pine trees and southern live oaks gradually diminish, though never disappearing altogether. We still have vestiges of the builder and silent generations' world in our midst (even though most of the people of those generations are already gone), but those vestiges are rapidly diminishing as the new postmodern era continues to emerge and mature. Each generation of church leaders must understand its own cultural context and whence it came.

As an American white baby boomer (the generation born between 1945 and 1965),[1] I must ask myself, "What was the boomer vision for the world?" In our early years, white baby boomers' vision was pretty much identical to that of the builders and silents. It was "the American Century," and we believed the United States *should* rule and that our nationalism was benign and "good for the whole world." We had been carefully taught in school and by the American news media that capitalism was good and communism was bad, *period*, with few shades or nuances.[2]

But the quagmire in Vietnam and the Civil Rights Movement, both televised daily in the 1960s, caused many of us to begin doubting our nation's definitions of righteousness and justice. Watching the events in places like Selma, Montgomery, and Birmingham, and the "body counts" in Vietnam served up nightly on the three major

---

[1] African American baby boomers shared many of the same cultural experiences and perspectives of white baby boomers, though there were, of course, significant differences because of the differing historical and economic circumstances between the two groups. I can speak only for my own white boomer experience.

[2] This was the clear message of the class, "Americanism v. Communism," which I was required to take in my Florida high school in the eleventh grade (1964–1965).

networks, made us wonder who we really were as Americans. A deep cynicism set in, first seen publicly on college campuses and in popular culture including music, the arts, and drama. This cynicism eventually led most white boomers away from a positive world view that we thought should be nurtured and fostered by the United States, to a kind of individualism that ultimately began to see the world through an often very selfish and self-serving lens. Thomas Wolfe began referring to us boomers as "the *me* generation." As I like to say it, "We white boomers went from wanting to save the world to wanting to buy a McMansion."

This atmosphere of cynical narcissism affected the generations of Americans following the boomers as well. We still see this selfish individualism playing out in the politics and economics of current times. The sad fact is that we white boomers had no new global vision to offer the world. We liked to *think* of ourselves as revolutionaries, in part because we saw through some of our national hypocrisy and in part because we distrusted institutions of all kinds as they had nurtured the lie of American exceptionalism. But most of us went from being fans of Superman's fight for "truth, justice, and the American Way" to deep disillusionment.

Of course, no one perspective can define a whole generation. Some of us didn't "get the memo" in the late 1960s that read, "It's time to leave the church now and become your own spiritual guide." There were many—me included, on my best days—who continued to want to make the whole world a better place for everyone. This was true of most of us boomers who were still in the church and trying to give positive leadership to the world, not because we believed in the American Empire but because we thought we were called by God to a greater vision of a world of justice and righteousness, whether the United States fostered it or not. Many of us caught this vision from our seminary educations as we experienced a critique of American culture and the church by our builder and silent generation professors, and other more mature (than us) Christian spirits, who had examined post-World War II American nationalism and found it wanting, while pointing toward a more genuinely Christian vision for the world.

I suppose this narrative *could* be read as a self-defense against charges that the baby boomer church leaders of the 1990s and early

2000s "blew it," that if we (and myself, in particular) had been more effective, the church would not have suffered the losses it suffered and continues to suffer in the 2020s. I will admit that my ten years as general minister and president (GMP) of the Christian Church (Disciples of Christ) shook my self-confidence often, and I have had plenty of days and, especially, nights (when my personal demons most often visit) when I have questioned my own calling, my own abilities, my own diagnoses, and most everything else.

But the plain fact is that the period of institutional decline—measured most often by numbers of participants, dollars for mission, and loss of cultural and political influence—that has swept over all mainline churches (and increasingly *all* churches, whether mainline or not) began in the 1960s and was going to increase no matter who the leaders were! The cultural forces at play in the late twentieth and early twenty-first century *guaranteed* institutional decline not only in the church but in nearly all social institutions (and set the nation up for the narcissistic and sociopathic appeals to authoritarianism we have been seeing in recent years).

Frankly, I think I had a better-than-average grasp of the cultural forces that were at work during my time of leadership and the changes in institutional life they demanded. But, like most leaders, I did not fully appreciate the degree of resistance to such needed institutional change that would be mounted from *within* the church. Some of that resistance came from people who were themselves excellent leaders who were doing the best they knew how in a rapidly changing context. Looking back, I can see many things I wish I had done differently or could have done differently, of course. But I do not feel much need to be defensive. I did the best I knew how to do, sought to do what I discerned I was called to do, and listened to and weighed every word of advice given to me. That's the best anyone can do.

So, this narrative is not intended to defend my leadership, or even to make me look better than I was (although any autobiographical account is bound to be at least somewhat self-serving). I own the good and the bad, the beautiful and the ugly, and I am mostly at peace. That said, I am writing because I think it is important for church leaders today to understand what happened and what I and other church leaders were trying to do during those ten years of 1993 to 2003, years of ferment and foment.

There were so many people—lay and clergy; congregational, regional, and general; denominational and ecumenical—who accompanied me on this journey and who gave their all to make things work, to make things better, to make me smarter and more faithful, to ensure the best possible result. I will forever be grateful to them. Some of them will be named here, most of them will not, because that is not the purpose of this narrative. But my gratitude to them and for them will never diminish.

I am also exceedingly grateful to friends and family who read my early manuscript and offered suggestions and corrections. These folks included Lori Adams, Ron Allen, Lois Artis, Chuck Blaisdell, David Hamm, Mindy Hamm, John Imbler, Belva Brown Jordan, John Mobley, Dan Moseley, Gary Straub, and Sharon Watkins.

How to Read This Book

There are two parts here: first, my life before becoming general minister and president, and second, my time as GMP, including reflections on what I learned. If you are not interested in the first part, I won't be offended: Skip it. However, I think everyone can learn from personal stories. Reading biographies is one of my favorite ways both to learn history and to learn about how people are shaped by their life experiences. If you are primarily or only interested in church history, the second part is for you. If you are looking for things to be learned about leadership of a mainline church during 1993–2003, you may want to skip to the last chapter. Feel free to read all, or part, as best suits your needs and interests.

If you are not familiar with the Christian Church (Disciples of Christ) in the United States and Canada, we are a mainline Protestant denomination that came out of the Presbyterian Church in the early nineteenth century. We are congregationally governed and speak of three "expressions" of church: congregational, regional, and general. Regions are our "middle judicatories," which other traditions might call conferences, synods, or dioceses. Some regions cover one state, some are less than one, and some more than one. We use "general church" instead of "national church" to describe the denomination as a whole because there are two nations involved (the United States and Canada). Due to early missionary efforts, there are also Disciples of Christ churches in other parts of the world (including China, Congo, India, Mexico, and Puerto Rico, among others). But those are free-standing communions, such as Iglesia Cristiana (Discipulos de Cristo) en Puerto Rico, or have become part of larger multidenominational bodies, such as the Church of South India.

—Dick Hamm
Indianapolis, 2025

Part I

Where I Came From

Chapter 1

My Own Beginnings

I was born in Crawfordsville, Indiana, in 1947 (an early baby boomer) to a sign painter and his wife. We lived on a one-acre lot in a neighborhood near Washington Street on the county side of South Boulevard. Our yard backed up against a farmer's field and over the farmer's fence was a world of nature to explore. Our white frame house was quite small, so there was room for a small orchard, a garden, a small garage, and my father's sign shop. Dad built a big sandbox for me (which later inspired me to build an indoor slide for our daughter). At night, I sometimes sat on the back stoop with my dad, gazing at the myriad of stars visible in those days before so much light pollution, and watching the horizon for the regular sweep of the rotating beacon of little Crawfordsville Airport some five miles to the southwest of us. (Some twenty years later I would joyously land my own plane there for a brief visit to the place where my father had arranged for my first airplane ride at the age of six.)

An aunt to whom I was very close once told me that as a baby I always woke up smiling. For as long as I can remember, I have awakened nearly every morning eager to meet the adventures of the day. While, like everyone, I have those down days and periods, I have mostly experienced great joy in living. My personality is marked by a strong sense of humor (occasionally inappropriate, but seldom mean-spirited). I regard humor as an important lens through which to understand the world.

My mother was born and raised on a farm near Hillsboro, just twenty miles from Crawfordsville, one of nine siblings. College was never a possibility for her, but she was a very bright woman with deep faith and great business sense. My father was a sign painter, a term that hardly describes what an excellent craftsman he was and that describes a trade that hardly exists today, as hand lettering has been almost entirely replaced by computers and vinyl cutters. After he returned from World War II service in the Army, he set up a sign shop in a war-surplus "Quonset hut" next door to the west of our house. Later, he moved to a larger building, just a few blocks away. To this day, I sometimes stop by a sign shop (of which there are fewer and fewer), stick my head in the door, and take a deep breath through my nose which fills with the unmistakable smell of lacquer thinner, found in every *real* sign shop, and I feel at home and sense my father's presence.

Dad worked a lot. Being the craftsman he was, his signs were in great demand; and having been a Depression-era child, he never quite felt financially secure. He wasn't much of a businessman, always undervaluing his work, but Mom compensated for that by managing well the money he earned. Like him, she was a child of the Great Depression, and an old family story suggests the money she managed was *literally* "cold" cash, since she always kept a roll of bills in a butter box in the fridge for emergencies. We didn't have a lot of money, but we always had enough, so far as I knew. Dad had an extremely tough childhood, often living on his own during his high school years. He was tender-hearted and if someone wanted to delay payment for services, he was likely to give his work away. So, mom handled the billing and collections, and things went better for it.

My older brother Charles and I were the only children in the neighborhood. But we had what must have been the best neighbors any kid could hope for, as they treated us with kindness, and we loved and respected them.

Bud and Hazel Layman, next door to the east, ran a poultry market right next to their house. I learned how to feed, round up, and "dress" chickens by the age of seven. My favorite Christmas gift ever was a chicken hook given to me by my Uncle Sam to use when I accompanied Bud on trips in his old Ford truck to pick up chickens he bought from local farmers. The first thing I "hooked" was the Laymans' old tom cat, so Bud kept the hook in his market to be retrieved when needed to hook actual chickens. I learned a lot about chickens!

Beyond the poultry market was a motorcycle shop where Red and Helen Cheney sold Triumph and Indian motorcycles. They had an extensive repair shop and a small test track. Red called Chuck

"Murphy" and called me "Little Murph" (we have no idea where those names came from). They, too, welcomed my brother and me into their place of business. Some days I would hook up our old garden tractor with its little trailer seat and drive it down to the motorcycle shop and go around and around the small oval test track they had for testing newly repaired motorcycles. That tractor moved about three miles per hour, so I wasn't setting any speed records, but it seemed a great pace for a six-year-old. This was 1953, and Power Wheels had not yet been developed.

To the west, there were the Hawthorns, also good neighbors, and beyond them "Shorty" Townsend's Shell station. Around the corner from Shorty's was a Dairy Queen. They sometimes let me pick up the trash on the driveway for ten cents, which I would instantly convert into a Dilly Bar!

Accompanying Bud to the city dump one day, I found some chicken hatchlings that had been discarded (born at the wrong time for some farmer, I guess). I rescued four of them, placing them in a shoe box. Two lived. Bud and Mr. Hawthorn, who raised a few chickens himself, regularly gave me cracked corn to feed those two birds. The two "survivors" soon grew to full size, but I found chickens to be poor pets. They don't come when you call them and they don't like to be petted. Bud, being a poultry man, one day jokingly offered me fifty cents apiece for them. In my mind, that immediately translated into two Dairy Queen Banana Splits! "Sold!" To this day, I must steer away from Dairy Queens lest I overindulge.

The adults in my life all seemed to have endless patience with my constant questions, assertions, and energy.

We attended First Christian Church (Disciples of Christ), a wonderful congregation it seemed to me, that thrives to this day. Some of my earliest memories revolve around First Christian. The adults there treated my brother Chuck and me with kindness. The sanctuary was (and still is) a classic space, with beautiful wooden beams and flourishes that extend high up into the ceiling and lovely stained glass. Our pastor, Rev. George Million, was a kind and authoritative leader whom I remember admiring as a small child, a grandfatherly image of God for me. The late 1940s and early 1950s were times of great optimism, as postwar prosperity was growing, and the church seemed always full. I fondly remember sitting in the pew with my family, Dad's bass voice resounding as we sang hymns.

One of my earliest memories of church was in the fellowship hall, where members gathered for fellowship dinners that always featured lots of homemade pies (still a weakness of mine—one of my early theological convictions was, "Any pie is better than any cake!"). It was a warm congregation that welcomed impetuous young boys who felt like they owned the place. I can't honestly say that I remember any sermon ever preached there, but the church felt like home as surely as did our small, one-story, white frame house.

Mom and Dad purchased an old shack just outside of town on Sugar Creek (a small river that runs along the northern edge of Crawfordsville). But after a couple of years, they were able to buy a somewhat *better* shack (a "cabin") just up the hill, with a deck that extended out toward the river, some thirty feet below. My brother and I enjoyed many happy hours along and on Sugar Creek, spending a week or two at the cabin every summer. Mom was less excited about it: no running water, the "bathroom" some seventy-five feet up a hillside path. But it did have electricity and an attached "spring house" in which spring water was directed through a low cooling box that kept watermelon, Cokes, beer, and anything else at a cool fifty-six degrees. There were bunk beds in one room and a double bed in the other. My brother and I came to know every bit of the woods, ravines, and creek for a half mile or so in each direction. One of my most pleasant memories of my father is when he would occasionally decide to spend a night out at the creek and would take me along. We'd stop at a small grocery store on the way to buy Ritz Crackers (for me) and a six-pack (for him). Ritz Crackers still remind me of my father (like the aroma of lacquer thinner).

Dad built a small pram (boat), which Chuck and I greatly enjoyed rowing up and down the river. But when Sugar Creek floods, it can rise more than twenty feet and widen to several hundred feet. The pram got washed away and we found it down river several hundred yards, smashed. The hills on our side of Sugar Creek rose about seventy-five feet above the water, and we made trails all along the hillsides through the trees, brush, and ravines. If you have visited Turkey Run State Park, about thirty miles downriver, you know exactly what this looked like. In the 1980s, a representative of the University of Illinois convinced my parents (then living in Florida) to give access to the ground for geological digs, as the area turned out to be one of the premier sites in the world for trilobite and crinoid fossils.[1] As children, my brother and I found crinoids scattered everywhere in the clay, but we didn't know what we were looking at, thinking they were some sort of art left behind by Native Americans who had lived there (we called them Indian beads).

Mom's family, the Janeways, often gathered for family reunions and other occasions on the old family farm near Hillsboro. How I enjoyed that extended family of aunts, uncles, and cousins! Characters to a person, they were the source of much fun and encouragement over the years. My Dad's sister and her husband, Thelma and George Douglas, and their son Bobby also lived in Crawfordsville, so we often spent time with them as well. It was the kind of extended family matrix that would bless any child and that today is missing for many in our highly mobile society.

A Move to Florida

A big upheaval came in 1957, when I was nine years old. Dad had been taken seriously ill with pneumonia in the Army during World War II and since then had never seemed to be able to get warm and stay warm enough in the cold months of Indiana winters, especially when he was working outdoors on signs using ladders, as he often did. So, in the summer between my third and fourth grade school years, Dad moved us to St. Petersburg, Florida. It was hard to say good-bye to our neighbors and to friends at school and church (it was especially hard for Mom). But I soon discovered there were other kids my age in our new neighborhood in St. Pete! In no time I had been drawn into neighborhood games of ball, adventures in nearby acres of jungle where no houses had yet been built, and there were beautiful beaches just fifteen minutes away! Dad bought an old wooden boat that was heavy and slow but seaworthy and better than nothing. My brother, already in high school, soon taught me how to water ski.

The rural elementary school I had attended outside Crawfordsville (Mt. Zion) was relatively small, but my new school, Pasadena Elementary, was larger and I met a host of kids as soon as school started. Many of my new friends were well-to-do and lived on or near the beaches, but others were working class like me and lived a couple of miles inland. I liked nearly all of them (as seems to be my

---

[1] Trilobites and crinoids were sea animals that first appeared over 500 million years ago.

nature) and reveled in having so many friends (or at least people I thought of as friends, whether they thought of me as a friend or not)! I didn't see much difference between the well-to-do and the rest of us, although I began to recognize and experience socio-economic differences and barriers in high school.

During our first few weeks in St. Petersburg, my brother and I rode the city bus to a municipal swimming pool downtown (The Spa). After a couple of trips with my brother, I was able to ride the city bus by myself. On my first solo trip, I got on the bus and immediately went all the way to the back seats. I had always sat in the back seats of our county school bus in Indiana because when the bus went over ruts in the road, those of us in the back would be thrown up in the air a few inches. So, naturally, as a nine-year-old, I headed for the back seats.

But the bus driver yelled at me, "You'll have to move forward!"

I asked, "Why?"

He replied, "Read the sign!"

That's when I spotted the sign over the back seats that read, "Rear portions of bus reserved for colored." I asked the driver, "How come *they* get all the good seats?"

Clearly, I was "not from here." There were very few Black people living in Crawfordsville in those days, and those who did live there seemed simply to be regarded as "people." I had no idea what Jim Crow was about ... but I learned quickly. I began to notice that all the Black people lived in certain parts of town (which I seldom saw or had reason to enter) and that none of them attended my new school or were in my neighborhood. Public places had separate restrooms and water fountains for "White" and "Colored." It was the beginning of a different kind of education and, I'm afraid, acculturation that took me decades with which to reckon.

St. Petersburg was (and is) a combination of Old South and, beginning in the 1920s, a warm weather mecca for Northerners. The population was roughly half true Southerners (including many African Americans) and half people who had migrated from elsewhere (about seventy percent from the Midwest, twenty-five percent from the Eastern Seaboard, and five percent from Canada or elsewhere). But both city and state politics were dominated by White Southerners. Living in my new home was a cross-cultural experience. I learned how to speak with a Southern Drawl and learned to love what both Black and White Southerners love about the South, while unconsciously also learning about "White supremacy," so-called "Christian nationalism," and hatred for "the Eastern Establishment."

We had joined Mirror Lake Christian Church in downtown St. Pete as soon as we got to town. I was baptized there by the Rev. Wayne Drash. But after just a year of our participation there, the Mirror Lake congregation decided to start a new church four miles west of downtown, not far from our neighborhood. Our family became charter members of the new congregation, which soon came to be known as Palm Lake Christian Church. We started holding worship on a ten-acre plot in an old poultry house (well-scrubbed!) where a farmer had been raising chickens. We became known among Florida Disciples as "the chicken coop church!" But the church grew rapidly under the leadership of Pastor Ken Dean, and soon the first church buildings (a fellowship hall and an educational wing) came up from the ground.

Palm Lake was (and still is) a wonderful congregation of adults who cared greatly about the children and youth who were there. They, including Rev. Dean, encouraged us young people constantly. I immediately felt drawn toward this new "extended family." We attended every Sunday (as many people did in those days), and I was nearly always glad to be there anytime the doors opened.

During our first year in Florida, my cousin Ellen came to live with us for several months while her older brother Tom received some treatment for congenital issues. I wasn't used to having a child younger than me in the house, and it took me a bit to get used to it. She was two and I was nine, but before long I was thinking of her as my younger sister. After she left for home in Illinois, it was years before I saw much of her, but in later years we became close and still enjoy a great friendship. I also feel close to her brother Tom, who lives in Springfield, Illinois. In fact, I remain connected to several of my Janeway cousins (including Nancy, Mary, Phil, Sharon, and Tim).

As I said, my father had a rather traumatic childhood. When he was just twelve years old, his mother was killed in a traffic accident (she got off a bus in their small town and was hit by a car while crossing the street). His father was ill-equipped to raise a child, so my father moved about during his teen years finding jobs in places in and around the Crawfordsville area, where he could also live. Knowing how he had been treated by his father, it was difficult for me to appreciate my Grandfather Hamm very much. But those experiences seemed to make my father determined that his own kids would have better lives. I think such experiences among the builder generation were more common than most of us born after World War II realize.

During the war, being older than most recruits, Dad was made a basic training instructor. He did not have to go overseas, but at one point he received word that one of the platoons he had trained had been killed while crossing a booby-trapped bridge. He took that very personally because he had taught them how to avoid such traps. I believe it was these kinds of experiences (his mother dying, his father not knowing what to do with him, and the tragedy of war) that led him to drink too much. By the time I was in junior high and my brother was overseas in the Air Force, Dad was coming home from work drunk most nights.

I saw first-hand what alcohol can do to a family, as well as to the person drinking. It was ugly. As a young teen, I didn't know what to make of it. But I was becoming what would eventually be described as an adult child of an alcoholic (ACOA). I loved my dad, and I never really doubted his love for me, but I saw the terrible impact his alcoholism had on my mother. While he continued painting signs on the side, the main family business became Hamm's Art and Sign Supply store, which he and Mother started in 1959. Mom's good management and sales skills and Dad's sign painting kept us financially safe, but it was not a very happy home. I was afraid to invite any kids over, or to have a party for friends, for fear of what they might see.

Dad was never violent, as there was no violence in him, thank goodness. He simply staggered in and went to bed and passed out. So, I tried to be with him whenever possible *before* afternoons. Mom worked all day in the store and came home to cook. All the while, she stayed active in the church and saw that my brother and I had what we needed. Dad was really a great guy in so many ways, naturally hilarious,[2] someone people (including me) wanted to be with. But

---

[2] Dad had a way of saying words in funny ways. Instead of "boy scout knife" he would say "boeing scout kah-nife". This always cracked me up. But then in seventh grade geography class I was asked to read aloud a story from our textbook about the Hindenburg explosion. I stood up and read as follows, "The Hindenburg explosion was the greatest cat-ass-trophy of the decade." Mr. Joiner, my teacher, looked at me and asked, "What did you say?" I repeated it. Fortunately, he accepted the explanation that "cat-ass-trophy" was the only way I had heard the word pronounced (which wasn't quite true, but I had certainly heard it most often with Dad's pronunciation).

somehow, he couldn't own his own worth. I think he was never able to overcome his father's apparent rejection. He continued going to church on Sunday mornings and he tried from time to time to give up drinking, but he never succeeded for more than a few weeks. He was in his late seventies before he was finally able to give it up.

Frankly, I hate to describe my father's alcoholism in print. In so many ways he was such a wonderful man, father, and grandfather, and I remain grateful to be his son. He taught me a kind of compassion that has blessed my life as a person and as a minister. Nonetheless, his addiction had a huge impact on the shaping of my own personality and my emotional and spiritual life, and to omit this reality from my personal story would simply be denial and dishonesty.

Upon our arrival in St. Pete, Jim Pfeiffer, who lived just a block away, quickly became my best friend. He encouraged me to get involved in Little League baseball. Jim was a pitcher, and being big for my age, and broad shouldered, I became a catcher. When opposing players would try to steal second base, I had a propensity for "pegging" center field! But I could catch pitches and pop-ups and I could hit and run, so I got to play regularly.

St. Petersburg was the spring training quarters for both the Yankees and the Cardinals. So, every spring our Little League coach would take us to see the great players of the day on those two teams and the teams they played in the "Grapefruit League." Among them were Mickey Mantle, Roger Maris, Yogi Berra, Elston Howard, Willie Mays, Hank Aaron, Ted Williams, Stan Musial, Whitey Ford ... on and on the list goes. I continued to play baseball until I was fourteen when, in a Pony League game, while at bat, I saw a fast high inside curve coming toward me. I stepped back and stepped back some more, but it hit me in the head and knocked me out, breaking my helmet. (Some people say this incident explains a lot!) It was difficult to stay in the batter's box after that, and I was beginning to be more interested in basketball anyway, so I quit baseball. But I still enjoy watching the "national pastime" and I have played on many a church softball team over the years.

Disston Junior High School was ... well, junior high school. Everyone was struggling to figure out who they were, and I was no exception. Though my grades were mostly okay, it was a difficult three years for me *except* for the basketball program. The young coach, Robert Thomas, was a wonderfully patient man who taught all of us on the team so much. In my freshman year, I did well, which gave me a new sense of value. It was a time in my life when I needed affirmation, and basketball provided it (along with church). However, I also got a lesson in humility. In the first game of our season, playing forward, I scored two baskets in a row with jump-shots from the corner. It was the first time I had heard cheerleaders yelling my name (and initially, some of them had to ask if anybody knew what my name was). It was so exciting that I lost my head and tried the same shot several more times, missing every one, so that the same cheerleaders began yelling, "Don't shoot!" That burned a lesson into my brain about "hotdogging!" Junior high is a challenging time for everyone, as we each begin to discover who we are, try on different personas, and experience rejection as well as the occasional triumph.

One October day in ninth grade (1962), the Cuban missile crisis came to a head. MacDill Air Force Base in Tampa was a Strategic Air Command (SAC) base and just eight miles from my house and from Disston Junior High School. We knew there were Soviet ballistic missiles with our name on them. The Cold War was such an ever-present reality in those days that we had to live in denial of the risk. But on that day in October, I remember getting a hall pass from Spanish class and going to the restroom. Looking out the window to the east toward MacDill, I wondered out loud if there would be a home to go to that afternoon. Thank God there were no miscalculations. As if *normal* fourteen-year-old anxieties weren't enough!

High school, however, was mostly great for me (though I realize not everyone feels that way about their high school experience). Boca Ciega was a large high school, with more than five hundred kids in my class, and I wanted to know every one of them. I played left tackle on the football team for a season but, after a particularly jarring hit from an opposing player who had a cast on his forearm, I decided that being a lineman held no good future for me. So, I quit and joined the choir. After that, while many of my friends were down on the gridiron doing battle, I was up in the stands with their girlfriends, cheering the team on. (Okay, that was smug ... but true.) I didn't go out for basketball because I didn't care for the new coach, who was a "screamer," but I did continue throwing the discus and shot put during the spring track and field season (which would come back to bless me a few years later).

Choir became my passion. Christine Baker, our teacher and choral director, was a tiny but fierce woman on a mission, and she got incredible music out of teenagers. The choir had one hundred and ten members and I became choir president my senior year. My voice wasn't great, but what I lacked in vocal quality I made up for in enthusiasm. So, I also got to be a part of the small show choir that sang around town (Baker's Dozen, we were called—twelve singers and a pianist ... get it?). But the big opportunity came when it was decided that the music department would put on the show "Oklahoma!" I got the part of Will Parker and played it to the hilt! (I think my friends were all glad when that show was done and I got my feet back on the ground.) I had good parts in a couple of other plays presented by the drama club. These were wonderfully affirming experiences and I learned a lot about presentation and speech. As a senior, to my amazement, I was chosen "Personality Plus" for the yearbook, and prom king (pretty heady stuff for a blue-collar kid).

I was beginning to be drawn toward ministry as early as junior high school. This was due to my appreciation of Rev. Dean, to my love of the church as I had experienced it to that point in my life, and to my mother's example of living the faith through compassion for and service to others—including the homeless people who lived around Hamm's Art and Sign Supply. Though I could not have expressed it so clearly then, ministry began to seem like a way one might internalize and embody these expressions of God's intentions for the world.

But I had always been interested in the sciences as well. Growing up in the late 1950s in Central Florida meant that, from our backyard, I could see the exhaust trails of rockets fired from Cape Canaveral, just ninety miles away on the Atlantic side. And on a clear night, I could see many rockets' last stages and watch satellites being boosted into orbit. I got very interested in rocket science and was part of a student project at the local science center called, "Marsflight," which simulated long-duration space travel. I wrote a letter to Wernher von Braun and received a response (something like Homer Hickam in the movie, *October Sky*). On several occasions my Little League coach took some of us boys to Patrick Air Force Base near Cape Canaveral to see displays of the latest rocket technology. My interest in chemistry was peaked when I learned I could make rocket fuel. Many a solid propellant-charged steel pipe was sent up out of our little backyard (yeah, my parents weren't home). My quest to build a liquid propellent engine ended in an explosion and fire that was (very fortunately) contained by a test hole I had dug three feet square and four feet deep. However, the flames shooting straight up twelve feet or so out of the ground were pretty impressive.

In sixth grade, I mowed several of our neighbors' lawns to raise thirty dollars to buy a 60mm Tasco telescope I had spotted at the nearby Eckerd Drug Store. That night I set up the scope in the yard and aimed it toward the brightest object I could see. It was Saturn, and the sight of that beautiful ringed planet *literally* took my breath away. I was hooked, and astronomy became a lifelong passion.

In eighth grade, my school friend Charlie Henry and I became ham radio operators. For the next ten years or so, anywhere I lived came to have a mast and radio antennas—my call letters were WA4RBT in Florida, which changed to WB9CYV when I moved north for college. Although I didn't have the words to say it just so when I was twelve, science felt to me like an extension of faith, because marveling at the physical world seemed like another way to worship God.

I also became very interested in airplanes at age six when Dad arranged for a flight for me in a small Ercoupe plane at the Crawfordsville Airport. In St. Pete, when I was twelve, I occasionally peddled my bike the five miles downtown to Albert Whitted Airport and sat on a bench in front of the pilot's lounge looking forlorn until someone would invite me to go along for a flight. The Piper salesman began to use me for a spotter in the rear seat while he demonstrated planes to potential buyers ... at least until the day I was sitting in the back of a two-engine plane piloted by a student, who couldn't seem to get the hang of engine synchronization, and I got sick (unfortunately, no one had yet introduced me to an air sickness bag). I joined the Civil Air Patrol in seventh grade, and by tenth grade I was cadet commander of a new squadron. I did more marching than flying in the CAP, but I learned a lot about aviation and weather, and there was one memorable trip in a C-119 "Flying Boxcar" late one night over to Guantanamo Bay, Cuba, and back.

Years later, the board chair of the church I served while in seminary had been a pilot in World War II and owned a wonderful grass airfield. He encouraged me to get my license and to buy an airplane, allowing us to keep it in one of his hangars for free. When Mindy and I started our family, we sold the plane for what we had paid for it. It had been a great way to get flying time. Upon moving to Kansas City, I joined a flying club that had two airplanes available to rent (a Cessna 172 and a Cherokee Arrow with retractable landing gear). I eventually gave up the club membership due to a lack of money and the press of work, which made it hard to fly often enough to stay safe (it's easy to get "rusty" if you don't fly regularly). I still miss flying as a pilot. These days, it is physical limitations that keep me out of the cockpit unless another pilot is riding along.

I was not an excellent student in public school. I got by okay with a B average and I learned a lot of "big picture" things, but my heart wasn't really in the day-to-day schoolwork. My heart was in singing, acting, science ... and, increasingly, in church. I loved summer youth conference at the Disciples' Silver Springs Conference Center in Ocala (just down the road from the famed Silver Springs attraction) and I became president of our Tampa District Christian Youth Fellowship and the Florida State Christian Youth Fellowship. As a youth in the Tampa District, I experienced the tutelage of Margaret Walstrom, a fiercely Christian lay woman who was the district youth sponsor. Being a state CYF officer gave me the opportunity to go to the World Convention of the Stone-Campbell Churches in San Juan, Puerto Rico, in 1965 (I love Puerto Rico to this day). There we saw and heard Martin Luther King Jr. speak. Ann Updegraff (later, president of the Division of Homeland Ministries) and I hung out together there, renting a motorcycle at one point and riding around the island. I also became part of the United Christian Youth Movement, which gave me my first real exposure to the Church Ecumenical. These leadership opportunities also provided the opportunity to see how the church beyond the congregation did its work, day to day, especially within the Florida Region. J. W. Cate became the new pastor of Palm Lake Christian Church, which delighted me, as I had already come to know him at district and state youth events, where he served as a sponsor. J. W. gave me lots of leadership opportunities at Palm Lake, including serving as a student minister one summer after graduation from high school. He was an encourager, like Rev. Dean before him.

My first car was one I purchased from a fellow high school student. It was a Morris Minor, a tiny English sedan from Morris Garages (MG). I quickly learned always to carry a spare fan belt and a tool to tap on the gas pump occasionally. Why in heaven's name would the *English* build a car that would drown out in a rain (England not exactly being a desert)? And how would such a car make its way to Florida, where it rains cats and dogs? Nonetheless, I loved that car. It needed paint, so I hand painted it in British racing green (which didn't make the car go any faster). The external hood hinges broke (as was common on Morris Minors) and so I had to remove the entire hood to check the oil (or to tap on the gas pump). The starter broke early on, but not to worry ... the car came with a crank you could insert through an opening in the front bumper. It was a very small engine, so it was easy to start with the crank. I drove that car for two years, until my parents bought a new car for me for college. The day I was to trade in the Morris Minor, my friend Rick Kear borrowed it. Somehow, in the process of trying to start the car, he got the crank into the radiator, and it sprang a leak. I told him not to worry about it, chewed some gum, pressed it into the hole in the radiator, drove it to the Chevrolet dealership, and turned it in. I'm certain they immediately towed it to the junk yard (or perhaps they used a bulldozer), but when I visited the salesman a few weeks later to pick up my new 1967 Chevy II, I saw the Morris Minor's crank painted gold and hanging on his office wall. It must have provided him with a good story.

Early in my junior year of high school, we moved from our house in a residential neighborhood to an apartment in the building that housed our art and sign supply business downtown. My parents had invested their savings to buy this building at the southwest corner of 18th Street and Central Avenue. It included several small store fronts on Central and on 18th Street, and two upstairs apartments. Because this was in a different high school's area, I wrote the Pinellas County School Board begging them to allow me to stay at Boca Ciega, where I had so many friends and interests. Happily, for me, they agreed.

I enclosed and remodeled a second-floor screened-in porch that spanned a gap over the back doors of the corner tavern that was part of our building (Jerry's Bar and Grill). It could get pretty noisy on a weekend night especially, and there were occasionally fist fights below my window, but that became my bedroom. There was a small door that let me out onto the flat part of the building's roof ("Up on the Roof," by the Drifters, was popular then and perfectly described how I felt going out on the roof and looking down on Central Avenue from above). The room also provided space for a closet, a desk, and my ham radio equipment. I put up a forty-foot radio tower on the roof, and I could look east to see space shots from Canaveral. Perfect.

I also got to know quite a cast of characters who lived on the surrounding streets. One night, coming home late from something, I climbed the inside stairs to our second-floor apartment and there, in the darkness, I stumbled over "Roy," a street person who slept wherever he could. I got to know Roy, and others, as real people rather than as "bums" or merely as alcoholics, and I watched as my mother often quietly did their laundry or slipped them a sandwich or some coins. Was she "enabling" them? Probably. But she was also keeping them alive with some measure of dignity. That made a lasting impression on my high school heart and mind.

Boca Ciega High School had no Black students or faculty, as Jim Crow continued to operate in St. Pete in the mid-1960s. However, we did have a significant number of Jewish students, many of whom were among my best friends. One night our singing group, Baker's Dozen, was scheduled to sing at The Beach Club in one of St. Pete's beach towns. Prominently displayed at the entrance was a sign that read, "No Jews Allowed." Two of our members were Jewish. So, we decided we would not be singing there and left. Though I had come to take "Whites Only" signs for granted, this was the first time I had seen (or noticed) a "No Jews" sign. It shook me, *because* I had Jewish friends. Some of us had just begun to hear about the Holocaust and I was just then dating Charlotte, a lovely Jewish girl. I wondered to myself, "What must it be like to know that there are people who want to see you and all your relatives dead?" This was incomprehensible. It was an important moment in my development of empathy for the marginalized and further kindled a desire to help build a more compassionate world of true community.

Graduating from high school in 1966, I still had not fully resolved the matter of science v. ministry. So, I did a year at St. Petersburg Junior College, living at home and working at the New England Oyster House, first as a dish washer, then at the raw bar (shucking oysters became second nature), and finally as a cook. I had a wonderful group of friends with whom to enjoy time off, all friends from high school days who had decided to go to junior college for a year or two before going on to various other universities. Like me, none were wild partiers or beer drinkers, so our times together were often spent around a bonfire on a beach singing folk songs (Peter, Paul, and Mary were still popular, despite the British Invasion). Most of us played guitars it seemed. Many of us remained lifelong friends.

During that freshman year in junior college, I connected with the local group of Campus Crusade for Christ. It was a theologically conservative group, but I learned about a different way of interpreting the scripture and it deepened my sense of personal connection with God. I wasn't buying the theology, but it was a group of very nice Christian people with whom to associate. However, on one occasion we had a guest speaker who obviously was *very* fundamentalist in outlook and argued for a six-thousand-year-old earth. I asked, "But what about the dinosaurs?" The speaker replied that "dinosaur bones were planted by Satan to fool us into believing in evolution." That was the last meeting I attended, but it had been an enriching experience in many ways, and I learned about parts of the Bible I had never heard mentioned in my Disciples congregation (and, yes, I had to unlearn some of that "information" later).

Back Home Again in Indiana

By the end of that first college year, I had decided on ministry. (I have often joked that taking trigonometry made up my mind, but not really.) Very few members of my extended family had attended college. But I did have an uncle by marriage (Col. Don Terbush) who had retired as an Air Force chaplain and lived in St. Pete with my beloved Aunt Mabel. He had attended Butler School of Religion in the 1940s, so he encouraged me to go to Butler University. I had long heard family stories of the great Butler coach, Tony Hinkle. Butler was not far from my first hometown, and I had no other ideas, so I said, "Okay."

Come September, I loaded up my Chevy II Nova, which my parents had provided (what a wonderful gift), and headed to Indianapolis. Mom packed five sandwiches for the trip, which I had eaten before I got out of Pinellas County. Dad, unfortunately, could not deal with my departure, so he was drunk and asleep that morning and I didn't get a chance to say goodbye. Thus, my joy and excitement about beginning a new chapter were tinged with grief.

I received half tuition because I was a Disciples student studying for ministry (a holdover from when Butler was a Disciples-related school), and half tuition for throwing the discus (a skill I had developed in high school).

I lived off-campus for a few months with friends of my uncle and worked as a fuel pump operator at a Blue and White Service truck stop. But this afforded me little time to develop friendships at school or to do much else but work and study (and it was pretty hard to get the smell of fuel oil out of my clothes and the grease off my hands). I enjoyed the people with whom I worked at Blue and White, even though I got teased a lot about being a "college boy."

One particularly dark and cold night, when I was still new at the job, a trucker brought his eighteen-wheeler into the drive and, leaving his engine running as truckers are wont to do, yelled to me on his way to the restroom to top off the fuel and the crankcase. I filled the fuel tank with diesel and then opened the cover and leaned into that pitch-dark growling engine cavity with my flashlight in one hand and pulled the oil stick out with the other. It was about a gallon low. So, I asked one of my coworkers how to add oil to the crankcase (having never oiled such a monster before). He pointed to a spout can that held about a gallon. I filled the can from the fifty-five-gallon drum of engine oil and went back to the truck. I found the oil cap and removed it. However, it took both hands to hold the oiler can above the engine, so I pulled the spout down and moved the can back and forth along the valve cover till I found the oil filler opening again. Unfortunately, and deliberately, my coworker had pointed me to an oiler can with a broken trigger, which meant the can was continuously open. Thus, I poured nearly a gallon of oil over this driver's engine while trying to find the opening. He came out of the men's room and saw his truck smoking like a wet leaf fire, picked me up by the collar, and said, "That's just what I needed ... an oil bath!" Fortunately, he didn't hit me (but he didn't tip me, either); instead, he got in his truck and drove off. The crew thought it was hilarious. It was hazing, but I knew enough to take it without getting angry.

Wanting to live on campus, I soon pledged Delta Tau Delta fraternity and became house treasurer (which paid my room and board).[3] I learned later that Delta Tau Delta had begun at the Disciples' Bethany College when Alexander Campbell, a Disciples founder, was still the president! Funny, or providential, how such interweavings of our lives occur. I put up a two-meter radio antenna secured to the chapter house chimney so I could continue my ham

---

[3] These kinds of scholarship deals are rare today, of course, and people are much more likely to have serious debt by the time they graduate. I am so grateful to have gotten through college as I did.

radio habit. (I was assisted in this rooftop project by fraternity brother Chuck Ritz, although I suspect he was eager to help mostly because he could see sorority houses from that thirty-feet high perch) and by my then day-roommate, Dennis Apple.

Though I loved Florida, it was great to be back in Indiana, where so many of my extended family members lived. As soon as possible, I drove the forty-five miles to Crawfordsville to see our old neighbors, whom I had not seen since I was eleven, when I accompanied Mom to see her brother, my Uncle Lowell, before he died.

After a brief reunion in the home of Bud and Hazel, now retired, Bud invited me to the garage. There, perfectly preserved, was his 1955 Ford pick-up in which we had hauled chickens. Also there, hanging on the garage wall, was the treasured chicken hook I had gotten for Christmas so long ago. What a welcome back!

I majored in religion at Butler and was able to take courses in Bible and in New Testament Greek. Robert Andry and Francis Reisinger were the religion professors. Professor Reisinger was the father of Don Reisinger of the Disciples Seminary Foundation in California, and his grandson was Rick Reisinger, who would one day head Church Extension. I would work with both Don and Rick many years later as GMP.

I minored in sociology because I found people fascinating. Most importantly, I met Mindy, the *most* fascinating person I met at Butler!

Mindy had grown up in Bluffton, Indiana, and was studying at Butler to become a medical technologist. On the first day of classes, I walked into my American literature class and there she was, and I was smitten! Having promised to help my Uncle Sam build a pole barn over the next several weekends, a month passed before I could ask her out. We finally went out on a weekend in October: Friday night, Saturday night, and Sunday afternoon. Harold Cline was serving then as a pastor in Kokomo, and his spouse, Ruby Cline, was taking religion classes at Butler. Ruby had become a confidant for me and several other of us young men studying for ministry. Having told her about that wonderful weekend, Ruby said, "Send flowers!" So I did ... and it worked! In a matter of three weeks, we decided we wanted to make a life together. But we were sophomores and had no money, so we had to wait three more years to get married.

Late that first November, Mindy and I went to Bluffton to visit her parents, Edna and Clarence. Edna was a New Yorker who had been a surgical nurse in the Army and had followed the Normandy invasion across France. Clarence, who had been raised on a farm outside Bluffton and attended Indiana University, had served as an Army Signal Corps officer in London on General Eisenhower's staff. They met in London before D-Day.

From my perspective, this first visit to the Fishbaugh home was a rather rough beginning. Clarence and Edna were delighted to see Mindy, their only child ... but not so delighted to see this kid from Florida who planned to marry her! My presence was obviously annoying to them (which I understand much better now as a father who was always concerned about any male who showed interest in my daughter). Looking back on it, we should not yet have shared our plans, and I should have made myself invisible on that visit. It took some years for us to overcome that shaky beginning, but Edna and Clarence both became dear to me. Eventually, giving them two grandchildren definitely sweetened the deal for them.

It was 1968, an election year, and Robert Kennedy was coming to town. We had caught sight of Ethyl earlier in the day on campus. So, a fraternity brother of mine, Pat Osting, and I decided to go to a downtown city park where Kennedy was speaking that evening. This was the terrible day when Dr. Martin Luther King Jr. was shot in Memphis. There were several hundred of us in the crowd at the park, and few of us had heard of Dr. King's assassination. When Kennedy announced what had happened, there was a collective gasp of shock and then the senator gave his impromptu speech that many have said was one of his best. That night, while there were riots in many cities, Indianapolis remained relatively quiet, and Kennedy's speech was credited by many for the peaceful night in Indy.

Just two months later, Robert Kennedy was himself assassinated. As a sophomore in high school, I had cried at word that John F. Kennedy had been shot. Now, as a college sophomore, I cried for his brother and wondered what we were coming to as a nation. Though Dr. King was obviously a major public figure in those days, I was not yet as spiritually and philosophically connected to him as I would later become. But Bobby Kennedy had captured my imagination with his opposition to the Vietnam War and his concern for the poor and marginalized.

In the spring of my sophomore year at Butler, through the Disciples Indiana Regional Church office, I became aware of a small congregation that needed a pastor. So, at the age of twenty, I started preaching every Sunday at Abington Christian Church near Richmond, Indiana. This church was in a little finger of Appalachia that sticks up into Eastern Indiana along the Indiana–Ohio border. Most of these folks were of Scots Irish descent and poor, working every day just to hold things together. It was an eye-opener for me, and why they put up with me, I still don't know. But they did, and I loved them dearly. I typically drove over early Saturday mornings to make calls, on Sunday preached and met with the youth group, and then drove home to Butler on Sunday evenings (to see Mindy before "hours"[4]). It was in the front room of the board chair's home (Bob and Ruth Taylor's) that I watched the moon landing in July 1969.

Abington Christian Church began to grow, and we had a good youth group developing, so I spent the summer of 1969 living in the church basement instead of going home to St. Pete. I got a job on the state highway mowing crew to earn a little money, but got covered in poison ivy the first week, so they let me drive a vacuum truck that was cleaning out storm sewers on all the state highways in the area. That was a new experience.

In December 1969, the New Testament professor at Butler, Dr. Robert Andry, told me about an open country church just twenty miles from school that needed a pastor. He was doing the interim ministry for them and said he would put my name in if I was interested. A twenty-mile commute sounded great, especially in comparison to a ninety-mile commute to Abington in all kinds of weather. So, after the customary interview, I accepted the search committee's invitation. Little Eagle Creek Christian Church understood itself to be a teaching church, and I had a lot to learn. Mindy and I were planning on marrying the following fall, and they had a lovely little parsonage that would be perfect for us.

I moved all my earthly possessions (which could *almost* fill my Chevy II, and which included a guitar and a banjo), piling everything in the middle of the living room floor of the parsonage right in front of a huge picture window (for which I had no curtains). I hurried back to school for the night and, upon returning the next day, found that my stuff had all been stolen. I'll never forget the sense of violation

---

[4] For younger readers, colleges had "hours" back then. At Butler, women students had to be in by 11 PM Sunday through Thursday, and by 1:30 AM on Friday and Saturday.

I felt, but that feeling became a resource to me as I worked with parishioners in the years ahead who suffered such property losses and personal violations.

I began working at Little Eagle Creek Christian Church that January 1970. Mindy was spending that academic year at Cleveland General Hospital finishing her medical technology degree with a year of classes and laboratory practicums. The following fall, assisted by two friends I had met on the "two-meter" wavelength ham radio band (Bob and Emmett), we put up a forty-foot radio tower outside a spare bedroom and got my ham radio station up and running.

Typical average worship attendance at Little Eagle was about seventy, but there was a heavy snowfall one Saturday night that February, just a month after I had begun as their minister. In the face of ten to twelve inches of snow, it was a pretty small crowd that Sunday morning. The small sanctuary had an annex to one side that had a large pull-down door so that a Sunday School class could meet in there. During worship the door was opened so it became a part of the sanctuary.

It is hard to preach effectively when a small number of people are scattered all over a space, so I asked the several people sitting in the annex if they would move over to the main part of the sanctuary where several other people were sitting. They all smiled but wagged their heads "no." I didn't know what to do. In my young head, it felt like my "leadership" was being publicly challenged, and my fragile ego didn't know what to do with that. So, I got up from my chair in the chancel, walked over to the annex, and pulled the door down! I walked back up to the chancel and sat down, but after a moment of reflection decided maybe that had not been the best way to address the situation. So, I stood up to go and open the door again. Unfortunately, an elder in the main part of the sanctuary got there first and raised the door.

People were no longer smiling. Some looked angry, some looked stunned, and some were crying! I apologized and somehow got through the service ... but I figured that was my last Sunday as pastor of Little Eagle Creek Christian Church. I knew it was too late to avert being fired at the regular board meeting that was scheduled for later that week. But I felt I had to apologize to these people individually for what I had done before I was sent packing. So, despite the snow, I went to the house of every single person who had been in that service, and I apologized to them, admitting it had been a stupid thing for me to do and I hoped they would forgive me.

Later that week, I attended what I was sure would be my last board meeting there. As the meeting began, the chairman, Les Wheeler, said, "In regard to the events of the past Sunday ..." (I thought, "Oh, here it comes!"), he said, "It takes a good man to admit when he is wrong."

That was it. I never heard another word about it during the four-and-a-half years I served that church. Nobody left the church. Nobody felt the need to punish me. Everyone treated me with kindness and respect. *That*, dear reader, is a *teaching church*! I learned more about grace and human kindness in that week than I had ever known before. I will forever be grateful to them.

It was that same board chair, Les Wheeler, who owned the Westfield Airport. We hit it off immediately. He was an adult, and a great mentor from whom I learned so much.

Les knew that I loved flying and had imagined taking flying lessons someday. Knowing I would be getting married later that year, he encouraged me to get started toward my pilot's license before the wedding. He knew how hard it would be to begin after the wedding. So, I began taking lessons at little Terry Airport (now Executive Airport) just a few miles from the parsonage. It was a stretch financially, so I took the hourly lessons once a week. By the time of our wedding, I had soloed and was about halfway through the required forty hours of instruction. Mindy, who had secured a good job as a medical technologist with Dow Pharmaceutical, encouraged me to finish getting my license.

Having been doing solo work for several weeks, I came home from school one day assuming I would be doing the usual touch and go landings that solo students do with instructors every few flying hours to demonstrate that you are "flying right" and haven't developed any dangerous habits. I was running late and hadn't had any lunch that day, so heated and consumed a can of spinach and quickly downed a Pepsi. Unfortunately, when I got to the airport, my instructor met me at the airplane having decided it was time to do some more dual training (both of us in the cockpit). Of all days, this was the one he decided to teach power spirals and recovery from unusual attitudes! After about forty-five minutes of these extreme maneuvers, I was turning as green as the spinach I had hastily consumed and told my instructor I needed to get back to the airport fast. Looking over at me, he could see the truth of my statement, so he tried to make a teaching moment of it. "Okay, you're seriously ill but your family is in the plane with you and depending on you to get them safely back to the airport!" It was a great role play, but about a thousand feet out on final approach, I couldn't hold it any longer. I asked him to take over, opened the little window within the window on the left side, and let "lunch" fly. We landed and I felt much better ... but the airplane's numbers were covered with dark green all down that side of the airplane. I had to get a bucket and clean it up, while the pilots in the lounge laughed out loud. After that, I paid careful attention to my pretraining diet!

Once I had my "ticket," Les said, "You'd better buy an airplane *before* you have kids." So, with his encouragement, Mindy and I found a wonderful, gently used, five-year-old Piper Cherokee 140, perfect for the two of us. It was a sweet little plane, N7248J. It got better mileage than our Oldsmobile Cutlass and cruised at a hundred and twenty miles per hour! Les gave us free hangar space at his airport. The local bank, of which he was an officer, loaned us the eight thousand dollars (that's right ... eight thousand dollars) to buy the plane.[5]

We enjoyed that plane immensely, flying it to Mindy's folks' place in Bluffton, and to my folks' home in Florida, to tent camp in Kentucky and Illinois, and many other places. When we sold it two years later, we got the eight thousand back. The exact same plane, a 1967 Cherokee 140, equipped as ours was, would sell for about fifty thousand dollars in 2020. Les had been right.

The parsonage where we lived was on Little Eagle Creek Avenue, which was more of a lane than an avenue and runs along the creek. It ran through an area some people called The Basin. Some of our members lived in that immediate area, and they called themselves the Basin Bunch, and I became designated The Basin Chaplain. This was the craziest, most fun-loving bunch of Christians anyone would ever hope to meet. For example (read the following paragraphs only when you are feeling strong):

---

[5] Obviously, Les was a well-to-do person, with a family farm, an insurance business, a car wash, the airport, and serving as a bank officer. But you wouldn't get that feeling from him. He dressed plainly, lived in a modest home, and was never ostentatious. He was extremely generous to everyone and to the church.

Mindy and I were married at her home church, First United Church of Christ of Bluffton. My brother served as my best man; my college roomie, dear friend, and fellow seminarian Skip Armistead, and one of my best high school friends, Rick Kear, served as groomsmen. The Basin Bunch all drove one hundred and twenty-five miles for the occasion. It was a lovely wedding. After the reception, through the hail of rice, we ran for my car with more than a hundred guests cheering us on. I opened the door for my bride and found lying across the bench front seat of my Chevy II a bale of hay, the bailing twine having been removed. Reaching in to pull it out, the bale disintegrated, and it took me several minutes to get it cleared out (with no one lending a hand to help, of course!). So, finally getting Mindy seated, I jumped in the driver's seat to leave. I stepped on the gas, but nothing happened. The engine was racing, but we weren't moving. I got out of the car and saw that someone had put a block of wood under my left rear axle. So, I opened the trunk, got all our luggage out (we were headed for our honeymoon in Florida, so it was *full*), found the jack, raised the rear axle, and removed the wood block. I repacked the trunk and got back into the car to leave. But when I put my foot on the gas, again, nothing happened! I quickly realized they had put chocks under both ends of the axle. So, I got out, emptied the trunk, applied the jack, raised the car, removed the other wooden block, repacked the trunk and got into the car.

All the guests seemed to be enjoying themselves immensely.

I finally was able to pull away from the curb, almost taking out the pastor's Volkswagen as we went, and took off, leaving my in-laws to pick up the straw, the wood, the rice, and all. We had reservations for that night at Hueston Woods State Park in Ohio, but I hadn't thought to fill the tank (see Mindy's eyes rolling). So, on the way out of Bluffton, we stopped to get gas. As the tank was filling, I began to smell something foul. I opened the hood and found that a pound of limburger cheese had been placed on the manifold and the engine was just getting warmed up! So, I pulled out the block of cheese, slammed the hood shut, paid for the gas (the attendant remarked that something didn't smell very good), and off we went. Seventy miles later we came into Richmond, and we stopped for dinner at Howard Johnson's.

We were finally beginning to relax and focusing on each other when a cake came to our table decorated with the words,

"Congratulations!" We panicked. How did the people in this restaurant know we had just gotten married? How could they have found out?

We paid our bill, walked out to the car, and found a note stuck under the windshield wipers, "See you at the hotel!" We looked across the parking lot and saw several heads duck down in a car. Oh no!

I had never driven so fast through Richmond, Indiana. Six of the Basin Bunch had followed us from Bluffton, and we were sure they would follow us all the way to Hueston Woods, so I aimed to lose them. We got to the lodge and saw no one coming in behind us. But all night we were awake thinking they would be coming to the door at any moment!

Well, we learned later, they hadn't followed us beyond Howard Johnson's, and so we were finally on our own (we hoped).

The next day we drove to Unadilla, Georgia, on our way to Florida. There was a little motel I had occasionally stayed in on my way back and forth between St. Pete and Indianapolis. We checked in and then saw my parents' car in the parking lot: They had stopped in the same place that night on their way home from the wedding! We had breakfast and a good laugh about it together the next morning.

We drove on to Ft. Myers, where we had planned to stay a few nights in exchange for listening to a real estate sales pitch. But we were the last guests to arrive that night and so they gave us what they had left ... a room so small that you had to crawl across the bed to get to the bathroom. The next morning, we asked for a change of rooms. They gave us a bigger room, but with twin beds! We left.

We spent a couple of nights at a place on St. Pete Beach, but we had hit a rare November cold snap in Florida, so we ended up going all the way to the Flamingo Inn at the southern tip of the Everglades. It was off-season, so we just about had the place to ourselves ... just us and the alligators.

But wait, there's more! We returned to our parsonage home ten days later. But remembering vividly what had happened in Bluffton, there was no way we were going to get undressed that night. A friend in the congregation had tipped me off to the fact that the Basin Bunch had drilled a hole in the oak floor under our bed, attached a mercury switch to the bed springs, and run a wire from it to a battery and all the way up to the top of my radio tower, where they had placed a red light. Whenever the bedsprings moved, the light flashed. So, we thought, "What the heck!" and jumped up and down on the bed so as not to disappoint our "friends."

Then, about midnight, we heard noises in our front yard. The Basin Bunch were beating pots and pans and firing off a shot gun. *Shivaree!*[6] They "made" me push Mindy in a wheelbarrow a quarter-mile down Little Eagle Creek Avenue to an elder's house. There we had refreshments, talked, and played snooker late into the night. Next day, I removed the red-light contraption, plugged the hole in the floor, and we had peace at last, though admittedly, all of this was a bit overwhelming at that point for Mindy, who may have begun to wonder what she had gotten herself into.

No one could ask for a better student church than that.

Christian Theological Seminary

In fall of 1970, I began classes at Christian Theological Seminary (CTS), having been encouraged to attend by my Uncle Don and by Howard Goodrich (later a regional minister and dear friend) who was on the CTS staff at that time. It is difficult to overstate how fortunate I feel to have been at CTS in those years. The faculty was composed of a marvelous combination of younger folks recently graduated from Chicago, Vanderbilt, Boston, and Yale and older faculty who were deeply rooted in church life. In addition to a wonderful faculty, the student body included some of the brightest people I have had the pleasure of knowing and calling friends. I would work with many of them later in regional and general ministry, including Bill Bass, Larry Brown, Rebecca Bunton, Larry and Janet Casey-Allen, Bob and Joyce Coalson, Cecil Cook, Joe and Ellen Culpepper, Jerry Fuqua, Claudia Grant, Kent Grimes, Lari Grubbs, Tom Jewell, Connie Nusbaum, Jim Powell, Pat Ramga, Peggy Richardson, Bob Shaw, Charles Webb, Pat Tucker Spier, Linda Weeks, Judith Hock Wray ... and the list goes on. Long conversations in the café complemented classes and visiting lecturers. A strong student body with which to interact is nearly as important as a strong faculty.

It is worth noting here that the women in my class were brave souls (as were the women in other seminaries across the land). They were preparing to do ministry in a world and church that was not yet willing to acknowledge the legitimacy of women in ministry. It

---

[6] A *shivaree* is a social custom rooted in medieval times, but in North America it is typically a good-natured hazing of newlyweds. Ironically (to me), a fine example of shivaree is found in the musical, "Oklahoma!"

wasn't just men who opposed their service, it was women as well (we *all*, male and female, drink from the same cultural cups). These female seminarians were pioneers in many ways and often paid huge emotional prices in their quest to be faithful to their authentic calling. I saw so many of them, among the brightest and best of seminary graduates, struggle to find congregations that could pay them a living wage. We all owe a great debt to these women who struggled to break the church's glass ceiling—and, unfortunately, that struggle is not yet over in many places. I was proud to call them friends and colleagues but did not, I fear, fully understand the toll they were paying for the needed transformation of the church they were seeking. I understand it better now, and yet it is easy to forget the prices they paid, and continue to pay, for gender prejudice and misogyny. I directly benefited from the excellent work of several of these colleagues when I was a congregational pastor, a regional minister, and as general minister and president.

Many of the same struggles have been and are still being faced by people of color and by people of differing sexual orientations. But in the early 1970s, these struggles were not yet visible to most of us in the church, stuck as we were in a frankly paternalistic, sexist, homophobic, and racist worldview. Not only did these people unjustly suffer, but the church has itself paid more of a price than most of us recognize for this unloving narrowness of mind that has limited the potential contributions of so many great people and that has flown in the face of Jesus' life and teachings.

One of our early flying trips in our Piper Cherokee was to St. Petersburg to see my folks. I learned a lot about life through flying. One of the most important lessons was about my own mortality.

We took off from Westfield Airport one morning before sunrise and headed south with high clouds that were forecasted to lift soon. As we flew, the cloud cover began to lower rather than lift, but clouds do sometimes lower right before they break up, so I flew on. We were soon flying through the high hills of Northern Kentucky and there I made a very bad rookie mistake: the hilltops were obscured by clouds so I flew between two hills into weather that I should not have flown into. I was soon *surrounded* by hilltops so that I had no navigational radio,[7] which meant I did not know exactly where we

---

[7] Navigational radio is line-of-sight, so being surrounded by hills cuts off the signals.

were, and the ceiling was still dropping and forcing us to fly closer to the ground to stay below the clouds. I couldn't find the pass through which we had come into this high valley so as to backtrack out. After a few minutes of following power lines (which always lead *somewhere*), we came upon a town, and so I flew in low circles around it trying to figure out where we were. We got so low that I finally confirmed our location by reading the sign at the edge of town which read, "Welcome to Greensburg, Kentucky." Consulting the chart, I now realized there was nowhere to land safely and no way *out* but *up through the clouds*. I was a visual flight rules (VFR) pilot, not qualified to fly on instruments, but I had no choice. Fortunately, every VFR pilot does get some instruction in instrument flying for just such a situation as this. But doing it with an instructor next to you and doing it with your trusting spouse next to you is a bit different. I was terrified! What if a new radio tower had been built since my chart was printed? What if there was another plane flying in the clouds above? How high did the clouds go? *How could I be so stupid?*

So, sweating bullets and with fear and trembling, I prayed for calm, turned south away from the closest hills, leveled the wings, pushed the throttle forward, and lifted the nose, hoping I would soon break through the top of the clouds. Instantly, I could see nothing out of the windshield but a grayish white and so I kept my eyes focused on the instruments. And then, *in a moment*, a calm sense of God's presence came over me. We were in the clouds for about twenty minutes, finally breaking out at eleven thousand feet, very close to the limit of where a normally aspirated piston engine airplane can fly and close to the limit of where a pilot can fly without an oxygen mask. The sky was bright blue up there and the sun lit up the beautiful white cloud deck now below, and we continued south for St. Petersburg. As we passed over Nashville, the clouds finally broke up and we were flying in clear skies. The rest of the trip, including the return, was uneventful. But I'll never forget the panic that had been welling up in my throat ... or the sudden sense of calm that overtook my fear as we ascended into that sea of clouds.

Soon after we got home, as I was reading the Bible, I came across Psalm 139 again. "If I take the wings of the morning and dwell in the uttermost parts of the sea, thy hand shall hold me ..." I remembered how a sense of God's presence and a resulting calm had come over me in that cockpit. It was not a miracle in the way that term is usually used. The skies didn't part. No invisible hand guided our plane. But that sense of God's presence and the ensuing calm in the face of imminent disaster had made it possible for me to do what I had been trained to do in an emergency. And I gave thanks to God again. I have drawn on that Psalm and that experience of God's presence time and again over the years ... in both ordinary and extraordinary circumstances.

That was a case when God's presence was so real, so palpable, that it helped me do what I had been trained to do. As a pastor who has been with many people in difficult life experiences, I know that many people have had the opposite experience. When people are utterly helpless in the face of a medical emergency for themselves, or for a spouse or a child, many have no sense of God's presence at all. Under such circumstances, we would all *love* to have an experience of God's presence that would comfort us. But sometimes *we just ... can't ... feel ... it.* That doesn't make us bad or faithless. It just means that our senses are so overwhelmed with fear, anxiety, and helplessness that we can feel little else.

The carelessness I had exhibited in the air on that trip to St. Pete carried over into other areas of my life, including my early days at seminary.

It was in seminary that I finally became a serious student. I now felt a strong sense of calling to ministry and I was challenged by professors to do my best. A turning point (a conversion experience, really) came for me one day in my first semester at CTS as I was walking down the hallway and came upon Clark Williamson (everybody who knew him has a Williamson story). I said, "Hi, Clark!" in my usual, lighthearted way. Clark looked at me and said, "You know Hamm, it's great to have the spontaneity of a child, but if you don't get some discipline about you, you're going to be a child the rest of your life!" It was a devastatingly true comment. It was also exactly what I needed to hear. I went home to examine myself and came back the next week a changed person and student. That's when I began squeezing as much information and wisdom as I could out of every seminary class and experience. It had finally dawned on me that to be able to spend four years in graduate school was a privilege very few people on the planet could have, and that discipline was a key to effective and faithful ministry, and so I began taking the opportunity seriously. I thanked Clark for that encounter many times and once more when I visited him in the hospital just a couple of days before he died.

Among the most challenging and invigorating classes for me in my first two years in seminary were in theology. I had enjoyed many good courses in biblical studies at Butler University, but I'd had no opportunity there to think systematically about the nature of God. So, at CTS I found courses in Tillich and Whitehead[8] to be particularly meaningful. Studying Tillich provided a frame for analyzing and understanding reality in Christian existentialist terms, which was a revelation to me. As a person committed to science, studying Whitehead gave me a way to reconcile the truths of science and religion. These studies in turn gave me a framework for studying ethics and the complicated relationships between individuals and cultures. The Old Testament prophets of the eighth century BC and the gospels became my primary windows upon what God desires from individuals, communities, and societies.

I was invited by the Christian ethics professor, Richard Dickinson, to be his student assistant, and I eagerly accepted. I'm not sure I provided much assistance to Dick, but he surely assisted me in gaining a greater understanding of how the world works and of the justice God desires. In addition to regular classes, I was able to attend a three-week seminar he led in Puerto Rico. There, I met many Puerto Rican Disciples and other church leaders (and reconnected with a few I had met there in 1965). It was a marvelous laboratory in which to study the socio-economic, political, and spiritual impact of American colonialism and its lasting effect on indigenous people.

While in Puerto Rico, I rented an airplane at the downtown San Juan airport and flew Dickinson and the general minister of the Disciples in Puerto Rico, Luis Del Pilar, on a brief air tour around the island, including a pass over the famous radio-telescope at Arecibo.

It was remarkable to see the changes that had come between my original visit in 1965 as a youth leader and this visit in 1974 as a student. I fell in love again with the island and its people. The relationship between Puerto Rican Disciples and Disciples in the United States and Canada remains close. The growth of the church in Puerto Rico is a case study of what happens when churches in

---

[8] Paul Tillich (1886-1965) was a renowned twentieth century theologian and Alfred North Whitehead (1861-1947) was a mathematician and philosopher who helped shape the post-modern perspective.

colonial lands (including Disciples in the U.S. and Canada) change from a colonial relationship with the indigenous church to a relationship marked by partnership and mutuality. These learnings served me well as GMP, especially as a member of the U.S.–Puerto Rico Commission that undergirds our partnership.[9] I have made many great friends in this wonderful sister church, including Luis Del Pilar, Ramon Goveo, Esteban and Annette Gonzalez, Miguel Morales, and Ferdinand Barbosa.

I also got to be part of a class Dickinson took to India for three weeks in 1974 (he and Nancy had lived there with their children for a time in the 1960s as part of a World Council of Churches assignment with the American Friends Service Committee). As his student assistant, I helped to make arrangements for the trip. Fortunately, Mindy accompanied me to India. The trip was so disorienting, reorienting, and ultimately life-changing that I am not certain our marriage could have withstood it had she not been there with me. As it was, we had the same experiences, processed them together with each other and with the group, and developed deeper social concerns and values in common. Other student friends with us included Bob and Coletta Eichenberger, Sally Smith, Jim Tingle, Judy and Mark Woldruff, and some additional outstanding people from beyond the Disciples.

After a twenty-four-hour flight in an Air India 747 that stopped in Kuwait for fuel, we arrived in Delhi and claimed our bags. As we walked out the airport doors into the teaming, dusty, and smoky streets of the city, it was for me like the reverse of Dorothy's experience when arriving in Oz. Instead of black and white yielding to technicolor as Dorothy opened the door, all the color seemed to drain out of the picture for me. It was a place so different from anywhere I had seen before that my brain couldn't process it. It was like walking into a *National Geographic* printed in black and white. Standing there, stunned by the sights, a "coolie" (an Indian porter) grabbed my large suitcase and hurried off with it. I thought he was stealing my bag, but he was simply taking it to a designated place where we could get in cabs. I turned and yelled to Dickinson, "He's

---

[9] In March of 2000, I joined Disciples leaders of Puerto Rico in demonstrating against the U.S. Navy's use of the Island of Vieques as a bombing test range, which left depleted plutonium fragments in the water and the soil all over and around that part of Puerto Rico. The Navy had used Vieques for this purpose since 1941. The Navy finally left in 2001.

taken my bag ... what should I do?!" Dickinson replied calmly, "You'd better follow him."

As we rode in our cab from the airport to our quarters, I saw cars, buses, stake trucks, auto-rickshaws, motorcycles, bicycles, women carrying jars and other containers on their heads, cows wandering about freely, children playing in tattered clothes, men driving horse and ox carts, and goats grazing wherever a blade of green could be found. It was overwhelming. But little by little over those three weeks as we visited villages and cities (Delhi, Agra, Mumbai, Cochin, Madras, Varanasi, Bangalore, Hyderabad, Mahabalipuram, and many more) and rode trains across the country in third class (meeting all kinds of people), the color began coming back into my perceptions. In fact, India is a land of so *many* bright colors and hues.

At Ernakulam, in Kerala State (the state with the most Christians per capita), while we were based at a convent, Mindy became ill (nearly everyone did sooner or later, as our digestive systems were unused to the local micro-organisms). The sisters of that convent cared for her in the most wonderful way and she quickly recovered. While we were there, we were visited by one of their colleagues from Calcutta, Sister Theresa (later known as Mother Theresa, and now Saint Theresa), who was in the area and had heard we were there. Theresa had what I call "Jesus eyes," she both looked at you *and* scanned you like an X-ray machine. While she was not yet widely famous outside India, you knew you were standing in the presence of a remarkable soul.

She asked why we were in India (although I'm sure she knew). I piped up and proudly said, "We are here to learn about the people and their culture." She replied, "Oh, so you have learned the language?" That was my last comment. Sister Theresa took no prisoners!

By the end of our journey, I had fallen in love with India and I had *begun* to understand what I was seeing. In fact, so rich are the cultures of India that when we arrived back at JFK and we walked out of the terminal to catch a bus to LaGuardia, the scene before me *there* appeared in black and white! All the New Yorkers looked incredibly obese and seemed rude and brash.

Dick Dickinson became a close friend and a wise counselor through the years. I returned to India for three weeks with him in 1992 as a regional minister and as a CTS trustee. Dick eventually became dean and then president of CTS. He died too young, but Mindy and I have stayed in touch with Nancy through the years.

I remained a full-time student at CTS for four years, earning a doctor of ministry degree in "culture and personality," a wide-ranging field that was perfect for someone like me who was fascinated by everything human and its relationship to the Divine. It included Christian ethics, organizational science, sociology, and pastoral counseling (these subjects are more closely related than one might think). We had a remarkably strong faculty in counseling, as CTS had been a leader in the whole pastoral counseling movement, including Lowell Colston, Sue Cardwell, Brian Grant, and Paul Johnson. My experience of clinical pastoral education at Methodist Hospital with Ken Reed, Stan Mullin, and Ed Alley was also formative. Having brought my lack of focus and my ACOA (adult child of an alcoholic) characteristics to seminary resulted in some extremely painful but necessary self-discovery that, again, resulted in life-changing experiences.

All of us, of course, are shaped in various ways and to various degrees by the circumstances into which we are born and by the experiences that life brings. In my case, being born white, in 1947, to a family whose roots were in farm life and church life (the Disciples of Christ, in particular) and who held aspirations for their children during those relatively prosperous and optimistic days after World War II, was key. I lived in places that were wondrous to a youngster (fields, woods and creeks, beaches, a town, and a city) and had the opportunity to travel as we took family trips to Canada, all around the Midwest, to Florida, and beyond. I was surrounded by many wonderful people of the builder generation and was mentored by them. As a boy, I was permitted huge freedom to move about, to get into things, to do stuff with my hands as well as my head, and to learn (sometimes the hard way). I learned that wealth and education didn't make one person better than another, though they can certainly make life easier, and I learned that wisdom can come from any quarter. My towns and neighborhoods were mostly safe. Anything seemed possible to me.

I remember singing a song in church camp, "I want to live in a friendly world." I felt like that was pretty much the kind of world I lived in (though I was puzzled early on by "duck and cover" exercises that seemed to suggest someone might want to kill me and my friends for reasons I didn't understand).

While my towns and neighborhoods were mostly safe, as a youngster I did experience molestation by a pedophile and once suffered sexual violence from a trusted church member, experiences far too common among *all* Americans. Also, like most who have suffered such violations, I have kept those things quiet out of shame and fear (also too common). There is no point of greater human vulnerability than one's sexuality and, like so many others I believe, those experiences of shame and fear clouded my attitudes toward my own sexuality and personhood. Recovering from such things is a lifelong project for most of us.

Part of being an adult child of an alcoholic means you must guess what reality is, because in a household with addictions, things are seldom what they seem to be. Everyone is playing roles in a larger script that no one realizes is being followed. However, most positively stated, once you understand this dynamic, it teaches you not to take things simply at face value, but to look for larger patterns that might consciously or unconsciously be in operation. Hostility experienced from others is not necessarily simply personal. Resistance to change from individuals and institutions is not necessarily personal or conscious. Recognizing that every institution and social group has its scripts and role players has been phenomenally helpful to me as a leader as I came to realize that conflict in institutions is often about something different than it seems, and identifying such elements is essential to moving forward. What seems "personal" is often an individual acting out an unconscious script rather than any real personal animosity toward others.

Still, couple this ACOA dynamic with my being, in Enneagram[10] terms, a "9" (9s are "peacemakers" who know little *inward* peace), and in Meyers-Briggs terms an ENFP (an external processor who is intuitive, significantly driven by feelings, and resistant to closing off options), and you get, among other things, a visionary who often sees possibilities where others don't (that's the upside) but whose feet are not always solidly planted on the ground (the downside). Some of the most important moments of my life have come in having to learn the difference between what is real and what is wishful thinking. Learning to fly helped me understand that harsh realities and risks must be taken seriously, and studying in places like Puerto Rico and India helped me see that my wealth is related to others' poverty, that

---

[10] The Enneagram is an ancient paradigm for understanding human personality and spirituality. If you are unfamiliar with this, I recommend, *The Enneagram: A Christian Perspective*, by Richard Rohr and Andreas Ebert (Crossroad Publishing, 2001).

God calls us to address the harsh human realities of the world, and that there are spiritual gifts in poverty that are difficult for me as a rich, white male to understand and experience.

Mental health is a lifetime project, and I learned at CTS to continue seeking counseling and insight into myself for the rest of my life as well as providing the same for parishioners. In addition to the pastoral counseling faculty, I had made lifelong friends among other excellent faculty members and staff as well, including Charles Ashanin, Robert Bates, Vinton Bradshaw, Al Edyvean, Les Galbraith, Gerald Janzen, T. J. Liggett, Lester McAllister, Ronald Osborn, Calvin Porter, Keith Watkins, Clark Williamson, Don Wismar, and others. All of these people played a role in helping my feet touch the ground.

Well, ready or not, the inevitable time came. I was ordained at Little Eagle Creek Christian Church on the morning of June 2, 1974, and graduated from Christian Theological Seminary in the afternoon of the same day. Some twenty-five extended family members showed up to celebrate the day with us. It was hard to leave Little Eagle Creek Christian Church and so many friends there, but it was clear to me that I needed to work with a more experienced colleague to learn some of the things one cannot learn in seminary. After a couple of interviews in other places, I accepted a call to Central Christian Church in Kansas City, Kansas, to be associate pastor working with Senior Minister Eldon Irving.

Chapter 2

"I Got to Kansas City on a Friday ... by Saturday I'd Larned a Thing or Two"

—Will Parker in "Oklahoma"

Perhaps the flight over to an interview at Central Christian Church, in Kansas City, Kansas, in April of 1974 should have been a warning that all would not be smooth there. We had sold our airplane by this time,[1] and so I rented a Cherokee 180 in Indianapolis for the trip. As we were flying west across Missouri at about five thousand feet, it suddenly became very quiet. The engine had stopped running, though the propeller was still "windmilling." I quickly went through the engine-out emergency check list (which had been drilled into my head by my excellent instructor): "carburetor heat on, master switch on, quarter-throttle, mixture full rich, switch tanks ..." As soon as I switched tanks, the engine came back to life. It was puzzling because, according to my flight plan, I should have had more than half a tank

---

[1] There were several reasons why we sold our plane. One reason was because Les Wheeler had been providing a hangar to us free in Westfield, and we didn't have the money to pay for a hangar in Kansas City (and I certainly didn't want to leave that beautiful airplane out on the tarmac day and night). A second reason, related to the first, was that we were planning to start our family. A third reason, however, was that in my seminary studies I had read *The Limits to Growth*, published by the Club of Rome. The essence of this book is that the resources the modern world is so dependent on (precious metals, oil, minerals, etc.) are not in unlimited supply. I decided that the world could not afford for me to own a plane full of aluminum and other precious metals when my flying was not essential. Thus, we sold the plane and joined a club in Kansas City, which meant several dozen people were sharing two airplanes, a much more ecologically and economically efficient arrangement. The club owned a Cessna 172 and a Piper Cherokee Arrow, both very fuel-efficient airplanes.

of fuel remaining in the right-wing tank, but it was when I switched to the left-wing tank that the engine restarted. I landed at the first available airport to see what was going on.

Having landed, I got out and inspected the right wing. Under each wing there is a "fuel sump" at the bottom of the tank that enables you to check the fuel to be sure it's the right color (different octane fuels are different colors) and that there is no water in the tank (water is heavier than gasoline and so sinks to the bottom of the tank). I realized immediately what was wrong. The sump was stuck slightly open and the gas cap on top of the wing was slightly loose. These two things together meant that, at cruising speed (one hundred and forty miles per hour in that plane), gas was being siphoned out of the tank faster than it was being used by the engine. I had the tank topped off with fuel, put a new gasket in the cap, and made sure the fuel sump was completely closed and taped for security. My first great lesson in flying mortality was the lesson about not flying into bad weather, which I had learned over Kentucky. Here was my second great lesson: Don't trust rented equipment to have been adequately maintained. Check *everything* mechanical before flying.

Lest readers think flying is just absurdly dangerous (or that *I* am absurdly dangerous), please know that I have enjoyed many hundreds of uneventful hours of flying. Admittedly, as someone has said, "Flying is hours of boredom separated by moments of stark terror!" But typically, the longer you fly the safer you become as you increasingly recognize your own mortality and learn to take *nothing* for granted!

Central Christian Church of Kansas City, Kansas was an incredibly difficult congregation in which to do ministry. As is so often true in troubled churches, the great majority of the people were wonderful, but the dynamics in the church were terrible. As I diagnosed the problem, there had not been an adequately long interim ministry after William C. Nichols (yes, *that* Bill Nichols, later interim GMP between John Humbert and me). Bill had been such a winsome pastoral leader and such a popular preacher that it is hard to imagine how *anyone* could have followed him without some time for the congregation to first grieve its losses.

It was an important lesson for me as a young minister. Lots of churches make the mistake of calling a new permanent pastor too soon after the departure of a popular predecessor. It is one of the mistakes regional ministers always warn congregations about but, in the midst of grief, congregations are often eager to get a new leader as soon as possible. It's akin to the fact that people who lose a beloved spouse are often tempted to marry again too quickly. People soon began trying to get me, the associate pastor, to help them undermine the senior pastor. I was at least smart enough to know that to do so would be unethical, and that if I then became senior minister, I would in turn be undermined by the same people.

Within a year, to stop the game-playing, I publicly announced that I would be leaving as soon as I received another call. (I don't usually recommend that pastors make such an announcement until they *have* another call, but this was an extreme situation.)

It was an incredibly stressful time, and yet three great things came out of it. First, our son David was born while we were there. Second, the youth group with which I worked as associate pastor was wonderful—beginning with their having unloaded our U-Haul on the day of our arrival and ending with the development of deep spiritual growth together. A particular gift from that youth group was that one of the youth, Donna Heim, felt a call to ministry and has greatly blessed the whole church these many years since (along with her husband, Bill Rose-Heim, who came along later). Third, Eldon Irving could not have been a better senior minister from whom to learn. A graduate of Yale Divinity School, Eldon was kind and emotionally supportive, and he helped me learn how to work more efficiently. He also taught me that it is good for a leader to surround himself or herself with people who have different gifts from your own and who will thus see things you don't see and bring greater balance overall to the work. That is priceless advice which has proved itself over and over.

The Disciples of Christ were amazingly strong at the time in the Greater Kansas City Area (now a region), with some eighty congregations in the metropolitan area that extends across the Kansas–Missouri state line. John Wolfersberger was the area minister at the time and a wonderful mentor. There were many outstanding and experienced Disciples ministers in the area who took me under wing and helped me do more than merely survive Central Christian Church. These included K. David Cole, Charles Duxbury, Tom Lieurance, Jack McInnis, Dan Moseley (who became a close friend for life), Jerry Porter, Bob Sweeten, Tom Underwood, and John Young. I was in peer support groups with these people and learned so much. So many others became good friends as well, including Lawrence Bash, Gene Brice, Forrest Haggard, Keith Strain, Terry Zimmerman, Area Associate Minister James Blair, Rick Butler, Fred Doris, Lloyd Gentry, Harold VanCleave, Wilma Little, and others. There was no better place than Kansas City to begin a full-time ministry.

Starting a New Congregation

Once I had announced my impending departure from Central Christian Church, the chair of the Area New Church Committee, Jerry Porter, approached me about the possibility of starting a new congregation on the far north side of Kansas City, Missouri. I had been a member of a new congregation in St. Petersburg (Palm Lake Christian Church). So, the idea was not foreign to me, even though mainline Protestants had largely ceased starting congregations after about 1965. It was 1975, and there were few people who had much idea about how to start a new congregation then, given the huge cultural shifts that had been unfolding during the past decade. But as my unhappiness at Central grew, I gradually became more open to the idea of starting a new congregation, thinking that I could perhaps "bend a twig" in a way that would help make a better Disciples congregation.

Finally, I agreed to be the first full-time pastor of North Oak Christian Church, a congregation of about sixteen people (pulled together in the previous months by retired ministers Virgil Nalley and Jim Hamilton) that had begun meeting in the basement of a Reorganized Latter Day Saints congregation just a few months before and had not yet been chartered as a congregation. I can't say that I felt a strong sense of "call" to that particular ministry, but I definitely felt "called out" of Central Christian Church.

North Oak was a practical move in the sense that our son had been born in May of that year (the same day that the initial small group of North Oak had first met for worship, unbeknownst to me), and I didn't really want to uproot our little family to move very far. So, I began work in Kansas City North in October of 1975.

We continued to live in the duplex we had rented when coming to Central, on what was then the far west side of Kansas City, Kansas. But it was only about a forty-five-minute drive out to my new "mission field." That gave us time to find a house we could afford in the Kansas City North (Missouri) area where the new church was being developed. We bought a small, older house with a walk-out basement, which provided a space in the lower level for an office with an outside entrance. It also had enough backyard for a small garden. It was a fairly easy move physically because we still didn't have a lot of furniture. Fortunately, we had saved some money during Mindy's four years of work as a medical technologist and had gotten our money out of the sale of our airplane so that we could make the required down payment.

Starting a new church brought some particularly personal challenges. We applied for a credit card, but when the company inquired about the location of my church, I had to give them our home address because the church had no building, no land, and no phone other than our home phone. Each credit card company to which we applied had the same reply: "Please contact us when your church has its own land and building."

I discovered that other Disciples congregations on the north side (but not quite so far north) were not necessarily excited by the prospect of a new Disciples congregation being started. Their attitude was, "Well, we might want to evangelize that part of town ourselves" (never mind that they hadn't done so in the twenty-plus years since that area, still mostly farmland, had been brought into the city limits). So, it seems, a new church pastor always has three tasks: First, convince the people coming to your worship services that the congregation is going to be viable and grow; second, convince the denominational folks who are helping foot your bills early on that you are going to be viable and grow; and third, convince the Disciples congregations within ten miles that they should support, or at least not oppose, your efforts. I expected the first two but not the third. But by the mid-1970s, the social disestablishment of the mainline church (including the Disciples) had already begun, and existing congregations were becoming somewhat anxious and defensive, and moving toward a survival mentality (more about this later).

The Congregation Takes Root

Despite the challenges, the congregation began to grow in numbers. We moved from the basement of the RLDS church to the New Mark Middle School, which had recently been built. The next challenge became the purchase of suitable land. As they say in real estate, the secret to most any public enterprise is "location, location, location." We began looking everywhere along the North Oak Trafficway and US 169, the two north-south roads that ran through the heart of our target area. There was still a lot of undeveloped land available, but when the Kansas City Metropolitan Airport moved from downtown out to farmland fifteen miles to the northwest to become Kansas City International (KCI became comically referred to as Kansas City Inconvenient), just six miles west of our projected church's area, land speculation began all around the new airport including as far east as our area.

This overspeculation drove land prices sky-high, and we found that most of the suitable properties were far out of our reach as a congregation. The Christian Church of Greater Kansas City had not anticipated having to help with funding for anything other than my salary, so when news came that the least expensive suitable site we could find was going to cost $220,000 ($37,500 per acre for six acres), the shock was palpable both in the congregation and in the Area Church. To his everlasting credit, John Wolfersberger got the Area to commit the dollars to help purchase the land. Without that help, the project would undoubtedly have died.[2]

Then the architects could be hired. We had a budget of about $200,000 for a fellowship hall (which would serve as our sanctuary for the foreseeable future) and a few classrooms. The drawings were completed, and the bids came in. The least expensive bid was $350,000. Wes Tyree, the chair of the building committee, came to my house to give me the news. He said that upon hearing $350,000, I turned white as a sheet. It was devastating news! So, we went back to the drawing board, literally, and came up with a plan that was closer to $250,000, which we thought we could swing if all went well. Again, that might not seem like a lot of money as I write this today, but $250,000 in 1977 equaled $1,250,000 in 2021 dollars, and at this point, North Oak Christian Church was composed of about fifty members, most of whom were young people of modest means!

Nevertheless, ground was broken in the fall of 1978, and the building began coming out of the ground in spring 1978. We were still meeting at New Mark Middle School, which was pressuring us to leave, as they did not want to appear to be providing space for a particular congregation indefinitely. We had been setting up chairs

---

[2] $220,000 in 2021 dollars is over $1,100,000.

and worship paraphernalia each Sunday for two years, and we were all eager to get to a permanent home. We had now grown to about seventy-five members and things were looking up, even though the anticipated growth in residential and commercial developments had not happened due to the high land prices, which continued to impact land and construction costs.

"Moving Sunday" finally came in the summer of 1979. We began worship that morning at the school and, with our church pianist, Cynthia Chambers, playing the theme from *Exodus*, we formed a caravan of cars and trucks to make the roughly one-mile trek to our new home. What a glorious day!

Now, with our own location, we could develop ongoing programs that drew new people. A first-class preschool was developed by Cindy O'Hara and Jayne Bruno, along with other innovative programs. The congregation continued to grow slowly, "organically," one might say.

It was soon after we made the move to our new building that a huge Roman Catholic parish to the south established a new parish in our area. The Trans World Airlines overhaul base that had been operating for decades in New Jersey was moved to the new Kansas City International. Many people made the move from New Jersey to KC, and many of them were Catholic. I made cold calls on hundreds of houses in the area inviting people to come to North Oak if they didn't already have a church home (which most didn't).

In those days, most people would actually answer their door, and ninety-nine percent of them were courteous, perhaps one to two percent inviting me inside to talk about the new church. But huge numbers of the new residents I contacted this way were Catholics who had moved from Jersey with TWA. So, when they responded that they were Catholic, I began asking them if they had enrolled yet in the Catholic parish. Most had not, so I handed them one of our North Oak brochures (in case they had said they were Catholic just to politely end the conversation) and also handed them a small piece of paper with the Catholic Parish's phone number so they could call and enroll if they were truly Catholic.

When the new Holy Family Parish began to be formed in our neighborhood, the priest, Father Patrick Rush, and I became fast friends. As a Disciples of Christ minister, I believed strongly in the unity of all Christians, so I asked our board to provide space for the Catholic congregation to worship at our place on Holy Days when the

Middle School (which Holy Family was now using) was unavailable. The board readily agreed. We soon began observing Ash Wednesday together at North Oak Christian Church. There was a rather hilarious moment as Father Pat and I began distributing ashes to those present by making the sign of the cross on each other's foreheads. Pat was as bald as I was, and it appeared to those present in the service that there was so much available space on our heads we could have written the traditional Ash Wednesday phrases there ("ashes to ashes, dust to dust") with room left over! North Oak continues to have a good relationship with Holy Family all these years later, even though that parish church has grown to many times the size of North Oak Christian.

Mindy wanted to earn some extra income for us as our finances were getting pretty tight, so she applied to be a census taker for the 1980 census. She was calling on people in our area who had not filled out the regular forms to ask them to fill out the forms on the spot. Most everyone was quite hospitable to her, but at one house there was a problem. A woman came to the door and Mindy explained who she was and why she was there. The woman wanted nothing to do with it and started closing the door. Mindy apparently held onto the storm door handle a little too long. The woman took exception to this and called the police. So, a little later I got a call from Mindy at the police station. She had been picked up and charged with "disturbing the peace"! Anybody who knows Mindy would have to laugh out loud at such a charge, but here she was at the booking desk. She was released on her own recognizance (apparently not being perceived as a threat to the community) and a court date was set. The complainant didn't show up. The judge dismissed the case and said, "I wish she was here today. ... I'd have made her fill out the census form right now!" It made for a good story, which I have told perhaps hundreds of times.

One great need "north of the river," as locals often describe Kansas City North (the "river" being the Missouri), was pastoral counseling. I had developed a close friendship in a small group with a person who represented herself as a Ph.D. clinical psychologist with a strong church connection. We invited her to begin providing counseling at North Oak Christian one or two days a week to bring the services to the neighborhood. After several months of providing this service, it was discovered that she had no Ph.D.—in fact, she had no degree of *any* kind. She was very good at pretending (remember the movie, *Catch Me if You Can?*). Some people have a remarkable capacity to fake while looking absolutely competent! Having considered her a close friend, I was devastated and felt totally betrayed. An attorney, Larry Larson, who was a member of our congregation and board chair (*this* was providential!) met her at the church the next time she was scheduled to meet clients there, collected her keys to the church, and told her never to come back.

Fortunately, North Oak was never sued over this, but the thought that a "friend" would fake credentials and counsel clients, thus putting them at risk and the congregation in legal jeopardy for the sake of her own aggrandizement, was a sobering reality and taught me a lesson about trusting "credentials."[3]

Peacemaking

In 1980, tensions between the teachers' union and the North Kansas City School District leadership began to develop around the matter of salaries and benefits. Things began to heat up as the local press began publishing statements from both the union and the administration. But labor negotiations conducted through the press are seldom successful. One afternoon, the president of the teacher's union (who knew me through some members of my congregation who were public school teachers) came to me to ask for any help I might be able to offer. I had no experience in negotiating labor agreements, but I could imagine how much long-term destruction would occur if there was a strike. Teachers who crossed the picket line would be resented by those who didn't, and the relationships between the union leadership and the school district's administrators would be poisoned for years. As a pastor, I had always had an affinity for both public school teachers and school administrators.

So, on the next Saturday, I drove to the house of the chair of the NKC School Board, who (luckily) was in his driveway working on a car. I parked my car at the curb and walked up and introduced myself. I told him that I was concerned about the impending strike and the impact it would have on teachers, administrators, and students. I could see the look on his face, "Oh geez, here I am trying to enjoy my Saturday and this guy is here to tell me what he thinks."

---

[3] One practical result of this episode was that years later as a regional minister, I insisted that congregational search committees be sure to check the credentials of any potential candidate no matter how good they *looked*.

However, his expression changed when I said to him, "If the teachers' union leadership would agree to sit down in confidential sessions without the press knowing about it, would the School Board be interested in conversations that might lead to a mutually agreeable settlement?" He asked, "Have they said they would do that?" I said a bit more than I really knew by responding, "If you are willing, they are willing." He said, "Yes, we would be interested in that possibility." I told him I would get back to him. I immediately met with the union president and told him, "They would be willing to meet in secret if you are." To my great relief, he agreed.

So, we set up a meeting on a weekday evening in downtown Kansas City (we didn't want anyone in the Kansas City North area seeing us together). As I drove the fifteen miles down US 169 toward the meeting, all the way to downtown I was berating myself, *What the heck do you think you are doing? You have no experience in mediation of contracts. You're going to make the situation worse and make a fool out of yourself!* But I was in too deep to get out now.

So, as I drove, I prayed: "God, this situation is not unlike pastoral counseling I have done between angry family members. Help me to do what I have been trained to do! Calm my nerves and grant me a sense of confidence as I walk into that conference room."

My confidence began to build as I remembered I was doing something God would want done and, since at that moment I was the only person in a position to mediate, I decided I'd better get over myself and do my best. I walked into that room quite calm (it reminded me a bit of flying into the clouds a few years before). There were three representatives of the union, two from the school district board, and the superintendent.

Both sides wanted to get through this without a strike, so we were able to lay out the basis of an agreement that night. The agreement was approved within two days by both the union leadership and the school board. Everyone behaved like adults and the school district moved forward. I was impressed by how much easier dialogue and agreement was accomplished by face-to-face meetings versus trying to negotiate (or, more realistically, trying to bring pressure to bear on each other) through the press. Besides settling the dispute without a strike, North Oak Christian Church's reputation as "progressive and engaged in the community" was enhanced, which made the church attractive to many new folks, especially teachers.

Over the years, the congregation was remarkably gracious to me. A lesser congregation might have been less generous with some of my less than stellar behaviors. For example, one Sunday morning came when I had no sermon. I had tried *really* hard to write a sermon, but I was just so exhausted by things I had been addressing that week that I simply came up empty handed. So, when the sermon time arrived, I said this (or something close to it): "I have no sermon to offer this week. I tried, but nothing came. I promised you I would never waste your time, and so I didn't want to fill this time with something less than what you deserve. I apologize, but I've got nothing worth saying this morning."

That might have gotten a preacher fired in some places, but this congregation gave me a pass. I imagine they could see the weariness in my face. I learned from the occasion, however, and soon after began taking an annual retreat to plan my preaching for the year and to get four sermons "in the bag": Christmas (it's hard to say something new every Christmas, but easier when you are not under pressure), Easter (same as Christmas); a sermon for my first Sunday back from vacation (so I didn't have to start preparing it the last few days of my vacation time), and one for any Sunday when I might have had such a week that I just didn't have the energy to create something. I also developed outlines for most of the other Sundays of the year, using the lectionary readings as a basis, but knowing that if last-minute inspiration hit, I could always set aside an outline and go with something that was more pressing. One such occasion was when a "skywalk" collapsed at the Hyatt Regency in Kansas City, killing one hundred and fourteen people (July 17, 1981). I set aside what I had prepared for the day and spoke to the theme, "Where was God at the Hyatt Regency?" I knew members would be asking themselves the age-old question, "Why do bad things happen to good people?" My conclusion, in part, was, "God *was* present at the Hyatt Regency, *grieving.*"

One Sunday in October 1980, the Kansas City Royals were playing the New York Yankees (including "Mr. October," Reggie Jackson!) in the American League Play-Off Series at Royals Stadium. As a diehard Royals fan, I *really* wanted to be there, but I had no tickets. So, I closed that Sunday service with the following benediction: "Now, O Lord, remember thou thy servant if there be any extra tickets to the game this afternoon. Amen." At 3 PM that day, Mindy and I were sitting directly behind home plate. Never mind my personal abuse of the liturgy, what a congregation! (The Royals swept the series 3–0, by the way.)

A Family Crisis

Our daughter, Laura, was born in 1977 in nearby Smithville, Missouri, and North Oak Christian Church had become a wonderful home for the four of us. The congregation was largely composed of similar families with children, and the congregation ministered to us deeply when our family faced its first real crisis.

At the age of three, Laura came home from our annual visit with her Florida grandparents with a fever. Not unusual for a three-year old, of course, but it continued to rise. Finally, early one morning, Laura said that her neck hurt. Red flags went off in our heads as we vaguely remembered something about a stiff neck being a possible sign of spinal meningitis. Mindy called the doctor's office and got her in as soon as possible. The doctor immediately arranged for her to be admitted to St. Luke's Hospital in downtown Kansas City, Missouri.

A culture was taken, and Laura was indeed diagnosed with spinal meningitis. We knew nothing of the disease, but we quickly learned that there are two types: viral and bacterial. The viral kind is usually not as severe in effect but cannot be cured with medications; the patient must simply be made as comfortable as possible while waiting it out. The bacterial kind tends to be more severe in possible side effects but can be aggressively treated with antibiotics. However, bacterial meningitis and the aggressive antibiotics used to treat it can have their own negative side effects, including hearing loss and other long-term issues.

The culture showed that Laura had bacterial meningitis. So, she could be treated, but we didn't know how profound any side effects might be. Within a day she lay totally listless in her hospital bed due to the disease and the medications given to her to provide comfort. To say we were concerned is, of course, putting it mildly! After three long days, the doctor was finally willing to say, "She's going to make it." But we still didn't know what lasting effects there might be. After several more days of intravenous antibiotics, she was looking much better and her energy was returning. Mindy and I took turns staying with her in the hospital, and Mindy's mother came to help care for David at home. For me, those times sitting with her in the hospital room were times of bonding between father and daughter. In particular, as Laura began feeling better, we watched *The Wizard of Oz* together at the hospital, and we watched that movie together many times in the years after (later, *Twister* became our favorite father-daughter movie to watch). There was no damage to her hearing, and we don't know of other lasting effects of the disease, so Mindy and I have always felt profoundly grateful.

The Kansas City Area had so many Disciples in it that I didn't have much time to cultivate ecumenical relationships other than that with Father Patrick. But the Kansas City Area Church gave me lots of opportunities for leadership development. I served on and then chaired several area committees including Congregational Revitalization (which helped me learn the importance of understanding the context of a congregation, new or old). Later, as chair of the New Church Establishment Committee, I learned how to select potential new church sites. Eventually, I became moderator of the area, serving with Area Minister (later Regional Minister) David Downing, who had become a dear friend. To this day, my advice to ministers is to serve on various committees (one at a time) in their region or area as a way of serving the wider church, of course, but also as a way of doing continuing education that will sharpen their skills and benefit every congregation they ever serve.

Having served for eight mostly wonderful but stressful years in Kansas City, I was getting restless. It had taken six years to build North Oak Christian Church from sixteen interested people to a congregation of about two hundred members. Our daughter Laura had been born during our second year at North Oak, and it was wonderful that both our children had so many contemporaries at North Oak with whom to begin their lives. But while new church development is so enriching in so many ways, it takes incredible amounts of time and hard work and, frankly, it doesn't pay very well. We had gone through the money we had saved in seminary when Mindy was working full-time and Little Eagle Creek Christian Church had provided a parsonage plus a small salary.

The folks at North Oak Christian Church were doing the best they could to pay me what they could while carrying the building mortgage, so I didn't feel I could ask for more. But I needed more and, looking back, I should have made my needs more clearly known so North Oak would at least have had a *chance* to increase my salary. I have advised new ministers to make their circumstances plain—gently but clearly—to their congregations' leadership and not to assume that they know what you need or will know what to do about it.

But I was also eager for an opportunity to work with a much larger program and more resources for ministry than were going to be possible for several years at North Oak, someplace where I was not the only ordained minister. So, I began to be open to a new call. My dear and long-time friend from seminary days, Jim Powell, was then serving as associate regional minister in the Indiana Region, and he told me that First Christian Church in Ft. Wayne was seeking a new senior pastor and, "I put your name in." This was just 20 miles north of Mindy's hometown of Bluffton (the scene of the "wedding capers") and her parents still lived there. First Christian Church had a reputation as a fine congregation. In addition to our children's maternal grandparents being in the area, I had an uncle (Charles Janeway) who had lived in Ft. Wayne most of his life working as a firefighter. It all seemed like it might be providential in many ways.

So, I flew over alone for an interview. This time I flew commercially. We had dropped our membership in the Kansas City flying club. This trip didn't go without incident, however. I had what I thought was a very good interview, but there was an ice storm the next morning, when I was to leave. The Ft. Wayne Airport shut down. I *had* to get home, because no one at North Oak knew I was in Ft. Wayne for an interview, and I had to preach that Sunday. So, the chair of the Ft. Wayne First Christian Church Board, George Bruckman, drove me (slowly on the icy roads!) to Indianapolis, where I was able to pick up a flight back to Kansas City. But that gave me an extra couple of hours to get to know George and to ask more questions about Ft. Wayne and First Christian Church. I left with a growing sense of call.

Chapter 3

Off to the City of Three Rivers

We enjoyed our 1974-1982 sojourn in Kansas City so much because it is such a wonderful metropolitan area. We hated to leave it. But it was *incredibly* difficult to say goodbye to North Oak Christian Church. These people—many the same age as Mindy and I, or nearly so—had become family (as congregations most always do). We had all invested blood, sweat, and tears in this new congregation. But, I also knew that this was *their* congregation, not mine.

On my last day in the office, I walked alone throughout our "first unit" building—with its fellowship hall/sanctuary, three classrooms, and kitchen—and remembered the trials and victories we had all shared together, the conversations, the joy and laughter, the tears, all of it. I thought for a moment, "Why am I leaving here? This is crazy!" But, in the midst of my own tears, I felt the Presence of God and the unmistakable sense of call to Ft. Wayne. It was time to go.

This was the first move we had made that did not involve a U-Haul truck or trailer. Our furniture was mostly no great shakes, but it was precious to us ... and there was my library of several hundred books. We bought a house just a mile west of the church and near the beautiful Foster Park, which featured fantastic annual flower displays and a golf course.

First Christian Church (Disciples of Christ) had moved from downtown Ft. Wayne to the south side of town in 1952. It had a beautiful stone building with a high steeple set on a four-acre lot at a busy intersection. Those who'd built the structure had great foresight in terms of functionality, in that there was wonderful space for just about any kind of activity. The one drawback was that, as with most postwar church buildings, it was built by relatively young people who gave little thought to the stairs they would have to climb thirty years later! There was no elevator to connect the various levels. But the sanctuary was lovely, with a very high ceiling and a "rock of ages" kind of feel.

My predecessor, Harold Cline (dear Ruby's husband), was an extremely competent minister. His good work in Ft. Wayne confirmed my suspicion that it is almost always easier to follow someone who is competent than to follow someone who struggles with leadership. Harold had left the church organizationally and missionally strong and relatively easy to lead.

That said, at the age of thirty-four, assuming leadership of a multiple-staff church, I had a steep learning curve, and some would say, I was in well over my head. But the wonderful lay leadership at First Christian must have felt I had potential, because they worked with me.

A Personal Scare

I left North Oak Christian Church exhausted, and I began at First Christian without a break (regrettable, but we couldn't financially afford a real break), preaching my first Sunday in Ft. Wayne on Palm Sunday, 1982. Of course, Mindy was exhausted, too, managing the move and the children while I focused on the work transition. It all caught up with *me* on Memorial Day weekend. In addition to preaching twice on May 30, my associate called in sick, which meant I unexpectedly had to speak at the graduation banquet that morning for our high school seniors.

During the night before, I woke up with a heart irregularity that was new and obvious. I didn't know if I was having a heart attack or what was happening. But it was taking my breath away. I decided I'd better get to the emergency room. Without fully explaining to Mindy what was happening, and with our children—seven and five years old—in bed asleep, I slipped out of bed and drove myself to the hospital (yes, dumb).

When you mention the word "heart" in an emergency room, they take you in as quickly as possible. They immediately put me on a gurney and wired me up to an EKG machine. After twenty minutes or so, the doctor told me I was not having a heart attack but was exhibiting signs of stress and exhaustion in the form of premature ventricular contractions (PVCs). He said to go home and sleep a couple of days and the signs would subside. However, he said, "You won't trust your heart unless you have a full work-up, so I am sending you to a general practitioner who specializes in heart care."

I drove home relieved, but still experiencing the PVCs and, as he had predicted, not fully believing that I was going to be okay. Premature ventricular contractions (sometimes called "premature heartbeats") feel like there's a recurring vacuum in your chest. I frankly don't remember who covered for me that next morning, but I stayed in bed. Gradually, over the next two days, the PVCs faded and then stopped, except for an occasional recurrence. I saw Dr. Jerry Andrews on Wednesday. He injected some radioactive dye, wired me up to a couple of devices, and put me on the treadmill. Within thirty minutes my test was complete, and I waited for the results.

The doctor sat with me and said, "The ER physician was correct, this is not going to kill you ... at least not very soon. But it is a warning. I am prescribing several things for you. You need to lose about twenty pounds, you need to stop drinking caffeine" (that was a low blow, as it was my custom to go in early and drain a pot of coffee before anyone else arrived at the office), "you need to stop taking yourself so seriously" (hmmm ... not the first time I had heard that), "and" (here it comes), "I want you to jog or run two miles every other day."

I immediately responded, "Doc, I'll do everything you've prescribed except running two miles every other day. I can't do that."

He said, "What do you mean you can't do it?"

So, I explained that I had thrown discus in high school and college and "always took a run around the quarter-mile track to warm up and always found that at the end of a quarter mile I was winded. I finally realized that I have small lungs."

He said, "You have *what?*"

"I have small lungs."

He looked at me with a smile and stifled a laugh saying, "Dick, I hate to be the one to tell you, but you *don't* have small lungs ... you have a fat [behind]!"

So, I went home and started running every other day, each time a little further than the time before, and lo and behold, within a couple of weeks I was running two miles. The weight came off and I felt a whole lot better. Little by little, I began to trust my body again, but I learned it takes a while for those who have even relatively mild cardiac events to regain trust of their bodies. The experience probably saved my life, and it certainly gave me a new appreciation for parishioners who experience such things. To this day I have worked at keeping my weight down and exercising regularly.

The "not taking myself so seriously" part has been more of a challenge. However, I know that I do not suffer this affliction alone.

New Opportunities and Learning New Ways

When I was four or five years old, I remember climbing up a step ladder to see what the world looked like from my father's height of six-feet-four-inches. It was frighteningly high! I thought, "Wow, being an adult is scary!" But, of course, one gradually grows taller so that with each inch of growth a new sense of normal develops and it's okay. The same happens with other kinds of challenges in life.

As the months of 1982 wore on, I grew into the new responsibilities and learned much about how to handle the various stresses and strains of ministry in general and of a multiple-staff church in particular. I began to fall in love with this new congregation and with Ft. Wayne as a city.

Ft. Wayne is situated at the confluence of two rivers, the St. Mary and the St. Joseph, which together form a third river, the Maumee. This made it an early hub of trade and, unfortunately, prone to flooding. It began as a fort built by General "Mad" Anthony Wayne in 1794 as a military outpost in the tragic subjection of the Miami Indians whose land was rapidly encroached upon by European settlers.

Today, Ft. Wayne is a city with major industry in the areas of electronics and automobiles and trucks. It is also a regional commercial, medical, and educational center with several four-year colleges and universities. Known for strong philanthropy, it has many lovely parks, a botanical garden, a restored classic theater, a beautiful minor league ballpark in the old downtown floodplain, a wonderful children's zoo, a performance center that is home to a fine symphony, a ballet company, and much more.

A person or church looking to do public advocacy found easy access to the news and editorial pages in two major newspapers, and to television coverage. I have often said that, "being a pastor in Ft. Wayne was great because you could get on television for something other than shooting someone!"

Gary Nunnally was serving as associate pastor when I arrived, but he soon resigned due to issues, not really his fault, that doomed his ministry before I arrived. He was followed by Don Wiltfong, an excellent Disciples colleague whom we recruited straight out of Christian Theological Seminary. Eventually we added a minister of music, Helen Donnell, and a minister of education, Linn Bartling, who was a licensed United Church of Christ minister. Together with our front office person, Diane Johnson, and our organist, Jerry Zimmerman, this was as creative and productive a staff as one could ask for. It was an immense pleasure to work with each of them. We also had a number of college and seminary interns, including Karla Dyer Buchanan, Jim Grimshaw, and Jeff Bates.

Soon after I arrived, one of our members who was a high school principal, Jack Weicker, invited me to join him at the Downtown Rotary Club. I joined this club, which was both a lot of fun and a "who's who" of city leaders. Rotary helped me rapidly find places of influence and service in the wider community and to hear and interact with speakers who were state as well as local leaders. Among the members were most of the Ft. Wayne School District executive administrators.

I made it a point to meet some of the other clergy of the city through the local council of churches, called Associated Churches of Allen County. Out of these associations came a progressive group called Clergy United for Action, which included the local rabbi, Richard Safran. Our aim was to advocate for issues in Ft. Wayne, such as racial and economic justice. Having become friends with the progressive editorial page editor, Larry Hayes (who had grown up in another part of the Stone-Campbell Movement), I was able to get op-eds written by me and other members of our group printed regularly, which called upon various groups and institutions (such as the school districts) to move on important issues.

Because First Christian was the site of a food bank, it was natural to develop a Bread for the World group. We met regularly to review what was happening in the world in regard to food security and to offer an annual "Offering of Letters" to our congressional representatives and senators.

Meanwhile, First Christian Church was beginning to grow a bit. We had somewhat of a challenge to growth in the fact that our building looked like something that would house an upper-socioeconomic-class congregation when we were, in reality, a very middle-middle-class congregation. So, getting the middle-class people who lived on the south side of the city to come and visit us at First Christian in our big, beautiful building was sometimes difficult. But my engagements across the life of the city, and those of our members, made the church seem more approachable and attractive.

Mindy and I love to go to the symphony, and some members of the Ft. Wayne Philharmonic decided to join First Christian (including cellist Sam Smith, who was the son of a Disciples minister; Sam's wife, Nancy, who was a bass player; and their symphony colleagues Lenelle and Dan Morse Ross). They in turn invited their friends to play at First Christian, and so we often enjoyed symphonic music in worship.

In 1984, a dispute arose between teachers and the Ft. Wayne Community School District. The tension lasted several months, with each side telling its story through various media. (Sound familiar?) I hadn't thought too much about all of this (except for the fact that this was our children's school district) until one day it hit me, "If no one intervenes to mediate, there is going to be a strike in our schools." I remembered how devastating strikes can be to a district for many years. Suddenly this sense of call came over me: "Who else in the city has experience in these things?" So, I suddenly became convicted that I had a responsibility to offer to assist as I had in the North Kansas City dispute.

I had relationships with both the leadership of the Ft. Wayne teachers' union and the Ft. Wayne Community School District administrators. So, I quietly went to each and asked, "Would you be willing to meet confidentially with the other side?" Again, no responsible teacher and no responsible administrator *wants* a strike. It is absolutely deadly to morale and will drive young families toward other school districts and private schools. The key is *confidentiality*. Neither side wants the public to think that it blinked first. This is an important learning: I would like to shake every senator and congressperson in the United States today and say, "Stop trying to negotiate through the press! It never works!" But I digress.

Both the teachers and the administration agreed to meet with me in secret. After weeks of intensifying rhetoric, to their credit, each side yielded a bit and an agreement was reached and approved in a matter of a couple of days. I was present when the public announcement of the settlement was made, but true to my word, I kept a low profile and spoke to no reporters. Nevertheless, my friends among both the teachers and the administration, and my congregation, knew what had happened, and it was appreciated. A plaque of appreciation from the school district showed up some time later. But, again, being an effective mediator often means remaining quiet and not allowing yourself to become a focus of attention. The parties must be seen as the primary enablers of the agreement (which they are), not the mediator.

Like the north side of Kansas City, the south side of Ft. Wayne was underserved when it came to counseling services. Thus, we brought a pastoral counselor to the church, providing an office, two days a week, in order to make such services more accessible. (But this time, I knew to check credentials and not take anything at face value!)

I soon found friends among young social justice proponents in the city, most of whom were not connected to any church but who shared my concerns for the marginalized. An older progressive leader in the community who became a friend was the CEO of Lincoln National Life, then based in Ft. Wayne, Ian Rolland. A younger man, Nick Kern, and I formed a small group to oppose apartheid in South Africa. Nick and I visited the CEO of the Lincoln National Bank, which was selling Krugerrands (South African gold coins) to ask the bank to stop selling them. We pointed out that the namesake of the bank (Abraham Lincoln) "would certainly not approve of them being sold in his bank." He didn't throw us out.

Racism is a huge issue in Ft. Wayne, as it is in all of America. The Ft. Wayne Community Schools had desegregated the high schools in response to court judgments in the 1950s and 1960s. However, the elementary schools had remained segregated by neighborhoods which, *practically* speaking, meant segregated by race, as most Ft. Wayne neighborhoods were quite segregated racially due to decades of red lining, steering, and other illegal but impactful practices. Clergy United for Action, and other groups in the city, pushed for desegregation of the elementary schools. But it was a hard sell for at least two reasons. First, few parents of any race wanted their kids to have to take long bus rides to school every day; second, the school board was appointed rather than elected, and few politicians were willing to touch the "third rail" that racial issues represented (and still represent) in Indiana.

I wrote op-eds about this in the *Journal Gazette* and occasionally was interviewed about it and other issues. I was becoming well enough known that TV stations would sometimes seek me out for comment on such matters as the school district's bond issues. It was satisfying to become a person of influence in that city. But there was also a constant red flag waving in the back of my mind and, sometimes, in front of my eyes, to be careful about either mixing partisan politics and religion or becoming too political in my strategies. It was important to maintain friendships on "both sides of the aisle" and on all sides of important issues so as to be able to share strong opinions face to face and not through public confrontations that make good theater and might enhance one's own visibility but do little to move the ball of justice down the field.

In 1987, our family visited my parents' home in St. Petersburg, as we often did. My Aunt Mabel (my mother's sister) and Uncle Don Terbush had purchased a used twenty-foot inboard/outboard boat in which Aunt Mabel could fish. She didn't operate the boat herself, but their next-door neighbor would take her out in it from time to time to fish. She very generously offered to loan it to me while we were in town, knowing that I had some experience with power boats.

It was decided that Laura would go with me to put the boat in the water, and we would then go across the bay to pick up David and Mindy so we could all go along. On the way to the boat ramp, I stopped at a gas station to top off the boat. Then we put in at a ramp on Boca Ciega Bay. I turned on the bilge fan to evacuate any gas fumes that might have collected there. While still tied to the dock, I had Laura stand at the back of the boat and I turned the "start" key.

The stern exploded, blowing the engine cowling forward, grazing my head before bouncing off the windshield and landing in the water a hundred feet away. A piece of something also flew off the engine and hit my ankle. I was stunned and dazed, of course, and all I could think was, "Laura's back there!" I turned around afraid of what I would see, but she was standing there also stunned but unharmed. I ran back and literally threw her onto the dock and told her to run because the boat was going to burn. Sure enough, the flames quickly grew to burn ten feet into the air as the gasoline poured out of the ruptured tank onto the engine. Thankfully, I hadn't been knocked out by that flying engine cowling or else I'm not certain either of us would have gotten out in time.

I followed Laura out of the boat and hobbled along the dock to get away from the fire. The boat burned into the water and our fishing gear and everything else on board went with it. A policeman happened to be coming over a nearby bridge, had seen the explosion, and called the fire department. Laura and I sat on the back end of the ambulance while the fire continued to burn, and a couple of news helicopters circled overhead.

I apologized profusely to my aunt and uncle, who were of course just relieved that Laura and I were okay. They said insurance covered the cost of the boat (and, in fact, they were probably getting past the point where they should have such a speedboat anyway). I was on a walker for several days while my ankle healed, but the kids wanted to go to Disney World that week. So, we went and the park provided a wheelchair for me and we got priority treatment at every ride. The whole episode felt pretty miraculous as it all could have been so much worse.

On the first Sunday after vacation, a couple I did not recognize greeted me after the service and said, "See you at the rehearsal!"

I said, "What?"

They thought I was joking, but I did not recognize them or know what they were talking about.

They said, "You're doing our wedding on May 15!"

I looked in my calendar and, sure enough, there were their names and the wedding date. Then it became apparent: I had some short-term memory loss from the boating accident. I didn't remember meeting with this couple.

I put a note in the church newsletter explaining that I'd had an accident while on vacation that resulted in short-term memory loss, so if anyone had said anything important to me in the week or so before my vacation, they should probably repeat it. A couple of days later I received a note from one of our deacons. It read, "Dear Dick, Sorry to hear about your accident and resulting memory loss. But that doesn't change the fact that I loaned you $200 right before you left for St. Pete! Sincerely, Mel." (No, I hadn't borrowed $200 from Mel!)

The next time we were in St. Pete, my uncle was trying to sell his pick-up but not having any luck. I asked him if he wanted me to blow it up for him, but he declined. The episode did put me in touch with a couple of old high school friends, however, who had seen the picture and article in the *St. Pete Times* about the explosion of the boat.

There was a movement in Indiana to convert from appointed school boards, such as we had in Ft. Wayne, to elected school boards. This became interesting to me, because they were to be nonpartisan elections. Thinking we might make progress on integration of the elementary schools if we had an elected school board, I recruited six potential candidates who seemed to agree with me that it was time to integrate. I asked the mayor, Paul Helmke, if he would provide some campaign training for these individuals, and he agreed to do a workshop held in First Christian Church's basement. Remarkably, when election day came, five of the six candidates I had recruited were elected. One turned out to be a wolf in sheep's clothing and totally changed her tune once in office, but the four others constituted a majority of the seven-member school board, so lots of good change occurred quickly after the election.

While many of the people of First Christian Church were generally conservative, I don't remember anyone ever complaining about my community involvement. I think it was because I genuinely cared about everyone, regardless of their political leanings, and because I remained steadfastly nonpartisan in my public statements. Most all the politicians in Ft. Wayne were moderates, regardless of party, and had the best interests of the city in mind, which made it easy to find common ground.

I do chuckle when I remember a particular comment once made by one of my favorite parishioners, Judy Church. Judy had a sharp wit and a keen ear as well as a compassionate heart and a deep faith. After an unusually pointed social justice sermon one Sunday, she came to greet me at the door and said in a playful voice, "Things going too smoothly pastor?"

Meanwhile, our children were having a good experience in the Ft. Wayne Community Schools. They both attended an excellent elementary school and a magnet middle school, which meant they were able to experience going to school with kids from many different backgrounds and races.

Another huge plus about being in Ft. Wayne was being a part of the Indiana Region, one of the best. Howard Goodrich was regional minister and he and his staff were always thinking of ways to support ministers and congregations. In 1988, I was presented the "Model Minister" Award by the region, which touched me deeply. I learned a great deal about regional ministry from Howard and other Indiana colleagues. I was elected to serve as one of Indiana's representatives to the General Board of our denomination, and that opened my eyes to the wider church in new ways. Among the wonderful people I met while on General Board was a young minister from Oklahoma named Sharon Watkins. Sharon demonstrated a deep love for the Disciples and a keen Christian commitment. Her father, Keith, had been a professor of mine at CTS and had become a good friend through the years.

My First Sabbatical

In 1989, after seven years as senior pastor at First Christian, I got the opportunity to take a three-month sabbatical. This was something I had been encouraged to ask to have in my contract when I arrived in Ft. Wayne. I was very tired, so I anticipated this with great joy. I had a book in mind that I wanted to write, and I wanted to deeply rest. I knew I would have to get out of Ft. Wayne if I was to really "get away," but I didn't have much in the way of funds for travel.[1] So, my plan was to go home to St. Petersburg and stay with my parents for several weeks, driving home to Ft. Wayne to see my family every couple of weeks, and finally taking my family on a train trip from Ft. Wayne to New York and then down to St. Petersburg together for a few days. This all sounded good to my parents. I hated to leave Mindy and the kids for a couple weeks at a time, but they all had busy lives and commitments in Ft. Wayne.

So, when the day came, I loaded up my car and headed south for my first stop, Nashville. Dan Moseley had remained a close friend after our departure from Kansas City. Not too long before I left Kansas City, Dan went to serve as senior pastor at First Christian in Midwest City, Oklahoma, and then on to historic Vine Street Christian Church in Nashville, where he had been a student pastor while at Vanderbilt Divinity School and then associate minister under Wayne Bell. Dan and I had continued to gather through the years for two-day retreats, first in Wichita and then in Louisville. So, Dan and his wife, Cindy, hosted me on my first night of sabbatical.

Dan had been on sabbatical not long before me, and so he warned me that I might experience some depression early in the process, but not to worry, that was a normal response to being out of one's "place," where one's identity and responsibility were clear. I thought he must be crazy—how could anyone be depressed in the face of having time off to think and just be? But just a few days later, depression set in, and I began to wonder if *I* was crazy! I was so glad

---

[1] This was before the wonderful sabbatical grants that are made available today through various clergy support programs.

for Dan's heads-up about this phenomenon and, sure enough, the depression lifted in just a few days as I got my bearings. I have often shared this learned wisdom with many colleagues approaching their first sabbatical.

I had hoped that these several weeks in St. Petersburg would be an opportunity for me to spend some quality time with my parents, as they were aging. On the one hand, it was a great reconnecting time with my mother. My father, however, was drinking the entire time I was there, so connecting with him had to happen in the early to mid-morning or not at all. That was a great source of sadness for me, of course, but the primary depression I experienced was more around what Dan had warned me about. Dad did stop drinking a few years after this, but I was never able to have the same kind of time to spend with him again.

Nonetheless, I did manage to rest, do some writing (the imagined book, *The Black Hole Syndrome*, has yet to appear!), and reset a bit.

I came home thinking I was good for another seven years at First Christian of Ft. Wayne, and why not? It was a great church, I had wonderful friends there, and the kids' maternal grandparents were just thirty minutes away. However (my, "however" is such a pregnant word), in just a few months I began to feel restless. I fell back into old patterns of working too hard (my own addiction). I thought it was just post-sabbatical stuff, and I tried to put it aside. But then a letter came from the Tennessee Region inviting me to apply for the role of regional minister.

I suppose because of my penchant for organizational leadership and my concerns for the denomination, the idea of becoming a regional minister one day had been rumbling around in my brain. But when that invitation to apply showed up, it was like a vocational bolt of lightning. I thought, "Rats! I just came through a sabbatical in which I struggled with my professional, personal, and spiritual identity, and now I'm back at square one!"

I loved the day-to-day work of congregational ministry, and the thought of leaving congregational ministry was painful. I worried about becoming "just" a church administrator if I ever received a call to regional ministry, because I felt called to do both pastoral care and justice advocacy. But Howard Goodrich was a very positive example of how regional ministers were more than just administrators. Also, at the Anaheim General Assembly of 1981, I had heard United

Methodist Bishop Leontine Kelly speak and realized that the middle expression of denominations (regions, conferences, synods, and the like) can be an effective platform for justice advocacy, offering an even wider audience than a single congregation.

So, in spite of my own reservations, there was no turning off the sense of call. I applied. In those days, lots of people wanted to be regional ministers for one reason or another, so lots of people applied. But I was inwardly convinced that this is where God meant for me to go next. Mindy wasn't excited by this prospect (see the above list of great reasons to stay in Ft. Wayne). However, she knew I felt that strong sense of call and she supported me. Mindy had worked as a medical technologist while I was in seminary, but when our son was born, she decided to stay home full-time. Had we continued to be a two-career couple, the decision to move would have been much more complicated.

As Mindy and I retired one night, she turned out the light and remarked, "You are laying here thinking you're going to be the next regional minister of Tennessee even though there are a slew of other people in the mix! But what's *really* disgusting is that you're probably right!" We both laughed and went to sleep.

I never lost my inner sense that Tennessee is where I was headed, and the call came after the necessary interviews. I truly hated to leave Ft. Wayne and all the wonderful people there (despite the gray winter skies), but there was no possibility of saying "no" to what felt to me like a genuine call. It was the same kind of call that had brought us to Ft. Wayne eight years before. I was now forty-two years old and, I realized later, I would be the first baby boomer in Disciples regional ministry.

The goodbyes were hard, especially to my staff and close friends like the Churches, Davises, Hayes, Johnsons, Millers, Mullens, Ohnecks, Olsens, Weickers, Vanderwalls, Zimmermans, and so many others. But the sendoff was wonderful. So many friends from both the congregation and the community came to wish us well, including Mayor Helmke, who had become a friend over the years. Our house sold within days, a further sign to me that this was right. Laura, just finishing sixth grade, was also ready for something new. But David, just finishing ninth grade, had made a wonderful cadre of friends and quietly grieved the move. I hated that. Happily, however, he has managed to maintain many of his Ft. Wayne friendships over the years.

Chapter 4

The Three States of Tennessee

In early July, we left for Nashville, where we had purchased a house on the west side of town (Bellevue). It was a four-hundred-mile trip. We loaded both vehicles with plants, clothes for the trip, and other things that couldn't go in a moving van—including our dog, Tiffie—and headed out, with Mindy following me in the minivan. Our Indiana license tags had expired in May, but I didn't want to pay for expensive Indiana tag renewal only to remove the tags when we got to Tennessee. What were the chances we would get stopped for expired tags on our way south?

As we approached Louisville—me in front, Mindy behind—an Indiana State Trooper came up behind her. I thought, "You've got to be kidding!" Sure enough, he saw her expired tag and turned on his red flashing lights. Mindy slowed down and began pulling over. So, *I had to make a decision.* Do I pull over, too, so she doesn't face this alone? Or do I keep going and get across the Ohio Bridge just a couple of miles ahead? We had no cell phones then, so I had to decide for myself. I kept going!

After crossing the bridge, I pulled over on the shoulder to wait for her. It was several minutes, so I began to wonder if they had impounded the car. My mind went back to the time I had pulled the door down on those people at Little Eagle Creek Christian. I thought, "Is Mindy ever going to forgive me for this?!"

She finally showed up and pulled over behind me. She must have seen the distressed look on my face because she got out of the car saying, "It's okay, you did the right thing ... no point in both of us getting tickets!" We had a good laugh and headed on south. Of course, I have enjoyed bringing this event up from time to time:

"You're acquiring quite a record, my dear! Disturbing the peace in Kansas City, expired plates in Indiana ... what next?"[1]

Meanwhile, our household goods were on a moving van that was parked in one-hundred-degree heat over the July fourth holiday. A box of Laura and David's fireworks had accidentally been packed into the truck by the movers, and I imagined the entire moving van going up in a huge ball of fire, but nothing ignited.

After getting moved into our house, the next order of business was to go to church at Vine Street Christian. The Moseleys welcomed us, and it was great to be together again in the same city and, now, in the same congregation. Dan introduced us to a few of their friends (most of whom went back to his days as a student pastor there in the 1960s): the Coles, Harrisons, Lees, Millers, Tallents, Whites, and Associate Pastor Linda Parker and her husband, John. It was great to have a ready-made community. Vine Street was a wonderful congregation of terrific people and a great new church home.

My installation service[2] was held at Woodmont Christian Church, another wonderful congregation in Nashville. It was a beautiful service that I will always remember.

The Tennessee Region of the Disciples is a fascinating entity. There were sixty-five congregations in those days, most of them west of Nashville. But they were scattered from the east to the west across some four hundred and fifty miles. Fun fact: It is actually fewer miles from the northeast corner of Tennessee to Canada than from the northeast corner of Tennessee to the southwest corner of Tennessee. In the 1800s, Nashville was at the heart of the controversy between the Churches of Christ (non-instrumental) and the rest of the Stone-Campbell Movement. In fact, the controversy climaxed at Vine Street Christian Church when David Lipscomb left the congregation in 1887.

Context Matters

Understanding context is a key to ministry in any congregation or institution of the church. The Tennessee Region is a case in point. Locals talk about the "three states of Tennessee," and there is good reason.

---

[1] For the record, I am not exactly proud of this episode!

[2] Having heard the wisdom of Regional Minister Bill Allen on the matter, I later came to prefer "commissioning service" to "installation service": one installs a water pump or a washing machine. Ministry is something we do together as part of a community ... thus a co-mission.

East Tennessee is part of Appalachia, and many citizens from there fought for the Union in the Civil War, even though Tennessee as a whole seceded. Slavery was not supported there in part because the land did not lend itself to the plantation farming of the west. People in the east are a bit slow to trust new people, in part because people there often lived in isolation before the mid-twentieth century. But once you are trusted, you are regarded as a friend for life. Religious expressions there include snake handlers and fundamentalism, and Dayton, Tennessee, is where the Scopes Monkey Trial occurred. But it is also the home of the University of Tennessee (Knoxville), who are the "Volunteers" (like those who voluntarily fought for the Union), and many other colleges and universities.

West Tennessee was divided in the Civil War because the cotton farmers sold their product in Memphis to Northern merchants who bought those goods (cotton was "king"), but it is Deep South culturally, with typically deep Southern accents and many Black descendants of slaves. People there are friendly, polite, and hospitable but not too quick to reveal themselves to you until they know who you are and what you represent. They'll invite you to "come over anytime," but be sure to call ahead because they don't mean that literally. Memphis is the cultural capital of the territory—within a couple-hundred miles radius to the north, west, and south—and celebrates the "blues" on Beale Street and Elvis Presley's home, Graceland. In many ways, Memphis is still "*Old* South," while offering many fine educational institutions, including the University of Memphis.

Middle Tennessee people are generally open and friendly. The Union captured and held Nashville from the early days of the Civil War, and there are lingering resentments among some lifelong residents. There is also a tendency to cook more food than needed, a cultural echo of food shortages suffered during the Civil War. Tobacco is still raised in some places, but more corn these days. Nashville is, of course, Music City and the home of the Grand Ole Opry and the WSM clear channel radio station where the Opry began. Nashville has become the center of every kind of music recording and has a wide range of cultural offerings. Vanderbilt University, Fisk University, and many other fine schools are there. Middle Tennessee is dominated by Nashville and can be called "New South." The population there has exploded in recent decades.

As both a Northerner (born in Indiana) *and* a Southerner (growing up in Florida), Tennessee seemed like just about the perfect place for me. Because we had so many congregations two hundred to three hundred miles from Nashville, I thought about getting "current" in private flying again, but decided against it, since the weather can be unpredictable (especially in the East Tennessee mountains). Feeling like one "has to get there" because a committee or congregation is waiting on you can make flying dangerous.

Settling in

The kids settled into good public schools and Mindy settled in to work in the Nashville Library branch in Bellevue. I hit the ground running and found regional ministry to be incredibly satisfying. Working with congregational conflict and search committees, and offering resources for mission and ministry was a joy. People there embraced me, and I embraced them. I thought this would likely be the ministry from which I would one day retire. As soon as possible I got into every congregation of the region (that took more than two years to accomplish).

I worked compulsively, however, as has always been my custom. I got to the Nashville office at 6 AM most mornings, no matter what time I might have dragged in the night before from Memphis or East Tennessee. There was so much good and seemingly urgent work to do that I found it hard to honor days off. The largest cluster of congregations was in the Memphis area, with a smaller cluster near Knoxville. These required a three-hour drive each way, but I never really got tired of driving in Tennessee. From the relatively low rolling landscape of the west to the large hills of the middle to the mountains of the east, it was all just beautiful. Springtime came so early, with a riot of blossoming trees and shrubs, and fall came so late, with a very short winter. Snow in Nashville was (and is) unusual ... it usually came in one-inch spurts (a prediction of which was enough to send everyone to the grocery store in panic!), and the snow was often gone by midday. One can't really blame Middle Tennessee folks for being fearful of driving in snow ... the hills can become icy very quickly, making it easy for drivers of cars and trucks to lose control.

Being rather frugal by nature, I bought a Toyota Corolla (T. J. Liggett's favorite brand and model), but I quickly discovered that my back needed more support. So, I traded the Corolla for a Plymouth Concorde, which proved to be an excellent car for the fifty thousand miles per year I was driving.

With a son-of-a-sign-painter's advertising mentality, I loaded that car up with Disciples of Christ decals and a front license plate my dad lettered for me. I encountered many people in the Pilot truck stops who either recognized the denominational name and symbols or wanted to know what I was advertising (automobile evangelism!).

I recognized immediately that the smaller congregations usually needed more help than the larger congregations, which had more resources, both human and financial (although large congregations have their issues, too, especially regarding a change of ministers and keeping a relevant sense of mission). I also recognized that the larger congregations were the ones generating the most denominational mission money (Basic Mission Finance), thus making my regional ministry possible. So, early on, I visited each of the senior pastors of the larger congregations saying essentially the following: "As *I* know *you* know, your congregation is disproportionately footing the bill for most of what the region accomplishes, and most of that work is, frankly, done among smaller congregations. So, I hope you see me as your missionary to the more needful congregations of the Region. I certainly want to be available and helpful to you, too, in any way I can ... but we both know most of my time will be spent with smaller congregations."

This honesty seemed to strengthen my relationship with the senior pastors of the larger congregations. Also, because I had been senior minister of a sizeable congregation, I did identify with them and had *some* advice and counsel to offer the larger churches occasionally.

Regional ministry is a place where one can minister to both congregations and individual ministers. Sometimes ministers think regional ministers always take the side of the congregation in any dispute between pastor and parish. This may be true with a few regional ministers, but I more often find the problem is that ministers don't tell their regional minister about what's happening until the conflict has gone so deep that it is impossible to restore the pastor's relationship with the congregation. I sometimes felt like a National Transportation Safety Board investigator sorting through the wreckage of a plane crash that could have been prevented if only someone had sought assistance sooner.

So, I worked hard, as every regional minister must, to develop relationships of trust with both lay and clergy leaders so they would call in the early stages of a conflict or other problems. My advice to ministers is always this: Keep your regional minister posted when there are issues in your congregation or between you and your congregation ... your regional minister may well be able to help you and/or your congregation work through the difficulties. At the least, the regional minister will be able to say in his or her reference for you that you sought help when needed, even if it didn't work out in your current congregation (and "seeks help when needed" is one of the most important and helpful references anyone can receive).

Some ministers fear their regional minister will "blackball" them for service in other regions as well as their own. But the truth is that most regional ministers bend over backward to find good places of service for *all* ministers and do not hold past issues against them so long as those ministers have been honest and receptive to assistance (and in some cases therapy or other redemptive work).

Regional ministers are called not only to be "administrators," but to be pastors. Like all good pastors, regional ministers develop strong relationships with those they pastor. In Tennessee, one example in my case was Jim and Joyce Blair. Not long after I began, I got word that Jim, a long-time minister in Kentucky and Tennessee, had been diagnosed with cancer and the prognosis was not good. Jim and Joyce gave me the privilege of being with them through many hard months of Jim's decline and death. Needless to say, a deep friendship developed, a friendship that Joyce, Mindy, and I continue to share. She became a vice-moderator of the General Church a few years later, and it was wonderful to serve with her in that setting as well.

I made *many* wonderful friends among the Disciples of Tennessee. (I made no enemies so far as I know!) Many of them remain lifelong friends. Of course, Mindy and I both enjoyed the wonderful friends we made at Vine Street Christian Church. Mindy and our son and daughter were immediately drawn into things, even though I was not there most Sundays because I was out in other congregations across the region. When we left Nashville for Indianapolis—half-joking, but mostly seriously—I told the Vine Street congregation that I knew they were going to miss Mindy... miss me, not so much!

I have often thought that regional ministry might be the main thing I was born for. I understood the role immediately, knew what was needed, and during my twenty-two years of congregational ministry had developed some skills and resources to offer the ministers and congregations in the region. I enjoyed nearly every day of it (except when we had to deal with misconduct cases).

The Spouses Group

As I was beginning regional ministry in 1990, there was a significant number of regional ministers' spouses and general ministry unit presidents' spouses who were occasionally able to travel with their husbands to denominational leadership meetings.[3] This group developed into a deep fellowship of mutual support. While the regional and general ministers were in meetings together, many of the spouses were enjoying each other's company and visiting interesting places in the cities where the meetings were being held. It was an informal but very well-organized group that included the following most active spouses as Mindy began: Virginia Acker, Anne Alexander, Gwen Allen, Martha Boswell, Berlina Brock, Sandy Finch, Georgia Flock, Marilyn Foulkes, Bonnie Frazier, Betty Lamb, Doris Lauer, Georgia Meece, Sheila Ratcliff, Susie Reid, Emily Smith, Karen Smith, Diane Steffer, Evelyn Watkins, and Ann Weisheimer.

I will always hold a special place in my heart for this group, because they were so supportive and helpful to Mindy as she made the transition to being a regional minister's spouse ... and then a GMP's spouse! It was a remarkable group of remarkably strong, loving, and gifted women who blessed the church in so many ways through the years.

Challenges and Opportunities

We Disciples were among the first denominations to take sexual misconduct with a new seriousness, which meant regions developed the means to identify and deal with misconduct in a way that assured due process for all involved and that removed sexual predators from ministry. As we have seen the damage recently to groups that did *not* take this issue so seriously back in the 1990s—including the Southern Baptist Convention and the Roman Catholic Church—I am grateful that we Disciples got on it when we did. But it required tremendous amounts of time and energy on the part of regional ministers everywhere.

---

[3] This was in a time when there were practically no female regional ministers or general ministry unit presidents, so spouses were almost all wives rather than husbands. Later, male spouses began joining the group, one of the first being Bob Frank Plumlee.

There was a range of offenders, from those predators who repeatedly victimized children and female parishioners to those who engaged in behaviors that were "middle-aged stupid." There was absolutely no room in the ministry for the former, but often redemption was possible for the latter through counseling and other discipline. Of course, the victims of misconduct were always the first concern. Fortunately, there are relatively few predators in Disciples ministry today because of these ongoing efforts. Most seminaries and regions now spend considerable resources to do ongoing education for the sake of prevention. But awareness and watchfulness remain appropriate.

Most regions owned campgrounds of some kind (and some still do). These are hallowed places where so many young campers and conferees first take faith seriously and where many decide to go into ministry. Bethany Hills, about twenty-five miles northwest of Nashville, was (and is) sacred ground for Disciples in Tennessee. Today, many regions have had to sell their campgrounds due to financial challenges, but it is always a traumatic process no matter how necessary it may be. Bethany Hills is a beautiful place nestled in the hills around a small lake.

Tennessee has a rich ecumenical community. The State Council of Churches included all the mainline Protestant communions, the Catholic Church, and many others. The fellowship with other bishops of the church ecumenical was wonderful, as we were able to share "best practices" and to otherwise support one another.

Soon after becoming regional minister, I took part in a Disciples "mission-funding conference" that would make allocations for each of the then seventy-two general, regional, and higher education ministries of the church *and* that would seek to resolve the growing tensions between these seventy-two partners that was the result of decreasing financial resources. Everybody had gotten along well so long as the number of Basic Mission Finance dollars was on the rise each year. But when a downturn began in the late 1970s and 1980s, tensions began to build. Not only did offerings to BMF decline, but inflation ate into the dollars that were contributed and further strained the budgets of the seventy-two partner organizations. The tension was not so much between individual regional ministers and general ministry unit presidents as between the regional ministers as a group and the general ministry unit presidents as a group.

The "mission funding system" at that point (and since 1973) featured a Commission on Mission Funding, composed of twelve earnest Disciples congregational leaders (four lay men, four lay women, and four congregational ministers) who were not recipients of BMF funds. This commission met annually to decide what percentage of congregational BMF giving in each region should stay in the region in which it was given to support the ministry of that region (staff, offices, campgrounds, administrative costs, program costs, and so on) and what percentage would go to general and higher education ministries. One percent of the overall BMF receipts were retained in an "adjustment fund," which the commission could use to address critical needs, emergencies, and perceived inequities.

Tennessee was in a stronger position than many regions because we had several very large congregations that contributed generously to Basic Mission Finance, so we could manage with a smaller percentage of return (thirty-seven percent) than some of the other regions could. For example, the Upper Midwest Region, Georgia, Virginia, Mississippi, and many others had a great many small congregations and only a few larger congregations. So they required a larger percentage of their congregations' denominational giving to stay in the region to support an adequate regional ministry.

Most all the regions had taken cuts in staffing (compared to just a decade before), due to decreasing BMF offerings from congregations (exacerbated by eroding value due to inflation). Tennessee was under financial pressure when I arrived, although it had earlier reduced its staff by one. Within two years, I had to eliminate my Associate Regional Minister Doug Meister's position, leaving me as the only regional minister on staff. I hated to cut Doug's position for several reasons, but I could not see how I could ethically maintain the size of my staff when most every other region was having to reduce theirs. Most of the general ministry units had development people out raising money for their unit's work, which regions typically did not. This meant there was less pressure to reduce staff in most general ministry units, and most (not all) general ministry unit presidents' salaries were quite a bit higher than most regional ministers' salaries. This increased the tensions among regional and general colleagues.

Consequently, most of us (both regional and general leaders) went to the mission funding conference of 1990 with fears about the future and some resentments about apparent inequalities in the system. A couple of regions had already rejected the current system of distribution by asking congregations to submit their Basic Mission Finance gifts to their regional office directly, and those regions then decided how much to pass on to the general ministries. But most regions were following the current protocol by asking congregations to submit their BMF offerings to Indianapolis directly for distribution by the current system. That current system depended on allocations being made by the Commission on Mission Funding, which was (as I mentioned before) composed of representatives of congregations from the wider church, none of whom was a recipient of BMF funds.

The fatal flaw in the system that became immediately evident to me as a new regional minister was that *many* came to the meeting assuming that if the system was truly *fair*, then *their* particular ministry would receive a larger share of the BMF pie. Somebody was obviously mistaken in this assumption! In fact, the BMF pie itself was shrinking at an alarming rate, and so discussions about how to increase the *size of the pie* would have been more productive than how to divide the pie that was remaining! Some of us (including a few regional ministers and a few general ministry unit executives) tried to shift the conversation in that direction, but many of these seventy-two otherwise fine leaders had moved into a survival mentality. They just couldn't seem to comprehend the decrease in giving that was confronting the whole church and how that meant changes were needed in the way things had "always" been done ("always" meaning "since 1973," which was before any of these regional or general leaders had come to leadership).

I had no idea that I was going to be thrust into the middle of this quagmire in just a couple of years! In the meantime, the congregations of Tennessee continued to give faithfully to BMF, and some congregations even increased their giving.

Unfortunately, in the midst of these mission funding struggles, the 1991 General Assembly in Tulsa (an assembly that was marked by controversy and turmoil) approved a capital campaign called Embrace the Future. The campaign's goal was to raise $30 million, and the proceeds (after campaign costs of ten percent) were to support the following: New Congregation Establishment, fifty percent; Overseas Capital, twenty-five percent; Vitalization of Congregations, ten percent; Clergy Care, ten percent; and the construction of a new denominational headquarters building, five percent.

As a new regional minister, I wanted to do my part to assure the success of the campaign. I asked Harold Goodwin of Memphis (who had become a dear friend and spiritual mentor) to chair the effort in Tennessee. Harold did a great job, and Tennessee was the *only* region to reach its campaign goal. In fact, when I later saw the results from other regions, I was dismayed to discover that the majority of regions had done very little to raise *any* money for Embrace the Future. It pointedly demonstrated how *un*united regional and general ministries really were! This was an eye-opener for me and made me realize how strong our Disciples tendency toward "autonomy" is and how much the denomination needed to be led toward greater unity of purpose and action.[4]

One of my primary concerns as a regional minister was the development of new congregations. There were so many places in the state that had no Disciples congregation and that seemed ripe for the establishment of such. I was particularly interested in Maryville, Tennessee, near Knoxville (and a gateway to the Smokey Mountains). However, a layperson from Alamo, Tennessee, wanted to start a congregation in Milan. She offered the resources to make it happen, and so that's where a new congregation was established. I still believe Maryville would have been a better place to start, but the region itself did not have the finances to support such a project.

Our beloved Fred Craddock, teacher of preaching at Emory and often voted one of the ten best preachers in America, was from Humboldt, Tennessee, Central Avenue Christian Church. I received an invitation to preach there one Sunday and looked forward to saying thank you to the congregation for having raised up such a fine preacher and educator. When I stepped into the pulpit to speak, I nearly tripped on something at my feet. I moved the object to the side and realized it was an old twenty-four-bottle Coke box. That struck me as odd. I learned later that the box was kept there so that whenever Fred came home to Central Avenue he would have that

---

[4] The good news is that the Embrace the Future Campaign did finally raise nearly $6 million, of which $1.7 million went for new congregation establishment, which did help fund the new church effort through the 1990s. Of course, $6 million was far short of the $30 million goal, but $6 million raised did make a huge difference in a time of great transition.

Coke box to step up on, being a man of giant *spiritual* stature but short *physical* stature!

Years after I stepped away from the Office of General Minister and President, at the Nashville General Assembly in 2011, I received a phone call from my friend Clay Stauffer, Senior Pastor of Woodmont Christian Church. He asked if I would be willing to preach at Woodmont on the Sunday morning during General Assembly. This was a high honor and I said, "Yes, of course." The Woodmont sanctuary holds several hundred people, and I knew it would be full on General Assembly Sunday with so many Disciples delegates in town.

Clay said, "Great! Would you like to preach first service or second service?" I thought for a moment and asked, "Who is the other preacher going to be?" Clay said, "Fred" (he didn't have to tell me the last name). I responded, "Do you think I'm *crazy*? I'll take first service ... no way I'm going to preach after Fred!"

Come that early Sunday service, sure enough the sanctuary was absolutely packed. So I rose and moved to the pulpit when the time came to preach. I began by saying, "I know why you are here at this time of the morning! You want to be sure you have a seat when Fred preaches! That's okay, I'm glad you are here and I am not offended in the least!"

The room exploded with knowing laughter. I went on, "To paraphrase Jim Croce's hit, 'Bad, Bad, Leroy Brown,' You don't step on Superman's cape, you don't spit into the wind, you don't pull the mask off the old Lone Ranger, and you don't preach after Fred!"

When the service was over, I met up with Fred in Clay's office and told him all had gone well, "But," I told him, "You better get in there pretty soon because there's only one seat left, and that's yours!"

A Fellowship of Concern

I had thought about the possibility of becoming GMP one day, but I had not seriously entertained the idea. I felt there were plenty of qualified people and many more qualified than me. The call to be regional minister of Tennessee had felt palpably real to me, and I was just getting started in that role, having begun in July 1990. However, soon after moving to Nashville, I began meeting occasionally with four friends to discuss the future of the church in general and the Disciples in particular. Rick Harrison was dean of The Disciples

Divinity House at Vanderbilt and had rapidly become a close friend (along with his wife, Mona). Michael Mooty was then senior pastor of East Dallas Christian Church. His father had been state secretary of Tennessee before Restructure created "regions." Dan Moseley was our family pastor at Vine Street Christian Church and had been my dear friend since our days together as pastors in the Greater Kansas City Area in the 1970s. Robert Welsh, who was becoming a friend, was then the associate ecumenical officer of the Council on Christian Unity. Robert had perhaps the broadest understanding of the global church ecumenical in our little group.

As an informal but influential group of friends and discussion partners, we jokingly referred to ourselves as "the Nashville Five." But, as Mona Harrison exclaimed, "It sounds more like Five White Guys to me!" Mona had a remarkable knack for calling a thing what it actually is.

The absence of women and people of color in this little group of five friends is striking to me now. But it reflected the fact that in 1990 the church was very much "white-centered," as we would say today, and white male ministers tended to be part of groups that were often devoid of significant input from women and people of color. In the Kansas City days, I had become friends with the excellent African American Disciples Pastor K. David Cole, but I had little other regular direct contact with Black Disciples. I began to have friendships with Black Disciples in Tennessee, including Alvin Jackson and May and Norman Reed, but we Disciples all still tended to move in racially defined circles. That is embarrassing to me now, but it also eventually helped me understand just how segregated the church still was (not that we have now moved so very far past those realities). The diversity of my friendship circles would be expanded exponentially very soon.

That said, the five of us had been drawn together by mutual concerns about our beloved church. We continued meeting for an overnight retreat twice a year for the next few years. Our conversations were wide ranging, but early on we all agreed that solid leadership from the Office of General Minister and President would be needed if the Disciples of Christ were to thrive in the years ahead (though none of us really wanted the job or saw ourselves as particularly well suited for it). All the mainline Protestant denominations[5] had been struggling since the iconic year of social change, 1968 (the very year the Disciples restructured as a denomination, and the year the United Methodist Church formed out of a merger)[6] All five of us felt that the denomination had lost focus both due to the rapid social change of the twentieth century that had been so disorienting to a church that had originated in the early 1800s, and due to having reorganized itself in a process primarily expressing the concerns of the 1950s and 1960s. We believed clarifying our sense of mission and developing a vision for the decades ahead should be a central task of the new general minister and president, who would be elected, presumably, in 1993 (since the church had failed to elect a new GMP in 1991 and was currently being served by an interim GMP, Bill Nichols).

Driving issues included the fact that our church was ninety-four percent white in 1993. I believe that, as important as overseas ministries are, North America was and is our primary mission field. North America was far from ninety-four percent white in 1993 (and is further from that now) and, when a church does not look like its primary mission field, there is a problem—in this case, the problem being the racism that is so deeply embedded in our North American culture and systems, including the systems within the church.

Another issue was in the fact that Disciples were (and are) still struggling with one of its four original values, "restoration." "Restoring the New Testament Church," an early part of the Stone-Campbell movement's "plea," had faded in the minds of Disciples as we began to realize in the mid-nineteenth century that there is no *one* New Testament Church to restore, no single biblical blueprint for how the church should be structured or live. We began to recognize that the church of Jesus Christ has often changed to reflect its new and changing geographical and cultural locations through the centuries. As I like to put it, *we had begun to realize that the New Testament*

---

[5] "Mainline Protestant" has been variously described as those denominations that were represented by congregations on the "main line" of the commuter train from downtown Philadelphia to the suburbs or, more generally, those denominations that helped shape and were shaped by the young United States. The eight generally identified as mainline are the following (some of which represent unions of previous bodies): the American Baptist Churches, the Christian Church (Disciples of Christ), the Episcopal Church, the Evangelical Lutheran Church in America, the Presbyterian Church (USA), the Reformed Church in America, the United Church of Christ, and the United Methodist Church.

[6] I wrote rather extensively about the year 1968 in my 2007 book, *Recreating the Church*, published by Chalice Press.

was created by the church rather than the church being created by the New Testament. But most of us Disciples ministers and other leaders had not effectively taught or articulated this truth, so it remained a point of contention among some.

Another issue was how the General Assembly sense-of-the-assembly resolution process was often dividing, rather than motivating and energizing, the church.[7] In addition, the weaknesses of the resolution process were being exploited by a so-called "renewal" group. I'll say more about this later.

We five friends had issues with the church of the 1990s. Robert Frost "had a lover's quarrel with the world" and we had a "lover's quarrel with the church" as it had developed in recent decades. We felt strongly that such issues needed to be addressed, and soon, if we were to move faithfully and effectively into the twenty-first century.

---

[7] Sense-of-the-assembly resolutions most often address social justice issues. They are submitted by a group of congregations and/or other expressions of the church to the General Board. The General Board recommends passage, or not, to the General Assembly and designates an amount of time for the Assembly to debate the resolution. The resolutions are introduced during an Assembly business session, followed by debate time as recommended by the General Board (typically 12 to 24 minutes are allotted, with the opportunity for the Assembly to extend debate by a majority vote if it desires), followed by a vote of the Assembly. The Assembly may instead vote to refer the resolution to a particular part of the church or to the Reference and Counsel Committee for reworking before being brought back to the Assembly floor for further consideration.

PART II

The Office of General Minister and President

Chapter 5

A Gathering Storm

I had attended General Assembly in 1973 in Cincinnati as a student at Christian Theological Seminary and every other General Assembly since, except for 1975. But the 1991 General Assembly in Tulsa, Oklahoma, October 25–30, was the first time I attended as a regional minister. This meant I had some idea of what was going on behind the scenes.

Michael Kinnamon had been nominated to become general minister and president in 1991. Michael was the academic dean of Lexington Theological Seminary. Many thought of him as an academic only, and thought the church needed a pastor for the role of GMP. However, I knew that Michael had pastored many a student in his years as a professor. I thought his brilliant intellect and deep roots in the ecumenical movement might help the church discern a new path forward. At the General Board meeting where he was officially nominated in 1991, I felt strongly enough about his selection that I had quietly started the General Board in singing the *Doxology* after the positive vote to recommend him to the Assembly.

However, as a regional minister, I perceived that, in addition to his being an academic, there was even greater opposition to Michael because of his position on human sexuality, a *very* hot topic in those days (and, unfortunately, yet today). Michael went about the United States and Canada, wherever asked, to explain his position on human sexuality. It appeared to some that he was *campaigning* for the role, which offended those who felt the election should be a matter of *call* rather than *politics*. However, Michael was *not* campaigning so much as he was simply trying to *teach* the church. Even though I intended to vote for his election, I went to Tulsa convinced that he would likely *not* be elected because so many opposed his teachings on sexual orientation and because he was perceived by many as primarily an academician and by some as a politician.

But as the five-day meeting progressed, attenders began to warm to one another, and the business of the church was carried out in a nonconfrontational manner. The mood of the General Assembly seemed to be rather positive and so I began to think, "Michael may be elected after all."

Mindy and I were staying a few miles from the Assembly Hall (the Tulsa Convention Center), so we drove in each morning for the gathering. On that Friday morning, the day of the election, we couldn't believe our eyes. There had been seven thousand or so attending (yes, General Assemblies used to be *very* large gatherings!), but on this morning it was hard to find any parking. Also, there were many buses that were bringing people in from somewhere for that day's session. (Who coordinated this busing in of folks is hard to say. At that point in America's "culture wars," there were lots of nationally organized efforts to influence such elections among the mainline churches.)

On that afternoon of the election, the hall was the fullest it had been all week. There was a spirit in the room that seemed very different from the gentle, pleasant spirit we had felt previously. When the time came for the vote on Michael Kinnamon's election, both the "ayes" and the "nays" were shouted loudly, and it was difficult to tell which was the majority. So, a standing vote was taken. But the hall was so crowded that it was difficult to get an accurate count and it was decided to take a written ballot vote.

Of course, counting the ballots took some time. Thus, the Assembly went on with its other business while the counters were working. A two-thirds vote is needed to elect a GMP. Finally, the moment came to announce the vote. Mindy and I were sitting high up in the arena with some friends. We prayed and hoped. The announcement finally came as the church in Assembly held its collective breath. Michael's election had failed by .4 of one percent!

Mindy and I looked at each other with disappointment about the defeat of Michael's candidacy. But we also looked at each other with fear of what might be on the horizon. We both thought in an instant, "The church wants to elect someone young like Michael, and they want a pastor who has some experience in the wider church.

I was (then) young like Michael, I was a pastor, and I was the first baby boomer to be called to regional ministry. We imagined the church might come calling in the next two years. It was a frightening thought. Who in their right mind would *seek* to become the head of a church in times like these, when churches were dividing all over North America? Besides, I had fallen in love with Tennessee and with regional ministry. I was anticipating many happy years in that new ministry.

Bill Nichols was selected as interim GMP. He was nearing retirement from ministry at Central Christian Church in Decatur, Illinois, and the congregation graciously let him leave a bit early for this "emergency" work. Everyone left Tulsa hoping Bill would help the church get its bearings after the Assembly. He did a fine job, in my estimation.

As a new search process for a new general minister began, none of us in the group of five who had been meeting in and near Nashville about church issues wanted to be GMP, although all of us had been nominated at one time or another. However, at least two of us felt strongly enough about the work to which we thought the new GMP needed to aspire that we allowed our names to go forward in the process. The other three of our group hoped one of the two of us would actually be selected.

Michael Mooty and I had an agreement (I thought) that if either of us decided to drop out, he would tell the other. However, as the nomination process unfolded, Michael dropped out of the process without telling me. (I still jokingly chide him about this to this day.) He encouraged me to stay in.

I remained in the process and, to my amazement, along with three other candidates, I was invited to a final interview with the search committee. The meeting took place in Dallas, and I arrived the day before the interview so I would be well rested. Michael Mooty was still serving East Dallas Christian Church then, so he and his wife, Sarah, invited me to lunch and, grateful for the opportunity to relax, I met them at a local restaurant. At one point in our conversation, Sarah (an intuitive) asked me if I had had any dreams the night before.

I didn't pay much attention to my dreams in those days (I have since learned to take them more seriously, as they often help clarify issues or to guide resolution of inner conflicts). But the previous night's dream had been quite vivid, so I shared it with them, still unfiltered and not having thought much yet about the content. "I dreamed I was in a big house. The windows and doors were all locked for some reason, and there was the unmistakable smell of natural gas filling the place. I kept trying to get out, but I couldn't. It seemed the place was going to explode! That's when I woke up."

There was dead silence for a few seconds ... then, recognizing the obvious meaning and significance of the dream, *we all exploded* in laughter! Having stayed in the process, perhaps past the time I should have, I now felt trapped, obligated to the church to see it through.

From the Dallas interviews with the search committee, the names of three of us were forwarded to the Administrative Committee, which interviewed us individually March 3–4 at the Mercy Center in St. Louis. Each of us retreated to our rooms after our interviews and awaited word while the Administrative Committee deliberated for what seemed like a very long time. After the decision was made, Marilyn Moffett, the general moderator in that biennium, came to each of our rooms to tell us which of our names would be forwarded to the General Board and General Assembly. Marilyn was a dear friend, and a lovely person, but on this night she seemed to me to be going from room to room like the angel of death! Part of me thought, "What if I am not selected?" But a larger part of me thought, "What if I *am* selected?!" I prayed fervently that God would grant me the serenity to accept what I felt I could not now change, whether yea or nay.

Eventually, Marilyn knocked on my door. She quietly informed me that my name would be going forward to the General Board. She congratulated me and told me I would be in her prayers as the process moved forward. I thanked her and closed the door behind her. I walked across the room to the desk and *literally* fell to my knees, thinking, "What have I done? Then, "What has the church done?" Then, "What has God done?" I then prayed fervently that God would help me conduct myself in such a way that I would not make the church regret the decision and that I would serve faithfully and effectively if elected by the General Assembly. I could have refused at that point but, having let my name go forward, had I withdrawn, the search process would have had to start over, and the church would likely have had another interim GMP, and the church needed the stability of a duly elected GMP.

I was reminded of that scene in the movie, *The Right Stuff*, when Alan Shepherd was sitting in the Mercury Capsule atop the Redstone rocket awaiting launch, sounding confident and ready on the radio, but suddenly offering an honest, if vulgar, prayer that he not "[mess] this up!"

My Approach

I have always been a combination of aggressively ambitious, confident (Mindy once said in frustration, "You've never had a humble opinion in your life!"), and self-doubting. Although not using the mythological imagery to make the point, my mother had drilled into my head the moral of the story of Icarus, who with wings of wax flew too close to the sun. This, and the old proverb, "Pride goes before a fall" prevented me from taking much delight in the occasion: I had now to adjust to this new reality and how I would present myself to the church and the media. I needed to demonstrate my confidence in the future of the church (because God is ultimately in charge) while not appearing to be either frightened or overconfident in my own capacities.

Once my nomination had been confirmed by the General Board, the media became interested. I was used to dealing with local media in Ft. Wayne and, in fact, had reached a point of being able to speak calmly with a microphone in my face or with reporters taking notes. I had learned how to say, "I have no comment at this point" and to pick and choose what I would or would not address. However, the folks of the media in Ft. Wayne were by and large friendly to me, and I had personal relationships with many of them.

So, it came as a shock to see articles about myself in the *New York Times*, the *Dallas Morning News*, and other major outlets. It was especially jarring when I realized that most of the articles had been written without anyone having interviewed me to get my perspective on a story. I was also struck by how often there were factual errors in the stories. Most of the errors didn't amount to much, but the whole process made me leery of reporters and sometimes prompted me to overexplain things, which I discovered was a whole *other* way of getting into trouble. I believe strongly in a free and *active* press, but I also believe in an *accurate* press!

The angle most often taken by the media was to contrast my approach with Michael Kinnamon's. As I said, Michael accepted every invitation to explain his positions on controversial issues *not* because he was campaigning but because he was trying to teach (he is, after all, a teacher). On the plus side, in this process he helped the church clarify some issues and learn some things about people who had been unfairly marginalized by the church. On the negative side, many people perceived him to be campaigning for the job. This perception was partly because the culture wars had heated up, and human sexuality was (and remains) at the center of the battlefield.

As for myself, I was still learning about the issues and was nowhere near as articulate about them as Michael. That said, there was very little difference between my position and Michael's. But, having seen what had happened during his nomination process, I knew that I had to resist the media's tendency to make me into a one-issue nominee as they had Michael. Even more important was the way in which the media was stirring up resistance in the church to any kind of constructive dialogue. Let me take that point a step further.

The first time the ordination of people with homosexual orientation had come before the General Assembly was in 1977. I saw that Assembly vote down a resolution that would have *removed* homosexual orientation as a bar to ordination. Not only was it voted down but, because ordination criteria are ultimately the province of regions, many people went home from that 1977 Assembly in Kansas City and introduced resolutions in their own regional assemblies specifically designed to exclude persons with homosexual orientation from ordination (just as we have recently seen state legislatures passing bills that were intended to render null and void federal legislation with which they disagreed). Thus, while many regions had practiced a sort of "don't ask, don't tell" policy, the door to ordination was now effectively slammed shut on those people seeking ordination who identified as gay or lesbian.

Fourteen years later, those absolute rules against ordination of persons who identified as gay or lesbian had begun to lose some energy in many regions, as some people were beginning to gain new understandings of human sexuality. But now the 1991 Tulsa Assembly had become a referendum on such ordinations and, again, people went home from that Assembly and introduced new anti-LGBTQ policies in their regions. So, what had been intended to lead the church toward a more inclusive approach to human sexuality issues had backfired and had, in fact, effectively tightened the rules again.

From my perspective, because many church members were being driven by cultural forces from *outside* the church, more than by Christian discernment *within* the church, trying to change the church's view and practices through bold General Assembly resolutions was a counterproductive approach. This is something pastors learn in congregational ministry: Church people are much more liberal in practice than they are in principle. What I mean in this case is that as members come to love individuals (sons, daughters, uncles, aunts, teachers, church members, and others) whom they have come to realize identify as LGBTQ, their fears diminish, and they often lose their taste for judgmental rules and policies that exclude.

In fact, while resolutions can be helpful under certain circumstances, the *real* change in attitudes among Disciples and other mainline Christians toward LGBTQ people has not been due to resolutions but to the courage of those LGBTQ folks themselves who have "come out" and risked rejection. While rejection has certainly occurred in too many quarters, and the pain inflicted by this reality must not be minimized and must be acknowledged, congregations have most often changed their attitudes as they realize, "This person whom we love and who has been an active Christian among us, demonstrating the love of Christ in their life, fully human like each of us, is obviously at least as Christian as us and so we need to reconsider our thinking about this or that particular human condition that we have thought might make this person 'other' or 'less than.'"

So, as the nominee, I knew the media could be either a help or a hindrance, and the person being focused on by the media must manage that coverage as best as he or she can, making it more friend than foe, more helpful than harmful to the cause. In a world in which controversy and conflict are more interesting to people than the factual substance of things (this has been called a post-truth era), and are thus more likely to draw readers/viewers/listeners and thus be more financially profitable to the owners of media, one must relate to the media on one's own terms. This meant for me, in part, to keep the focus on what *God* might be trying to do in and with and through the church rather than what *I* might be trying or planning to do.

The *New York Times* reported my candidacy as that of a moderate. That was close enough for me. It was much better than trying to explain to reporters that I believed my call meant I needed to hold together *two* challenges: one, to help the church more deeply understand what God was calling the church to be and to become (more deeply *Christian*, really) and, two, to help the church thrive as an institution so that it could bring more people to the knowledge of Christ and God's intentions for the world. I was quite pleased when my old friend and mentor, Dick Dickinson (then president of Christian Theological Seminary), told the *New York Times* I was an *evangelical liberal*. I *am* an evangelical in that I want more people to come to know God through Christ, and a *liberal* (today, I prefer the term *progressive*) in that I believe God wants the world to be as open, loving, just, and gracious to all as God is; that the arc of history really *does* bend toward justice, and it is our responsibility as Christians to help bend it progressively in that direction.

I am also *ecumenical* in that I do not believe the Disciples of Christ have the only or best way to be church. In fact, to say or believe such a thing would be most un-Disciples-like! All the Christian traditions (Catholic, Anglican, Protestant, and Orthodox) have some parts and pieces of the truth, including us Disciples. And when we recognize one another as all on the road to Emmaus together, we are all closer to the truth.

I am also *interfaith* in my outlook because, like John 1:1, I see the *logos* (generally translated into English as the "Word") that came to rest in Jesus in a special way to nonetheless be present *throughout* creation and in *many* religions. It is the recognition and surrender to the *logos* that saves, not a mere recognition of Jesus the man. That said, I yet confess that which Jesus taught and lived is the way and truth I have chosen as *most* representative of the *logos*, and the Disciples of Christ is where I feel most at home as a Christian always seeking to become more Christian, more attuned to the *logos*, more committed to the gospel of love. But I also recognize *all* those who sincerely seek the truth to be brothers and sisters.

As I have thought in ensuing years about Michael Kinnamon and myself, I have come to put it this way. Michael is a thought leader in the search for justice. I am something of a thought leader in the search for effective and faithful organization. It is not a difference in belief (I believe "faithful" means the same thing Michael believes it means ... faithful to God's desire for justice). It is, rather, a difference in emphasis and expertise. To put it another way, I am a thought *follower* in the search for justice. I am inspired by thought leaders in the search for justice, which is why I have listened carefully to people like Dr. King, Jim Wallis, Ron Sider, Mother Teresa, Walter Brueggemann, Allan Boesak, Michael Kinnamon, Bill Coffin, Marian Wright Edelman, Archbishop Tutu, and so many others. But as I listen to these inspired icons, I am also constantly asking myself, "How can the church as an *organization* be helped to understand these truths and to incorporate them into their way of being and doing?" This, it seems to me, is a question that every general minister and president, every regional minister, every minister, and every lay leader of the church needs to be asking constantly.

Life Begins to Change

On April 7–9 (after the General Administrative Committee had named me the sole nominee, but before the General Board meeting that would be asked to confirm it), Mindy and I drove the five hours from Nashville to Indianapolis to begin house hunting. While there, I was invited to meet with the general ministry unit presidents based in Indianapolis. We met at the Pension Fund offices, which were then located on "the Circle" downtown. I parked my car on the Circle and met with these mostly older, white, male colleagues for an hour or so, my first opportunity to be in conversation with them as a group. While the conversation was still going, someone came into the meeting and said, "Dick's car is being towed!" In my eagerness to get to this meeting, I had inadvertently parked in a tow-away zone. Lester Palmer (who has a sense of humor I very much appreciate) was greatly bemused by this and gave me a ride to the police lot where I could reclaim my car. I thought, "Great start, Dick!"

The General Board met April 17–20 in Chicago and confirmed my nomination. I went home to Nashville, and we put our house up for sale, contingent upon my election by the General Assembly (given what had happened at Tulsa in 1991, no one could take such an election for granted). We listed the house on May 13, and it sold on May 23, a more promising sign than was the towing of my car!

The General Assembly, meeting in St. Louis during a monumental flood, confirmed my election on July 17 (ninety-two percent "yes," 3720 of 4058 ballots cast by voting delegates). This was what I had hoped for, as it would signal that there had been desire on the part of the church to move ahead and accept new leadership.

It all seems like such a whirl now, but three things stand out in my memory. First, the photographer who was recording the Assembly took a photo of me (before the election) with the four previous GMPs. He then asked me to step aside and took a picture of the four without me. It seemed to me a stark reminder that I had not been elected yet and that, in fact, since Tulsa 1991, no one was taking my election for granted!

The second thing that stands out in my mind was that Archbishop Desmond Tutu was our Assembly guest that week, and I had the opportunity to meet him for the first time. I was introduced to him as the nominee and he looked me up and down and, with that trademark grin and sparkling eyes said, "You have an episcopal smile!" It felt like an endorsement (even though at that point he didn't know me from "Adam's cat").

Third, about fifteen of my relatives on my mother's side, all Disciples, came to the Assembly for the election, along with Mindy's parents, Edna and Clarence. We invited them up to our hotel room so we could have a little time together. We were put up in the Hilton's Presidential Suite, which overlooked the St. Louis Cardinals' Busch Stadium. That suite was nearly as big as our house! I spent much of that family time explaining that the room had been "comped," so the church didn't actually have to pay for it! (I *am* my mother's son.) Over the next ten years I admit that my immediate family and I grew very fond of these "presidential suites"! I didn't get to spend much time in them, but they were impressive.

Well—wisely or unwisely—the church had skipped a generation in its search for a new GMP. My relative youth, forty-five years of age, was obvious, as all my predecessors had been elected in their late fifties or sixties and had retired from the job. But I think the church recognized that it was time for leadership from a younger person who had come of age during the turbulent 1960s and who thus might help the church find its way forward in the postmodern era. Whether or not they had selected the *right* young person was now moot. At some level, conscious or unconscious, most of the church knew we Disciples *had* to move forward and we had to get clarity *quickly*.

So, in a moment, on July 17, 1993, I went from being regional minister of Tennessee, confident in my work there, to being the new and not-so-confident general minister and president of the Christian Church (Disciples of Christ) in the United States and Canada. As soon as the Assembly closed, our family of four drove back to Nashville and began saying goodbye to friends and packing. It took me four days to close out my regional office (I hadn't wanted to be presumptuous about the outcome of the election, so I had not begun packing in earnest before the Assembly). I commuted to Indianapolis for several weeks. We left as a family for Indianapolis on August 29 and closed on our new home in Indy on August 30.

The move was relatively easy for son David. He had graduated as valedictorian that May from Nashville's Hillwood High School and was preparing to begin college that fall at Harvey Mudd College in Claremont, California. The goodbye to Nashville was more difficult for daughter Laura, who had just completed her sophomore year at Hume-Fogg Magnet High School. Laura and I are much alike in temperament and personality. I knew how important high school had been for me, and I hated to interrupt her high school experience. To help her feel more at ease, we toured some of the better high schools in the Indianapolis area and let her choose which one she wanted to attend. She chose Lawrence Central High School, noted for its excellent performing arts program, its diverse student body, and a recent renovation. So, we bought a house in that area, near Geist Reservoir.[1] In September, David left for college in California and Laura began at Lawrence Central.

I will never forget the day we took David to the airport. Like a lot of parents, I had not thought much about the fact that our children would leave home before we were ready for them to do so. I had given so much time to work, thinking that there would always be time for family. That day, the words of Cat Stephens's song, "Cat's in the Cradle" kept playing in my brain. "Wait! He can't be leaving already!"

Not spending more time with family in those formative years of our children's lives is the one great regret of my life. I have since learned that this is a regret of too many ministers, and especially of the churches' bishops. We carry that regret deep in our souls, recognizing that we were ultimately in charge of our own schedules and should have set aside another time for family whenever family time was interrupted by work demands. "Too soon old, too late smart" (young ministers, hear me!). Getting to the office in the morning at 6 AM to get organized for the day, no matter if one got

---

[1] I have often joked that our house was "just a million dollars from the water," which meant a couple of blocks.

home at 10 PM or 1 AM the night before, and without compensating time, seemed necessary then. Now it does not seem as wise as it once did, especially with respect to home life.

I later apologized to my children for this error. David accepted the apology diplomatically, responding, "You modeled a strong work ethic for us." Laura was less diplomatic, and I thought back to my experience of my own father's emotional absence and realized that, despite my best intentions, I had repeated the old family script, though substituting work for drink. Thank God for grandchildren, who give some of us a second chance to be the kind of presence we wish we had been for our children. The presence of grandchildren in our lives is a bright light to Mindy and me, and we love them deeply.

Our house was in the northeastern part of the Indianapolis metropolitan area, and the Missions Building, the old headquarters of the denomination, was on the east side, in a neighborhood called Irvington. The drive to work was only about twenty minutes. However, the airport, which I used most every week and often twice or three times a week, was on the opposite side of town. In 1993, it was thirty-five minutes to the airport, but due to the rapid growth in northeastern Indianapolis, by 2003 the trip had become fifty-five minutes. So, after I finished as GMP, we moved to our current home on the west side, twenty minutes from the airport, which I would continue to use for my post-GMP work (consulting and ecumenical work), and twenty minutes from Christian Theological Seminary, where I would be teaching occasionally. I would like to have moved sooner but, until I finished as GMP, the time and effort that moving across town required just seemed impossible.

Chapter 6

Getting Started

I visited Indianapolis within a week after the 1993 General Assembly. Ann Updegraff Spleth, president of the Division of Homeland Ministries, picked me up at the airport. This was a comfort because Ann was also a baby boomer and had seen many of the same dynamics I had seen over the years, and we had been friends since high school days, when we were both part of the Disciples Florida State Youth Program. Her father was state secretary in those days (soon to be retitled "regional minister") and I was state CYF president. Ann and I both went to the World Convention in San Juan, Puerto Rico, in 1965, and we hung out together that week and had the opportunity to hear Martin Luther King, Jr., speak to the gathering. Now, twenty-eight years later, on our way into town, we had a good laugh about the fact that we were both now in general church ministry.

I "inherited" three associates, each of whom brought his or her own individual gifts to the office. Don Manworren was the chief administrator and very good at detail, had mounds of institutional memory, and was deeply committed to justice and ecumenism. He had once been a candidate for GMP, so he understood the vicissitudes of that process. Claudia Grant, who had been a fellow student with me at Christian Theological Seminary (and who had been a key contributor in seminary days to the undoing of my naïve, white male American worldview), was an excellent pastor and worship leader. John Foulkes knew the story of Black Disciples inside and out and had lived much of that history, and so was invaluable in helping me understand it. This was a good team, in my view, and I depended on them to help me understand my new work and context. Frankly, all three had been deeply disappointed when Michael Kinnamon was not elected, and it took them a bit to understand my very different approach to the office.

Mary Collins was my executive assistant and stayed with me for my entire time as GMP. She kept confidences and was totally trustworthy. She often ran interference for me in the office, and she kept me from being negatively surprised whenever possible. A good and kind listener, I found that when regional ministers called the office, it was often because they wanted to talk to *her*! All these years later, Mindy and I still enjoy an occasional luncheon with her.

I found there were *so many* excellent employees in the General Offices who served with passion for the church. One of these was Neil Topliffe. Though director of public relations for the Board of Church Extension, he spent much time handling the considerable communications opportunities and challenges surrounding my nomination and election. He was a great help to me in those first days of my service.

Decision about the Headquarters Building Project

In 1991, the denomination had entered into the capital campaign called *Embrace the Future*. There were five key projects to be funded by the hoped-for goal of thirty million dollars. One of these was a new headquarters building in downtown Indianapolis. Since 1928, most of the denomination's General Offices in Indianapolis (exceptions including the Board of Church Extension and the Pension Fund) had been headquartered in the old School of Missions Building, part of the former campus of Butler University.[1] Several additions and modifications had been added to the building over the years as the general ministries grew. When I visited the Missions Building in 1974 as a student at Christian Theological Seminary, I remember there being secretaries with their desks in some of the hallways because the staff had grown so much during the 1950s and 1960s that there simply wasn't room in the offices proper.

However, by the 1980s, the Missions Building had become more sparsely populated, as the size of denominational mission budgets

---

[1] Butler University was started by Disciples abolitionists in 1855 as an alternative to Bethany College, which began in a slave state (in Virginia, before that part of it became West Virginia) in 1840. Butler's campus had been in Irvington (on the east side of Indianapolis) until it moved to its current Fairview campus on the near northwest side of the city in 1928. Most of the former Irvington campus buildings were torn down and the land sold for housing development. The Bona Thompson Library remained and was part of the School of Missions.

had decreased. The "Building" had also become extremely expensive to maintain, to heat, and to cool (without central air conditioning in most of the complex, more than a hundred window air conditioners were needed in the summer). Despite the church's deep emotional attachment to the Missions Building, a move was needed to lower expenses.

A triangular plot of land in downtown Indianapolis near the Canal had been put together to accommodate a beautiful new headquarters building that would house the current occupants of the Missions Building plus the Board of Church Extension and the Pension Fund. The Community Development Department of Lilly Endowment had pulled the parcels together at a cost of seven million dollars as part of a renewal project for downtown Indianapolis and they were *giving* it to the church! The church was to shoulder the fourteen-million-dollar cost of the building construction itself.

Soon after I arrived, the campaign committee (which now included me as GMP as well as the presidents of those general ministry units that planned to reside in the new headquarters) met to review progress on the campaign. Of the thirty-million-dollar goal, only one and a half million had been raised in over two years (the Tennessee Region was the only region that had reached its campaign goal).

Though, naturally, the campaign fundraisers had put a bright face on the progress made so far in the overall campaign, I had come to my new role with serious doubts about the building of a new headquarters building, as beautiful as the architect's rendering was and as wonderful as it would have been to be a part of the renewal of downtown Indianapolis.[2] The country was clearly in the midst of a major change in its religious landscape, as denominations were beginning to diminish in their ability to garner loyalty, trust, and dollars. The old Missions Building, once full to the brim with workers, now had empty rooms that were cordoned off to save utility costs. I had serious doubts that donors would or even *should* support a new headquarters project, and its inclusion had been dragging down the Embrace the Future Campaign as a whole. When I heard the report, I was stunned at how little money had actually been raised by the

---

[2] Indianapolis, like many major cities at the time, had a weak core, with many empty store fronts and a great need for revitalization. Revitalization of downtown Indianapolis had begun in the 1970s, but had slowed to a trickle in the 1980s.

campaign as a whole and by how many donors had specified that none of their gifts should go toward the proposed headquarters project.

I did not have the executive authority to decide by myself the fate of the headquarters building project. But in view of the report we had just received from the campaign, I blurted out to the group, "We can't proceed with the building project given this lack of support for it!"

There seemed to me to be a collective sigh of relief among the general ministry unit leaders present, who had apparently been waiting to hear what the new GMP would think about the project. No one argued. That was effectively the end of the headquarters building project (it was officially terminated by the Administrative Committee a few months later, in February 1994).

There remained the problem of the seven million dollars the Lilly Endowment had spent creating the proposed site. Would we have to repay that money, since we were abandoning the project? I explained to the Lilly Endowment the reasons for our backing out of the project. Fortunately, and incredibly generously, the Endowment did not ask for repayment, and the property was used by the city for another renewal project later.

Over the course of the next several months, a committee composed of Missions Building leadership, assisted by Disciples member and broker Drew Augustine, looked for possible buildings to renovate or to lease. Among other places we looked at was the Pan Am Building downtown (built in association with the Pan American Games in 1987). Ultimately, we found a twelve-story building in the center of downtown at 105 East Washington Street in which we could lease several floors. At a May 31, 1994, meeting of the Christian Church Services Board,[3] decisions were made to move forward. We renovated four and a half floors, and this became the new "Disciples Center," in which our Indianapolis General Offices would reside for the next twenty years. The lease provided that every five years we could renegotiate our agreement and thus increase or decrease our space or move on to another location if we thought it appropriate.

---

[3] Christian Church Services was a small organization set up to act on behalf of the general ministries housed in the Mission Building and, later, in the new location on East Washington St. The president of this organization, Ryan Hazen, facilitated building equipment and repairs, managed leases, maintained general building services, maintained common areas of the building, and so much more. Ryan was wonderful in this executive role, and was later succeeded by another excellent leader, Steve Belding.

It gave us what we needed for those twenty years in the face of a rapidly changing cultural and ecclesial context: *flexibility*.

As hard as it was to leave the Missions Building at 222 South Downey Avenue, with its deep Disciples history and tradition, it was time. We knew that the mounting costs of staying in the historic building were wasting precious mission dollars.

The Irvington neighborhood, which had been home to the Disciples Mission Building for so many decades, was naturally concerned about what we intended to do with the old rambling facilities when we left, and those of us responsible for the move wanted to be sure we did not leave a problem or an eyesore for the neighborhood. On January 5, 1995, a public meeting was conducted by the Irvington Community Council to consider the church's proposals for disposing of the Missions Building. A large crowd showed up, and there were 499 votes for the proposal to create a retirement facility and 309 for demolition and redevelopment, but most present agreed they would be happy with either usage.

On January 30, 1995, we held a worshipful ceremony, planned by Disciples historian Peter Morgan, to close the Missions Building. Former GMPs, retired missionaries, regional and general ministry staff people, and many other Disciples were present as we decommissioned the building and walked the two blocks in the snow to Downey Avenue Christian Church to give thanks for all the Missions Building had meant to us all. On June 25, 1995, when the weather had warmed, an open house was celebrated at the new Disciples Center International, downtown.

In July 1997, after much work, we approved a proposal for redevelopment of the old Missions Building from Mansur Real Estate Services, Inc, a redeveloper of historic properties, and approved the use of Browning, Day, Mullins, and Dierdorf, Inc., as architects. Craig Mullins (a partner in the firm and a Disciple) became the primary liaison between the architects and the church. Mansur's proposal required a nonprofit partner in Indianapolis, so we eventually partnered with the Indiana Black Expo Economic Development Corporation, a nonprofit in Indianapolis, to form the Missions Building L.L.C. Limited Partnership to redevelop the Missions Building into the Mission Place Apartments, an affordable senior housing facility with seventy-nine units. This newly remodeled facility generally delighted the neighborhood and duly honored the historic role of the Missions Building in Disciples life and ministry.

Some will wonder why, since we needed a new headquarters facility, we did not propose to complete a merger with the United Church of Christ and share facilities with them. There are several reasons why this was not pursued, including the following. First, denominational mergers were largely a thing of the past. Having observed mergers that occurred earlier in the century (including the United Church of Christ, itself a product of merger in 1957, and the United Methodist Church in 1968), the costs in time and energy made mergers seem less desirable than previously thought. The model for denominational ecumenism had moved on to "ecumenical partnership." The Disciples have such partnerships with a number of denominations, so that we achieve much of the *benefit* of merger without the *cost* of merger. Second, the United Church of Christ had already secured a new headquarters in Cleveland, which is near the geographical center of their congregations. For Disciples, the geographical center would be closer to St. Louis. Third, moving to a new headquarters outside of Indianapolis (even St. Louis) would have meant uprooting dozens of employees, which would also have had a negative impact on Indianapolis-area Disciples congregations where so many of these employees and their families were participants.

My Purpose: To Move the Church Forward

I had no formal "mandate" provided to me by the General Board or General Assembly, although I could sense that people just wanted me to make things work again (not because anyone before me had failed, but because the times were changing rapidly and the church felt like it was falling behind). Of course, this is exactly what every expression of the church wants from every key leader: Make it work again! However, there are a couple of underlying assumptions in that desire, of which a wise leader must be cognizant.

First, the unspoken part of the plea to "make things work again" is that we will go back to doing what we used to do because it worked then. This assumes that what worked then will work now, despite changes in context. Things "worked" pretty well after the 1968 Restructure ... until annual budgets stopped growing and began shrinking. But beginning in the 1970s—due to inflation and the fact that North American culture as a whole was moving away from the "mainline churches," including the Disciples—many congregations' own budgets, and thus their contributions to denominational work, began shrinking both in amounts and in dollar value, which put the whole denominational system under stress. This stress increased dramatically over the next several decades. This is exemplified by the fact that the regional and general ministries redesigned the church's funding system *three times* during my years in regional and general leadership! (I will say more about this.)

Another unspoken part of the plea to "make things work again" is the assumption that they can be made to work again "without changing anything that directly affects me personally." Many a pastor-candidate has been fooled by a congregation's desire for a minister to help them grow, but *without changing anything*! The same is true in every expression of the church. It is part of the human condition: We *all* want success and effectiveness ... without change to anything we personally care about.

However, "making things work again" was not all I was called to do (at least not as I understood my call). So, what *did* I understand my call to be? Four things primarily: (1) to help the church deepen its spirituality (its relationship with God), in the face of an increasingly secular culture; (2) to clarify its mission; (3) to bring our structures into line with that mission: and (4) to help those structures function as effectively as possible. This is really what I thought the church was calling me to do, and what I thought God was calling me to do. Obviously, this is not something any one leader can do by him- or herself. It requires leaders from all expressions of the church to accomplish this to any great measure. But in our system, the GMP is called to lead this parade, or at least to point it in the right direction and cheer it on.

I cannot objectively judge my own effectiveness in this quest—that is up to the church and its historians to do. But I can tell you that if the General Assembly of 1993 thought they were electing a GMP who was just going to keep the machinery running as it was established in 1968 (however appropriate that machinery may have been then), they chose poorly.

I still find joy in the successes I experienced, and I am at peace with my failures. As one of my cherished, if curmudgeonly, CTS professors (yes, Clark Williamson) said to me on a golf course fifteen years later, "At least you tried to *do* something." While not exactly a ringing endorsement, I was grateful he had at least noticed my effort!

My First Cabinet Meeting (September 1993)

Although not mentioned in the original Design of the Christian Church (Disciples of Christ), the General Cabinet has been an essential regular gathering place for the heads of the various general ministry units of the church and the general minister and president. It was begun by the first GMP, Dale Fiers, and offered a place for the executive leadership of the general church to think together and plan for the work of the denomination.

Note: these "general ministries" were named "general administrative units" by The Design in 1968. That typically got shortened in common usage to "general units." When The Design was amended in 2005, the name was changed to "general ministries," a much more churchly title. I will refer to these as general ministry units, in order to avoid confusion with the Office of General Minister and President and other "Recognized Ministry Partners" and "Related Organizations."

Each of the general ministry units represents important core values of the Disciples of Christ and was developed to address those values. The Board of Church Extension (now referred to as Disciples Church Extension Fund) was established in 1888 to assist existing congregations in their sustainability and growth and to help new congregations that were being developed across North America. The Christian Board of Publication was founded in 1911 to resource the church's commitment to an educated and informed faith. The Christian Church Foundation was developed in 1964 to help all Disciples be good stewards of accumulated financial resources for the sake of the mission of the church.

The Council on Christian Unity (now called Christian Unity and Interfaith Ministry) was established in 1910 to help Disciples live out our commitment to the unity of the whole church of Jesus Christ (our "Polar Star"). The Division of Higher Education (later referred to as Higher Education and Leadership Ministries—HELM), was established in 1914 and reflected the Stone-Campbell Movement's commitment to education as a gateway to faith and to the need for an educated clergy. The Disciples of Christ Historical Society, established in 1941, has sought to help us remember who we are and from whence we have come, which gives clues as to where God may be leading us now.

The Division of Homeland Ministries (now known as Disciples Home Missions—DHM) reflected the need to resource congregational life so as to strengthen congregations in their local mission. The Division of Overseas Ministries (DOM) is at the core of Disciples' commitment to share the Good News of Jesus Christ with the whole world in a way that enhances justice and genuine community. These two ministries, DHM and DOM, grew out of the missionary societies and boards of the 1880s and 1890s.

The National Benevolent Association was founded in 1887 to tend to the needs of the poor and marginalized of our church and beyond. The Pension Fund of the Christian Church was founded in 1895 to assure that those whom the church employs are financially secure in their time of retirement and disability.

The Office of the General Minister and President (OGMP) is not a general ministry unit, but (and this is often confusing to people) is located in the Disciples Center building, which is often referred to as the General Offices (because there are many general ministries housed there as well as the OGMP). As general *president*, the GMP is the chief executive for the denomination as a whole (signing legal documents and so on); but as general *minister*, the GMP is the chief pastor and spokesperson for the denomination. These two roles are sometimes difficult to exercise in a combined role (which is one reason congregations usually have a pastor *and* a chair of the board). It is, in part, the ambiguity of this combination of roles that can make the relationship of the GMP with the Cabinet somewhat sticky.[4]

Although I had served congregations for many years and had been a regional minister, I had a rather naïve view of the Cabinet as I approached my first meeting with them. Some of them I knew only from afar, and some had been mentors and important influences in my ministry without their even knowing it. I had become friends with Jim Seale, president of the Disciples of Christ Historical Society, because it was located in Nashville, where my regional office had also been. I had accepted an invitation from Paul Crow to observe

---

[4] Other ambiguities in the relationship between the GMP and the general ministry unit presidents include the fact that most of the general ministry units were formed long before the Office of the GMP (formed in 1968), and thus each had its own long-term history and particular ethos and had enjoyed a high degree of self-direction before The Design of 1968. In addition, each had its own board, recruited in large measure by or with the approval of the general ministry unit president, which meant they approve their own budgets, hire their own staff, and shape their own life and mission in large measure.

a Central Committee meeting of the World Council of Churches in Geneva while a regional minister, and so got to know him somewhat. Of course, I had known Ann Updegraff Spleth of Homeland Ministries since CYF days.

Years before, I had been approached by Hal Watkins of Church Extension about the possibility of working for Church Extension, but I had said "no" only because I had just recently started a new congregation in Kansas City and felt an obligation to stay with them. I had known and appreciated a friendship with Jim Johnson of the Christian Church Foundation. I had known Robert Welsh of the Church Finance Council as a friend and discussion partner for a few years. I had served on the Board of the Division of Overseas Ministries for several years, so I knew Bill Nottingham.

But I had never met Jim Spainhower, president of the Division of Higher Education, and I had never had any real relationship with Lester Palmer of the Pension Fund, Jim Suggs of the Christian Board of Publication, or Rick Lance of the National Benevolent Association.

I was a bit anxious about meeting with them as a group, because it is not unusual for individuals in a group setting to interact differently than they do as individuals. Yet, I was also excited at the prospect of meeting them all together.

My staff and I thought it might be helpful to meet in a "retreat setting" rather than meeting in one or another of the offices in Indianapolis, Nashville (at the Disciples of Christ Historical Society), or St. Louis (at the offices of Christian Board of Publication, the Division of Higher Education, or the National Benevolent Association). So we gathered at the Four Winds Conference Center at Lake Monroe near Bloomington, Indiana.

From my perspective, the General Cabinet had not had ongoing leadership from a general minister and president for a while. Bill Nichols had been a two-year *interim* leader since the Tulsa General Assembly and had spent his time and energy providing pastoral care to an anxious denomination, which was appropriate; but he did not have the time to initiate much direction or programming. So, I presumed they would eagerly embrace new leadership from a settled GMP. Thus, I came to my first Cabinet meeting with a long list of possible issues for us to discuss and prioritize. Perhaps I should have spent more time listening to Cabinet express members their concerns and hopes *before* launching into a list of my concerns and hopes. However, I was eager to demonstrate leadership, thinking they would be pleased, maybe even comforted by the knowledge that the new GMP was not merely a maintenance person.

I think some of the Cabinet members did feel this way. However, two or three had become used to being unencumbered by a GMP's opinions of how the church should move into the future, especially a GMP so new to the scene. Some, I think, were just anxious about the future of their own ministry unit and how they could help it survive or increase in the face of a church that was beginning to show signs of institutional decline. I think a few had come to a place of seeking to *protect* their ministry unit from a church embroiled in the controversies of the day rather than seeking ways their unit could help the whole church thrive.

But, to a person, we *all* felt a deep sense of responsibility to the general ministry units and offices we served and *that* sometimes overtook even our commitment to the *whole* church. The challenge was not so much in the quality of the individual Cabinet leaders, although we all had our strengths *and* weaknesses, to be sure (as is true of every generation and every group of leaders). The challenge was in the fact that mission dollars were eroding in number and value combined with the fact that our system puts general ministry units (and regions, for that matter) in competition with one another for funding. I said something about this before, and I'll say more about this later; suffice it to say here that this tendency toward a competitive attitude on the part of general ministry unit presidents and regional ministers was one of the things that would eventually wear me down as GMP. But I'm getting ahead of myself.

Here is the list of things I named at that first Cabinet meeting/retreat so the group could begin thinking together about priorities and how we might move forward together.

- **The need for a Disciples mission statement.** I felt the church was drifting badly in its own sense of mission.
- **Clergy morale.** This was an issue among *all* groups: white male, female, racial, ethnic, all generations. *Every* constituent group had a morale problem in the face of the challenges of the times.
- **Disciples' identity.** There was a need for member education. Most members did not understand who Disciples are and how we are put together.

- **Distances between groups.** There were widening gaps between various perspectives as groups were turning inward: between congregational/regional/general expressions, racial/ethnic constituencies, and conservatives and liberals.
- **Our lack of programming for and inclusion of Gen X,** the generation born between 1965 and 1982. There was a need for strong camp and conference programming and campus ministry. The oldest of this young generation were in their twenties, and many were disappearing from church life.
- **Clarification of the role of regions and their revitalization.** I planned to be active with regions in the selection and support of regional ministers and in interventions, as needed. Like units and congregations, without adequate resourcing from outside, regions were apt to make poor personnel decisions that created problems for the whole church.
- **Clarification of roles of General Board and Administrative Committee.** There seemed to me to be a lot of overlap. Could the General Board be a churchwide planning body in off-Assembly years?
- **Stewardship education.** Not much of this was being done anywhere.
- **Clarity in mission funding.** What exactly does Basic Mission Finance *fund*?
- **Spiritual climate of general church offices.** Life in the general church offices had, in many cases, become dominated by secular administrative practices; spiritual life was not being addressed in many offices, although it was rich among some.
- **Restructure.** Clarity of mission is the first step. The Restructure of 1968 had been incomplete in some respects and obsolete in others. For example, regions were hardly considered in the process.
- **Strategy with "renewal" groups.** The church was being roiled by so-called renewal groups that were being funded by right-wing interests.
- **A Sunset Rule for resolutions.** Shouldn't resolutions have a limited time frame when they ask for general ministry units or regions to do something specific?

- **The purpose of General Assembly.** We needed to reconsider length, connection to congregational life, and general ministry unit work. How could Assemblies foster lay education, enable community building? How could we better coordinate general ministry unit reports? How could we bring better focus through Assembly themes. General Assemblies had been stand-alone events, each with its own theme that was not directly related to the one before. Assemblies also seemed like wonderful opportunities to provide educational resources specifically designed for congregations and leaders.
- **Clarification of the role and a name change for the Council of Ministers.** Some congregational ministers resented the idea that a Council of Ministers would be so named when no congregational ministers were invited—it was for leaders of BMF recipient organizations only.
- **Common strategies for "crossover" clergy.** Some of our best ministers came to the Disciples from other traditions, but because there were no universal processes for how regions granted standing to ministers who were coming from other denominations, there were "low places in the fence" that had sometimes allowed authorization of clergy with troubling histories and behaviors.
- **Effective orientation for new regional ministers.** There was little in the way of orientation for new regional ministers, so problems sometimes ensued as new regional ministers were often "thrown into the deep end."
- **Connection between general ministry units and the General Board.** Each general ministry unit had its own board, so how do the general ministry units relate to the church's General Board?

Of course, I was not asking the group to resolve all of these issues in this brief cabinet retreat. I was just trying to get some important issues on the table for ongoing discussion in the year ahead. But I must have failed to make that clear. Although most of the (then) eleven general ministry unit presidents understood what I was doing, a couple of them apparently thought I was planning on "turning over the tables" and demanding responses to all of these items that very day.

I mentioned at one point in the conversation that I intended to write a book on some of the cultural challenges I thought the church needed to face up to. The anger of one general ministry unit president, in particular, boiled over, and he made his feelings known in no uncertain terms! He asked with great energy, "Do you think Christian Board of Publication is going to publish a book for you just because you are General Minister and President?" After a momentary pause, I responded, "Well, yes, I thought that would be the case." That exchange told me a lot (though I later came to count that president as a friend).

Some of them seemed to feel (incorrectly, but understandably, as I look back on it) that I was blaming them for the church's ills. It was quite an initiation into general church life. It was a baptism as surely as if the Cabinet had dragged me the hundred yards or so down to Lake Monroe and thoroughly dunked me (as I had once been "laked" by college fraternity brothers when I was a pledge). If I thought this was a group of leaders who were waiting for directions from a new "green" GMP, that illusion had been punctured!

I *then* (better late than never) explained what I was doing: I was presenting some concerns that were top of mind for me as an outsider coming into the general expression of the church and wanting their feedback, additional concerns, and so on. Everybody calmed down and settled in then for a healthier discussion of the challenges that were facing the church we *all* loved. We departed the retreat as friends, but it had been a bit of a rocky start with this important leadership group.

By the way, still smarting a bit, when I finished my book manuscript, I did not ask Christian Board of Publication to publish it. Instead, Professor Tony Dunnavant, a friend who thought my analysis was worth the church's study, saw to it that my first book, *From Mainline to Frontline*, was published by Lexington Theological Seminary. CBP *did* publish my next two books without reservation, for which I am grateful.

The further from general church staff a GMP candidate comes, the more orientation is needed. That orientation needs to be historical, philosophical, and relational. As a regional minister when elected, I thought I understood the general church. But I really had not much clue about the General Cabinet and general ministry units. Of course, the three regular GMPs before me (Dale

Fiers, Ken Teegarden, and John Humbert) had all come directly from general staff and started with a much more realistic picture of the general expression of the church (including an understanding that the general ministry units had begun as separate agencies formed independently from one another and still operated as essentially individual units). As I later departed office in 2003, I tried to impress upon the General Committee for Renewal and Structural Reform the importance of providing a thorough orientation for newly elected GMPs. Ironically, I was asked years later by the United Church of Christ to help orient *their* new GMP, Geoffrey Black, in 2009, and I hope he found it helpful. I was never asked to formally help orient *our* future GMPs (although each of my successors has approached me individually with smart questions).

How Would I Spend My Time?

This was an important question for me as a leader (as it is for every leader of anything). After eighteen months or so as GMP, I had begun to understand the nature of the job and to think seriously about priorities and how I should spend my time. As a regional minister, I had heard the complaints of congregational ministers and members about how they felt denominational leaders seldom communicated with them unless they were asking for something. This was overstated, of course, in that regional ministers and representatives of Church Extension spent *most* of their time with congregations. The staff of the Division of Homeland Ministries spent a lot of time in men's gatherings, women's gatherings, and youth gatherings. Christian Church Foundation staff spent a significant amount of time in congregations helping them establish endowments and otherwise safeguard their financial assets. The other general ministry units were *always* willing and happy to visit congregations when invited to do so. Nevertheless, the *perception* was that denominational folk visited only when they needed something (usually money). It was true, however, that GMPs seldom visited in congregations (most often for good practical reasons, as shall be seen).

Thus, I decided I would try to be as available as possible to congregations and regions as a sign that "We are all in this together!" However, this was more challenging than it initially seemed. There are many general church meetings that occur over weekends to make lay participation easier, including General Board meetings;

General Nominating Committee meetings, General Assembly Planning Committee meetings, racial/ethnic assemblies (National Convocation, National Hispanic Ministries, and North American Pacific/Asian Disciples), and ecumenical assemblies of the National and World Councils of Churches. Regional assemblies typically occur on weekends, as well. Each of these is a place in which a GMP should be present from time to time. Of course, occasionally a GMP needs to stick his or her head into his or her *home* congregation to worship and be a part of that local community, too. There are vacation days and sometimes family gatherings that require a weekend. By the time these are added up, there are not a lot of weekends left for a GMP to be out "showing the flag."

Nevertheless, I did manage to get into about twenty-five congregations a year on Sunday morning. Sometimes these were the morning after a regional assembly I had participated in, or a special anniversary of a congregation (I preached for quite a few hundredth anniversaries), or for other occasions, or "just because." So, over the course of my ten years, I was in about two hundred and fifty congregations. That was still a small proportion of our then 4,000 congregations, but it required a significant amount of energy. Nevertheless, I always enjoyed those visits.

I did soon learn, however, that while most *ministers* knew what a GMP is, few members of most congregations had much idea (or cared). Many members dismissed it the way members of service clubs often skip on the week the state governor of the club is visiting (my Rotarian experience is showing). They didn't realize how few congregations ever get to host a GMP. I remember many times standing at the door after worship and having some members shake my hand and ask, "Now, where is the congregation you serve?"

So, I tried to get pastors to impress on their people that my visit was not just one from an "outside speaker" who would preach long and be boring (although that may have happened a time or two), but that my visit was worth their time. I refused to go if the senior pastor was not going to be present to host (to avoid being seen as "mere" pulpit supply). My primary purpose in being there was always to express appreciation for the congregation's ministry "on the front lines of mission" and to thank them for their participation in the whole mission and ministry of the Christian Church (Disciples of Christ) through their financial support and through any persons their congregation might be contributing to regional and general work.

I also made it a point to have a "forum" or open conversation with any who wished to participate during the Sunday school hour or a fellowship meal, or whenever the congregation wished. In these forums, members could ask *any* question they might have about the denominational or ecumenical world. It was an opportunity to correct misinformation and assumptions and to replace skepticism with enthusiasm or, at least, accurate information. It was in these settings where I had the opportunity to address prophetic issues in a way that made it possible for me to *personally* take any heat rather than the denomination taking the heat. I believe being prophetic means personally taking such heat, not making the church as a whole pay the price for the truth one proclaims. There were always questions about human sexuality, the nature of biblical authority, nationalistic perversions of the gospel, and so forth. I always tried to be respectful (however disrespectful questions sometimes were) and to be honest. It generally seemed to be appreciated by folks, even if they disagreed with me.

I didn't spend much time promoting those ministries of the church that were already doing well. For example, Week of Compassion—already a marvelous mission and ministry—had, under Johnny Wray's leadership, more than doubled in contributions. They didn't need much help from me, although Mindy and I certainly contributed financially to it through our home congregation, and I lifted up that ministry when visiting congregations and regions.

In retrospect, perhaps I spent too much time on the road (which is to say, on airliners) and not enough time in Disciples Center and at home. However, it was evident that I needed to spend time with the regional ministers.

The Regional Ministers

I came to the Office of the General Minister and President *from* regional ministry, so I knew the weaknesses in our system regarding how regional ministers were called, supported, and held accountable. I decided it was important for me to continue meeting with the Conference of Regional Ministers and Moderators in order to maintain trust and to enlist their help in the changes I was seeking to foster in church life.

Done well, regional ministry is one of the most important ministries in the life of the church. Pastors and congregations depend on regional ministers to be of assistance in a variety of ways that are essential to the health of our congregational ministers and our congregations. The reason this is true is that we Disciples are not people who respond well to instructions to "just follow the rules." Therefore, telling folks how things *ought* to be done, as purported in various manuals or even in The Design, does not ultimately fly in this church. Rather than rules, our first loyalty is to *relationships.* Regional ministry done well means, in part, that regional ministers carefully cultivate relationships with and between their ministers and congregations, thus engendering trust that will lead the minister and/or congregation to communicate regularly with the regional minister and to call when help is needed (or to accept help when it is offered).

A typical congregational search committee has people on it who have never participated in a ministerial search process but who may be accustomed to participating in, or even leading, secular search processes in their workplaces. Sometimes these folks will encourage the committee to "skip all that search and call process stuff" the regional minister touts and just go "head hunting" on their own. How many congregations have ended up exploding because they hired a wolf in sheep's clothing, someone who was willing to "cut a deal" outside the regular search and call channels? How many? *Many!*

Search committees often grow weary and, in their impatience, short-circuit the process. Many search committees take the attitude of "God will provide!" That may be true, but it doesn't mean the congregation doesn't have to do its homework to find the one God is providing. This means, for example, *actually calling references!* Most of us would be amazed at how many search committees, having been captivated by the personality or other traits of a candidate, will somehow then decide that no further work is needed, that no deeper reference checks are warranted. References may seem to check out fine on paper ... but we don't know the whole story for sure till we actually *talk* to the references! Thus, my advice to search committees is always, "Do not take written references at face value (few people are willing to tell the whole truth in writing). *Always* check with the candidate's previous regional minister. If the previous regional minister suggests there might be a problem with a particular candidate, *carefully check it out before going further!"*

As for regions seeking a new regional minister, most regional search committees were working alone in the early 1990s, without any substantial help from anyone beyond their region. The Conference of Regional Ministers and Moderators[5] offered "recommended processes" in print, but few regional ministers had the time and energy to meet with the regional minister search committee of another region as an in-person resource. So, in September 1993, I offered myself to the Conference of Regional Ministers and Moderators as the primary consultant to those regional minister search committees. This work took a lot of time, but I felt it was crucial to maintaining high quality among regional ministers.

Equally important to me, it gave me the opportunity to encourage committees to look at women and people of color, who were grossly underrepresented in regional ministry at the time. It also provided a trust relationship for me with new regional ministers. This made me more helpful to them when challenges came. Most regional search committees were extremely glad for the assistance, although a few wanted to "do it their own way" (which sometimes ended in disasters). All in all, I feel the work I did with the Conference (and then the College) and with regional minister search committees was among the best and most productive ways I could spend my time. It is partly because of this effort that the profiles of regional ministers went from only one white woman and *no* people of color in 1993 to five white women and five men of color in 2003. That was a great return on investment![6]

On the other hand, I must confess my own naivete at this point. Simply getting women and people of color before search committees was essential, but there also needed to be some kind of systemic work done to support these pioneering women and people of color when they got the opportunity to serve. A system that has been white-male dominant forever does not easily welcome women and people of color into leadership. There are a hundred ways in which a system

---

[5] The Conference of Regional Ministers and Moderators was an organization that met annually for mutual support and edification. It was a place where regional moderators could see the larger picture of regional life and work and be oriented for their roles. This organization later divided (1998) into the College of Regional Ministers, which met and continues to meet two to three times per year, and the Forum for Regional Moderators, which meets during General Board and Assembly.

[6] Of course, the major factor in the growth in numbers was that the church had many excellent female candidates and candidates of color. But it must also be said that we had such candidates long before regions became open to seriously considering them. My successors wisely continued such encouragement to regional search committees.

can sabotage such leadership. I both salute the courage of these new leaders and warn us all that we must actively support these people and help ward off systemic sabotage that is an expression of latent misogyny and racism. These were things I was still learning about myself as a white male leader.

Taking a Populist Approach to Change

Change is difficult for any institution, perhaps most of all for the church. In seminary, the joke was to sing (to the tune of "Onward Christian Soldiers"), "Like a mighty tortoise moves the church of God ..." This should not be surprising, as institutions are created to *preserve* things: values, beliefs, ways of being and doing. If one has no anchor point, the winds of the culture can blow one around mercilessly and life becomes a muddle. On the other hand, if institutions are not careful, their "anchors" can become "lead sinkers" that can drown an institution in the comfortable past. Thus, one of the primary jobs of any leader of any institution or organization (whether ecclesial, governmental, educational, social, or commercial) is to strike a dynamic balance between anchorage and needed change.

Resistance to change is endemic in every church. It often comes from members, but it often comes from the very leaders who are *called to bring needed change!* In most churches, including the Christian Church (Disciples of Christ), resistance comes from both *some* members and *some* leaders. So, I realized early on that I would have to build a sense of urgency, a *consensus* that change was needed among general, regional, and congregational leaders, and the membership in general. As I liked to say it, we didn't need to change *everything*, just the stuff that was killing us!

To name a few examples: We Disciples needed to clarify our mission and our goals as a denomination; congregations needed to focus on reaching out into their local context to do mission rather than focusing on merely keeping things comfortable in their own buildings; General Assembly needed to have a clarified purpose and methods that would address that purpose; some general ministry units needed more focus on helping congregations *engage* in mission rather than merely doing mission *for* congregations; all expressions of the church needed to deal with the systemic racism we had inherited from North American culture and previous generations;

we all needed to focus on the mission rather than focusing on institutional survival. The list goes on.

Thus, I didn't feel there was just one fulcrum point within the general, regional, or congregational expressions where I could gain leverage for needed change. Change was needed *everywhere!* So, I tried to build a sense of urgency for needed change just about everywhere in the church. My calls for change and explanations of the change needed became pedantic to some, I suppose. As I look back on my addresses to general and regional church leadership, I can see how my explanations may have gotten old to them.

However, in the face of the active resistance of a few and the passive resistance of many, I continued to advocate for it and presented my case to the entire church membership in any way I could (through speaking, articles, and a couple of books, among other means). My thought was that if I got enough lay people and congregational ministers stirred up about the need for change, it would bring some pressure to bear on the rest of our structures to respond. This would be called "populism" in the political world, and I made no apology for it. It's the only way I knew to try to move an organization as big, as diverse, as scattered, and as anxious as the Christian Church (Disciples of Christ) in the United States and Canada. It felt like what I was called by God to do. Someone else may have had different or better methods to offer, but this seemed right to me and for me. It was the same way I sought to lead each of the congregations I had served.

As some wag observed early in my tenure, "Leading Disciples is like herding cats." This is true, but it helps when the cats being herded know that you love them, and that God loves them. Both of these statements are also true and remain true. Populism, at least as I lived it, can be exhausting for a leader. But it does bring some measure of success among Disciples. (See Appendix 1 for a brief discussion of how these dynamics work among Disciples.)

Chapter 7

Challenges and Initiatives

I have previously alluded to some of the concerns that made me willing to serve as GMP, including my perception that the church was drifting in its sense of mission; the lack of new church starts in the past twenty-five years; and the failure to reach large portions of the people of North America, including African Americans, Hispanic Americans, Asian Americans, and others. Finally, there were some organizational deficiencies that needed to be addressed, such as help for regional search committees and equitable application of operational and ministerial standards across all regions.

Some of these, such as clarity of mission, were long-term projects that would require several years of work; others were relatively quick to address. The following is a look at some of the challenges I chose to address and the initiatives I tried to foster. Of course, all these initiatives required the support of various individuals and groups involved in management, governance, and programming, and none could be successfully addressed by a GMP alone. Each involved group effort—sometimes by staff, sometimes by the General Administrative Committee and Board, and sometimes by ministry partners across the three expressions of the church. I was grateful for these partnerships in needed change. Whether I chose the right issues in the right order is up to someone else to decide, but my choices were most often made based on where I thought change was possible. Not only choosing the right issues, but also selecting the right "fulcrums" by which change can occur, is an important function of leadership anywhere.

As a community called together in response to God's grace and love for the world, there were five questions I believed were key for

Disciples as we faced the headwinds of the postmodern or (as some prefer to call it) the post-establishment era.

1. Who are we, and what is our mission now?
2. How can we best organize ourselves for doing this mission?
3. How will we fund our mission?
4. How can we reconcile the various divisions among us and bring ourselves together in common mission?
5. How can we develop and better support faithful and effective leadership for the church?

I encourage you to read my address to the Administrative Committee meeting on January 29, 1995, in which I offered an overview of these questions and how I proposed getting started on answering them (see Appendix 2).

The Foremost and Overarching Challenge: Autonomy

"Autonomy" is not a word that appears in the New Testament. The word comes from Latin and literally means "a law unto oneself," but it is most often interpreted as "self-ruling" or "independent." The word has been used throughout the Stone-Campbell Movement in part because the Movement was an effort to get free from *denominational* rules and governance in favor of *local* (congregational) decision-making and governance. Both Barton Stone and Alexander Campbell split from the Scottish Presbyterian Church as it appeared on the American frontier. Ever since, the Movement has struggled to find an appropriate and workable balance between local freedom and belonging to a larger community.

The Christian Church (Disciples of Christ) decided in the Restructure of 1968 that we wanted to be part of a larger community that would express our co-commitment to one another as "church." The other two branches of the Stone-Campbell Movement (the Independent and the non-instrumental Churches of Christ) did *not* want to belong to a larger expression of church, which they rightly believed would somewhat curb their local freedom. For them, the congregation was the ultimate expression of church, and anything beyond the congregation is a fellowship or an association but not truly church.

The concept The Design uses to describe a balance between local freedom and belonging to a larger community is *covenant*. We have been trying to define exactly what that means for us ever since 1968!

We have most often defined covenant in such a way as to mean voluntary cooperation. But as every Disciples member knows, voluntary cooperation sometimes breaks down, especially when it requires sacrifice for the sake of the larger community and one another's needs. The temptation to meet one's own needs first and foremost is *always* the temptation for congregations, regions, general ministries ... for *every* expression of the church.

Most of us in regional and general ministries have a clearer notion of what "breaking the covenant" means than what "keeping the covenant" means, especially as the terms apply to our own way of participating in the larger body. To put it another way, born as we were in rebellion against what was perceived as unreasonable control from church hierarchies, we tend to be more sensitive to our *rights* than to our *responsibilities* within the covenantal body. We also tend to spend more time and energy protecting our turf than thinking together about how all of us can thrive together. It is one of the key issues we must face as a whole body if we are to thrive into the future.[1]

"Autonomy-thinking" was and is everywhere—in congregations as well as regions and general ministry units. So, getting people to talk to one another seemed essential to me. The funding system debates had been detrimental to the relationships between the general ministry units and regions, as well as other BMF recipients. Thus, trying to position the various groups for dialogue with one another was a key to my strategy. I had attended three of these annual funding system meetings as a regional minister, and I hadn't found them particularly useful in developing collegiality or working on solutions to important matters together.

---

[1] As I look back on this period of the mid-1990s, I think I should have pressed harder for a process aimed at reducing the amount of overall denominational structure rather than focusing as we did on relatively minor efficiencies and apparent redundancies. However, I don't think many of us fully realized at that point how much of a reduction in size and resources we Disciples were going to experience in the next twenty-five years. We were still thinking that significant increases in giving to Basic Mission Finance were possible and thus that the financial picture would somehow improve. We were wrong. In our defense, however, neither did any other mainline denomination's leadership fully foresee the depth of the coming reductions. It began to become abundantly apparent to me by the end of my service as GMP, and I began talking about a fifty-percent reduction in size within the next two decades. Many Disciples leaders rolled their eyes when they heard me say that, but it turned out to be true.

The Council of Ministers typically met in December of each year, so I decided to use that occasion in December 1993 as an opportunity to get people talking to one another about something besides money ... something *more important* than money.

The Council of Ministers was arguably misnamed because it included only general ministry unit presidents and regional ministers. No congregational ministers were invited. This was a source of some irritation for congregational ministers who were aware of it. However, the *function* was legitimate: The general ministry unit and regional leaders needed a place to talk to one another about how their ministries could best *together* serve the whole mission and ministry of the church. The name implied that we are a hierarchical church, which we are most certainly *not*!

So, after my first Council of Ministers meeting as GMP (in 1993), I changed the name to the Leadership Team Conference. We were key leaders of the church, but not the *only* key leaders of the church. It was thus a somewhat humbler name and expressed our aspiration to lead as a team rather than as a bunch of individuals. By 1997, at Karen Frank Plumlee's suggestion, I had begun calling it the Team Leadership Conference (TLC). We were, after all, seeking to be a team of leaders, conferring and mutually caring for one another and for the church with "tender loving care."

To initiate the conversation in 1993, I presented four keynotes to the Council of Ministers. I aimed to avoid being accusatory or judgmental and instead focused on identifying some of the challenges I believed we needed to address, encouraging the entire group (around seventy leaders) to engage in dialogue regarding the ideas I presented. I did not seek simple "approval" for the concepts I articulated; rather, I encouraged meaningful dialogue, welcoming amendments and alternative suggestions for each idea. I considered the meeting a success because the whole group took what I was "putting out there" seriously and, in several instances, improved ideas and enhancements to my suggestions emerged from the group in response. This allowed me to bring several proposals that were stronger and had broader ownership to the subsequent Administrative Committee and General Board meetings.

I think the content of those four brief keynotes and some summation of the follow-up conversations will clarify what I was thinking about in these first months of my service as GMP, so I have included those in Appendix 2.

The dialogue in small groups that developed out of these keynotes was most heartening. The overall response to the ideas and process was positive, and there were very helpful questions and concerns as well as affirmations. At the General Board meeting in July 1994, I continued to develop these themes of working together and clarifying mission.

General Commission on Ministry 1993

In 1993, two groups were primarily responsible for ministry concerns. The Conference of Regional Ministers and Moderators addressed concerns raised by regional ministers in a *Committee on Ministry*, chaired by Bill Allen, regional minister of West Virginia. Meanwhile, the General Board's *Standing Committee on the Ministry* addressed concerns from the general church perspective, chaired by Lester Palmer, who had been appointed by Dale Fiers shortly after the Restructure. These two groups shared many overlapping concerns and functions. Each group was focused on ensuring consistency in rules and their application regarding the ministerial relocation process, clergy misconduct, clergy support, and the like. The concern was not driven by a bureaucratic desire for control, but rather reflected the reality that inconsistencies allowed unhealthy individuals to victimize the church and its members. This issue became even more urgent following the Jim Jones affair in 1978, as Jones had been a Disciples minister *with standing*!

I met with the existing General Board Standing Committee on the Ministry and the Conference of Regional Ministers' Committee on Ministry (which were meeting together at the time) and heard concerns expressed about overlaps of responsibility between the two groups and how this was inefficient and weakened the effectiveness of both in seeking to provide for healthier Disciples ministry and ministers. So, we together developed the idea of a General Commission on Ministry (what would come to be known as GCOM— yes, we Disciples have acronyms for everything). This Commission, the concept of which had been officially blessed by the General Board in 1993, brought together representatives from all three expressions of the church and began working through the commonly identified issues in June 1995. The original members of the newly formed

General Commission on Ministry, whom I appointed in consultation with the two groups, included Bill Allen, regional minister of West Virginia, who served as chair; David Alexander, regional minister of Georgia; Bill Boswell, regional minister of Louisiana; Joyce Coalson, DHM vice president for the Center for Leadership and Ministry; John Foulkes, executive secretary of the National Convocation (and associate general minister); Karen Frank-Plumlee, regional minister of Montana; Richard Guentert, regional minister of the Upper Midwest; Tom Jewell, regional minister of Oklahoma; Diana McKee, lay person from Milton, Canada; Saundra Michael-Bowers, Pension Fund staff; Nancy Stalcup, lay person from Dallas, Texas; Bill Tabbernee, president of Phillips Graduate Seminary; and myself, *ex officio*. Lester Palmer, who had become president of the Pension Fund by this time, took the opportunity to step off after more than twenty years of faithful service. Bill Allen, regional minister and chair of the Conference of Regional Ministers Committee on Ministry, accepted the role of chair of GCOM and did an outstanding job for ten years as the first chair of the new body.

The issues constituted a lengthy and challenging list:

- Women in ministry were (and are) still struggling for equity.
- The "relocation process" (later called "search and call") was not serving some categories of ministers and congregations very well, and we needed to educate both ministers and laity about how the process works.
- There were differences in the relocation process from region to region (what some of us referred to as "low places in the fence").
- There were similar inconsistencies regarding the recognition of ordination from other denominations.
- We needed to implement a system for the electronic transfer of records from the Center for Leadership and Ministry in DHM to regions.
- There were inconsistencies in how various regions viewed licensed ministry.
- A group was needed to review appeals regarding standing (not to overrule a region's decision but to determine whether a region had followed its own processes adequately).

- A study was needed of how many ministers would be needed in the years ahead, and how retired ministers could most helpfully relate to their former congregations.
- Finally, we needed to bring about the reconciliation of the ministries of the Disciples of Christ and the United Church of Christ.

The General Commission met for the first time June 2–3, 1995, and went right to work. The second meeting was February 2–3, 1996, and three subcommittees were created from Commission membership: Relocation, Standards, and Support.

Various resource people were invited to meet with the Commission and its subcommittees periodically. Disciples historian Newell Williams, then of Christian Theological Seminary, attended the first meeting to lead the group in a theological reflection on Article I of the Disciples "Policies and Criteria for the Order of Ministry." In the second meeting, Richard Harrison, president of Lexington Theological Seminary, facilitated a similar reflection on Article II of the "Policies." Chuck Blaisdell, who was then the associate regional minister of Indiana, participated to work with the Standards Committee. Additionally, Randy Clay from Suran Systems and Joyce Beloat from DHM's Center for Leadership and Ministry attended to support the Relocation Committee.

I have given quite a bit of space to this discussion of the formation of the General Commission on Ministry because the challenges it faced were many, and I believe it has been one of the most positively contributing governance structures Disciples have ever created. I can remember when every regional office had banks of file drawers filled with relocation papers from over the years. It had become difficult to find and track candidates in many of these individual regional filing systems, and effective record maintenance became more than could be afforded in some regions and a huge financial burden in others. The electronic search and call process developed by GCOM has made it so much easier for all concerned: regional ministers, candidates, and search committees. Developing common ordination standards and relocation practices across regions was also essential.

During my time as regional minister of Tennessee (1990–1993), the ugly issue of sexual misconduct was consuming vast quantities of many regions' staff time. Even in my mid-size region, such cases were taking up to a third of my time and half of my emotional energy. By standardizing procedures and providing education on the subject, GCOM helped regions squeeze out the sexual predators from the ranks of Disciples ministers so that, within a few years, sexual misconduct cases became exceptional rather than routine. I am so grateful that we Disciples got a handle on this issue in the 1990s, rather than waiting, as some others did, to cut through our denial and deal with perpetrators before more people and congregations were victimized. No system is perfect, of course, and an unhealthy minister occasionally slips in, but when his or her unhealthiness becomes apparent, congregations and their regional ministers have recourse, and all ministers accused of misconduct of any kind receive due process.

The new GCOM addressed these issues and more (including designing alternative pathways to ordination) over the years, and their work was gladly received and embraced by the regions and by DHM and the other general expressions of the church. It continued the initial pattern of meeting twice a year, for two to three days each time. In 1997, new members were added to the Commission including LaTanya Bynum of Broad Street Christian Church in Columbus, Ohio (formerly of DHM); Charles Shorow of First Christian Church, Salem, Oregon; and Gene Kraus of the United Church of Christ Office for Church Life and Leadership. So, throughout these years, GCOM has gradually changed in membership and leadership but has continued to bring clarity and support to the many issues surrounding ministry that have challenged the church. It has served as a "court of appeals" for those ministers who felt they were denied due process by their regional committees on ministry and has become the place where ministers working in the general expression of the church are certified and supported (a great relief to regions in which general church institutions are located, especially Indiana and Mid-America). In 2003, Bill Allen retired and stepped down as chair, and Tom Jewell assumed the role and continued Bill's tradition of excellent leadership.

Early Staff Changes (1994)

Claudia Grant had served well and long as a deputy general minister, having been brought on by John Humbert in 1985. In 1994, she resigned. She had been a primary source of pastoral care for many leaders across the life of the church and was much loved and appreciated. In the wake of her departure, I felt the need to add a new person to staff, but I did not have sufficient budget to support another full-time associate (in addition to Don and John), so I asked Linda McKiernan Allen, a gifted pastor and leader, to step in part-time until we could decide what was needed staff-wise for the long term. Linda agreed and went to work immediately in early 1994 as program director for General Assembly, helping to plan and prepare for the Assembly coming up in fall of 1995.

I also extended a call to Lori Adams in 1994 to work half-time at developing the concept of "processes of discernment." Lori, too, was and is a gifted pastor and leader.

The Cabinet expressed the desire for a restructuring of the Office of Communication. Thus, I created a new role of director of communications, which had been done part time by Claudia Grant as part of her work as associate general minister.

While senior pastor of First Christian Church in Ft. Wayne, I had encouraged Curt Miller and his family into Disciples membership. Curt had a long history of work in communications, most recently serving as the news director for the Clear Channel, 50,000-watt Ft. Wayne radio station, WOWO. After conducting an open search, Curt was selected and became our new director of communications, a position he held for eight years. I always marveled at seeing Curt standing in the front of an Assembly Hall while several thousand attendees on break were greeting each other and creating a din and commotion. Curt would be standing there with the video camera recording, reporting on what had happened so far that day at the Assembly. It was as if there was no one else in the room. When he interviewed people, he was always prepared, but unlike so many TV news personalities today, he didn't just ask questions from a scripted list. He asked questions based on the interviewee's actual response to the previous question. Curt oversaw an office including four others: Cliff Willis, director of news and information; Cathy Hinkle, staff writer; Ted Nottingham, director of video production; and Elizabeth Frazier, administrative assistant.

With a new director of communications in place and two half-time colleagues (Linda and Lori) joining Don, John, and me in the OGMP, we were getting up to speed staff-wise in 1994. Robert

Welsh had become president of the Church Finance Council in 1992, having been the associate ecumenical officer, serving in the Council on Christian Unity for many years with Paul Crow. This made him a resource to me as I began relating to the National and World Councils of Churches and other ecumenical groups. Robert's father, W. A. Welsh, had also been one of the primary framers of The Design, so Robert brought a deep understanding of the philosophy behind the creation of The Design. Later, after Paul Crow's retirement, Robert would become president of the Council on Christian Unity and the Disciples ecumenical officer, and we would continue to work closely together.

The component parts of the Office of General Minister and President included, in those days, the Office of the Yearbook (which produced the annual *Disciples Yearbook and Directory*), managed by Shirley Cox until 1995 and then by Larry Steinmetz; the Office of Research (which tracked various data related to giving to Basic Mission Finance—later renamed Disciples Mission Fund—and provided other statistical research as needed), directed by Frank Helme; and the Office of Communication. However, over the years, as inflation continued to take its toll on BMF giving, there were several consolidations and reductions. The elimination of one associate general minister position (that vacated by Claudia Grant) was the first such reduction. Later, the Office of Research would be eliminated (when Frank Helme retired), and the Office of the Yearbook would be given added responsibilities (which *Yearbook Director* Larry Steinmetz kindly accepted). These sorts of reductions made sense in the face of the changing financial picture, but each had its inherent costs in the reduced capacity of the OGMP. In terms of energy, each of those reductions took something out of the hide of those who remained, including me. But I refused to yield to the temptation of a deficit budget. Don Manworren was especially helpful in keeping the budget balanced while finding ways for us to get done that which needed to get done.

Financial Challenges in the Office of GMP (1994)

At the end of 1993, as I was just getting settled in, the OGMP financial reserve had dropped from $380,000 to a low of $120,379. Since the OGMP is almost totally dependent on Disciples Mission Fund giving, I established a goal of $300,000 in reserves in order to cover our low-income months (August–November) without having to draw on our line of credit. Also, because in any general or regional ministry that is BMF/DMF-*dependent*, you don't know how you are doing budget-wise until mid-January of the following year (when all Mission Funding gifts for the preceding year have come in). Thus, it is essential to have sufficient reserves to endure a year of deficit spending, as you may not even realize you are *doing* so until the following January.

Having served in growing congregations in Kansas City and Ft. Wayne, with *increasing* budgets and staff, it was an adjustment to move into Tennessee regional ministry and then the OGMP, where budgets were *shrinking* due to gradual decreases in Basic Mission Finance (now Disciples Mission Fund). As previously noted, during my ten years as GMP, I had to eliminate several staff positions to maintain a balanced budget.

Early on, I realized that a sizeable portion of the budget of the Office of General Minister and President was paying the healthcare premiums for those who had previously retired from the OGMP. Paying the healthcare premiums of retirees made sense when such insurance premiums were incredibly low (the 1970s), but as they began to skyrocket, we were reaching a point at which paying the premiums for retired personnel was becoming an existential threat to the OGMP. We had a moral obligation to continue the practice with those who had "hired in" under such an agreement. We also had a moral obligation to provide healthcare insurance to those who were actively working. But we had no obligation to offer "health care for life" to new employees. So, I discontinued offering that lifetime coverage for anyone hired after 1993. This kept faith with those already retired and those currently working in the OGMP but ended the practice of lifetime coverage for those yet to be hired. Of course, not many people had retired from the OGMP in recent decades, so it was a nonissue for most. But it has made a huge difference over the past thirty years in the OGMP budget.

Clarifying Our Mission as Disciples (1994)

Feeling as I did that we Disciples had become rather foggy about our mission as a church *now*, the first order of business was to help the church clarify our mission. I was not the only one who felt this need. In 1992, Robert Welsh proposed to the General Board that the Church Finance Council develop "a whole-church strategy involving visits with congregations to receive input for mission and to report on current ministries of the church." The General Board affirmed the idea and the Church Finance Council did a great job of collecting observations and insights. Between September 1993 and June 1994, nearly six hundred congregations were involved in "mission conversations," and these congregations ranged from the very small to the very large.

The results of these conversations were summarized in a "Report to the Church" for the General Board on July 6, 1994. Many of the questions that Disciples were asking were identified, along with the emphases congregations hoped to see from the regional and general church expressions.

Predictably (to those of us working in and with congregations), many of the expressed concerns reflected the themes of human sexuality, biblical interpretation, and the nature of salvation that align with the "culture wars." Frequently, the "social pronouncements of General Assemblies" were singled out for critique, as well as the communication gap between congregations and the regional and general expressions of the church.

Suggested priorities for the next decade included helping congregations minister effectively to children, youth, and young adults, including those encountering drugs, abuse, homelessness, gangs, AIDS, and more. Regional and general expressions of the church were encouraged to minister visibly and directly with these groups as well as helping congregations do so.

Additional priorities suggested included evangelism, helping congregations carry out ministries of justice and compassion in their own localities, clarification of our Disciples of Christ identity and mission, fostering stewardship education, and communication across the life of the church.

The mission conversations were deeply appreciated by the vast majority of participants as an earnest attempt to seek the wisdom, and to understand the felt needs, of the congregations. Many expressed the hope that the mission conversations, or something much like them, could become a regular feature of denominational life. Yet, there were those who doubted that the "system" would really hear what congregations had expressed in these conversations—a predictable response in the face of the anti-institutional attitudes that had gripped the country, the high anxiety of regional and general leadership in the face of financial and numerical decline, and the perceived "distance" that had developed between congregations and the rest of the church.

The results from these mission conversations confirmed my own thoughts about our future direction. As a church, we needed to reverse the flow of energy from congregations to the denomination (which had perhaps been appropriate in the mid-century, but not so much in the 1990s). This was a flow that mimicked the larger culture's flow of energy from the local to the national as the nation fought World War II in the wake of the Great Depression, which had pushed Americans (*and* Canadians) into a pattern of local isolation. Now, in the late twentieth century, the denomination needed to begin to use its energy and resources to start new congregations that could most effectively reach new and younger people and reinforce and redevelop the established congregations, which had begun to dwindle institutionally and in cultural and spiritual influence in the 1960s.

The Sunset Rule (1994)

In February 1994, I asked the Administrative Committee for a "sunset rule" that would require that all actions taken by that body, or by the General Board, be reviewed every seven years rather than automatically continued. This was just a way of recognizing that organizations have a way of piling up rules, programs, and the like without ever revisiting them to see if they are still needed or effective. To make room for initiatives to come, some things needed to be discontinued. Don Manworren did an audit of General Board and Administrative Committee actions from past years to identify possibly obsolete items so they could be allowed to expire without further action.

Mission Imperatives (1994)

The mission conversations of 1992–1993 were an effective prologue to a General Board process of developing *mission imperatives*, which we incorporated into the design of the General Board meeting of 1994 (my first as GMP). This was the first time, so far as I know, that the General Board had been used as a planning body for the whole church, and nearly three-fourths of the agenda and time of the 1994 General Board was given to thinking through the identity and mission of the Christian Church (Disciples of Christ). We met at Washington University in St. Louis.

The resulting mission imperatives were tested with a large number of congregations, with regions, with general ministry units, and with other ministries of the church after the General Board meeting. A video in which I described the imperatives was sent out across the church, along with a guide to potential responders.[2] The imperatives were widely affirmed and stimulated input from across the church about how they might be realized moving forward. This was a first and important step in the development of what would eventually become the 2020 Vision.

The Mission Imperatives developed by the General Board, to be effective 1996-2000, were as follows:

Mission Imperatives of the Christian Church (Disciples of Christ) for 1996–2000

Ephesians: 4:11–13, 15–16

The gifts he gave were that some would be apostles, some prophets, some evangelists, some pastors and teachers, to equip the saints for the work of ministry, for building up the body of Christ, until all of us come to the unity of the faith and of the knowledge of the Son of God, to maturity, to the measure of the full stature of Christ. But speaking the truth in love, we must grow up in every way into him who is the head, into Christ, from whom the whole body, joined and knit together by every ligament with which it is equipped, as each part is working properly, promotes the body's growth in building itself up in love.

We believe God's mission for the church is to be and to share the Good News of Jesus Christ, witnessing and serving from our doorsteps "to the ends of the earth" (Acts 1:8).

As the Christian Church (Disciples of Christ), led and empowered by the Holy Spirit, **we believe God calls us to strengthen congregational life for this mission.**

---

[2] Researchers can find the responses to these mission imperatives in my GMP files at Disciples of Christ Historical Society.

To accomplish this, we shall:
- Prepare Disciples for Christian service by nurturing faith; teaching and practicing the spiritual disciplines of worship, Bible study, prayer and stewardship, and fostering our Disciples identity.
- Emphasize ministry with children, youth and young adults.
- Engage in outreach ministries of reconciliation, compassion, unity, and justice.
- Renew congregational life, do evangelism, and establish new congregations.

In accepting these imperatives, we affirm our need to strengthen the relationships among congregational, regional, institutional and general ministries; receive the gifts and testimonies of our diverse multi-cultural church family, ecumenical friends and global partners; and share our life in Christ more fully.

> —*Offered by the General Board, July 1994, in response to conversations across the Christian Church (Disciples of Christ). We invite Congregations, Regions, General Ministry units, and Institutions of Higher Education to join in implementing the imperatives.*

Reading these mission imperatives, one can easily see the results of those six hundred mission conversations echoed. One may well be impressed by how a board of more than two hundred people could arrive at such a focused document. Four plenary sessions and multiple small-group sessions were required, along with hard work by the general moderators (Duane Cummins, Cynthia Hale, and Joyce Blair) and a number of staff, but the end result was worth it in the opinion of the participants (based on their post-meeting written evaluations of the meeting). Soon, these mission imperatives would begin to broaden into a *vision* for the future of the denomination.

Structural Renewal, Right-Sizing, and the Vision Panel (1994–1995)

Few significant changes in structure had occurred in the general church since the Restructure of 1968. That Restructure process, as painful as it sometimes could be, was the culmination of thinking and work that had begun in the early 1950s (e.g., "The Panel of Scholars"). We had hoped for a structure that would prepare us for the twenty-first century, but what we got, although well-designed and very well-intended, was a structure that prepared us for the 1950s and early 1960s. Many of the organizational assumptions that were operative in the 1940s and 1950s in the postwar period that influenced Restructure were no longer operative. Beginning about 1968, the world entered an era that in many ways would be built on the exact opposite of the builder generation's assumptions and values. As Disciples "saint" and historian Ronald Osborn put it, "we restructured just in time to be obsolete."[3]

It was clear to me that the general and regional church structures were in some ways hampering efficiency, effectiveness, mutual planning, and mutual accountability. Now that we had the mission imperatives in place, I thought it was time to begin looking at needed structural changes. So, I asked for the establishment of a Vision Panel[4] whose purpose was to review The Design with an eye to what change might be helpful and recommended.

In this process of creating the Vision Panel, I underestimated two factors: (1) how committed many of my older colleagues, especially, were to The Design as implemented in 1968[5]; and (2) how difficult it would be to identify specific needed changes. The

---

[3] For a fuller discussion of this change in generational perspectives, see my book, *Recreating the Church: Leadership for the Post-Modern Age* (Christian Board of Publication, 2007). I wrote this book too soon to be able to offer much characterization of the shifts from baby boomers to generations X, Y, and certainly Z. But the book does a pretty good job of describing the shift from the builder and silent generations to baby boomers, and these shifts are still being felt in everyday church life as of this writing.

[4] Structure Panel might have been a more accurate title, as I was not yet thinking in terms of a larger vision such as that which became the 2020 Vision. But the mere mention of the word "structure" would have engendered resistance to an honest conversation about how we were organized, so divisive had conversations about structure been in our immediate past.

[5] There were three reasons, I think, why my older colleagues resisted thoughts of change to The Design. First, The Design had been implemented at a very high cost in terms of the time and energy required of general and regional leadership over the past twenty-five years. In some ways, it had been a bitter struggle to implement The Design and so the thought of new struggles that would be inevitable in the process of changing further were anathema to them. Second, as cohorts of the silent generation, they believed in the underlying assumptions of The Design and were committed to preserving the organizational vision of their builder mentor/colleagues that had given rise to it. Finally, they had learned how to carve out a leadership role for themselves within the context of The Design. Change might jeopardize their positions. I think this last reason was the least frequent source of resistance, but it is only human to experience such feelings.

Vision Panel tended to take a high-level view, which was helpful and needed. But members found it difficult to identify and recommend specific changes in structure. It was useful, and I think necessary, as we began building an openness to change. But it fell far short of my unrealistic hopes. Nonetheless, the Vision Panel did important work and I was very grateful to the co-chairs and all the members: co-chairs Kris Culp (Disciples Divinity House Chicago) and K. David Cole (Swope Parkway United Church, Kansas City), Chuck Blaisdell (associate regional minister, Indiana), Carlos Cardoza (Columbia Theological Seminary), Tony Dunnavant (Lexington Theological Seminary), Deborah Hull (Bethany College), Dan Moseley (Vine Street Christian Church, Nashville, TN), Doug Skinner (First Christian Church, Amarillo, TX), Maureen Osuga (laywoman, Youngstown, Ohio), and Jeri Sias (lay woman, Wichita, KS), along with me and OGMP staff support.

Of course, even in the midst of these organizational/institutional dynamics, the church was still called to teach and to embody justice. It was not an either/or proposition. But continuing to press for justice *without paying attention to our institutional decline was, in my opinion, tantamount to writing checks for social transformation against organizational accounts that had insufficient funds.*

There is a dilemma faced in any restructure process in any organization. On the one hand, those on the inside will typically resist structuring proposals that come only from those outside of the parts being restructured. On the other hand, if restructuring proposals are generated only by those on the inside, the proposals will likely be short of a truly robust proposal for change.

To their credit, the members of the General Cabinet had some very helpful and creative discussions regarding possible restructure of the general ministry units[6] They generated several concrete ideas. One of these was to move the Council on Christian Unity, the smallest general ministry unit, into the Office of General Minister and President. This made sense to me for several reasons. Although Paul Crow had provided leadership in the ecumenical organizations to which we as Disciples related (National Council of Churches, World Council of Churches, etc.), it was difficult for him to bring his ecumenical insights and engagements into the denomination as a whole because he was rather marginalized by having a small

---

[6] See General Cabinet notes of April 4–5, 1995.

general ministry unit that did not have ready access to the rest of the denomination. While the president of the Council on Christian Unity was always regarded as the practical day-to-day ecumenical officer of the church, The Design specifies that the GMP is the chief ecumenical officer of the denomination, so to have the Council on Christian Unity operating outside the OGMP made little sense. As I saw it, Paul needed to be at the OGMP staff table as an associate general minister, bringing his ecumenical insights to General Assembly planning and all the other activities of the OGMP.

Paul Crow initially affirmed this idea, but later changed his mind. To this day, the Council on Christian Unity (now calling itself the Council on Christian Unity and Interfaith Ministry) is steadily losing influence and has become even more marginalized within a church that claims, "Christian unity is our polar star!" The GMP thoroughly participates in the life of the Councils, but the insights and counsel of the day-to-day ecumenical officer (the president of the Council on Christian Unity and Interfaith Ministry) is mostly lost on the larger body.

Again, to their credit, most of the general ministry unit presidents looked for new ways to work together and to enhance their combined efficiency and effectiveness. On the other hand, most regional ministers were so focused on their own regional financial survival and needs that they had little appetite for talk about restructuring regions. Any useful plan would have meant the merging of some regions together for the sake of efficiency (and I would add "effectiveness, if done well"), but that was simply a nonstarter for most of those who served smaller regions.

Early in the Restructure process that culminated in The Design in 1968, there were those who believed *bigger and fewer* regions were the way to go for the sake of efficiency and effectiveness. But there were also those who thought *smaller and more numerous* regions was a better route to follow. Having read over these discussions[7] and having had many conversations with regional ministers, I concluded that (1) the best way forward was to combine the two ideas so as to produce regions that were larger and fewer in number (perhaps twelve regions instead of thirty-six) for the sake of administrative efficiency, but (2) smaller pastoral centers within those larger

---

[7] A paper written by John Wolfersberger was especially helpful in this conversation.

regions, which would be served by individual regional pastors who would not have the administrative burdens (which would be handled by the larger regional office) and who would thus be able to give full-time to providing direct pastoral care, consulting, and programmatic assistance to ministers and congregations.

However, because most of the regions in those days were very small (eleven of the thirty-six had fewer than fifty congregations), some were very large (some had more than two hundred congregations), some were spread over considerable geography (Canada being the most extreme example of huge geography and only about thirty congregations), some had self-financing areas within a region (the Southwest and Mid-America, most notably), a few had some endowment, some had many large congregations whereas some had many small congregations, some had one or more campgrounds and some had none, and many other variations, discussions about possibly changing the configuration of regions became extremely complicated. Those complications were true even *before* one factors in natural resistance to change.

My experience as a regional minister suggested that, on average, it takes about one regional minister per forty-five congregations to be viable (assuming there are the usual administrative and pastoral tasks of maintaining search and call processes, supervising the management of a campground and administrative staff, dealing with congregational conflict, as well as the usual necessary pastoral care, programming, and promotion). But again, in the face of all the variables, some of which are listed above, it is difficult to come up with a plan for uniformly sized regions.

Nonetheless, some mergers between some small membership regions seemed to make obvious sense. Some of these have now been realized (some toward the end of my tenure, some well after): Arkansas, Louisiana, and Mississippi came together to form the Great River Region; South Idaho contributed some of its congregations to join with Oregon in creating the new Oregon–SW Idaho Region; a few South Idaho congregations, along with Montana, joined with the Northwest Region, forming the Northern Lights Region; Michigan and the Illinois–Wisconsin Regions have begun relating in new ways; and other possibilities are being considered. This is heartening, and I am grateful to those who led these efforts, including Ruth Fletcher, Barbara Jones; Sandy Messick; Theresa Dulyea-Parker, and Cathy and

Doug Wirt. One regional minister, Thad Allen, is serving three regions at the time of this writing (West Virginia, Pennsylvania, and the Northeastern Region). This is heroic on his part but, in my opinion, unsustainable for the long term. I am grateful for his plowing this soil, but these three regions really need to look at how they might integrate their work in a more humane way.

Obviously, if one examines each of these successful mergers of regions, it takes a *long* time and an incredible amount of energy on the part of leaders to bring it about (one reason mainline denominations as a whole are no longer discussing mergers with one another). While further regional mergers are no doubt appropriate and needed, I see other issues as even more important now. For example, regional ministry is still being done in a "pastor-centered" way (to use "consultant language") in many places, and the affiliative forces that hold a denomination together are being eroded by forces at work in the larger culture with little effective response by most regions.

These are issues for another forum; I mention them here simply to point to how change is not something that is made once and forever, but is a continuing process that has to move as fast as the cultural context within which an organization lives—in this case, the Christian Church (Disciples of Christ) in the United States and Canada. When it comes to our general, regional, and congregational expressions, we Disciples are still over-organized (boards too large, committees too large, etc.) and, in some cases, under-led (partly due to our own ambivalence about leadership) and overmanaged (due to having too much to do). These are ongoing issues we will have to continue to address as a church. I am greatly heartened by current GMP Terri Hord Owens's ongoing efforts in these matters.

One useful outcome of the regional ministers' discussions of realignment of regions was the affirmation of the idea of regions meeting in fellowship groups annually or as needed for mutual support. This became a place where trust could be built and regions could develop partnerships with one another for various purposes. This had occurred before I became GMP in the Northeast (NIRF: Northeastern Inter-Regional Fellowship) and Southeast (SERF: Southeastern Regional Fellowship), but a group was now formed for the Midwest (Heartland Regional Cluster), the South-Central regions (ROSES: Regions of the Sun Equipping and Serving), and the West (WRIM: Western Regions in Ministry). These are settings in which new configurations and approaches can and have been explored together with nearby regions.

A Churchwide Promotional/Communication Strategy

This was an initiative that I had hoped would be led by Curt Miller, director of communications. I hoped such a strategy would help strengthen the sense of affinity and identity among all Disciples congregations. There had been such a strong sense of affinity between congregations of the Movement in the nineteenth century based on a common sense of mission and purpose. But in the twentieth century, and especially since 1968, the sense of "belonging" to one another and being the same "family" had eroded in the face of various cultural pressures.

Unfortunately, as capable and effective as Curt Miller was in the technical aspects of communication, he was not a strategic thinker. The idea of a denomination-wide promotional/communication strategy eluded him. I should have secured someone for whom this was a strong skill to help him in this, but due to financial pressures I kept putting off such a hire. I regret this. Eventually, Curt left the office and Melinda Mains became the interim director.

Seeking to Be Both Prophetic *and* Sustainable

It seemed to me that there were those who felt the church must be prophetic at all costs. Others felt the church needed to pay more attention to its sustainability. But the truth was *not* that the church had to choose between being prophetic and being sustainable. In fact, the only way to *be* sustainable, and to be *worth* sustaining, in the face of a rapidly changing culture, is to be prophetic. But if the church is to be a credible and sustainable witness to the wider culture, the first subject of our prophetic mission needs to be the church itself. *Along with the world, the church is always the subject of its own mission!* We needed, and always will need, to get our own house in order! A church that was still mired in racism, homophobia, misogyny, and nationalism would not be up to the challenge of providing a credible witness for justice to a world afflicted with these same ills.

Having experienced nearly every General Assembly since Restructure, I had come to see how General Assembly "sense-of-the-assembly resolutions" were brushed aside by politicians and other cultural leaders. Even early on, General Assembly resolutions were crafted to speak to a world in which the church had little credibility instead of speaking to the church itself, a church that needed to address its own lack of integrity before it could speak authoritatively to the world. Again, the world is not the only subject of the church's mission—the church is the subject of its own mission.

While General Assembly resolutions are not without value (for example, they sometimes embolden or provide a sense of authority for pastors and other leaders who seek to be advocates for justice), *real* transformative change within institutions, including congregations, seldom comes via resolutions and distant proclamations from bodies that are not very representative of the people in the pews. Transformation more often comes from leaders who do the hard work of prophecy where they work and live every day, among the people in the pews, hard work done with love for the institution, with all its foibles and limitations, as well as love for the marginalized and dispossessed.

The prophets of the Old Testament did not work by committee or resolution; they took personal responsibility for proclaiming the truth. They often took heat, or worse, for speaking God's truth to a people and a world that didn't want to listen. I think trying to do prophetic truth-telling *simply* through a General Assembly resolution amounts to "cheap" prophecy: The institution takes the heat instead of the individuals who are telling the truth. I've seen ministers, in particular, who have voted for prophetic resolutions and then gone home and acted like they didn't know anything about it. ("Gee, I don't know, I must have been in the lobby when that resolution came up!") Typically, these same ministers had not invited their congregations to discuss the issues before the Assembly, and most of the members found out about what the Assembly had voted from the media or from biased groups instead of from their pastor or other delegates. That has often generated a great deal more heat than light. I am not averse to heat, but that should be primarily born by the truth-teller, not by the institution, except when the institution *itself* needs to change.

Again, there *are* times when a General Assembly sense-of-the-assembly resolution is appropriate, especially those times when the institution itself needs to be called to accountability. But simply passing resolutions without preparatory work and without provision for reception by the church is akin to firing a gun into the air with no thought about where the bullets might land and what they might strike. Any regional minister can tell you about the collateral damage from controversial resolutions, because they are left to clean up the mess made within the congregations in their charge.

Admittedly, I suggested in my article in *The Disciple* in June 1994 that I thought it was time to eliminate sense-of-the-assembly resolutions. (I was not alone in this. Dr. Ron Allen, Ellen Culpepper, David Kagiwada, and Rick Jensen had suggested the same in an article they jointly wrote for *The Disciple*.[8]) Clearly, I struck a nerve, as I received letters and other messages of affirmation from many in the church while also being chided by some who thought I was trying to "neuter" the church's prophetic witness. Soon after having suggested the elimination of controversial resolutions, I began to backpedal, recognizing that there *is* a legitimate place for sense-of-the-assembly resolutions, while also seeing the truth in both sides of the debate.

I began to find a way forward in 1994 when a member of the Cabinet (Jim Suggs, president of Christian Board of Publication, who had worked on previous adjustments to The Design's provisions for Assembly business) helped me see that this was not an either/or matter. The Design already provides four different means by which various subjects can be brought before General Assembly for consideration. "Sense-of-the-assembly resolutions" were and are one means, but also available are the vehicles called "reports," "operational items" (addressing organizational needs), and "items for research and reflection." I realized that some particularly controversial items that had been addressed previously as sense-of-the-assembly resolutions could be brought by other means under items for research and reflection. Although sense-of-the-assembly resolutions were *sometimes* the best choice, I came to believe (and still believe) they should be used carefully and sparingly. Other approaches are often more productive in the end, however inconvenient or time-consuming they may be.

Introducing Processes of Discernment (1994)

Understanding the differences between the four kinds of General Assembly business items opened the door for the development of an experiment I called "processes of discernment." "Discernment" is not a word that modern Disciples (or Protestants in general) had

---

[8] "Is Assembly the Same Old Stuff?" *The Disciple*, Vol 10, #17 (1983), pp. 16–17.

used often. I came across the concept in my contacts with the Roman Catholic tradition and, in particular, through my study of Ignatius of Loyola, as I was seeking to deepen my own spiritual life. Ignatius (1491–1556) was a co-founder of the Jesuits, and he devised "rules for discernment" for his monastic community that sought God's desires for them and for the world while *maintaining community.*

All the mainline Protestant churches, including Disciples, had been pronouncing judgments on various matters through assemblies, synods, conferences, and so on throughout the last half of the twentieth century at least. These were often perceived in the congregations, especially as seen through the media (which has most often been members' first notice of such votes), as "lines drawn in the sand." While I have agreed with the content of almost all of these pronouncements, I have also seen the fracturing of community that results when the wider church is ill-prepared to understand and truly receive such. Disciples especially, as a church born in the United States, have assumed that democracy and discernment are the same thing, while any serious study of history shows that the majority is often dead wrong and that attempts to force a majority opinion upon a minority simply results in resistance rather than compliance. On the other hand, when people are invited into a process of seeking truth—a process bathed in prayer, vulnerability, and serious dialogue and struggle together with serious study of current scholarship and, importantly, in the presence of some of those most impacted by the truth or its absence—hearts are often softened and changed (without minds being either softened or set aside).

This is what the processes of discernment sought to do: to open minds and hearts and to encourage serious and humble engagement with important questions so that God's desires might be sought out, understood, and realized. These processes sought to provide the space for people to safely explore alternatives and to imagine different answers to questions than those that had heretofore been *assumed* and culturally determined. But such work requires more than the twelve minutes of floor debate that had usually been given to sense-of-the-assembly resolutions.

Of course, developing such a way was (and is) no simple matter. As I jokingly put it at the time, "All we need to do is find a way to adapt Ignatius's rules of discernment for his communities of a few brothers into a process that will work for several thousand Disciples in General Assembly!" No one had done this before to my knowledge. But I knew a young woman who had been working on similar ideas as a staff member of Vanderbilt University in Nashville, so I asked Lori Adams to join my staff. She began as a part-time person, because that's all the Office of General Minister and President could afford. She quickly established herself as a credible leader, a great colleague, and an effective developer of processes.

As I thought, discussed, and prayed about what the most challenging issues facing the church at that time might be, and which might be amenable to a process of discernment, I identified two key issues: the nature of biblical authority and racism.

1. The nature of biblical authority was (and is) so important because it was easy to see that Disciples who came from various perspectives, whether left or right, were all using the Bible to make their arguments. However, their assumptions about biblical authority and "what the Bible says" were different, and thus they were talking past each other. Every congregational pastor sees the conflict such differences in assumptions can make in community life and witness. The nature of biblical authority was especially important in regard to conversations about sexual orientation, but I thought perhaps clarifying the authority of scripture *before* discussing sexual orientation would be most helpful.
2. .Racism has been a topic of discussion in this country for five hundred years, but those discussions often tended to generate more heat than light. I grew up a white male with privilege in the Jim Crow South in the 1950s, and my growing faith had continued to challenge my inherited assumptions. I believed (and still believe) that to be a faithful church, we have no choice but to grapple with the stunning gap between what we as a nation and church *said* we believed and what we actually *did* and *do* in national, ecclesial, and organizational life.

So, I proposed these two possible topics of discernment to the General Board at its meeting in July 1994. I thought perhaps the Board would choose one of the two. To my surprise, the General Board decided to attempt both. Thus, Lori Adams went about gathering two steering committees, one for each of the two topics.

The steering committee chosen to develop a process of discernment on the nature of biblical authority included Carmelo Alvarez (Christian Theological Seminary), Chuck Blaisdell (associate regional minister, Indiana), Eugene Boring (Brite Divinity School), Toni Bynum (Broad Street Christian Church, Columbus, Ohio), Judy Church (Ft. Wayne, Indiana), Bob Coalson (Indianapolis, Indiana), Stephanie Crowder (Nashville, Tennessee), David Darnell (Central Christian Church, Coral Gables, Florida), Ruth Fletcher (associate regional minister, Northwest Region), Deborah Hull (Bethany College), Nobi Kaneko (First Christian Church, Tucson, Arizona), Rick Lowery (Phillips Theological Seminary), Marti Steussy (Christian Theological Seminary), and Lori Adams (OGMP staff).

The steering committee chosen to develop a process of discernment on racism included Lois Artis-Murray (Raleigh, North Carolina), Garth Baker-Fletcher (Claremont School of Theology), Angel Bonilla (pastor of Second Spanish Christian Church, Bronx, New York), James Demus (pastor of Park Manor Christian Church, Chicago, Illinois), Robin Hedgeman (associate regional minister of Ohio), John Lau (Battery Park, New York), Dan Moseley (pastor of Vine Street Christian Church, Nashville, TN), Mary Alice Mulligan (Indianapolis, Indiana), Don Shelton (regional minister of the Pacific Southwest), Tanya Tyler (Lexington, Kentucky), David Wu (Lexington, Kentucky), and Lori Adams (OGMP staff).

The process of discernment on biblical authority struggled to make headway. The group finally decided that the diversity of thought on the matter was so broad that a "process of discernment" was not an effective way to address the subject. Thus, they stopped meeting after a year or so of work.

Both steering committees brought their reports to the Denver General Assembly in 1997. While the biblical authority steering committee closed out its work, the process of discernment on racism brought a very positively received report. It became, under chairman Robin Hedgeman's leadership, the process of discernment on racism in the church, a much more focused topic than racism in general. It became a process to organize for change. Ultimately, the Anti-Racism/Pro-Reconciliation Initiative grew out of this process of discernment.

Since the process of discernment on biblical authority had closed out its work, I proposed a process of discernment on the role of gay and lesbian persons in the life of the church. The role of LGBTQ persons in the life of the church was so important because the world as a whole was (and is) in conflict about human sexuality. There were (and are) those who argue for the exclusion of LGBTQ people from the military, from family life, from ministry, and from the church itself. To me, this represented a misunderstanding of scripture, and these were judgments made on the basis of culture rather than the gospel. We were adding insult to injury to those brothers and sisters who were being excluded from church life and community. Could the church back up a bit and start by examining our assumptions rather than making judgments based on the world's fear-based or anger-based conclusions?

The steering committee chosen to develop this process of discernment included Greg Alexander (associate regional minister of Kentucky), Peter Browning (Drury University), Dana Bainbridge (Southside Christian Church, Omaha, Nebraska), Jo Ann Bynam (Los Angeles, California), David Cortes (pastor of Deltona Christian Church, Florida), Ron Greene (Spokane, Washington), Alvin Jackson (pastor of National City Christian Church, Washington D.C.), Mark Johnston (Boston, Massachusetts), JoAnne Kagiwada (Oakland, California), Stephanie Paulsell (Princeton, New Jersey), Maria Perez (Bronx, New York), Doug Skinner (pastor of Northway Christian Church, Dallas, Texas), Mary Smith (Kallispell, Montana), Judith Hock Wray (New York, New York), and Bill Paulsell (OGMP contract staff).

The team offered its remarkable report to the General Assembly of 2001 in Kansas City, Missouri. The report included a written report but, more impactful, brought a discussion of the theme of "the role of gay and lesbian persons in the life of the church" to the Assembly stage. There, a team of people representing tremendous demographic and philosophical diversity held a public discussion with one another in front of the entire Assembly. They modeled the kind of conversation that discernment of such a challenging subject requires. There were also video resources provided for the church to enable such conversations in congregations. I was so appreciative of the work that Bill Paulsell and Lori Adams did to make all of this happen. It was truly a gift to the church.

Worshipful Work

"Worshipful work" was a subject being discussed in many mainline churches. Charles Olsen had brought the idea to church leaders' attention with his books on the subject. As some of us in the OGMP thought about the culture of our Administrative Committee, our General Board, and even our General Assembly, we felt it was time to soften the lines between "business" (in the Robert's Rules of Order sense) and worship. We had both business and worship in our plenary meetings, but why not begin to do business in a worshipful way as suggested by Olsen? Thus, Linda McKiernan Allen and Lori Adams looked for ways to structure our business meetings in a more worshipful way.

We sought to model this in General Assembly business sessions in 1997. Many congregational ministers and members appreciated this new way of doing our work together. It was another step beyond discernment processes to help move our business meetings into a *discernment culture* instead of a political culture in which people came to "win" a debate and a vote rather than to learn and seek consensus.

Used well, Robert's Rules of Order[9] can help groups arrive at consensus in an orderly fashion. But, in a conflicted atmosphere (such as that we find most everywhere in these postmodern times), the Rules are easily "weaponized" and sometimes used in ways that are divisive and manipulative. Roberts Rules are too often used to prevent those with little power from being heard and included. We too easily confuse "democracy" with "discernment," equating the will of the majority to the will of God.

The scriptural approach of "Come, let us reason together" (Isaiah 1:18) was the hoped for outcome of incorporating "worshipful work." It helped our plenary bodies become more rooted in humility and less in anger. These practices have continued to the present day, and I think the church is better for it.

Reforming the Process of Resolution Submission (1995)

Yes, I had stated in my column in *The Disciple* magazine in June 1994 that I thought the sense-of-the-assembly resolution had "run its course" and we should find different ways to accomplish that work. However, I made no actual move to eliminate sense-of-the-

---

[9] These were created by U.S. Army General Henry Martyn Robert to make decisions in boards and other groups more civil and to bring order to the chaos that was common in public meetings of the 1870s. They were largely successful when used skillfully but can be easily weaponized when used by people with ill-intent or when used in settings in which the participants do not fully know or understand Robert's Rules.

assembly resolutions because we now had another tool to use in helping the church struggle with controversial issues, and because there were occasions when such sense-of-the-assembly resolutions were appropriate, needed, and could not be replaced by discernment processes. But I did begin managing the sense-of-the-assembly submission process more aggressively than had my predecessors.

The Design originally specified that proposed General Assembly resolutions had to be submitted to the Office of General Minister and President and postmarked one hundred and twenty days before Assembly. However, because The Design also required that resolutions be reviewed by the General Board, which met ninety days before General Assembly, this left only thirty days for the GMP to work pastorally with submitters to change wording or even to convince them to withdraw proposed resolutions that were divisive by nature or design. Because "postmarked" meant the mail still had to be delivered, opened, and reviewed by me (who was out of the office traveling in the church most of the time), there was often *no* time to do anything in consultation with the submitters or anything else but to pass them along to the General Board to review and act on.

So, I asked the General Assembly in 1995 to change The Design to require resolutions to be submitted one hundred and eighty days before General Assembly instead of one hundred and twenty. This gave me (and future GMPs) time to work with submitters to help them make their resolutions better (and therefore more likely to be recommended by the General Board for approval by the General Assembly), *or* to totally rewrite their resolution, *or* to encourage them to withdraw the resolution altogether. This change was approved, and it enabled me to keep most (although not all) politicized and/ or poorly formed resolutions from reaching the General Assembly (though always with the consent of the submitting parties, because I didn't have the power to simply block a resolution if the submitting party was determined to send it forward). I felt this was (and is) an essential tool for the GMP to use in fulfilling his or her pastoral role with the church. I'll talk more about this in the discussion of "renewal" groups.

Reform of the General Assembly Planning Process

Since the first General Assembly in 1969, each biennial gathering was planned independently of the others. An Assembly Planning

Committee would meet and choose a theme that seemed inspired and relevant for the moment, and speakers were chosen to elucidate that theme. I saw the General Assembly in a different light. It seemed to me that General Assemblies were marvelous opportunities to bring the church together around key issues of mission clarity and needed change in the way we go about doing our work as the church.

Thus, as soon as possible, I began encouraging the Assembly Planning Committee to see its work as building from one assembly to the next toward the change we needed and the direction we were seeking to move as a church, rather than seeing each assembly as a one-off event. This enabled the General Assembly to become a tool for change as well as education and inspiration.

The Bethany Project (1995)

I came into my role feeling strongly that the denomination as a whole needed to rediscover its spiritual roots and to move away from so much "democracy" (which seeks to know the will of the people), toward more "discernment" (which seeks to know the will of God). Sometimes democracy arrives at the same conclusions as discernment, but not always. Sometimes the majority is wrong; sometimes the minority turns out to be right. Democracy, when responsibly led, is generally the best system for civil governments, in my opinion. But I believe *churches* need to go beyond democracy to joint discernment.

Through mutual friends, Disciples minister Martha Grace (Gay) Reese had heard of my interest in developing the Christian spirituality of our whole church. Since this was an arena of intense interest to her, we met in Indianapolis for lunch one day in 1994 at a Pizza Hut on East Washington Steet (near the old Missions Building where the Disciples' General Offices were located until 1995). We immediately discovered that we were thinking similarly and feeling a common call to help the church rediscover a "deep Christian spirituality" (a phrase that would become one of the three primary marks of a faithful growing church in the 2020 Vision). We believed that a mature spirituality was a key element in the health of pastoral leaders and, in turn, in the health of congregations, which could then be more effective missionally and evangelistically.

Both of us were drawn to the ancient practices of spiritual retreat in which participants engage in a time of extended personal silence (in community) as well as in times of community dialogue and personal discernment. We began some initial experimentation with retreats with mutual friends of ours (including Gary Straub, Jim Powell, Ann Azdell, Harold Goodwin, and Robert Welsh), and these folks eventually became regular intercessors for me, praying for me and for the church and providing a kind of spiritual protection and direction that we Disciples seldom actively pursue or discuss.

As we discussed how the church as a whole could be drawn into this spiritual discipline and way of discernment, we agreed that the best place to pilot such an approach might be with regional ministers, as they are called to be examples and pastors to pastors. So, in 1996, we selected a list of regional ministers to invite to participate in one or two groups of about eight persons each. Enough of them responded positively that we established two groups over the course of a year: Group 1 included Bill Allen of the West Virginia Region, Darwin Collins of the Pennsylvania Region, Tom Jewell of the Oklahoma Region, Barb Jones of the Arkansas Region, Bill McKnight of the Mississippi Region, John Mobley of the Alabama/NW Florida Region, Howard Ratcliff of the Ohio Region, and Guy Waldrop of the Kentucky Region. Group 2 included Chuck Babcock of the Bluebonnet Area of the Southwest Region, Bill Boswell of the Louisiana Region, Jim Hartley of the Trinity Brazos Area of the Southwest Region, Chris Hobgood of the Arkansas Region, Chuck Isbell of the Coastal Plains Area of the Southwest Region, and Charles Lamb of the Northeastern Region. Each began with a retreat at "Old Bethany" (the preserved home and grounds of Alexander Campbell) in Bethany, West Virginia. The curators of the Campbell properties graciously gave us the run of the place. So, we dialogued and prayed in the Campbell Mansion, and as we took individual prayer walks we could retrace Alexander Campbell's footsteps into his study beside the house, into the cemetery where he and so many family members and early lights of the Stone-Campbell Movement are at rest, and up to the college and the old church. We were reminded that Alexander Campbell was a highly disciplined Christian whose insights often sprang from prayer and discernment and not merely from intellect alone.

Our retreats typically consisted of a time of hymn singing together; time for two of our number to share their spiritual journeys with the group; twenty-four hours of "grand"[10] silence for rest, prayer, and reflection, with optional offerings of centering prayer and one hour of individual spiritual direction; group reflection on what had been learned/experienced in the time of silence; a meal of celebration; and a closing communion service.

Through Gay's efforts, the Lilly Endowment became involved, providing resources ($260,076) that made it possible to expand the pilot groups to several new groups composed of Disciples pastors across the country (five hundred pastors eventually participated). Gay became director of the Bethany Project. To this day, more than twenty-five years later, there is a group of those original participating regional ministers (now retired) with whom I meet twice a year, and there are still some groups of local pastors across the life of the church who continue to meet in their groups. Although the movement did not ultimately spread as broadly as Gay and I had originally hoped, it blessed, and continues to bless, scores of pastors.

The Bethany Project also became a model for the annual retreat for the "heads of communion" of the National Council of Churches (more about this later). The Bethany Project also led to Gay's development of the Bethany Fellows for promising young pastors.

Looking to the future and realizing that the primary way to transform the church was through younger ministers, including the newly ordained, Gay envisioned the Bethany Project in a new form. The Lilly Endowment was launching their Transition into Ministry initiative for new clergy and liked the new proposal, and Bethany Fellows was born! Gay and Don Schutt served as the staff for this initiative, soon adding Kris Tenny-Brittian. In 1999, they began by bringing together groups of leaders who would become the mentors of young pastoral leaders (among the first of these were Kim Gage Ryan, Bob Hill, and Gary Straub). The Bethany Fellows program continues functioning and has blessed scores of new ministers in their first four years out of seminary. Like the Bethany Project before it, Bethany Fellows seeks to bring the resources of intellect and Spirit together in lively interplay, creating a community of mutual support and discernment.

Another outgrowth of the Bethany Project is the Mainline Evangelism Project, beginning in 2002 and also funded by Lilly. This

---

[10] "Grand" silence is a classic term for silence in which retreatants not only do not speak but also avoid eye contact and other nonverbal forms of communication during the designated time of silence.

drew on the relationships Gay and I had developed with the heads of other mainline churches and ultimately resulted in her writing the series of books and resources called *Unbinding the Gospel*.

Mission Imperative Fund (1995)

The mission funding conversations of 1993/1994 that resulted in the approval of a new mission funding system in 1995, established a Mission Imperative and Adjustment Fund. This new fund was based on two percent of Basic Mission Fund receipts, half of which would be used by the Commission on Mission Funding[11] to fund initiatives that sought to address the mission imperatives that had been identified out of the mission conversations and the other half of which could be used to "adjust" the amount provided to individual regions and general ministry units that might have special needs or emergencies during the year. At the end of each year, any remaining balance in the Mission Imperative and Adjustment Fund was to be distributed to all regions and general ministries based on the same percentages as the ninety-eight percent of BMF had been distributed.

As the discussion of the idea of the General Board serving as a Church-Wide Planning body unfolded in 1997 (discussed below), the Commission on Finance recommended that the Mission Imperative Fund become a separate fund to be administered by a method that would be approved by the General Board. The establishment of this new Mission Imperative Fund was exciting to me because it represented the willingness of BMF-supported general ministry units and regions to give up control of a full percent of BMF for the sake of new initiatives. One percent in 1996 dollars was approximately one hundred thousand dollars, which may not sound like much even in 1995 dollars, but one has to understand that some general ministry units and many regions were teetering on the edge of unsustainability, so to give up any bit of money for new initiatives represented a huge leap of faith.

A Consultant Is Secured (1996)

Because we were seeking to discern and implement new directions in the life of the church, which had structural and

---

[11] The Commission on Mission Funding no longer exists (having been replaced by another approach by a yet newer Mission Funding System developed in 2002) but was at that time the body that made decisions as to how BMF funds would be distributed among the various general ministry units and regions that were supported by BMF.

programmatic implications as well as missional implications, it was thought by many (including me) that a process consultant would be helpful. I contracted with Dr. Paul Dietterich of the Center for Parish Development in Chicago. I found his analysis of the cultural shift that the church was and had been undergoing since the mid-1950s was practically identical to my own. However, when we began designing steps toward transformation, the process quickly became too complex and expensive. Had there been sufficient funds available, I think we would have worked through to a satisfactory and helpful process of transformation. However, as tight as money was becoming in the general church, I necessarily concluded Paul's services before we developed a full plan for change. Nevertheless, the work Paul and I did together was helpful and informed my next steps.

Churchwide Planning (1996)

The fragmented nature of the church's structure made common and coordinated planning difficult. Without a regular time and place to think together about the big picture needs of the whole church, each general ministry unit, region, and related organization naturally tended to operate in its own silo to some degree, each doing its own analysis of needs and its own planning. This was understandable, as the leaders of each of these general ministry units and regions were called to care primarily for the health of their own organization, the assumption being that what was good for their organization was good for the whole church. The Design, as originally approved, did authorize the General Board to provide a means to do common planning, but the Board had seldom been actively used to do so.

In 1994, I set an agenda for the General Board that was built around clarifying our mission. Meeting in St. Louis, the Board had developed the Mission Imperatives for the whole church.

With mission imperatives still fresh, I proposed to the Administrative Committee in February 1996, and received approval, to convene a Planning Design Team Conference to develop a framework for regular churchwide planning in relation to the church's mission imperatives that would invite participation and ownership. The members of this team included Judy Church (layperson, Ft. Wayne, Indiana), Scott Colglazier (pastor, Indianapolis, Indiana), Conchita Delgado (layperson, OGMP staff), Jim Hartley (area minister of the Southwest Region), Mark Reid (regional minister of Oregon), Ann

Updegraff Spleth (president of Division of Homeland Ministries), Guy Waldrop (regional minister of Kentucky), Guenhee Yu (American-Asian Ministries, executive minister), Jim Powell (president of Church Extension), Donna Rose Heim (minister, Odessa, Missouri), Lucas Torres (National Hispanic Pastor), Robert Welsh (president of Church Finance Council), and Marilyn Dubasak (ecumenical representative of the United Church of Christ). This Design Team brought a proposal to the 1996 General Board meeting that would officially make the General Board a whole-church planning body in its off-assembly meeting years (the even years). This would provide a widely representative body that could think together about various programs and initiatives.

The 1996 General Board approved the concept and a new Design Team was called together in fall of 1997 to sharpen the proposal and to design a process for use by the General Board in 1998 (the next off-assembly year). The new team included Ruth Fletcher (regional minister of Montana), Nobi Kanecko (pastor, Brea, California), Chris Hobgood (regional minister of Arkansas), Noel Baker (layperson, Franklin, Indiana), Carolyn Ledford (layperson, Washington, North Carolina), Jim Rivers (pastor, Roanoke, Virginia), Michael Mooty (general moderator), and OGMP staff Dick Hamm, Lori Adams, and Robert Welsh.

The Design Team's report was approved by the 1997 General Board, and the 1998 General Board meeting was the first "biennial planning session" of the Board. The pattern thus established continued: the General Board serving as a churchwide planning body in off-assembly years.

The OGMP and Church Finance Council Enter a New Relationship (1996)

Robert Welsh, president of the Church Finance Council, and I were informally looking for ways to model consolidation of some administrative structures. He proposed that we model a form of such consolidation by his becoming an associate general minister and president of the Church Finance Council. Thus, the Administrative Committee became the new board of CFC (as it is for the Office of GMP), and Robert and I were able to share administrative resources and to directly represent one another's work when out among the congregations and regions.

Robert resigned as associate general minister and president of the Church Finance Council in 1998; in 1999, Lois Artis Murray was elected his successor. This arrangement of having the president of CFC also serve as an associate general minister worked very well until, ultimately, the Church Finance Council ceased to be a general ministry unit and many of its functions (Treasury Services, Reconciliation, and Week of Compassion) migrated directly into the OGMP.

Clarifying the Role of Disciples in Canada in the Wider Church

The role of Canadian Disciples in the denomination has been a subject of conversation for many years. Canadian Disciples leadership has not seen the designation of Canada as a "region," much like any other region in the United States, as an adequate way to relate the congregations north of the border to those south of the border. The complications are myriad: It is difficult to get Christian Board of Publication materials and other denominational materials into Canada due to import restrictions; laws applying to financial transactions of various kinds are very different in our two countries, which complicates the work of Church Extension and the Pension Fund; the furthest eastern congregations are separated from the furthest western congregations by three thousand miles. Ecumenically, Canadian Disciples relate to the Canadian Council of Churches and are considered a separate entity by the World Council of Churches. In ethos, many of the Canadian congregations were heavily influenced by Scottish Baptist churches and others in a way the congregations in the United States were not.

The complications are difficult to navigate, and yet the Disciples in Canada bring a perspective (including a different perspective on international justice issues and the American role in the world) that I think is helpful to U.S. Disciples and could be even more helpful if a clearer relationship were shaped. I worked at this for several years, along with Robert Welsh and colleagues in Canada. Unfortunately, we did not get to a place of clarity before I left the OGMP. I know my successors have spent some time and effort on this as well. Other issues among the Canadian congregations have often taken precedence on the part of their leadership.

Broadening the General Cabinet (1997)

Because the Christian Church (Disciples of Christ) in the United States and Canada had been overwhelmingly white in racial composition during its first two hundred years (not surprising, as the movement originated among Scots/Irish immigrants), other racial ethnic groups often struggled to have their voices heard and to receive the resources they needed to grow in number. African American Disciples were the largest racial minority in the church, and they had negotiated a place for themselves at a number of important Disciples tables when the National Christian Missionary Convention merged with the United Christian Missionary Society in 1968 to form the newly structured denomination. But Hispanics and Asian Americans were not so well represented.

Thus, in an effort to provide these folks a fairer representation, I invited the National Hispanic Pastor (Lucas Torres) and the executive pastor (Geunhee Yu) of North American Pacific Asian Disciples (NAPAD) to be part of the General Cabinet. It seemed important to me so they could represent the needs of these growing segments of our church to the leaders of our general ministry units. John Foulkes, administrative secretary of the National Convocation, was already meeting with the Cabinet as an associate general minister.

In addition, the general church leadership and the regional church leadership were most often meeting separately. I attended the College of Regional Minister meetings, but I could not alone represent the regional ministers to the Cabinet or vice versa. So, I also expanded the Cabinet to include two representatives of the College of Regional Ministers, beginning with Charles Lamb and Karen Frank Plumlee. It was my hope that this would foster communication and lower the sense of "us vs. them" that often tinges relationships.

Public Issues Coordinating Council (1997)

Various responses to various justice issues were popping up in different places around the general church. Homeland Ministries would usually be the unit to address domestic issues, while Overseas Ministries would often address issues in other places in the world. It seemed to me that it might be helpful to have representatives of the various groups that engaged in public witness to meet occasionally, not to make formal statements but to coordinate efforts, to support one another, and to avoid blindsiding one another.

Thus, I proposed and began calling together a Public Issues Coordinating Council to meet to review how we *together* might further the church's witness for justice. It included representatives of Homeland Ministries, Overseas Ministries, the National Benevolent Association, Week of Compassion, Reconciliation Ministry, the Office of GMP, the National Hispanic Pastor, and the coordinator of American-Asian Ministries.

I think the PICC served a good purpose and was a good idea, but as units continued to shrink and feel the pressure of increasingly hectic schedules, attendance became spotty, and we stopped meeting. Sharon Watkins later instituted a similar group she called a "justice table."

Seeking to Restructure and Right-size the General Board (1997)

I was not the first, or the last, to recognize the need to right-size the General Board. In fact, the Standing Committee for Renewal and Structural Reform had brought a proposal (GB Business Item No. 9251) to downsize for the consideration of the General Board in 1992 after a couple of years of discussion. That proposal was not approved. Because we had just had that conversation and decision, I did not want to immediately go there again. While four-year terms on the General Board meant that a substantial amount of turnover would have occurred by 1996, the reality was that the resistance to downsizing the Board came more often from regional ministers than from congregational representatives, and all regional ministers were on the General Board throughout the time of their regional ministry.

Restructuring is seldom the first step taken by a new leader of a nonprofit organization. This is, in part, because nonprofit CEOs (including heads of denominations) can't *demand* changes of culture and behavior from employees through fear of termination or demotion as in a for-profit organization. With nonprofits, the employees and the entire organization must be "won over" to new ways of thinking and behaving (although this dynamic functions in for-profit organizations as well to various degrees). This is one reason why change typically comes slowly in nonprofits. This is especially true in the Disciples denominational structure, as the GMP has no "employees to boss" except those within the Office of General Minister and President itself. Change among Disciples—whether in a congregational, regional, or general setting—requires lots of conversations and opportunities to work through varied personal and structural resistance. The larger the organization, the more effort real change takes. As I like to tell my "Disciples History and Polity" students at Christian Theological Seminary, "Any minister who has a one-year plan for the transformation of his or her congregation will find a year later that the only thing that will have changed is the name of the pastor!"

So how *does* one go about changing an institution? Clarification of mission and methods is usually the starting place. But restructuring becomes even more urgent when (1) the current structure is inefficient and is thus draining the financial and other resources of an organization, and (2) the current structure actually *hampers* decision-making, thus making it difficult for the organization to adapt to new needs and methods. In my view, both conditions were present and had been present since the Restructure of 1968, which had been approved as "about all that was really possible at the time." The framers of The Design had known that the restructuring proposal was yet incomplete in some significant ways, but it was nonetheless a giant leap forward at the time.

I fully understood why the decision was made to move forward with Restructure even though it failed to address some key matters. Reorganization is always somewhat experimental and incomplete in *any* organization, and it is seldom possible to get all the needed change passed in an initial package of structural change. In fact, The Design was initially approved as The Provisional Design, the assumption being that there would need to be adjustments in the future as more experience was gained. Unfortunately, the "provisional" part of the title was removed by the General Assembly in 1977, the apparent assumption being that The Design was pretty much fine as it stood. But it *wasn't* fine. It was so right in so many ways, but in my opinion, it was both *too much* organization overall and *inadequate* in some regards. It addressed the role neither of regions nor of colleges and seminaries in the life of the church.

One of the problems, as I saw it, was the size of the General Board. In typical builder-generation style (and it was mostly builder-generation folks who constructed The Design), it was thought that there needed to be plenty of representation from all quarters of the church. To put it simply, the General Board was designed to be the most representative of the church's governance bodies,[12] and thus it was made so large that it became difficult for it to actually make decisions. We see the same pattern in congregations that were structured by the builder generation with boards that, to this day, are often larger than the congregations' average worship attendance! The theory was to give everyone a place at the table and ensure effective communication and transparency; however, there are more effective ways to accomplish the ideals of giving everyone a voice and communicating and being transparent to everyone in the congregation.

Having been a General Board member for seven years before becoming GMP (four as a representative of the Indiana Region and three as a regional minister), I had seen these problems play out in the General Board's meetings. The Board spent much of its annual meetings in five "section meetings" of approximately forty-five persons each, reviewing and discussing the business items coming before the Board in plenary session later in the meeting. With forty-five members, these section meetings tended to be dominated by extroverts (who, I must admit as something of an extrovert myself, are not *always* the most thoughtful or creative participants) and by general and regional staff who were permanent members of the Board and who were often respected for their leadership roles and knowledge of the wider church (which is understandable, but which biased the sections toward the way things have always been done and represented by those who had always been doing things in those ways). So, beginning in 1994, I increased the number of General Board sections (the *relatively* "small" groups that discussed business items before they were brought with recommendations to the floor of the whole General Board) from five to ten, thus reducing the size of each to something more like twenty-two or twenty-three. This did result, I think, in better discussion in the section meetings and better questions and ideas being brought to the General Board in plenary sessions.

---

[12] One might think the General Assembly is the most representative of our governance bodies, but the General Assembly actually tends to be heavily weighted toward those parts of the church that are able to afford attendance, which means small congregations (with smaller budgets), congregations more distant from a General Assembly's location, and congregations with financially challenged members (including many people of color and ethnicity other than Euro-American) are typically underrepresented. Also, since clergy with standing all have a vote at General Assembly, and many have expense allowances for travel, clergy are greatly overrepresented compared to laity.

However, it was difficult for a Board of two hundred and twenty-five people to stay focused or to have meaningful discussion and debate when the section reports were brought to plenary. Again, the discussions tended to be dominated by extroverts, staff leaders, and people of the dominant culture, and thus the full discussion one would hope for continued to be somewhat truncated and biased.

So, my second proposal (much more controversial), brought to the Standing Committee for Renewal and Structural Reform and ultimately to the General Board itself, in 1996, was to reduce the size of the General Board from about two hundred and twenty-five (including *ex officio* members) to something more like ninety (I would have preferred something closer to fifty, but I knew that was a bridge too far in an initial downsizing proposal). The expected objections were raised. These concerns were not without validity ("Won't some groups in the church be underrepresented? Won't communication and transparency be damaged?"), but I maintained there were better ways to address these concerns than having a General Board that was bigger than ninety-five percent of our congregations!

After much discussion, the General Board approved the proposal and it was thus forwarded to the 1997 General Assembly. It included the provision that the then thirty-six regional ministers would be represented by five, whom they could select from among their own ranks, and the eleven general ministry units would be represented by three of the unit presidents), although all General Board meetings would continue to be open to any member of the church, and thus all regional ministers and general ministry unit presidents *could* be present if they wished. Predictably, the opposition voices came from a few regional ministers who raised the specter of underrepresentation of some other groups in the life of the church (although I was certain that their concern was primarily their own loss of voting membership as thirty-six individual regional ministers).

The concerns of those few regional ministers, voiced at the "no" microphones at the Denver General Assembly in 1997, were enough to convince a substantial minority of the Assembly to vote "no" to the proposal so that it failed, seventy-one percent to twenty-nine percent (seventy-five percent being needed to change The Design). So, regrettably, downsizing the General Board was a matter I had to pass on to my successors. It was a great disappointment to me, but I was not going to fall on that particular sword or allow the disagreement between me and these few regional ministers to become a problem in our working relationships and friendships. I felt, however, that the resistance to downsizing (or, in my parlance, "right-sizing") the board was, in part, a function of the denial we were collectively expressing about the growing financial crisis we were facing.

Immediately after the vote, I could feel some tension in the room as the Assembly wondered how I would respond, having heard me strongly support the proposed right-sizing. So, I made the following statement immediately following the vote:

> I do not want this discussion about the size and structure of the General Board to be misunderstood as bureaucratic wrangling or politics. Though I voted for reformulation, I accept this decision and am glad to lay the question to rest. I will wholeheartedly continue to work to improve the way our current General Board structure works, and I know I will have the help and cooperation of all regional ministers and general ministry presidents in this quest, along with the elected members of the General Board. This is not about winning and losing. While various ones of us have had differing opinions as to how to achieve this goal, *all* of us want the General Board to be as effective and representative as possible. We will move forward together.

That said, part of the reason the proposal failed was because The Design required seventy-five percent of the voting members at General Assembly to approve any amendment to The Design. I realized that *any significant* structural change would be unlikely unless that seventy-five-percent bar was lowered! So, I turned my attention there next.

Proposal to Reduce the Percentage of GA Votes Needed to Change The Design (1998–2003)

It is difficult to imagine seventy-five percent of Disciples agreeing on almost anything! It's not because we are contrary people (although there may be an element of truth in that characterization), but because we are so democratic in our approach to church life that it is difficult for leaders to garner a consensus about almost anything.[13]

In the face of this reality, I suggested that we should change provisions for amendment of The Design from seventy-five percent approval by the General Assembly to two-thirds approval. Two-thirds is still a pretty high bar, but it is possible to attain while assuring that no *widely* opposed proposal can succeed.

So, in 1998 I brought this proposal to the Standing Committee on Renewal and Structural Reform and it became a resolution, approved by the General Board, that came before the 1999 General Assembly. Ironically, seventy-four percent of the voting delegates approved the change, so the resolution failed to pass. I strongly urged the General Board to bring the resolution back to the 2003 General Assembly. Happily, in my view, the amendment passed in 2003, and it is now the rule that changes to The Design can be passed with a two-thirds majority. This did not make amending The Design *easy*, but it made it *possible*, which I considered a gift to my successors and a needed improvement in structural flexibility.

Six Vital Issues and the Mission Council (1998-2005)

Two very notable results came out of the General Board Church-Wide Planning Session in the summer of 1998: the identification of six *vital issues* and the authorization of a Mission Council, which I had proposed to develop ways of addressing those six vital issues. The six vital issues identified by the General Board were (1) spiritual vitality and faith development; (2) leadership development; (3) inclusiveness, diversity, and hospitality; (4) evangelism and witness; (5) worship; and (6) justice, reconciliation, and service.

The first meeting of the Mission Council was held January 5-7, 1999, in St. Louis with the following invited to be participants: Laura Bailey (layperson Seattle, Washington), Rafael Gonzalez (layperson, Oviedo, Florida), Chris Hobgood (regional minister, Capital Area Region), Barb Jones (regional minister, Arkansas), Dennis Landon (president of Division of Higher Education), Janet Long (chairperson, Washington, Ohio, clergywoman, former general moderator), John

---

[13] Just a reminder that "consensus" does not mean unanimity. Consensus means that, while a particular proposal may not be *everyone's* first choice, nearly all people can accept a particular proposal as a viable way forward.

Mobley (regional minister, Alabama–NW Florida), Max Morgan (clergy, Ft. Worth, Texas), Zola Walker (layperson, Jarvis College, general first vice moderator), Karen Warren (clergy, Vincennes, Indiana), Russ White (president, Christian Board of Publication), Chris Wilson (clergy, Albuquerque, New Mexico), and Gaylord Yu (layperson, Chicago, Illinois), with OGMP staff support from Don Manworren and me.

The Mission Council sought to ground its work in worship and prayer. Members reviewed previous attempts to do whole church planning in the 1970s and 1980s. We thought this was a "Kairos" moment in part because general, regional, and congregational leaders had come to understand that the church's call now required the *strengthening of congregational life for mission.*

The Council recognized that it was critical to keep in mind that churchwide *planning* does not equate to *programming.* In fact, the group struggled to resist the temptation to think in terms of programmatic responses to the six vital issues. It was increasingly understood that transformation would come only through creating contexts in which information can be exchanged and developed, and new relationships formed and nurtured. Thus, the Council determined that its role was to facilitate processes that included broadcasting the vital issues for mission; bringing people into relationship around those issues; exchanging information across the life of the church; developing and pursuing avenues of accountability; and, *lastly,* recommending funding of initiatives from the Mission Imperative Fund (one percent of BMF).

It was decided that the Council would meet twice a year: in the first quarter of the year to consult regarding ongoing responsibilities, and to review proposed initiatives and provide coaching to submitters as needed; and in the third quarter of the year to make Mission Imperative Fund allocation decisions. The Mission Council spent much time getting its purpose and criteria right.

In 2001, John Mobley, regional minister of Alabama–Northwest Florida, became chair and was amazingly effective in managing all the Council was seeking to do. Others joined the Mission Council as original members rotated off: Allen Harris (clergy, Cleveland, Ohio), Eric Cole (clergy, Greensboro, North Carolina), Alvin Jackson (clergy, Washington, D.C.), Belva Brown Jordan (clergy, higher education), John Lau (layperson, New York, New York), and Bill Edwards (as the new associate general minister and vice president, who had begun when Don Manworren retired).

Many good projects were funded by the Imperative Fund Grants made by the Mission Council. One of the most important early on, in my view, was seed money provided to Board of Church Extension for the New Church Establishment program. A goal of one thousand new congregations by the year 2020 had just been approved by the 2001 General Assembly (part of 2020 Vision) and the New Church Ministry was just getting started.[14]

There were a number of other significant grants made as well—some to projects originating in congregations, some in regions, and some in general ministries, many cutting across all three expressions of the church. Among these were seed money for the Bethany Project, which sought to deepen Disciples' spirituality, and the Nazareth project, which lifted up licensed ministry and developed alternative paths to ordination—which was an important way of strengthening leadership in the life of the church (one of the original vital issues and a subject of the 2020 Vision). Seed money was provided to help establish a Korean Studies Program at Brite Divinity School that aims to raise up new Disciples ministers who have a Korean cultural background (which continued to thrive under the leadership of Professor Dr. Timothy Lee and Dr. Newell Williams, president of Brite Divinity School). Seed money was also provided for the Shalom Congregation Program.

The work of encouraging, reviewing, granting, managing, and holding accountable the use of Mission Imperative Grants became too much for the Mission Council to accomplish by itself, so working groups were formed around the six vital issues to facilitate much of this work.

Later in the six-year life of the Mission Council (1999–2005), when increasing financial stress was consuming so much of the church's energy, the Council helped the racial ethnic ministries continue and grow through the National American Pacific/Asian Disciples and the Central Pastoral Office for Hispanic Ministries. These are just a few examples of the lasting impact on the church of the Mission Imperative Fund and the Mission Council. Yet another new "mission funding system" ended the Mission Imperative Fund

---

[14] The Board of Church Extension is now identified as Disciples Church Extension Fund (DCEF).

and so, too, was the Mission Council ended. But it had done some great work.

General Ministry Unit President Search Committees (1999)

Each general ministry unit has the right to establish its own procedures and policies regarding searches for new leadership. On the one hand, the general ministry units have almost always chosen *very* capable leaders. However, there have been a few occasions when general ministry presidential search processes have followed secular models, and occasionally the results have been disastrous. In any case, it seemed to me that general ministry unit search processes should be transparent to the rest of the church, and the wider church should have the opportunity to express its current priorities and concerns to the search committee itself. How could this be best accomplished? The simplest answer to me was to be certain the GMP was consulted at the beginning of every general ministry unit presidential search process (just as regional minister search committees had begun doing).

The language of The Design at that time (Paragraph 58)[15] read, "The chief administrative officers of the various administrative units shall be elected by their respective governing bodies following consultation with the General Minister and President and with the advice and counsel of the Administrative Committee of the General Board."

That paragraph sounds fine but, in practice, my experience was that the Administrative Committee and the GMP were seldom consulted before a search process had been completed and a new general ministry unit president had been elected by the unit board. If the GMP is not consulted until after the internal election process is complete (as is usually the case), the opportunity for the search committee to be oriented by the GMP as to what the larger church needs from that general ministry unit and its new president is lost. (Happily, in conversation with Sharon Watkins, I learned that her experience was different, perhaps because of the Executive Search Process protocol that was an outgrowth of the Anti-Racism initiative.)

My purpose was certainly not to make it possible for the GMP to *control* who would or would not become a general ministry unit

---

[15] The Design has some added language now, but the new language does not address this matter any more effectively.

president. Rather, it was to provide connection between the search committee's work and what was happening in the wider church, and to provide churchly counsel to committees that would ensure outcomes that would be good for the whole church. This is parallel to the way regional ministers work with congregations.

Although I proposed language through the Standing Committee for Renewal and Structural Reform to the Administrative Committee to add a bit of language to Paragraph 58 for clarification, this was not forwarded to the General Board. However, in the General Cabinet meeting of January 12–13, 2000, I requested an addition to general ministry units' bylaws/constitutions: "When a vacancy in the office of unit President occurs, the Board Moderator of the unit shall consult as soon as possible with the General Minister and President regarding interim arrangements, a search process, and the wider church's hopes and expectations regarding the unit." Some of the general ministry units added this or similar language to their bylaws, but not most. I still think it is needed.

Commission on Faith and Understanding (1999)

Still seeking ways to handle complicated and/or controversial issues more helpfully (and less divisively), I proposed the idea of a Commission on Faith and Understanding to the Administrative Committee and General Board in 1999. This idea first surfaced when the Steering Committee for the Process of Discernment on Biblical Authority recommended that a different kind of process was needed for such a complex matter as biblical authority, about which many people have differing opinions. Practically *everyone* affirms the authority of the scriptures, but what that actually means in regard to particular passages of scripture and subjects is often a matter of contention. So, the Steering Committee recommended the development of a standing commission that could give in-depth biblical and theological consideration to specific issues coming before the church. The Commission was somewhat similar in concept to the Commission on Theology, which was being discontinued and had been housed in the Council on Christian Unity.[16] So, I asked that

---

[16] The main difference between the two was that the Commission on Theology wrote lengthy documents on general subjects of theology (often appearing as booklets published, for example, as "The Nature of the Church Series," with themes like baptism and the Lord's Supper), whereas the Commission on Faith and Understanding was envisioned to address narrower subjects of immediate concern.

the proposed Commission on Faith and Understanding be similarly housed in the Council on Christian Unity.

I asked Chuck Blaisdell (regional minister of Northern California/Nevada) to serve as chair and invited the following persons to an initial meeting of the Commission: Kristine Culp (dean of Disciples Divinity House, Chicago), Tony Dunnavant (dean of Lexington Theological Seminary), James Duke (professor at Brite Divinity School), Emily Jackson (layperson, Mississippi Boulevard Christian Church, Memphis, Tennessee), Verity Jones (pastor, Terre Haute, Indiana, Central Christian), Dennis Landon (president of Division of Higher Education) Timothy Lee (lecturer at UCLA), William Lee (pastor of Loudon Avenue Christian Church, Roanoke, Virginia), Chad Martin (layperson, San Francisco, California), Carmelo Alvarez (dean of Christian Theological Seminary), Scott Colglazier (pastor of University Christian Church, Ft. Worth, Texas), and David Vargas (vice president of Division of Overseas Ministries).

This was an outstanding group of people, and as chair and supporting staff, Chuck and Robert did great work, but the Commission turned out to be too cumbersome to function as we had hoped. Nevertheless, before being dissolved, the Commission did bring a very helpful paper drafted by Chuck Blaisdell to the General Board regarding the nature of the covenant that is at the heart of our polity and life.

Experiments always have the right to fail, so long as we learn from them. The Commission on Faith and Understanding was discontinued after two years as it was overwhelmed with potential subjects of study. In addition, it was discontinued because we "discovered" that a panel of generalists, even as well informed as this group was, will tend to generate overly general responses that are satisfying to few. But it did point the way toward new approaches to be attempted in the following years. We concluded that individual groups of "experts" in particular areas responding to particular issues would be more productive and efficient.

I resigned as GMP before I could propose a successor to the Commission on Faith and Understanding that might have proven to be less cumbersome. If I were to make such a proposal today, I might ask each of our seminaries to address a particular matter as context for major issues being brought to the General Board and/or General Assembly. I know my successors have continued to struggle with the challenge of how to help the church work through important and complex issues in a way that does not politicize or divide but that can enhance the church's voice and our unity as Disciples. I support these continuing efforts.

A New Vision for the Church: 2020 Vision

As I have said many times here, from the start, my primary concern was to help the church come to clarity about its purpose and direction in the twenty-first century. From that first conversation with the Cabinet in September 1993, to each meeting with regional ministers, to the Mission Conversations, the Administrative Committee, the General Board, and the General Assembly, getting clarity of purpose and direction was my priority. All of this work came to fulfillment when I presented the 2020 Vision to the General Board for approval in 2000 and to the Assembly for affirmation in 2001.

Together with the other statements and summaries that had been developed during those years since 1993, the Vision pointed the way forward toward what we were to become. The Vision is as follows: "To be a faithful, growing church, that demonstrates true community, deep Christian spirituality, and a passion for justice." This vision is based on Micah 6:8, which represents a high point in the prophetic tradition and points directly to Jesus' desires for the church. I believe it also represents some of the best of our Disciples history and tradition, as we have always emphasized faithfulness to one's understanding of what God desires, a commitment to evangelism (sharing the good news of God's love and grace for all), the unity of all Christians (in spirit, if not always in doctrine or method), and actively participating in God's desire for a just world.

Perhaps the newest element of the 2020 Vision is the emphasis on "deep Christian spirituality." We were born out of Enlightenment ideas, and *thinking* has been our strong suit. As the culture has turned increasingly secular (a process that was beginning even as we Disciples were being born in the nineteenth century), we have emphasized *thinking* and *doing* more than *being*. Thinking and doing are great, and certainly are *part* of the Christian life, but if we are to be sustained spiritually over the long haul in the work of transforming the world, we need to have our being rooted in the life of the Spirit. This is what the Bethany Project was about, and I am convinced that we need to pay more attention to the nurture of the spiritual lives of all Disciples: members, ministers, and denominational leaders. This is one of the primary antidotes for the burnout we see among so many leaders these days. It is also that which makes it possible for us to live faithful and productive lives in the face of the chaos in the world around us.

In addition to this qualitative statement of vision were four quantitative goals to be achieved by the year 2020: (1) to start one thousand new congregations; (2) to revitalize one thousand of our existing congregations; (3) to become an anti-racist/pro-reconciling church; and (4) To develop the leadership necessary to make these goals possible to achieve.

I know when people heard "one thousand new congregations by 2020," many thought I (and anyone else involved in formulating the vision) was engaging in fantasy. This is understandable in the face of the fact that we had started new congregations at a rate of only about twelve per year for the previous twenty years. To suddenly seek to start an average of fifty per year did, in fact, seem absurd. In fact, in a new church consultation led by the Board of Church Extension, during which we were deciding what number to put forth, I had initially recommended a goal of about six hundred and fifty new congregations by 2020. But the consultant to that meeting, George Bullard, made a hard case for one thousand. Jim Powell, president of Church Extension, said later that I went pale upon hearing this number! Nonetheless, the group affirmed one thousand as the goal. I am so thankful now that we accepted that higher number, because the church actually achieved *more* than one thousand as of the year 2020!

New congregations had typically been started by existing congregations (although few existing congregations chose to start new congregations after 1965 as existing congregations increasingly thought of new congregations as a threat to their own survival rather than as an expression of mission) and by regions (assisted by the Board of Church Extension, for whom new congregations have always been a part of the mission). Few regions any longer had the resources to start a lot of new congregations (especially using the expensive pastor–developer model), so the leadership for new congregation establishment fell back to Church Extension. To facilitate this, Church Extension President Jim Powell and Vice President Rick Reisinger sought out Rick Morse, the pastor of a new congregation, Lake Washington Christian Church in Kirkland, Washington, to lead the effort.

Rick Morse moved to Indianapolis and called together an outstanding team that included Judy Turner of Homeland Ministries (minister of congregational growth), Dee Long, and Gilberto Collazo of University Christian Church in Rio Piedras, Puerto Rico. Gilberto's selection was especially interesting because he amounted to a Disciples missionary *from* Puerto Rico *to* the United States and Canada, and the flow of missionaries had always been the opposite. It made sense to bring Gilberto to work in new congregation establishment because the church in Puerto Rico had been *growing* for many years, whereas the church in the United States and Canada had begun shrinking. Later, Nadine Burton and Charlie Wallace would join this excellent team. In Resolution 0117, at the 2001 General Assembly, the first fruits of the new congregation initiative were reported in the form of fifty-two new congregations!

At Rick's retirement, I told those assembled to celebrate him because he had "changed the face of the Christian Church (Disciples of Christ) through the work he and his team had done." The new congregations represented huge diversity in race, culture, and ethnicity. We were no longer a ninety-four-percent white denomination, and we are much better for it! We Disciples still do not completely reflect our primary mission field (North America), but we are moving in that direction as we become increasingly diverse.

Revitalizing one thousand of our existing four thousand congregations was a goal that was met with enthusiasm, as *many* of our existing congregations were in obvious need of such revitalizing. This work was taken on in partnership between the Board of Church Extension, the Division of Homeland Ministries, and the regions of the church, as this work fell naturally into the mission of each of these entities.

The number of congregations actually revitalized is a bit harder to identify than the number of new congregations started. A new congregation is either started or not, but revitalization is a process that occurs over years. However, between 2000 and 2020, I can safely say that there were more than a thousand congregations with which Church Extension, Homeland Ministries, and regions worked toward revitalization. Furthermore, there were some congregations that experienced revitalization more than once during those twenty years.[17]

---

[17] Years later as a church consultant, I recommended that congregations revision their life and ministry every seven to ten years as part of an ongoing revitalization process.

The fact is that the cultural and socioeconomic context in which congregations live and serve has been changing at an incredible rate. Some congregations respond to those changes by adapting their own approaches to ministry. Others simply hunker down and *refuse* to change due to fear or denial. The former have a chance, whereas the latter most often die eventually. As I learned in my many years of church consulting (after my GMP years), most congregations that die do so by suicide—either by making bad decisions in the face of the change around them or, more often, by refusing to make *any* decisions in a timely fashion. Thus, the work of helping congregations understand the changes in their context and to make better decisions in a timely way is incredibly important. But, as they say, "You can lead a horse to water, but you can't make it drink." As is so often true of the human condition, we often *say* we want to grow and thrive, but we most often want to do so *without changing*.

"Becoming an anti-racist/pro-reconciling church" pushed the church to go beyond the simple sentiment, "Can't we all just get along?" or the mere charity that has often been extended from White congregations to people and congregations of color. Like our two nations (the United States and Canada), we of the church needed to go beyond simply addressing individual racial prejudice. We needed to go to the roots of the issue by addressing *systemic* racism, within our church systems and within our nations. We had learned this, in part, through the significant work of the Process of Discernment on Racism, which had been authorized by the General Board in 1995 and reaffirmed in 1998.

This work led to the adoption of an Open Executive Search Process (drafted by Lois Artis Murray, a member of the Anti-Racism Steering Committee, who would later become president of Church Finance Council) to assure that all people had a fair chance at employment within our general ministry units and regional ministries, and with development of anti-racism/pro-reconciling workshops for general ministry units and then for regions.

We began by using the services of a provider called Crossroads Ministry, based in Chicago, which had been identified by L. Wayne Stewart, director of Reconciliation. L. Wayne authorized Reconciliation funding to provide for the first three years of our partnership with Crossroads. Soon we began developing our own trainers and programs (Lori Adams and Jessica Vazquez of the Office of GMP were pivotal in this work), and we were providing anti-racism training for the General Board and Administrative Committee. Not long after, training was being provided to regional anti-racism teams, one of the first of which was in the Capital Area and led by Brenda Cardwell, Ken Brooker Langston, and regional minister Chris Hobgood. Chris, who was born in Congo, a child of Disciples missionaries, and would become interim GMP in 2003–2005; his commitment to anti-racism is perhaps his most important legacy to the whole church.

Today, many regions require regular anti-racism/pro-reconciliation training for ministers to maintain standing (just as they require "boundary training"). Many congregations and Disciples-related colleges and seminaries have now undergone the training, and the movement remains strong. I believe it is essential that we Disciples lead the way toward "true community" by transforming ourselves, our congregations, and other systems into a *whole church* that is anti-racist and pro-reconciling.

Developing the leadership necessary to make these other elements of the 2020 Vision reality is, of course, an ongoing challenge. Leadership for the church comes through many sources: congregations that encourage people to accept the call to become ministers and other leaders; camp and conference programs, which have always been so important in leading young people to hear a call to Christian vocation and lay leadership; and colleges and seminaries that further encourage and develop persons for leadership in the church and world. All of these sources and more must be continually nurtured and supported. This is essentially the work of the Division of Higher Education, which changed its name to Higher Education and Leadership Ministries (HELM). Under the leadership of HELM President Dennis Landon, this general ministry unit developed an important program called Leadership Fellows, which has helped develop transformational clergy leaders for the church. In addition, the Bethany Project (described earlier) developed a Lilly-supported program called Bethany Fellows, with the same aim of developing transformational leaders. Some of our best and brightest congregational leaders have come through these programs.

My book, *2020 Vision for the Christian Church (Disciples of Christ)*, was published by Christian Board of Publication in 2001. It was a great opportunity to support the launch of the vision, and the 2020

Vision began taking hold across the life of the church. Having led this process of envisioning from 1993 to 2000, I believe the 2020 Vision is *my* most important legacy as GMP. But it is the hard work and commitment of so *many* people in the general, regional, and congregational expressions of the church (some of whom I know and many of whom I do not) that has begun to make the vision real, and they all have my undying gratitude and affection.

Important Changes in Leadership

Leadership changes are always important, of course, but some were particularly significant for the change I was working to bring to the church. Below are some examples, in addition to those already mentioned.

I described previously how important it was for Lori Adams and Linda McKiernan Allen to come onto the staff of the Office of GMP after Claudia Grant's departure. As program director for General Assembly, Linda helped shift the planning for General Assembly so that each subsequent assembly built on the one before, rather than each being a stand-alone event, and helped keep the assembly related to the newly defined mission imperatives. A progressive herself with strong pastoral skills, Linda was also able to relate well to some of our more conservative folks, so that they felt heard and knew their ideas would be seriously considered.

Lori was key in our experimentation with processes of discernment and "worshipful work." She helped keep the anti-racism/pro-reconciliation initiative on track. After a couple of years, I wanted to "promote" her to the role of associate general minister, but she refused the offer because she was a new mother and didn't want to be away for the travel that would have been required. But for all practical purposes (except salary and travel), she *became* an associate general minister. She was a voice of honesty, unafraid to tell me the truth whenever I needed to hear it ... whether I wanted to hear it or not. That was priceless. As a person in a same-gender relationship, raising a family, she helped me in my own growing understanding of LGBTQ identity and helped me navigate the complicated dynamics of church life around human sexuality issues. Though she was not often "front and center," it is impossible to overstate her value to my leadership and to the whole church.

Pat Tucker Spier became president of the Division of Overseas Ministries in early 1994. She and her then-husband, Rik, had earlier served as missionaries in Japan and, at the time of her selection, Pat was serving on the pastoral staff of West Street Christian Church in Tipton, Indiana. While I had nothing to do with her selection, as I was just starting as GMP, Pat's election was significant for both personal and churchly reasons. She had been a fellow student at Christian Theological Seminary, so we had shared history, and I knew her to be exceedingly capable, which was important for anyone who was following the very capable Bill Nottingham. She was also coming onto the Cabinet as the second woman to serve as a general ministries unit president, which meant Ann Updegraff Spleth would no longer be the only woman there.

Pat inherited important work, as her predecessor had been working toward the development of a Common Global Ministries Board with the United Church of Christ, which meant there would be some merger of staff and that all missionaries of our two churches would go on behalf of both. Bringing this new board together was both important and challenging work, as any kind of merger always is. It gave concrete expression to our ecumenical partnership with the United Church of Christ and created efficiencies that blessed the work and both churches. Both the Division of Overseas Ministries and the United Church Board of World Ministries retained their own integrity and accountability to their own church bodies, while also bringing the work and the workers together in new and powerful ways. It was groundbreaking for the North American mainline Protestant Church.

Pat's successor in 2003, David Vargas, brought the first Hispanic general ministries unit presidency to the Cabinet. This was a sign of the change that was beginning to take hold in the whole church and a sign of the wisdom of the DOM Board in choosing David.

Jim Seale, president of the Disciples of Christ Historical Society, had become a dear friend while I lived in Nashville as Tennessee regional minister. When Jim retired, Peter Morgan became president and continued in Jim's excellent pattern. Peter had come from congregational ministry to the Division of Homeland Ministries, and he knew the Disciples backward and forward. As a member of the Cabinet, he was always supportive of the 2020 Vision, personally encouraging to me, and actively developed resources for congregations to help redevelop our sense of Disciples identity.

Robert Welsh was always an important conversation partner. His familiarity with the history of Restructure and with the ecumenical world was invaluable. So, when the Church Finance Council was brought into the Office of GMP and Robert became an associate general minister, it made consultation and cooperation even easier. After Paul Crow's retirement on December 31, 1998, Robert became president of the Council on Christian Unity.

Following Robert, Lois Artis Murray was selected to become associate general minister and president of the Church Finance Council. Lois had served the church in various ways and places through the years and was a certified public accountant. She was the first Black woman to serve as a general ministry unit president and as an associate general minister, and thus the first Black woman to be a member of the Cabinet. She served with distinction. Lois was an essential part of the anti-racism initiative, having served on the original Process of Discernment on Racism Steering Committee.

A part of Lois's work as president of Church Finance Council was to supervise the director of Reconciliation, L. Wayne Stewart, who had begun in 1993. L. Wayne had identified the anti-racism organization Crossroads, which was the only provider addressing racism among religious groups and which became our partner organization in the new anti-racism/pro-reconciliation initiative. Lois's engagement and contributions to that initiative were essential.

However, as president of the Church Finance Council, Lois knew what was happening to Basic Mission Finance, how it was shrinking despite all efforts to increase congregations' contributions to it. Thus, she felt the same urgency I did to reduce structure and increase efficiency wherever possible to make every mission dollar count. To accomplish this, she needed a dedicated board that was closer to the day-to-day issues of the Church Finance Council's work than was the Administrative Committee and that could provide the needed support and advocacy for change. Thus, the CFC Board was restored and the associate general minister part of her title and work was removed. As envisioned by Lois and her restored board, the closure of Church Finance Council, placing responsibility for BMF promotion on the recipient partners, coupled with the creation of the Office of Treasury Services within the OGMP to assure that money was spent properly and as intended, reduced administrative structure and increased accountability. Reconciliation Ministries and Week of Compassion migrated to the Office of General Minister and President.

This creation of Treasury Services eventually paved the way for regions and other related ministries with shrinking resources to receive financial accounting assistance through Treasury Services and to participate in a uniform audit process. Financial audits are extremely important in any church organization, but they are also expensive. More than two-thirds of our regions, the nine ministries that report through the OGMP, and nine other ministries, use Treasury Services as of this writing. This saves these ministries money and provides accountability through an annual audit. John Goebel, originally brought on staff by Lois Artis Murray, continues to be crucial in the development and provision of these services.

Jim Powell became president of Church Extension in 1995 after Hal Watkins's retirement. Jim brought experience in congregations, regions, and Church Extension. He had been director of the Church Advance Now program of Church Extension back in the 1980s, when few were thinking about new congregation establishment. Jim was a great colleague who helped redefine the church's mission and who pushed hard for new congregation establishment and congregational revitalization. Also, as a long-time friend, he was a comfort to work with and an important encourager for 2020 Vision even after I resigned.

Deborah Thompson, and later Vertie Powers, had done a good job with Church Advance Now (CAN), and a new effort called Vision Builders, developed to encourage individuals and others to give to new congregation establishment. From 1990 to 1999, one hundred and eighty new congregations were established. However, these were begun under the old assumptions about how congregations were to be started, which included the expensive pastor–developer model, and few regions had funds left to invest in such new congregations as of 1999.

In 2000, Homeland Ministries President Ann Updegraff Spleth left after fifteen years of service. Ann was the first baby boomer and the first female to lead a general ministries unit (a remarkable accomplishment in itself). She effectively guided Homeland Ministries through some terrifically turbulent years and worked hard to position Homeland Ministries for the postmodern era. Ray Brown, one of the great African American leaders of our church, served in the interim until the arrival of a new president, Arnold Nelson, in 2001.

Jim Suggs served as president of Christian Board of Publication for eight years (1989–1997). They were tumultuous years of change, as CBP had to adjust from an old business model that had worked well for nearly a hundred years to a model suitable and sustainable for the twenty-first century. His publishing of the *Chalice Hymnal* and other Disciples resources was a boost both for the church and for CBP's budget. Russ White (a friend from Nashville days) followed Jim and sought to build on Jim's innovations, including the Chalice Press imprint, although Russ deemphasized Disciples-specific resources (including *The Disciple* magazine) in favor of resources with broader appeal to Christian communities beyond the Disciples.

It was hard to think about the OGMP without the presence and skills of Don Manworren, who retired in 2000. But Bill Edwards became associate general minister and rose to the challenge, providing fine organizational leadership.

There were changes of leadership at the Pension Fund (as the presidency passed from Lester Palmer to Art Hanna), but the same basic excellent fiduciary care and care for the church's employees, including clergy, through the years. Our Pension Fund is the envy of so many other denominations and represents perhaps the most concrete way in which the church cares for and affirms its ministers and other employees.

Lucas Torres had been a delight to work with as National Hispanic Pastor, but Pablo Jiménez, Lucas's successor in 2000, was also an effective leader with whom I enjoyed working.

Of course, unchanging leadership is also important. Jim Johnson remained president of the Christian Church Foundation during all my ten years as GMP and oversaw remarkable growth in the Foundation's assets while hiring excellent people to staff. Guenhee Yu gave excellent leadership to the American Asian Disciples, which became North American Pacific Asian Disciples (NAPAD), and encouraged and nurtured scores of new American Asian congregations. John Foulkes was with me in the OGMP during all my ten years, retiring in 2003 after so many years of faithful service to the National Convocation.

Pablo Jiménez became the first Hispanic to serve on the Cabinet, and Guenhee Yu became the first American-Asian to serve there. Together with John Foulkes as executive secretary for the National

Convocation, the three brought thoughtful and helpful participation to the Cabinet.

Regional ministers also have a great impact on the church as a whole, even though their primary service is to a particular region. I counted all the regional ministers as friends. Several served as mentors as I began work in Tennessee. The regional ministers were extremely helpful during my ten years as GMP, as coworkers, counselors, and friends. Many of these colleagues piloted projects for various general ministries and for the OGMP. They serve as indispensable connectors between congregations, and between congregations and the rest of the church.

The General Moderators

According to The Design, the general moderators of the Church are elected every two years and hand off leadership to a new team at the end of each General Assembly. The people I got to work with in these important roles were exceptional to a person. Each became a trusted friend, dialogue partner, and confidant. I'm listing these folks here because each is precious to me. I could tell a story about each of them (but will refrain, as each could also tell a story about me!). They are listed in order as moderator (responsible for presiding at general plenary bodies, including General Administrative Committee, General Board, and General Assembly), first vice moderator (responsible for working in the development of the General Assembly program), and second vice moderator (responsible for working with the business items of the general plenary bodies).

1993-1995: Duane Cummins, Cynthia Hale, and Joyce Blair

Duane Cummins was president of Bethany College, having served previously as president of the Division of Higher Education. A historian, Duane has written many helpful books about us Disciples. He was a tremendous source of encouragement and wisdom. Cynthia Hale is the founding pastor of Ray of Hope Christian Church in Decatur, Georgia. She is widely recognized as one of the finest preachers in the country and comes from a rich lineage of African American Disciples. Joyce Blair was a professor at Belmont University and became a dear friend of my family while I was regional minister of Tennessee. We worshiped together at Vine Street Christian Church in Nashville.

1995–1997: Janet Long, Saundra Bryant, and Paul Rivera

Janet Long was senior minister of Washington Avenue Christian Church in Elyria, Ohio. I came to know her through general church life, including her service as chair of the board of the Church Finance Council, and I appreciated her insightful leadership and good humor. Saundra Bryant, a social worker by education, was executive director of All Peoples Christian Center in Los Angeles, a remarkable urban ministry. Paul Rivera was an architectural engineer for the New York City Schools. He had served as regional moderator of the Northeastern Region, and as a trustee of the New York Theological Seminary.

1997–1999: Michael Mooty, Zola Walker, and Don Lacey

Michael Mooty was Senior Minister of Central Christian Church in Lexington, Kentucky. He had been a conversation partner for several years and had become a close friend. He had served as board chair for several Disciples ministries, including Church Extension, Christian Board of Publication, Lexington Theological Seminary, and Week of Compassion. Zola Walker was church relations director of Jarvis Christian College in Hawkins, Texas. She had been moderator of the Southwest Region and served on the boards of the Council on Christian Unity and the Division of Higher Education. Don Lacey was a physician in private practice as well as serving as a clinical professor at the University of North Carolina. A member of Hillyer Memorial Christian Church in Raleigh, North Carolina, Don helped organize the Urban Ministries Center in Raleigh and served as an elder, youth group sponsor, and CMF president.

1999–2001: Paul Rivera, Lanny Lawler, and Minnie Smith

Paul Rivera did such a fine job as second vice moderator in 1996–1997 that he was selected to be moderator this time. Paul was one of the smartest, kindest leaders I have known. Lanny Lawler was senior minister of Eastwood Christian Church, Nashville. Our paths had crossed in Indiana and again in Kansas City and Tennessee, and I counted him a good friend. Minnie Smith worked in the Social Security Administration in Hannibal, Missouri. A member of Willow Street Christian Church in Hannibal, she was a member of the Board of Church Extension.

2001-2003: Alvin Jackson, Patricia Payuyo, and Ted Waggoner

Alvin Jackson had transformed Mississippi Boulevard Christian Church in Memphis, Tennessee (which is when we became friends), and was now senior minister of National City Christian Church in Washington, D.C. A past president of the National Convocation, he had also served on the Board of the Division of Overseas Ministries. Unfortunately, Alvin was unable to attend the General Assembly he had helped prepare for, due to other events in his life. Patricia Payuyo rose to the occasion and gave sterling leadership to the Assembly business sessions. A member of Filipino Christian Church in Los Angeles, she was moderator of the Pacific Southwest Region and a member of the Board of NAPAD. Ted Waggoner was an attorney in private practice in Rochester, Indiana, where he was an active member of First Christian Church. He was a member of the Indiana Regional Board and of the General Standing Committee for Renewal and Structural reform as well as having served as a parliamentarian for General Assembly.

I should add that I did not personally choose these leaders. Rather, they were chosen by the General Nominating Committee and presented to the Administrative Committee, General Board, and General Assembly for election. However, I did have the opportunity to offer my own input into these nominations, and I was delighted by them each.

These wonderful and gifted leaders brought a huge diversity of race, ethnicity, geography, age, and church experience to their offices. Amid the turmoil that was being experienced by anyone who was working in the regional or general ministries of the church during the tumultuous years of 1993-2003, these moderators brought a love of the church, remarkable faith, and wise counsel, which helped those of us in the church's employ stay grounded and (mostly) sane. Thanks be to God for these Disciple friends! I know every GMP has felt and feels the same about the moderators with whom they have worked.

It is a point of pride for me as a Disciple to recall the selection of women and people of color for various roles in the life of the church, including in my own office and in general ministry units, regions, and other ministries of the church. But like "ceiling breakers" everywhere in our North American culture, being the first woman, the first person of color, or the first person of LGBTQ identity in a particular role is never a cakewalk. There is always personal resistance to such leaders from some colleagues, coworkers, and members. Some of the resistance is outward and obvious, but much more of it is inward and often even unconscious, so that resisters may not even know the degree to which they are resisting. Because of this, in *my* estimation, such ceiling breakers are heroes and sheroes of the church. Those of us who love the church should recognize these pioneers for who and what they are and appreciate them.

Chapter 8

Controversies and Catastrophes

'Renewal Groups'

One of the significant contextual challenges confronting the church was (and is) the culture wars that spawned so-called "renewal groups" in the 1990s. Rapid social change brings high anxiety in people and in their institutions. Fear begets questions like, "What is going to become of us?" "What will happen to our cherished values and ways?"

Both people and institutions can respond to this anxiety in a number of ways. One is to be *reactive*, to try to nail down anything that seems to be loose or coming up. Fundamentalism, not only in Christianity but in *every* religion in the world, has been growing and is a product of fearful reaction to rapid change. It is not only in religions, but in every arena of life in which people can *react* by refusing to change or to allow anything to change.

The other primary way to respond to anxiety generated by change is to seek to understand the changes and be *responsive* by seeking new ways of doing things that are respectful of the past yet appropriate to moving forward. Religion itself has the purpose of both conserving and preserving that which is appropriate to conserve or preserve while also facilitating needed change when and as it is needed. Living institutions, and those that will continue to live, are those that figure out how to hold these two seemingly contradictory purposes together.

Very conservative Christians had gained a lot of visibility in the United States in the 1980s. It's hard to imagine now, but when Jimmy Carter self-identified as an evangelical Christian in 1976, most Americans had little idea what that meant. Evangelical Christianity had not been very visible in the United States as a category of

Christians, although it had been growing in numbers over the decades. It had become more visible in large part in reaction to the fact that mainline Protestant churches, so long at the heart of American culture, had been embracing the results of archeology, linguistics, and other modern sciences as they applied to the Bible. Mainline Christian thought leaders had moved away from literal interpretations of the scriptures to more nuanced understandings. Over the years, we mainliners spoke less about sin and hell and more about grace and human potential. The word "evangelical" began to be used by the media to refer to "fundamentalist" Christians specifically, a particular kind of conservative position that refers back to theological and philosophical battles being fought in Presbyterian circles in the 1910s–1920s and then spreading to other branches of Western Christianity and then to churches in the Global South, where very conservative and even fundamentalist missionaries were being sent.

By the 1970s, some conservative evangelical Christians—represented by people like Jimmy Swaggart, Jerry Falwell, Pat Robertson, and others—had begun to use television in very powerful ways to garner followers and to preach a fundamentalist point of view. Falwell and others began mixing their fundamentalist Christianity with American politics to create a potent brew that swelled the ranks of those who identified as very conservative Christians and that called into question the faithfulness of those more progressive Christians who comprised the mainline churches. More thoughtful evangelicals, including my personal friends Jim Wallis and Ron Sider, began to feel uncomfortable with the way the label "evangelical" was being used in the media.

During the 1980s, many politicians were aligning themselves with these TV personalities and their traditional morality (more preached than lived in many cases, unfortunately) and their fondness for wrapping it all up in the American flag. Right-wing leaders of industry and some conservative foundations began pouring money into these "religious" organizations and into political action committees (PACs) and domestic operatives who sought to further undercut the mainline churches. Rather than referring to themselves as fundamentalists, these ultra-conservative Christians began using the word "orthodox" to identify their beliefs, which implied that their position was "normal" rather than "fringe." The term "orthodox" reveals their discomfort with change.

One such group was the so-called Institute for Religion and Democracy (IRD), which continues to this day. Funded by foundations and individuals, this group, and others like it, sought to sow the seeds of unrest in mainline churches. Articles often appeared in popular media (most notably and surprisingly, perhaps, in *Reader's Digest*), which touted lies about the mainline church. Two of the most outrageous examples are articles that appeared condemning the National Council of Churches and World Council of Churches for being sympathetic to communism"[1] These sensational accusations were absurd, but the mere headlines were enough to convince many Americans that the mainline churches were themselves drifting into communism.

If such groups fairly debated differences in theology with mainline groups, I would have little problem with it. I believe I could hold my own in such a debate (as could any number of Disciples leaders and scholars). But these groups were (and are) steeped in secular *political* tactics and have used them to undercut trust among mainline members for their own denominational leaders and pastors. Their purpose was to drive citizens out of the mainline religious groups and into more politically and religiously conservative camps. The IRD helped foster and train many of these so-called renewal groups.[2] The Disciples' "renewal" group was called, "Disciple Renewal," which later renamed itself, "Disciples Heritage Fellowship." I put these names in quotation marks because they were neither about being Disciples nor about renewal. They were seeking to stir up resistance to denominational leadership and to lead people into their own politically and theologically conservative camp.

Beyond such culture war issues, in my conversations with leaders of these groups, it became clear to me that, in contrast to The Design of the Christian Church (Disciples of Christ), they had no understanding of "church" as extending beyond the local congregation (an ecclesiological disagreement).

When I became GMP, Disciple Renewal had many of us in general and regional leadership in a frenzy, thinking that the denomination

---

[1] These sorts of attacks continue today, of course, as we hear right-wing extremist leaders talking about moderate social justice policies, which are supported by moderates on both sides of the aisle, as being "socialist" or even "communist," when they are no such thing.

[2] See "Funding the War of Ideas: A Report to the United Church Board for Homeland Ministries," by Leon Howell, October, 1995.

would be divided (as had already happened twice in our history, even as a church for which Christian unity is supposedly our polar star!), or so diminished in size that we would be unable to have any impact on our culture. Some regional ministers were doing damage control constantly because of the disinformation and accusations being published and distributed among Disciples churches. As GMP, I received scores of letters from people who had obviously all read the same material coming out of Disciple Renewal and were asking me why the church was doing this or that and expressing their distrust of denominational leadership. It is puzzling to me how people can withdraw trust from their own leaders so easily when they receive accusatory materials from people they don't even know—but this continues unabated in today's culture as credence is given to wild conspiracy theories and as so many suspect "someone" is "trying to distort the gospel," or to "do them in."

After responding to several hundred letters from individual Disciples members (most of which contained identical language) and finding my time and energy being sapped by these letters and accusations (I tried to respond to them all in writing), it occurred to me that I should see exactly how many congregations were propagating or forwarding these accusations and making so much noise.[3] It sounded like an army, but was it? So, I reviewed the newsletters and other materials Disciple Renewal was sending out. What I found was that about forty Disciples congregations belonged to Disciple Renewal (by their own count), mostly located in Texas and Illinois—forty out of four thousand congregations: That's one percent. I decided then that the group had little life other than the life we were giving them by reacting to everything they wrote or said, however absurd. They were like a parasite growing on a tree: Eventually they would kill the tree (their host) and they would then die as well, but all the destruction was apparently worth it to them to kill the denomination the rest of us appreciated.

My new strategy was to not publicly mention their name as an organization, while continuing to reach out to their individual leaders to seek healthier relationship. (I did not dislike the individuals giving leadership to this reactionary group, but I felt they were being

---

[3] My friend and seminary classmate, Bob Shaw, reminds me of something CTS professor and theologian Clark Williamson once said: "The church is like a swimming pool: Most of the noise comes from the shallow end."

used by forces beyond their own understanding ... and they would probably say the same about me.) I commended a strategy of public silence to everyone else as well. As our denominational leadership stopped responding in public ways, sure enough, their support and the damage they were doing to the Church began to wane. They have been able to sow the seeds of distrust through a relatively few more congregations through the years, but the church itself mostly ceased offering them a platform to spread their division.

This same strategy of distrust and division was being implemented in every mainline denomination in the United States (it was called "Biblical Witness" in the United Church of Christ, "Presbyterian Lay Committee" in the PCUSA, "Good News" in the United Methodist Church, and so on).

Of course, these days we see the same strategy being used by extreme groups around the world to weaken democracy itself in favor of more authoritarian approaches to government. These secular groups now have an even more sophisticated internet and media presence, plus the "assistance" of internet operatives in Russia, China, North Korea, Iran, and elsewhere.

I confess that one of the reasons I personally respond so negatively to such inuendo and dirty-tricks *politics* in the United States today is because these same tactics were used against me, and the denomination I love, to sow doubt, distrust, and division rather than being true reform movements. We Disciples needed (and need) some reform, to be sure, but reform that seeks to address and to adapt to the *postmodern* world ... not the *premodern* world!

The Closing of Phillips University

Phillips University was established in 1906. Located in Enid, Oklahoma, through the years it educated scores of ministers and lay leaders for the Christian Church (Disciples of Christ). It was a small school by today's standards (fewer than five hundred students by 1998), but its impact was mighty!

However, it proved increasingly difficult to attract students to Enid, especially as other colleges and universities sprang up in Oklahoma and beyond. In the 1980s and 1990s, various school administrations had developed various proposals to keep Phillips sustainable. In the end however, there were just not enough dollars. Unfortunately, for years the church had been told that everything was fine. Phillips's leaders were probably fearful that, if church members came to see Phillips's future as tenuous, they might withdraw the financial support they *had* been contributing. By the time the church found out what the actual financial picture was (I was part of a group of five or six general church leaders who went to campus to see for ourselves), the school had amassed ten million dollars of debt, with no reasonable means to pay it off.

Some Phillips enthusiasts begged the denomination to pay off the debt. I tried to explain that the denomination doesn't have large amounts of cash just laying around! The money we had in our general financial institutions—such as the Pension Fund, the Christian Church Foundation, and Church Extension—had all been given for dedicated purposes and could not legally or ethically be redirected to a project like Phillips.

Frankly, some of the people who were asking the denomination to redirect mission dollars *knew this was not possible*, but they thought by characterizing the denomination's leaders' refusal as a shameful rejection of a Disciples institution in need, they could motivate Disciples lay people to contribute directly to Phillips (this was as vexing to me, frankly, as was Disciple Renewal). In 1998, not only did Phillips close, but there were many, especially in Oklahoma, who believed the denomination had been derelict in "letting it happen." Thus, the Disciples not only lost what had been an important school, largely due to mismanagement by university administration, but the whole church took another "hit" in terms of distrust.

Fortunately, Phillips Graduate Seminary (now Phillips Theological Seminary), another important Disciples institution that shared the campus with Phillips University in Enid but had separate administration, had separated from the university several years earlier and moved to Tulsa, where it continues to thrive. Also fortunate, once the university's assets were liquidated and the debts were paid, a charitable foundation resulted that provides funding for Disciples student scholarships and educational projects, so the university's legacy of Disciples education goes on.

The Disciple Magazine

The Disciple was a long-standing publication of Christian Board of Publication. It had resulted from the merger of two predecessor publications: *World Call* and *The Christian*. It has often been said that the Stone-Campbell Movement didn't have bishops, we had editors.

There is much truth in this, and even though *The Disciple* was a freestanding publication that did not receive editorial approval of general church leadership, it performed a valuable function in reporting news from across the life of the church and offering thoughtful articles and editorial opinions about the big issues of the day.

Many church members thought it was a "house organ" and always reflected the thinking of denominational leaders. I can say with certainty that this was not so. I often agreed with the *stance* of *The Disciple* toward particular issues, but I often disagreed with the magazine's *approach*. Nevertheless, its editors had the right to write what they wished in any way they chose. Despite occasional disagreements on my part, I recognized *The Disciple* as being an important contributor to church life and thinking. As GMP, I enjoyed a good relationship with the magazine and its last editor, Patti Case (who remains a close friend and with whom I have worked in a number of other settings and projects), and the previous editor, Bob Friedly (with whom I frequently had lunch). In fact, I wrote a column for the magazine regularly.

So, it came as a great disappointment when CBP President Russ White told me in December 2001 that the magazine would soon be closing. Although there was nothing I could do about the closure, I appreciated the heads up, because I knew this would be perceived by many as a further sign of decline in the denomination as a whole, especially on the heels of the closing of Phillips University.

Christian Board of Publication had been experiencing financial stress for many years, and it was only careful management by Jim Suggs, the previous president of CBP, and Russ White, the president when the magazine was closed, that had kept this important general ministry unit alive. In earlier decades of the twentieth century, CBP made so much money from sales of graded Sunday school curriculum (primarily) and other denominational materials (such as worship bulletin covers) that it actually contributed significant sums of money to Basic Mission Finance. But as Sunday schools began to wane and to use materials other than printed curriculum and other than Disciples-branded items, and as subscriptions to *The Disciple* decreased, CBP became a financially struggling general ministry unit.

Thus, the closing of *The Disciple* made some financial sense in the face of new fiscal and cultural circumstances, but many in the church saw it as a betrayal or a sign of the denomination's demise.

Partly to offset this impact, former CBP President Jim Suggs and former *The Disciple* Editor Bob Friedly started a new magazine, *DisciplesWorld*, which operated successfully and helpfully for several years with Verity Jones as editor. No one could have made a more skilled or devoted effort. But the same economic forces that had brought down *The Disciple* eventually brought down *DisciplesWorld* as well. It may be time to consider the development of a digital version of such magazines, which would go beyond the sharing of information about various programs and initiatives done by the Office of Communication (as important as this information is). Such a digital magazine could offer the opportunity for discussion of the larger issues of the church and world, including theology, justice, interfaith relationships, ecclesiology, and more.

The National Benevolent Association

The president of the NBA from 1996 to 2004 was Cindy Dougherty. She was beloved by many who had known her for her work in church relations at more than one Disciples college. Her apparent desire was to build NBA into an even larger enterprise than the one she inherited from her predecessor, Rick Lance. Rick was an excellent administrator and a fiscal conservative in the sense that he was very careful about how NBA invested its money. He took a route that depended on the gifts of individual Disciples and local investments by Disciples congregations, by government, and by others to grow the number of homes serving older people, children, and youth, always careful not to overextend the resources or credit limits of NBA itself.

Cindy, on the other hand, imagined growing the number of new NBA projects at greater speed, building income-producing facilities and leveraging NBA assets to do so. The idea arose to build a large, high-end facility that would draw the well-to-do and earn money for NBA to use in other projects. The problem was that NBA and Cindy herself had no experience in the development of such properties. When the property did not sell as quickly and profitably as she had hoped and anticipated, a considerable debt was amassed by NBA, with its other properties being used as collateral to keep the project alive. Although a reasonable settlement was offered early on by the financiers, the NBA board, with Cindy's leadership, chose instead to declare bankruptcy in hopes of a better outcome.

She did this while keeping at arm's length those who might have given her different advice. As GMP, I found that the NBA's financial reports had become highly complex and not revealing of much. I'm not an accountant, but I began to suspect there might be a problem of overextension. I asked for more information on a number of occasions, beginning in 2000, but always received replies that revealed little to nothing. I still trusted Cindy's intentions, but I had become concerned that the NBA was operating outside its core competencies.

Just as I was completing my service as GMP in 2003, it became apparent that my fears (and the fears of many others) had been confirmed. In early 2004, with ninety-five facilities in twenty-two states, the NBA declared bankruptcy and many of the NBA homes went on the sales block. They were "bargains" for potential buyers, because they were available for a rather small percentage of what it had cost the NBA to build them and because they were filled with residents who had signed contracts to remain, so there was ready-made occupancy, without which no such facility can survive.

The people hurt by the bankruptcy of NBA were primarily those who had made gifts to the NBA over the years, and the ninety-five hundred residents of NBA facilities who suffered the huge stress of wondering what would become of their savings that had been invested in lifetime contracts, and for staff who had given their all for NBA as a matter of belief in the mission and ministry. The credibility of the entire institutional church took a serious hit, of course.

There's a reason why church institutions need to be rather conservative in their investing approaches, and why church institutions need to be "open books," so that anyone can see what their strategies and practices are. I have learned over the years that if an "outsider" can't make sense of an institution's accounts, something is likely not right.

Another Kind of Tragedy

I had promised Gene Trester for some time that I would visit a training session for facilitators of the Adult Bible Interdependent Learning (ABIL) program he had developed. So, on April 19, 1997, I flew to Columbia, Missouri, Regional Airport to visit the ABIL Training session were being led by Kim Gage Ryan. I had been invited to preach the next morning at Broadway Christian Church, where Kim was associate pastor and Rick Frost was senior.

The Columbia Regional Airport is about fifteen miles south of Columbia, in the midst of farmland. Bob Combs was a professor at the University of Missouri (in Columbia) and a member of Broadway Christian, and he graciously agreed to pick me up at the airport. As we passed by fields of tall green corn, we struck up a conversation on the way to town. Coming to a "T" intersection, Bob rolled through the stop sign into the intersection and into the path of a large pickup truck traveling perhaps sixty miles per hour. Bob froze and I just had time to turn my head straight forward in the hopes of avoiding serious neck injury. The truck T-boned us on Bob's door.

Bob's car was an old Mercedes, built like a tank. Still, the truck pushed the car sideways several feet. I was rendered unconscious and, when I awoke, I called out to Bob. His side of the car had borne the brunt of the damage, and he was still unconscious. His breathing was labored, and it was obvious there was fluid in his lungs. He did not respond to my calling out his name.

There was a car immediately behind us which, remarkably, was driven by a physician. The doctor immediately called 911 and then came to us to see how we were. The truck driver was okay, as his air bag had protected him. Though I had been knocked out, I appeared to be okay. But Bob was in serious trouble.

In just a few minutes the fire department arrived and, as they were cutting Bob out of the wreckage with the "jaws of life," a life-line helicopter arrived, too. They loaded Bob into the helicopter, and off it went to the Columbia Hospital. In the commotion, I had unloaded my bags and placed them at the side of the road, realizing that a wrecker would be coming to tow away the car. I was still a bit dazed by it all and I sat down along the road next to my bags. It was then that the fire department folks realized I had been in the accident, too. They offered me a ride to the hospital to get checked out (which I foolishly refused). Someone took me to Broadway Christian Church (I don't remember who), where word had been received of the accident. I know I greeted the group, but I have no idea what I said to them. Somehow, I got back to the airport and flew home either that night or the next morning. I don't remember anything else about the trip, including whether I preached at Broadway the next morning or not.

Bob died a month later. He remained comatose until he died, although the first responders had done everything they could to give him a chance. I felt so badly for Gertie, his widow, a delightful person.

I was okay, but deeply shaken. Since the "flying in the clouds" incident, I had felt an uncritical sense of being protected by God, but how could I claim special protection when I walked away from this accident and my companion did not? Moving forward I felt a sense of vulnerability that often presses on me (as it does on most of us humans), along with a bit of survivor's guilt, I suppose. I have continued to feel that *ultimately* I will be okay, because I reside in the everlasting arms of God, but not in the sense that God will physically intervene to protect me from the daily risks that living implies. This accident laid bare for me the fact that one must navigate the gap between one's childhood faith and one's adult faith. I think we all have some kind of gap there, large or small, with which we must each wrestle honestly.

Engaging in conversation with someone is natural and normal for me. I had never thought that being in conversation might be distracting to a Disciples volunteer driver ... until then. From that time forward, I insisted on arranging my own transportation whenever I needed a ride.

Another Tragedy

Ralph Glenn was regional minister of the Southwest Region (Texas and New Mexico). It had been my pleasure to participate in his commissioning to regional ministry in 1998. Like so many who knew him, I deeply appreciated Ralph's ministry and his personal warmth. He was very capable in so many ways.

However, Ralph had addiction issues that were known only to a few, including me. A few leaders from the Southwest Region and I staged an intervention in my office in August 2000 to confront him about these behaviors and to seek to work with him to make a change. I understood myself to be Ralph's pastor in a very real way.

In 2002, Ralph took his own life. That was a tragedy for the Southwest Region and for all who knew and loved Ralph. Frankly, it hit me like a ton of bricks. I had just been to Ft. Worth the week before to participate in Ken Teegarden's funeral (less a tragedy, as he was advanced in years, but nonetheless a personal loss for me as well as a loss for the whole church) and now, here I was participating in a funeral for a relatively young and active colleague. Every local pastor knows the pain of burying their members who have become friends. The experience is no different for those in regional and general ministry.

Chapter 9

Ecumenical and Interfaith Engagements

As GMP, I was expected to participate in various ecumenical bodies. We Disciples have been instrumental in the formation of almost every ecumenical body in North America and the world. In fact, the historical record of Disciples in the ecumenical movement is legendary.

We were among the founding members of the old Federal Council of Churches of Christ in America in 1908 and of its successor, the National Council of Churches of Christ in the USA, in 1950. We were also among the founders of the World Council of Churches in 1948. Disciple Rev. Roy G. Ross served as general secretary of the National Council of Churches from 1954–1963. Disciples minister Joan Brown Campbell served as general secretary of the National Council of Churches for many years, and the remarkable Disciples lay leader, J. Irwin Miller (chair of the Cummins Diesel Corporation), served as president of the National Council of Churches from 1960 to 1963.

Every GMP since 1968 has participated deeply in the life of the Councils. Disciples have also given leadership, through the National Council, to Church World Service; to the programs for immigrants, refugees, and migrants (through Jennifer Riggs of DHM); and to so many other ecumenical efforts. At one time (in 2007), Disciples ministers held the executive leadership roles for three national ecumenical groups in the United States simultaneously: the National Council of Churches (Michael Kinnamon), Churches Uniting in Christ (Patrice Rosner) and Christian Churches Together in the USA (me).

Whenever a local council of churches or similar organization has been formed, if there were Disciples in that place, they were nearly always key players in the founding. In fact, the Disciples' engagement in ecumenical councils and organizations of all kinds is far disproportionate to our size. Christian unity was a core value for Disciples from the beginning, and that has been evident ever since.

In 1993, I attended my first board meeting of the National Council of Churches in New York City at NCC headquarters (nicknamed "the God Box"). Soon after, I was asked by General Secretary Joan Brown Campbell to serve as vice president of the Council and chair of the Board of the National Ministry Unit, and I did so gladly. Of all the "heads of communion," I believe my attendance at NCC Board meetings and other occasions was among the most regular.

I also made it a point to attend World Council of Churches meetings when they occurred in New York (in those days, there was a U.S. Office of the WCC that brought United States church leaders together regularly). Being elected to the Central Committee of the World Council in 1998 meant spending a week annually in various places around the world (most often, Geneva, but also Berlin and Harari). My successors have continued to do the same.

These sorts of trips are not junkets. They provide opportunities to be regularly updated on what is happening around the world, from many and various perspectives, and to exchange ideas and resources with leaders of churches on every continent. The National Council of Churches (U.S.A.) includes more than thirty-eight communions with forty million members, and the World Council includes three hundred and fifty communions with more than half a billion members of every imaginable stripe (including Anglican, Catholic, Orthodox, Protestant, and Pentecostal).

My role with these organizations also made it possible to meet fascinating people from many walks of life, from the White House to South Africa, Cuba, the Middle East, and China. My successors have continued this tradition of ecumenical leadership.

The 'Head of Communion' Retreat of the National Council of Churches

When I joined the National Council of Churches Board in 1993 as a head of communion,[1] several efforts had been made through

---

[1] "Head of communion" is the term used in worldwide ecumenical circles to designate the person who is the administrative/spiritual head of a denomination. In the case of Disciples, it is the GMP; in the case of other denominations, it may be called presiding bishop, or general secretary, or something similar.

the years to establish an annual Heads of Communion Retreat for the heads of NCC member churches. In 1995, Gay Reese and I had just started the Bethany Project among Disciples (which featured regional minister retreats of forty-eight hours over three days, including twenty-four hours of silence). I thought this would be an excellent model for NCC heads of communion as well. So, I volunteered to try anew to start such an annual heads of communion retreat, and General Secretary Campbell gave me the green light.

To my great pleasure, several of the heads of communion picked up on the idea. I think it was an idea whose time had come because there was so much stress in all the churches in the face of the massive cultural shifts that had been occurring, and so much cynicism and hostility directed toward denominational leaders, that many recognized the need for time away for prayer, reflection, mutual support, and sharing of ideas and best practices.

So, in 1998, eight heads of communion gathered at the College of Preachers (part of the National Cathedral complex in Washington D.C.) for retreat. The following year we did a Bethany Project-style retreat, with Gay and me serving as retreat leaders. Apparently, word had gotten around about the first year's retreat, because fourteen came to the 1999 retreat.

We all appreciated the twenty-four hours of silence with the "run" of the cathedral, so that we could sit individually high in the balcony or in the side chapels, or wherever we wished, to pray. The grounds were free to roam also. The sharing that followed our time of silence was deep and significant. These leaders of churches were no assemblage of "bureaucratic hacks," but a group of deeply rooted Christians committed to the mission of Christ and the health of their communions.

Perhaps the highlight of the 1999 retreat was a foot-washing ceremony. This was offered as a substitute for taking communion together, as some of our churches do not allow taking communion together (a great loss for me as a Disciple, because we will take communion with *anyone* who claims Christ). We all understood that some traditions wish to reserve taking the Lord's Supper together until we manifest a more visible unity than we do at present. I will never forget having my feet washed by the presiding bishop of the Episcopal Church, Frank Griswold. Likewise, it was a significant moment for me to wash the feet of my American Baptist colleague, Dan Weiss.

Some folks may find it hard to believe that heads of communion could engage in twenty-four hours of silence, but it was a welcome relief for those of us who were always expected to "have a word" for every occasion and situation. During the time of silence, participants were encouraged to engage in any of the following as they wished: centering prayer, an hour of spiritual counsel/direction, private pilgrimage around sacred spots of the Cathedral, journaling, Bible study, meditation walks, and exercise. At the completion of the twenty-four hours (including silent meals), the group debriefed by sharing what insights or personal experiences of the Spirit they had had during the time.

Over the years 1998–2003, the heads of the American Baptist Churches (Dan Weiss, then Roy Medley), the Church of the Brethren (Stan Noffsinger), the Christian Methodist Episcopal Church (Bishop Nathaniel Linsey), the Disciples (me), the Episcopal Church (Frank Griswold), the Evangelical Lutheran Church of America (George Anderson, then Mark Hanson), the International Council of Community Churches (Michael Livingston), the Moravian Church (Bob Sawyer–South, Burke Johnson–North), the Presbyterian Church U.S.A. (Clift Kirkpatrick), the Reformed Church in America (Wes Granberg-Michaelson), the United Church of Christ (John Thomas), the United Methodist Church (Bishop Bill Grove, then Bishop Mel Talbert), and the Orthodox Church in America (Father Leonid Kishkovsky) participated regularly. It was a sweet fellowship that I miss to this day.

The annual retreat has continued over the years since my departure (pausing only for Covid), which pleases me greatly. Sharon Watkins once told me, "Every single one of us [heads of communion] told our successors, 'If there's one thing you must do, it's participate in the HOC retreat.'" Terri Hord Owens has likewise affirmed it as an important resource to her and her head of communion colleagues.

The World Convention

The World Convention is a gathering of people from all three "streams" of the original Stone-Campbell Movement (Disciples, Christian Churches/Churches of Christ [also called Independent Christian Churches], and Churches of Christ). The gathering occurs every few years and, as previously mentioned, I attended my first one in San Juan, Puerto Rico, as a Florida State Christian Youth Fellowship representative.

After the Restructure of 1968, Disciples' interest in the World Convention waned. It had been seen as the one place where the three "cousins" could remain in dialogue in the hope that reunification, or at least a lessening of growing hostilities between the three groups, could be fostered. However, the Churches of Christ had separated from the larger Movement in the late 1800s, and the Independents had begun separating from the Disciples in the 1920s, and we had all continued to move further away from each other throughout the mid-twentieth century so that any kind of reunification had begun to appear to be hopeless as hostility between us grew in the face of our isolation from one another.

The hostility was fed by the fact that *some* Independent Christian ministers were actively seeking to take congregations out of the Disciples. Many of us Disciples felt that "stealing Disciples congregations" had become the "new church program" of the Independent Christians from the 1950s through the 1980s. This perception was often reinforced by false claims around our Restructure processes, including the claim that "the Disciples denominational organization was trying to get the deeds to the properties of local congregations" (untrue). The fewer opportunities we had for open and positive interaction with each other, the greater the hostility became.

We Disciples are dyed-in-the-wool ecumenists, believing that all Christians are made one by our common commitment to Christ and our common dependence on God's grace. We cooperate with and engage in dialogues with Christian groups that hold very different theological and ecclesial assumptions (including, for example, the Roman Catholic Church). Yet, there was this growing rift between us Disciples and our cousins of the Stone-Campbell Movement. This seemed to many Disciples to be incongruous.

When I was asked to serve on the board of the World Convention, I agreed to do so, even though most Disciples leaders had given up on the Convention as a useful engagement. As one who had family members on both sides of the Disciples/Independent lines, this ugly church family fight was well known to me. I felt that my serving on the board might demonstrate a new openness to dialogue and friendship. I was encouraged because New Zealanders Lyndsay and Lorraine Jacobs (who had become dear friends during my Tennessee sojourn, as their office was in Nashville) were the new co-general secretaries of the World Convention. Even more significant, a young generation of church historians representing the three streams (Newell Williams, Paul Blowers, and Doug Foster) had become friends.

So, in one of my first board meetings, I made a statement:

> I believe the time has come for us to *actively* seek reconciliation between the three streams of the Stone Campbell Movement. Further, I believe this reconciliation will best be approached in a spirit of confession. Over the past fifty years, we of the three streams in North America have lied about one another. We have related to one another on the basis of distorted "histories" and false assumptions and impressions. We have often sought to "save" one another as though one is saved by one ecclesiology or another rather than by faith in Jesus Christ. Thus, we have brought pain and damage to one another and to the whole body of Christ. I am not suggesting that we will reunite organizationally, but that we ought to recognize each other as fully brothers and sisters in Christ and be friends.

The rest of the statement can be found in my files at the Disciples of Christ Historical Society. The statement was met with shock on the part of some, but welcomed by others, including Dr. Henry Webb, a church historian from the Independent Christian tradition who became a dear friend. There was enough support for the idea that a "Stone-Campbell Dialogue" was created, in which several individuals from each of the three streams met together at various sites around North America for the next several years.[2] Robert Welsh provided administrative support for these meetings, which began in 1999 and continued through 2005.

Although the hoped-for formal reconciliation did not result, friendships were developed, written study resources were produced, and the tensions between the three streams lessened greatly. Part of this lessening of tensions occurred, it must be admitted, because younger leaders of the three groups were no longer interested in

---

[2] The division and rancor that had marked the relationships of the three Stone-Cambell groups in North America had not been so pronounced in other parts of the world, so this was primarily a North American problem which begged a North American solution. So, a separate dialogue, outside of the World Convention itself, was deemed appropriate. Still, the World Convention leadership supported the idea, and the Jacobs often attended the dialogues.

the old internecine issues, and were thus content to let the three groups move forward separately, without relationship or reference to our common histories. But there were new relationships of trust built as well.

Memorable Ecumenical and Interfaith Occasions

On the one hand, being GMP was the hardest work I ever did in my life. Trying to hold things together while also trying to move things forward demands everything a leader has these days. One must draw on every ounce of experience, skill, and talent one has while looking to colleagues, friends, and the Holy Spirit for guidance and strength. It is truly exciting when one sees how one has contributed to positive change (sometimes with public acknowledgment, sometimes in total anonymity). But one's shortcomings also become all too apparent, of course. A GMP, like any pastor, must depend on so many others, because no one person has everything that is needed by him- or herself.

All this said, there are some things about being a head of communion that are pretty awesome. I'll name a few of the occasions that were memorable for me.

Visiting the White House

Not every president of the United States is open to having progressive clergy visit the White House. I was never invited by George H. W. Bush or George W. Bush (nor were the presiding bishops of their own Episcopal and United Methodist communions). In large measure, of course, this was because we church leaders often disagreed with presidential policies (especially in the cases of the Iran-Contra affair and the Iraq war). However, Bill Clinton often invited progressive clergy to visit and even to offer counsel. Early in my tenure, I was invited to a White House breakfast of religious leaders, where I met Al and Tipper Gore and Hillary and Bill Clinton for the first time.

Soon after, I was invited to participate in a ceremony on the White House lawn. I was sitting just twenty feet or so from the table where Yitzhak Rabin, and Yasir Arafat famously shook hands in front of President Clinton and signed a peace agreement.

I was also part of a small delegation of six or seven heads of communions invited to the Oval Office to offer counsel regarding the situation in Haiti and the custody case involving the Cuban child, Elian Gonzales. The president was very generous with his time, giving us perhaps thirty minutes.

To a sign painter's son, these were heady occasions. The White House is an impressive place, no matter *who* is president. I had mixed feelings of, "What in the world am I doing here?" and, "Wow, this is cool!" Visits to the White House came several times, but they never became routine. There was always a "gee whiz" factor, and one had to be careful to navigate these feelings lest one be "used" in one way or another by politicians.

Dinner with Carl Sagan

Another exciting opportunity came in the form of an invitation from Joan Brown Campbell to join a few others in a dinner party with Carl Sagan. As an amateur astronomer (emphasis on *amateur*), this was almost more than I could stand. When introducing ourselves, my temptation was to tell Dr. Sagan, "I have a computer-driven Meade Schmidt-Cassegrain telescope with a ten-inch aperture." Fortunately, I remembered an experience I'd had many years before when I set myself up for extreme humbling in a conversation with Mother Theresa, so I kept my astronomical passions to myself.

Sagan was an impressive individual in person, just as he was on television in his famous series *Cosmos*. Many referred to him as an atheist, but he was clearly (and by his self-description) an agnostic and, I would say, a seeker (as every scientist should be). In a predinner conversation that included Father Leonid Kishkovsky (of the Orthodox Church in America), it became clear that Sagan was conversant with a number of foundational Christian theological doctrines.

Lunch with Pope John Paul II

The year 2000 was celebrated as a Year of Jubilee by the Roman Catholic Church. Robert Welsh (then the Disciples ecumenical officer) had many friends in the Vatican, partly because of our Disciples–Roman Catholic Dialogue but also because of his connections through the World Council of Churches. The Jubilee Celebration in Rome was set for the week between Christmas and New Years. Robert and I were invited to attend and to stay in the newly constructed *Domus Sanctae Marthae* (newly built by John Paul II to house the church's cardinals during papal election processes), thirty feet across the brick pavement from the Sistine Chapel.

We spent nearly a week as the guests of the Vatican. During that time, we got a private tour of the Sistine Chapel from the Cardinal who was head of the Pontifical Council for Ecumenism, we ate in the guest hall with various Catholic leaders, and we spent evenings out on the town exploring Rome (becoming familiar with members of the Swiss Guard who let us in and out of the Vatican's Sistine gate).

On the day of the Jubilee Celebration, we were taken to the Papal Basilica of St. Paul Outside the Walls, a massive Cathedral rivaled only by St. Peter's itself. There were thousands of people all around the Cathedral, hoping to catch a glimpse of the general minister and president (that was my joke to Robert). They were awaiting the Pope's arrival, of course, and he came the short distance from the Vatican by helicopter.

Including Robert and me, there were perhaps two dozen representatives from churches around the world. Among the others were the Ecumenical Patriarch Bartholomew I, Archbishop of Constantinople, and the Archbishop of Canterbury, who, with the Pope, tapped on the Jubilee Door of the Cathedral, breaking through the bricks that had been placed over that door twenty-five years before at the end of the last Jubilee Celebration. The three other Basilicas had already been "opened" several days before, but January 18, the beginning of Week of Prayer for Christian Unity, was chosen by John Paul II as the day the holy door of St. Paul's would be opened. After the pope opened the ceremonial door, our procession of representatives of churches from Europe and North America entered the Basilica. It was my great honor to assist in the liturgy with a reading.

After the Jubilee Celebration at St. Paul's, the representatives were taken back to the Vatican, where the Pope had a lunch prepared for us. It was a grand day, indeed.

Meeting Andrew Young and J. Irwin Miller

In 1994, soon after becoming GMP, I became friends with J. Irwin Miller, then in his mid-eighties, retired CEO of Cummins Engine Company, a well-known Disciples churchman who had served as the first lay president of the National Council of Churches in 1960-1963. Once a year or so, I would sit in Dr. Miller's living room in

Columbus, Indiana, and discuss the church and the world with this brilliant man (who was the prime force in building Christian Theological Seminary's facilities in 1965 as well as making Columbus an architectural mecca). It was always personally thrilling to sit in his guest chair partly because Dr. Miller was such a formidable discussion partner and partly because I knew that many U.S. presidents—and other political and cultural leaders of the United States and the world of the previous forty years—had sat in this very chair to discuss the affairs of the day.

On one such occasion, Dr. Miller spoke of how leaders of some mainline Christian denominations of the National Council and some U.S. business leaders had met together with some regularity in the 1960s to discuss issues and seek partnerships between the churches, businesses, and government for the sake of the common good. It sounded like an interesting idea, and I took it as a suggestion upon which I might follow up.

I mentioned to Dr. Miller that Andrew Young—who had served as Dr. Martin Luther King Jr.'s lieutenant; then as a congressman, U.S. ambassador to the United Nations, and mayor of Atlanta; and *then* as founder of Good Works (an organization that sought to develop business between the United States and Africa)—would likely be a good partner in such an undertaking. Dr. Miller thought this was a good suggestion and mentioned that he had never met Andrew Young and wished that he could.

Andrew Young was born in New Orleans in 1932, son of a middle-class African American family (his father was a dentist and his mother a teacher). He had to travel out of his neighborhood to attend a segregated public school. Eventually he attended Howard University and then Hartford Theological Seminary, becoming an ordained minister of the United Church of Christ. As a young man, he worked as a pastor in Georgia and led voter registration drives. Before joining Dr. King and the Southern Christian Leadership Conference, Andrew Young served on the staff of the National Council of Churches' youth department in New York from 1957 to 1961. I became acquainted with him when he served as president of the National Council of Churches in the late 1990s. I was at first, admittedly, star-struck to be chatting with this Civil Rights icon, but he immediately asked me to call him Andy, and we quickly found common ground as we shared stories of our calls to ministry.

In 2000, having spoken with J. Irwin Miller, I scheduled an appointment with Andy at his office in Atlanta to discuss Dr. Miller's idea and to invite him to meet with Dr. Miller at his home in Columbus (travel was difficult for Irwin at this point, in 2001, at the age of ninety-one). I also invited Robert Welsh to join us. We found a date agreeable to all of us and met in J. Irwin Miller's front room on May 9. It was fascinating to watch these two lions of industry, government, and social justice meet and identify mutual friends, memories, and hopes for the future.

After that meeting, I invited two other heads of communion friends (John Thomas of the United Church of Christ and Wes Granberg-Michaelson of the Reformed Church in America) into the conversation, and we made plans for another meeting in Atlanta at Andy's offices. Unfortunately, soon after the meeting in Columbus, Andy was diagnosed with cancer and had to undergo a very difficult surgery. His recovery was long and complicated, and by the time he was feeling better, I was leaving the OGMP. I regretted not being able to see this project through to bring together current leaders of church, government, and business. It was a different time than the 1960s when Dr. Miller was doing this as a leader of church and industry. Perhaps it would not have been possible to create such an alliance after 2001, but it would have been worth a try. Dr. Miller died in 2005 at the age of ninety-five. Dr. Young is still going as of this writing at ninety-one.

One other word about Andrew Young. When we were visiting about our personal backgrounds, he told me that he had received his call to ministry while spending a few days at the Southwest Region's Lake Brownwood Christian Retreat in Brownwood, Texas. I have often shared this story with regional ministers and others who labor to provide camp and conference experiences for our young people (and our not-so-young). One never knows when a "future Andrew Young" is in our midst and seeking a call.

The World Council of Churches

The World Council of Churches is a remarkable fellowship. It includes many wonderful spiritually and intellectually brilliant people. Serving on Central Committee—composed of one hundred and fifty members and seven presidents from around the world and always having many observers and visitors present—is an opportunity to meet church leaders from every continent (except Antarctica ... there are no penguins on Central Committee!). Admittedly, the meetings can be long, as all parts of the worldwide church are represented on every issue (the first session may seem especially long if one has been traveling overnight by airplane to attend the meeting from another continent). But hearing all these perspectives is so important, and the opportunities to visit with colleagues over (incredibly strong) coffee during breaks are always worth it.

The Central Committee meetings are most often located in Geneva, Switzerland, at WCCC headquarters, but sometimes the gatherings are in other locations. A particularly memorable Central Committee meeting for me was in Berlin, where I had the opportunity to visit the Brandenburg Gate, the new Reichstag, remnants of the old Berlin Wall, the "spy bridge" in Potsdam (where prisoners were sometimes exchanged between East and West), and the jagged remains of a church in downtown Berlin commemorating the destructive bombing of World War II.

The World Council General Assemblies, which occur about every seven years, are marvelous occasions of worship and inspiration, with incredible colors, sounds, and cultural expressions from every corner of the world. In 1998, the Assembly was in Harari, Zimbabwe. Tom Jewell and I roomed together at a hotel near the university campus where the Assembly was held. I bought several very heavy soapstone sculptures, wondering if the plane would get off the ground when we headed for home since I knew I wasn't the only delegate on board who had "over-bought" soapstone! (We made it.)

During the Assembly, Nelson Mandela, then president of South Africa, was a featured speaker. At the appointed time of his arrival, the air was electric with anticipation. Now advanced in age and showing the physical effects of his harsh treatment during the apartheid struggles, the great man entered as the drums were beating and he came down the center aisle gently dancing to the rhythm. The Africans in the hall (most of those present on this day) were overjoyed.

As an American, a citizen of a country that has too seldom been on the right side of history in matters of colonialism, I was extremely excited to see Mandela, but also anticipating a well-deserved scolding for those of us from the Global North whose governments had been slow to oppose apartheid. What we got instead was an eloquent statement of gratitude for the missionary schools our churches had supported. President Mandela spoke of how he would never have been able to lead an anti-apartheid movement or attain any office in South Africa had it not been for those schools that had taught him, a dirt poor and oppressed child, how to read and write. It was the most gracious statement of genuine gratitude one could imagine, and it brought tears to the eyes of nearly every white church leader in the crowd (as we were familiar with our own nations' and churches' history of colonialism). What a moment and memory.

I also attended a government reception (not a function of the Council itself) where we met Zimbabwe's President, Robert Mugabe. He also had learned how to read and write in missionary schools, and while he led the independence movement that had freed then-Rhodesia from the British Empire, he was as different from Mandela as night and day. Mandela sought to reconcile Black South Africans with those who had been their oppressors (and his), bringing the possibility of real democracy and a better life for all. Mugabe used his position to increase his own power and wealth at the expense of *all* Zimbabweans.

There before us were two extremely different human responses to the attainment of power. Would that Mugabe had been a Mandela. Would that Africa had never been subject to the colonialism that fostered oppression and autocracy.

The Attack on The World Trade Center

Mindy, Laura (then living in New York City), and I were in St. Petersburg, Florida, at my parents' home on September 11, 2001, when the World Trade attack occurred. I was watching TV and saw the news alert flash onto the screen. The first airliner (American Flight 11) had just crashed into the North Tower. No one knew yet whether it was an accident or an actual attack.

Laura had become a United Airlines flight attendant. I called for her (and everyone else) to come into the living room to see what had happened. As we watched in horror, the second plane crashed into the South Tower (United Flight 175). This was traumatic for all of us to watch, but especially for Laura, who was based in New York City for United. She soon began making calls to find out who of her colleagues might have been on Flight 175. Then, American Flight 77 crashed into the Pentagon and, soon after, United Flight 93 crashed in Somerset County, Pennsylvania. Anyone who was alive and aware of the world around them knows this tragic story and where they were when they heard about it.

All airlines were grounded, so we kept the car we had rented in Tampa and drove home to Indianapolis. (I will always be grateful to the car companies for allowing people to keep their rented vehicles to get home.) Laura was home with us for a few days until the airlines (including United) could fly again. We were glad for some time to process the events with her. We were so proud of Laura when she went back to work. Flying out of LaGuardia each day right over the smoldering remains of the Trade Center must have taken an amazing amount of courage on her part. I know I wasn't eager to fly anywhere for a while.

Of course, the attack led to a wave of Islamophobia in the United States, never mind that a significant number of innocent Muslims had been killed (thirty-one) and the mosque that was on the seventeenth floor of the South Tower had been destroyed in the attack. While I was, of course, mourning the tragic losses that 9/11 represented, I was also concerned about the impact it would have on American Muslims.

The Islamic Society of North America is located just outside Indianapolis, in Plainfield, Indiana. I reached out to the then-president of ISNA, Dr. Sayyid Syeed. As we talked about the horrific events of the day before and the impact it would likely have on Muslim citizens, we decided to make a joint statement in which we condemned terrorism and expressed our sadness for the lives lost. We thought it important for Muslim Americans and Christian Americans to stand together in this time of national tragedy, to acknowledge our loss as a people, and to condemn the barbarism of the terrorist attacks.

We scheduled a press conference at the Islamic Center for a time of day we knew would be best for local news media. We invited television, radio stations, and print media. We hoped we might help avert the typical xenophobic responses that would no doubt marginalize Muslim Americans, as though they or mainstream Islam had something to do with the destruction of the attacks ... the same kind of xenophobic response that created the Japanese American Internment Camps of World War II.

When the appointed time came, two reporters showed up. *Two.* There was nothing about it on local television, and just a small article buried in the back pages of the local newspaper. Period.

It demonstrated to me how we are addicted to fear in this country. Fear draws viewers, listeners, and readers, and thus sells advertising. So, it seems there is seldom interest in telling or reading stories that demonstrate that American Muslims are as disgusted by and fearful of terrorism as any other Americans. This experience is part of what later interested me in a U.S.–Pakistan relations program that I participated in after leaving the OGMP. My friendship with Dr. Syeed continues.

Standing on the Balcony of the Lorraine Motel

In January 2002, the Consultation on Church Union (COCU) had finally yielded a visible expression called Churches Uniting in Christ (CUIC). The inauguration of this new ecumenical body, which included eleven American denominations (including the Disciples, of course), was held in Memphis, Tennessee. Because we were in Memphis, we marched in the footsteps of the sanitation workers who were on strike during Martin Luther King Jr.'s visit in April 1968.

The assassination took place as Dr. King was standing on the balcony of the Lorraine Motel in Memphis. Most everyone who lived in that era remembers the picture of King lying on the balcony, and the Revs. Abernathy, Jackson, and Young all pointing across the way to a boarding house from which the shot had come.

One representative of each of the CUIC denominations was invited to stand on the spot where Dr. King was martyred and to make a brief statement. On the parking lot and street below, several hundred were present to listen. Frankly, I don't remember what I said on that occasion, so touched was I to be standing on that spot. I do remember John Thomas (of the United Church of Christ), who spoke after me, taking off his shoes as he moved to the makeshift podium to speak. It was a very cold day, barely above freezing, but all the rest of us wished we too had thought of removing our shoes on that holy site. That act said more than any words could say. I will never forget standing in that spot, remembering Dr. King's sacrifice.

Chapter 10

My Resignation and Life after GMP

GMPs are typically elected to six-year terms, with a maximum of two. Twelve years is a long time. Dale Fiers, the first GMP, served five years before retiring (1968–1973). Kenneth Teegarden served a full twelve years and retired (1973–1985). John Humbert served one six-year term and retired (1985–1991). Bill Nichols served as interim GMP for twenty-one months and retired. I was elected at forty-five years of age and served until I was fifty-five, having served ten years and three months. I have never understood "call" in terms of a certain number of years. As I understand it, call means one serves as long as one feels called to serve in a given situation and then moves on. "Terms" are an administrative concept and really don't mean much to me other than being an opportunity every so often for the church to decide whether *it* thinks the minister is still called to serve in that situation.

The reasons for my twenty-month "early" departure are complex, interrelated, and deeply personal. Though, let me say at the outset, I feel I left at the *right* time, rather than *early*.

A Personal and Theological Crisis

First, as any recent General Minister and President (GMP) will attest, the role is an incredibly taxing undertaking, in part because the Disciples of Christ structure (including the Office of General Minister and President) was approved in 1968 and implemented as a culmination of a generational perspective that was rapidly passing away. Of course, 1968 was an iconic year of change in American (and world) culture that carried a new perspective and a new way of being that had been developing since the 1950s. As the groundbreaking book *Bowling Alone* (by Robert Putnam) documented, Americans were becoming less loyal to their social institutions, including the church, less willing to trust institutional authority and leadership, and generally moving toward a kind of individualism that made public ministry more difficult in *any* setting, but especially in denominational settings.

Due in large measure to the culture's increasing distrust of leadership (something that had always been second nature to Disciples from the beginning), the office of the General Minister and President was created with great responsibility and practically no formal power or authority. This made *everything* more difficult. I had to depend on *informal power and authority* to accomplish anything.[1] That meant I had to earn the respect and support of Disciples across North America before being able to do much of anything beyond maintaining the status quo.

Having been a local pastor for twenty years and then a regional minister for only three, I was hardly known beyond the communities in which I had served (unlike Dale Fiers, Ken Teegarden, and John Humbert, who had all served in churchwide roles previously). To many of those who had been working in the general church for years, I was an outsider and they were not sure I could be trusted. My ideas were born of recent congregational and regional experience, not general church experience, and these ideas often seemed threatening or radical to some. Thus, I felt the populist route (earning the trust of local Disciples and thus enabling *informal* authority) was the only path available to me. That involved travel to all parts of the church, speaking at regional assemblies, preaching in congregations, being available to regions when they had problems or were making changes of leadership, and responding to every communication from any quarter within the church as quickly as possible.

This meant flying all over North America and, because of our ecumenical commitments, the world. Often, I went to the airport three times a week to catch flights. (I actually tracked this and found that I flew 758,455 miles during my service as GMP.) To stay on top of the ongoing work, on the days I was not traveling, I was most often at the office by 6 or 6:15 AM to get things done before anyone else got there, and I usually left at 5:30 or 6:00 PM.

---

[1] See a brief discussion of formal and informal power and authority in Appendix 1.

I'm not asking for sympathy. I *chose* to work that way and was never able to figure out a better way to do the work that needed to be done. It was both a systemic issue (lots of responsibility, too little formal power or authority) and a personality issue. I had always worked hard in ministry, but this was truly all-consuming.

As the first GMP with children at home, I don't think anyone (including me) realized what the impact would be for a GMP who was a parent in his forties and early fifties. As I said before, what a shock it was when we took our son to the airport to fly to California for his first semester as a college student in the fall of 1993. As I watched the MD-80 back away from the gate with its precious cargo, it hit me like a brick: "My God, he's gone!" For so many years, I had told myself, "So and so is hurting; the church needs this and that and can't wait. ... I'll soon have time to spend with the children, but meanwhile they will understand that my work is really important." But now, there he was leaving. There would never again be time for regularly spending days and evenings with him, witnessing his life events, discussing his days, and playing games with him.

Of course, exactly the same feeling came when, two years later, our daughter went to college in Texas at Texas Christian University. I had apparently learned nothing from my experience of our son's departure. Or, at least, I had gotten in so deep that I had no real idea how I could escape the demands of ministry as GMP.

This is really my only true regret in ministry, becoming attached (addicted) to work and not knowing what to do about it. It is easy to see it now, but at the time I was blinded by my own issues. I began to recognize that, as an adult child of an alcoholic, I was separated from reality by something like a layer of wax paper ... I saw through a "glass darkly." But I didn't know what to do about it. My father's addiction had been to drink; mine was to work. Working too much and too hard gets you a lot more rewards than alcohol, but one is deluded in either case, and both are ultimately destructive to you and your family. Yes, I apologized to the children, and to Mindy, who was so often left to fend for herself, but we will never get back those years.

While I was GMP, a dear aunt died and several of my uncles died. Then, unexpectedly, my father died. He had been seriously ill a few weeks before, and I was unable to get to his bedside because I was out of the country. So now, as he was doing better and seemed to be out of the woods, I was on my way down to St. Pete to see him. But

I stopped over in Atlanta to preach. It was in the wee hours of that Sunday morning that the news came from my brother, "We've lost Dad."

Wait! Wait! I'll be there in a few hours. He can't die without me being there with him! Yes, he could ... and he did. Not long after, my mother died as well. Parents die, of course. That was not the issue. It was the fact that I had not been there for them in their dying days that was so troubling to me.

I had come to a point in my life when I recognized that I was dying spiritually because of the demands of my work and my work addiction. I was not experiencing the abundant life that Christ promises, a life that can be lived only in freedom (not freedom from any job per se, but freedom from *anything* to which we become enslaved, anything that we give control over our life, thus abdicating our responsibility to be free from *any* external fact or circumstance. This addiction was not the church's fault, although the church as a system does reward overworking and thus encourages ministers to become addicted (as do many other nonchurch systems ... it is, in fact, endemic to the American way of life). The responsibility for my work addiction lay squarely on my own shoulders.

While I could not articulate this clearly at the time, at some intuitive, emotional, and spiritual level, I began to understand that I had to break the addiction. But work had become so powerful that staying in the role of GMP would have surely killed me. I needed to get out and away, as surely as a drunk must stop spending days and nights in bars! I knew the God of grace, whom I had loved all my life, was not trying to kill me or punish me. It was me who had taken the office of GMP and turned it into a spiritual death trap.[2] It was me who had to break the chains and escape my enslavement.

My first thought was, "I'll be letting the church down." Of course, that was my first thought! That is always the siren song that calls out to anyone trying to break an addiction: "Stay the course till you are dashed on the rocks!" Addiction fights dirty! Never mind that I had been letting down my family, myself, and (in a real sense) the church itself through my addiction. Thus, *simply recognizing the means to quitting my addiction* was generating guilt in me! The chorus to this song is this: "It all depends on me!" So, now I was becoming God? I was in grave spiritual danger.

---

[2] A favorite book of mine is Gerald May's, *Addiction and Grace* (HarperOne, 2007). If any of this sounds too familiar to you, I commend this book as a great window on the issue, no matter what your own addiction may be.

A Long-Term Systemic Issue

The longer-term issue that had worn me out was the Mission Funding System (how Basic Mission Finance dollars and other gifts were promoted and distributed among the general ministry units, regions, and other church-related organizations that depended on those dollars). The system that had been worked out in the 1960s had worked quite well as long as there were more dollars available each year. But in the 1970s and 1980s, as mission dollars began to shrink in number and in spending power due to inflation, incredible pressure was being put on the system.

Ironically, the mission funding system had been developed to mitigate competition between recipients for mission dollars and to protect congregations from being solicited for gifts from all sides. However, once the available dollars began to shrink, all the BMF-dependent structures of the church (general ministry units, regions, colleges, and seminaries, among others) began to compete for a larger share of the shrinking pie. There was an attempt to fix these issues in 1991 (while I was still a regional minister). However, that system lasted only a couple of years, so by 1994, we were working on it again. But neither could that *new* funding system hold in the face of shrinking dollars ... and *eight regions* pulled out of the system.

Each iteration of the mission funding system required many days of time, energy, and meetings on the part of all the leaders to redesign and implement. Relationships were strained to the breaking point in some cases. The assumption so many leaders still brought to the negotiations, despite the shrinking pie, was "if the system is *really fair*, my ministry will receive more dollars." There was little appetite for any proposals that might have combined some structures to create greater efficiency. It was the typical culture of scarcity, which inevitably leads to competition among otherwise generally excellent leaders. The "commitment to mission" mindset that had created all the various organizations (some many decades ago, some in recent years) began to give way to a survival mindset. It was exactly what I had warned my colleagues against ever since becoming a regional minister.

The new system cobbled together in 2001 effectively ended the Mission Council and the Mission Imperative Fund. Without *any* project capital available, it seemed to me that the transformational processes we had been seeking to implement for the past several years had little hope of continuing. At least *I* couldn't see a way forward at that point, and, having seen some very fine leaders at their very worst, I was discouraged and emotionally exhausted.

Meanwhile, the day-to-day work of the Office of General Minister and President went on and on, relentlessly, and I became increasingly "fried." I felt I was becoming a part of the problems confronting the church rather than a part of the solutions. So, after an emotional and spiritual struggle that lasted several months, an impromptu overnight retreat with several close colleagues (Lori Adams, Alvin Jackson, Michael Mooty, Dan Moseley, and Jim Powell) in mid-March 2003, and conversations with Mindy, I decided to step down. I had no place to go next, really ... but I was in no shape to go anywhere, anyway. I needed a deep, extended rest and time to reflect on what had happened and sort out the causes.

On the way home from that overnight retreat, in the car by myself, I suddenly began whistling! I hadn't whistled for years. Something in my spirit was celebrating because the incredibly difficult decision had been made.

Lori Adams, Patti Case, and Melinda Mains (interim director of communication) helped me plan how the announcement would be made. It was important that the word get out to as many as possible at the same time so as to leave little room for speculation (there was no scandal, no cover-up, nothing unseemly ... I was simply exhausted). A few days later in March, I called a meeting of the people who worked at Disciples Center and announced my intention to step down at the Charlotte, North Carolina, General Assembly that fall (2003); an announcement went out to the church; and there was a press release, followed by this letter of resignation:

> Dear Friends in Christ,
>
> As of General Assembly in Charlotte, October 17–21, I will have completed more than ten years of service as General Minister and President. These have been remarkable years. The church has been weathering a tumultuous period of cultural change which continues unabated. Although we began on the frontier some 200 years ago, our organizational Design was conceived and implemented in the 1960s. While I believe our core values (taking the

Bible seriously, Christian unity, faith and reason, freedom) remain exactly on target today, some of our traditional ways of functioning have proven inadequate to the challenges of the 2000s.

While my second term of service does not conclude until August of 2005, I feel that I have completed the work that I was called to do, and I believe "call" supersedes "term." I have prayed much and consulted with my spouse and a few friends in seeking to discern what I should do now. It is, therefore, with a profound sense of gratitude to God and the church for the opportunity to serve these ten years that I tender my resignation effective at the conclusion of the Charlotte General Assembly.

Some will interpret my resignation negatively, but let me say clearly that, while I admit I am tired, I am neither discouraged nor depressed. I'm just done. I believe that 2020 Vision ("to become a faithful, growing church that demonstrates true community, deep Christian spirituality, and a passion for justice") is right on target, and I am excited and energized to see us rising to the challenge of our goals to start 1,000 new congregations, to revitalize 1,000 of our existing congregations, to develop the new leadership needed, and to become an anti-racist/pro-reconciling church. Insofar as my tiredness is concerned, I am simply applying the advice I have preached to my colleagues over the years: Take responsibility for your own health and well-being.

I felt called in 1993 to help heal divisions in our church, to help restore trust in regional and general church leadership, to begin to address some of the systemic issues that have sometimes interfered with our effectiveness in mission. I will close my service as GMP with a sense of satisfaction that, while we are still a shrinking church, we are a healthier and stronger church in many ways and that we will soon become a growing church again. I take pleasure in my own small part in helping increase trust in the midst of our tremendous diversity, in the development of the "process of discernment" concept, in raising the quality of regional ministers, in diagnosing the implications of the cultural shift in North America, and in casting 2020 Vision.

I have seen my task, in part, as adapting our structures to our changed (some would say "postmodern") cultural context. However, I feel that we have adapted and pushed our vintage 1960s structures about as far as they can go. We need to take a fundamentally new look at how we can mobilize for our mission as a whole church.

For a time, I thought perhaps I was called to lead us in this period of review and transition. However, I think I am too tired and too identified with our current structures to effectively lead in this task. In addition, I think it will take four years, rather than the two years remaining in my term, to address and implement the needed change. I don't believe the church can afford for me to spend two years as a "lame duck" leader. Thus, I prefer to step aside and allow the process of review and transition to begin immediately.

This has been a marvelous ten years for me personally in so many ways. I have been pushed to grow in ways I never imagined. The friendships developed across the life of this church and of the church ecumenical will bless me all my days, and I have had the opportunity to be in so many wonderful places and to participate in so many wonderful events. It has been my privilege to see firsthand the marvelous mission that is accomplished by this church across North America and around the world every day. So, while I will have a chance to say it again in Charlotte, I want to take the opportunity to say now also, thank you for your trust, your prayers, your friendship, and your many kind expressions of support for me and my family.

I am not sure what I will be doing after October. I am clearer that my current call is completed than I am about what my next call might be. But you know I will be doing something in the church to contribute toward the realization of 2020 Vision. I'm not "abandoning ship," I'm just moving from the wheelhouse to the engine room—with maybe just a little "shore leave" on the way.

Within a week or so, Moderator Alvin Jackson will announce a process to lead us in the next steps in our journey as the Christian Church (Disciples of Christ). I ask for your continued prayers even as I shall be praying for you and this church we love.

Grace and peace, Dr. Richard L. Hamm

At the Assembly, I tried to explain to those gathered something of why I was stepping down. I could only name exhaustion at that point because I hadn't had a chance to really think through and identify all the reasons. It was complicated. Drawing on an old Rolaids TV commercial, I joked at the end of my statement to the Assembly, "How do *you* spell relief? I spell it 'H-O-B-G-O-O-D'!" Thus, Chris Hobgood, who had been selected by the General Board to stand for election as the twenty-one-month interim, was elected later that day.

I remember the morning after the Charlotte Assembly well. Mindy and I got up, packed, and walked out of the Convention Hotel. Frankly, I felt like a great weight had been lifted off my shoulders. Rather than feeling sadness, I was feeling satisfaction that the 2020 Vision was in place and that I had done everything I knew how to do to help the church prepare for the twenty-first century.

I still loved and appreciated my church, the Disciples of Christ, and the regional and general leaders who, together with me, had failed to find a way through the mission funding crisis (they were all good people, most were excellent leaders, and I considered nearly all of them friends), but I knew that after ten years, three months, and two days, I was done. I had felt called into this ministry, and now I felt called *out* of this ministry. I was "taking the wings of the morning" secure in the knowledge that "God's hand was leading me and holding me fast" (Psalm 139:9–10).

We drove from Charlotte to our son's home near Raleigh to spend a night and then drove home to Indianapolis. We had no idea what I would be doing next or where I would be doing it. But I had managed to escape the sense of obligation and the guilt that systems use to keep good leaders in the saddle until they have been ridden into the ground. It was time to rest.

We had enough money saved to enable me to take three months off to recover. During that time, a seminary (not of our denomination) called to ask if I might be interested in its presidency; "Thanks but no thanks" was the only responsible answer I could give. There was an inquiry about the possibility of doing an interim ministry at National City Christian Church, but my mother-in-law was in the final stages of her life, and Mindy and I needed to be near her in Indiana. I could have looked for a regional ministry somewhere, work I had enjoyed so much, but unlike my predecessors who had *retired* from the OGMP, I felt that no matter where I might have served in regional or general church life, I would have been in my successor's way. (This was my own feeling and *none* of my successors has *ever* made me feel like I was *in the way* or unwelcome to serve in any way I might feel called.)

Late in January 2004, after I'd had three months or so to rest, Rick Spleth, regional Minister of Indiana, called and asked if I might be interested in being interim senior pastor of West Street Christian Church in Tipton, Indiana. By this time, I had begun thinking about doing consulting, and I was wondering if, having been out of the congregation for thirteen years doing regional and general work, I still understood how congregations work. There couldn't have been a better place for me to land than West Street! The congregation had enjoyed excellent leadership in years past and was a foundationally healthy place.[3] It felt like home, with so many warm and supportive folks (not all of whom agreed with me on everything ... so it also kept me interested).

It was just an hour from home, so I could serve without moving. I spent a most enjoyable year or so with these wonderful folks. Most importantly, I realized that I still knew how congregations work (and don't work) and what they needed to be doing to begin adapting to the new context of the twenty-first century.

So, after I had been at West Street for a year (and had left it in the capable hands of my interim associate, Erin Reed Iobst), I called my friend George Bullard, whom we had used as a consultant in the development of a Disciples new church goal. I told him I was thinking of starting a church consultancy and asked him for advice. He immediately replied, "Let's work together!" So, I became a part of the newly forming Columbia Partnership in 2005.

Happily, I had built up a lot of trust within the Disciples and beyond through the years, and so my consulting work grew rapidly and I was soon making a living again while doing something I loved

---

[3] I attribute much of this health to the excellent ministry there of Rev. Rick Hull and to marvelous lay leaders who understood what it means to be the church.

and that I felt fit perfectly with the 2020 Vision, which included the revitalization of existing congregations. My very first consulting client in this new ministry was the Oregon region, whose regional ministers, Cathy and Doug Wirt, kindly invited me to work with them.

For the next fourteen years, I did consulting with congregations and middle judicatories of many mainline denominations, including more than a hundred Disciples congregations and several regions. I wrote a third book, *Recreating the Church* (published by Chalice Press in 2007), in which I laid out many of my ideas and learnings.

Along the way, a new national ecumenical organization was being formed: Christian Churches Together in the USA. In 2007, I agreed to become the part-time executive director of Christian Churches Together in the USA while I continued my consulting work on a somewhat reduced basis. I also agreed to teach Disciples history and polity at Christian Theological Seminary with Dr. Scott Seay, and I taught a few Doctor of Ministry classes (which I still occasionally do, as of this writing).

This all kept me engaged in ministry, but out of the way of my successors (again, not that Sharon Watkins or Terri Hord Owens ever made me feel like I was encroaching). I didn't attend another General Board meeting after 2003 until 2023. I felt very welcome there, and it was fun to be in the board meeting twenty years later watching someone *else* give leadership! (Bless you, Terri Hord Owens!)

In 2012, at the age of sixty-five, I retired from Christian Churches Together in the USA, but I continued consulting, writing, and teaching for another five years, until the age of seventy. Thanks to the Pension Fund of the Christian Church (bless 'em!), Social Security, and other resources, Mindy and I are enjoying time together gardening, camping, practicing amateur astronomy, travel, and—best of all—grandchildren. This has also been a time for volunteer activities that bring me joy and satisfaction.

Volunteer Engagements

Mindy and I are active at Central Christian Church in Indianapolis, our home church since 2003, where I have served as an elder, a trustee, and in various committee chairs and activities. Mindy has also served in various roles in the congregation, including currently being a deacon and coordinator of Central's Free Clothing Ministry.

I have been a trustee for Christian Theological Seminary most of the years since 1999. I went off the board briefly to serve as director of a Lilly Planning Grant in 2004 and was then invited back on the board. I went off the board when I was asked by interim president Bill Kincaid to serve as interim vice president for advancement in 2018, and was then invited back on the board. Each time I returned to the board the twelve-year "clock" was reset. Because CTS provided me with a very real kind of spiritual and emotional transformation when I was a student, I have served these many years with gratitude for the opportunity to give back. One of the joys of trusteeship was the opportunity to meet and get to know a brilliant and delightful woman from Chicago named Terri Hord Owens, who was also a trustee of CTS for several years until becoming the church's GMP.

In 2023, I finished fourteen years as chair and then vice chair of the National City Christian Church Foundation Board. These were years of great transition at National City Christian Church, and it was a joy to work with Senior Pastor Stephen Gentle and to help stabilize the National City Christian Church Foundation's endowment.

Beginning in 2012, I became part of a group called the U.S.-Pakistan Interreligious Coalition (UPIC). This was a group formed under the leadership of an old friend, former director of communications for the United Church of Christ, Bob Chase, and Professor Dr. Mumtaz Ahmed, president of the International Islamic University of Islamabad. Every year or so, we took a small group (ten to twelve) of American Christian clergy (Protestant and Catholic), rabbis, and Muslim educators and imams to meet with Pakistanis. We met first in Oman and then several times in Pakistan (in Lahore and Islamabad). Although a bit unnerving at times (especially when we ventured into the Northwest territories), it was wonderful to be back in Southern Asia and to meet so many wonderful people in Pakistan. When Dr. Mumtaz died, our group stood at his graveside to offer a memorial service (we think this was the first time there was a graveside service in Pakistan that included Muslims, Christians, and Jews). When Covid arrived and extreme instability developed in the Pakistani political picture, our journeys were interrupted, but many friendships remain, and hope remains for greater friendship and cooperation between the various religious groups and our two countries in the future.

As of this writing, I am currently serving as chair of the board of the Center for Congregations (a Lilly Endowment-funded program). I also served for a time on the board of the Center for Interfaith Cooperation in Indianapolis, and for five years was on the advisory board of the National Fund for Sacred Places. I am a member of the Leadership Team for Bread for the World in Indiana. These are all great organizations and have been great engagements for me. Mindy and I also enjoy serving monthly as volunteer ushers at Butler University's Clowes Hall (where, together, we first saw Peter, Paul, and Mary in person in 1968).

My love for the Christian Church (Disciples of Christ), and my passion for our mission, still burn strong. I give thanks to God and to the church for all I have been able to experience and do. Now, I daily give thanks to the Pension Fund of the Christian Church (Disciples of Christ), which has been our partner since I was a seminarian!

Chapter 11

What I Have Learned

Some of these things I already knew, of course, but I have learned them more deeply. Other things were indeed new to me altogether as I became GMP. Here is a summary of some of the key learnings I consider most important.

It Isn't Easy to Be a Disciple

My experience is that it isn't easy to be a *real* Christian, *period*, no matter what your denominational affiliation may be.

Yet, I know many people think it *is* easy to be a Disciple. The argument goes something like this: *"Being Disciples of Christ is easy because it doesn't matter what you believe since the Disciples don't really believe in anything in particular other than a rather vague notion of God and Jesus. You don't have to believe a particular creed, or a particular interpretation of the Bible; there are no rules you must follow; anything goes."*

People who think this way, even if they are members of the denomination, clearly do not understand who we Disciples really are. The word "disciple" means follower or student. To be a follower or student of Jesus is not easy. It means more than memorizing some favorite Bible verses or a creed (though there is nothing wrong with some memorization). It means constantly seeking to better understand the character and intentions of Jesus and constantly seeking to align one's own life with Jesus's life and teachings. This is hard to do for many reasons, including the fact that the scripture does not provide a complete and unambiguous picture of Jesus. Also, there is the human tendency to see scripture through the lens of one's own time and culture and to find ways to make Jesus *agree* with one's own time and culture. Much more challenging is to understand the time and culture of Jesus and then measure one's own time and culture, as well as one's life, against the life and teachings of Jesus. This is made even more difficult by the fact that the New Testament was written many decades after Jesus lived and taught in Galilee, and the New Testament itself was assembled in the 4th century. Therefore, there is already some distortion in the story of Jesus presented in the Bible due to the passage of time and rapid cultural changes in the first few centuries of the Christian era.

Alexander Campbell, one of our earliest leaders (1788-1866), taught that to understand the Bible on its own terms, one must follow seven rules of interpretation. These "rules" included the following (paraphrased): in reading any of the book of the Bible, one must consider the historical circumstances of the book (the order, the title, the author, the date, the place, and the occasion for it); who is speaking and their perspective; the same laws of interpretation that apply to the language of other books must also be applied to the language of the Bible; the meaning of words must be discerned in relation to the context and parallel passages; do not extend the meaning beyond the point being illustrated by the passage; and finally, we must come within an "understanding distance." That is, we must be familiar enough with the whole to be able to understand the meaning of the particular.[1]

The Disciples of Christ of the early 1800s did not agree with the common practice of the church of the Middle Ages, an educated elite interpreting the scripture to uninformed congregations. They thought every true Disciple should equip himself or herself to read the scriptures critically, following those "rules of interpretation," and allowing each other the freedom to arrive at somewhat different conclusions about the meaning of particular passages. As Disciples historian Mark Toulouse put it, we Disciples have a commitment to both "toleration and diversity."

The seven rules were a reflection of Renaissance thinking and were the precursors of what would soon after Campbell be called "Biblical criticism." The growth of Biblical archeology, language sciences, and literary studies in the 19th century and to this day,

---

[1] I recommend Mark Toulouse's good book, "Joined In Discipleship" for a fuller discussion of these seven rules, especially Chapter 2. "Joined In Discipleship," by Mark G. Toulouse, Chalice Press, St. Louis, 1997.

means there is a lot to understand and, most importantly, that some long-standing perceptions of what the scriptures mean must be reconsidered in the light of new evidence. *To be clear, what is today popularly understood to be the plain meaning of particular Biblical passages is sometimes the exact opposite of what the Bible was originally understood to say.*

It is hard to be Disciples of Christ because there is no one person or creed or church tradition that can tell you what to believe or what the Bible means. One must ferret out the meanings for oneself. The good news, however, is that when we do this work together in community (in classes, in discussion groups, in personal conversations, in worship), we can help each other to come to deeper and truer understandings.

Questions I have often heard from newcomers to the Disciples include, "What do Disciples believe? Is there a book I can read to find out?" One of my favorite Disciples members once responded to such a query, "We have a brochure!" That joke had just enough truth to it to strike me as hilarious. We *don't* have volumes of carefully curated beliefs or creeds. What we *have* is the Bible and a way of understanding it that involves hard work, humility, and tolerance. If one is looking to be spoon fed, the Disciples of Christ may not be the best place to be. But if one is looking for spiritual and intellectual honesty that takes the scriptures *seriously*, the Disciples of Christ is a good place to be. We are not the only church/communion/denomination that takes this approach to understanding the Bible and to following Jesus, but we are one when we are at our best.

As I said before, *the New Testament was created by the church rather than the church having been created by the New Testament.* The church in every era must work hard to understand the life and teachings, the message and meaning of Jesus, for each new era, not allowing current cultural biases, or past cultural biases, to define them, but seeking to understand afresh what the implications of the Gospel are for our day. "Church" is not simply a place to be reassured each week, but a place to think critically about the world and what God is seeking to do in it now. This requires humility and tolerance as we all together engage in this ongoing work.

Finally, *as* we together discern the implications of the Gospel and what God is seeking to do in the world *now,* we are expected to align ourselves with the Gospel and *participate in what God is seeking to do*! Easy? Nope. Faithful to our Disciples of Christ calling? Yes!

Family Members and Friends Can't Simply Wait Until We Finally Get Around to Spending Time with Them

Note: If you haven't read, "A Personal and Theological Crisis" in Chapter 9, I suggest you do so to understand this "learning."

The challenge of helping to move our denomination in some ways from the 1950's to the 1990's was so great, I threw myself into the work. On days when I was in Indianapolis, I would be at my desk typically by 6 am and would leave after 5:30 pm. But I was traveling many days, visiting congregations and regions, participating in ecumenical gatherings of various kinds around the globe. This seemed necessary to be equipped to effect change in the Christian Church (Disciples of Christ). But 80-hour work weeks, month after month, year after year, took their toll on my personal health: physical, emotional, and spiritual. My calendar was 98% *filled for two years out* most of the time, so that *my calendar began to feel like a prison*, and I felt like a prisoner.

Meanwhile, while I was barely thinking about things going on close to me and what they meant, significant events and changes came to my immediate and extended family....all in my emotional absence....because my emotional energy was all being directed toward work. Close relatives died, our children changed in all the ways they do between the ages of 16 and 28. Mindy soldiered on, but often alone. My family still loved me, but I began to realize that I missed *so much*. The fact is, no one can hold back time and change, not even in the name of important work, not even in the name of the church's work.

In reflecting on my childhood and adolescence and on my family of origin's dysfunctions, I realize I wanted the church to be a place where people would know and affirm one another, assume the best about each other, and lift the world to where God wants it to be. There is nothing per se wrong with these desires, but one cannot relate effectively to a denomination of three-quarters of a million people as though they are your family. Trying to do so led me to sometimes assume all Disciples were friends and family and to sometimes share personal feelings and humor inappropriately. I thought they would understand my intentions when, in fact, they had no real basis for such understanding because most didn't really know me. It wasn't long into my time as GMP that I realized not everyone "assumed the best" about me and I would have to demonstrate who I was and my hopes for the church. I could mostly accomplish this in ministry with a congregation, and even with a mid-sized region like Tennessee. But one can never embrace or feel the embrace of an entire denomination at once. Being an adult child of an alcoholic is a "gift" that just keeps on giving! I know many others in ministry have similar traits with which they may continue to struggle.

I'm not the first person to make these kinds of mistakes, but I am one. I wish I had established a better work-life balance in all my years of ministry. Being present with actual family and friends is a holy vocation as much as is church work.

The New Church That Is Becoming Must Not Require Unhealth from Either Clergy or Laity

Like so many in my generation, I was *socialized* to work at the expense of my family and person. For so many, this has resulted in the loss of the abundant life Jesus says is supposed to be ours. This must stop for the sake of both the church's faithfulness and its effectiveness.

Almost always when I have interviewed for a new ministry somewhere, an astute search committee will ask, "You have told us about your strengths, can you tell us about your primary weakness." This is what one might call "lobbing a softball pitch right across the plate"....it's just too easy. The "correct" answer is always, "Well, I tend to work too hard." It is the *right* answer because every search committee wants to hire someone who "works too hard." *Everyone* is socialized to think working too hard is a virtue. "Hard work" is fine, but "working too hard" is no virtue – it is out of line with what God asks of us and ultimately leads to illness and setting an example that perpetuates unhealth.

It is not simply a problem for ministers, but for laity as well. There is a cultural "commandment" by which so many of us have been consumed: "Be perfect!" Jesus never said it, and it isn't really in the Bible. Oh, there is that passage, rather inadequately translated in our English Bibles (Matthew 5:48, from The Sermon on the Mount), "Be perfect therefore as your heavenly Father is perfect." But the meaning of "perfect" in the original Greek of the New Testament does not mean "do everything you can do and do it without flaw," which is obviously impossible for us mortals, which is why we all must depend upon God's grace and each other's. "Perfect" in the

Sermon on the Mount is more accurately translated as "live with integrity," or "be whole," or "be healthy." To put it another way, we are called to be human *beings, not* human *doings*! Ministry, that of clergy and laity alike, is intended to be a "team sport." Ministers are not called to *be* the saint (in the cultural sense), but to *equip the saints* (Ephesians 4:12).

Denominational Systems are Subject to the Same Human Condition as Congregations and Individuals Everywhere

I brought many illusions into the office with me. I don't think I was exceptionally naïve, it's simply a matter of fact that there are things you can't know about an organization of any kind until you have a "bird's eye" view. I had experienced a view of us Disciples as a pastor of congregations for 25 years, and then as a regional minister. But I was unprepared for some of what I would discover from my new denominational perch.

First, the good news: there is a lot of good work that gets done by denominational agencies and programs. A *lot* of good work! One thinks of programs like Week of Compassion and Overseas Ministries, and these are, indeed, stellar examples of what denominations can do. But much less "spectacular," yet nonetheless necessary work is also accomplished: ministers, lay leaders, and congregations receive care and support: smart and dedicated Christian leaders help the whole church think about the new things God is doing in the world today regarding contemporary issues; ministers are recruited, educated, and encouraged; camps and conferences educate and inspire young people; congregations receive loans and capital campaign assistance; endowments are created and maintained; core values are affirmed; and so much more.

The bad news: *denominational systems are subject to the same human condition as are congregations and individuals everywhere*! We Disciples are no different from any other church or other human organization in this regard.

This wasn't a total surprise to me, of course, but it was truer than I had allowed myself to admit because so many of my personal mentors and heroes were serving or had served in denominational roles. On a couple of different occasions, as a local pastor involved in facilitating settlements between teachers and school districts, I was amazed at how human the PhD's who run the school systems are.

After one particularly childish outburst by a school administrator, I thought, "Robert Fulghum[2] was right, everything we need to know we learned in kindergarten (or *should* have learned in kindergarten) ... too bad we keep forgetting what we learned."

Anyone who has served on a church board or committee knows the truth of Fulghum's premise *and* knows how easily those kindergarten lessons are forgotten when one moves into an organizational setting at any level. Still, because this *is* the human condition, God has *only* crooked sticks, like the church, with which to work. Yet God can use even crooked sticks, as has been repeatedly demonstrated throughout history. As Dr. King observed, "The arc of the moral universe is long, but it bends toward justice." It bends toward justice slowly because the human condition is real and we are imperfect. But it bends nonetheless, because God raises up leaders and people of courage in every moment to serve the cause of justice and all of God's hopes for the world. Thus, it is essential that we remain committed to God's vision as revealed through the prophets and by Christ, even when our tools, including our institutions (*including the church itself*), seem not to be up to the tasks at hand. As many of my African American colleagues remind us, "God finds a way out of no way."

The fact that the church is something of a crooked stick is not a reason to leave it. It *is* a reason to be realistic in one's expectations of the church, and it is a reason to *nurture* the church into greater health. I find many new ministers are not only surprised by the imperfections of the church but come to hate it because they think the church does not live up to Jesus's hopes for it. *Of course* the church doesn't live up to Jesus's hopes for it...because the church lives within the same human condition we all do. Confusing the church with the actual Reign of God will *always* lead to disappointment and disillusionment.

Indeed, *denominational systems are subject to the same human condition as are congregations and regions and individuals everywhere.* We must not pretend this isn't true, or we can get badly hurt. But good institutions are important, and institutions such as the Christian Church (Disciples of Christ) are worth repairing and improving in any way possible because they are tools that help us participate in God's transformation of the world.

---

[2] Robert Fulghum, *All I Really Need to Know I Learned in Kindergarten* (Random House, 1986).

The Covenant at the Heart of Our Denominational Life is Weak

We Disciples *covenant* to be church together. It is the underlying assumption of our denominational life. The Design of the Christian Church (Disciples of Christ) in the U.S. and Canada puts it this way (Paragraph 2): "Across national boundaries, this church expresses itself in covenantal relationships in congregations, regions, and general ministries of the Christian Church (Disciples of Christ), bound by God's covenant of love. Each expression is characterized by its integrity, self-governance, authority, rights, and responsibilities, yet they relate to each other in a covenantal manner, to the end that all expressions will seek God's will and be faithful to God's mission. We are committed to mutual accountability."

This language of covenant is beautiful, but the covenant remains weak among us. We are much quicker to speak of "rights" than we are to speak of "responsibilities." Each expression (congregations, regions, and general ministry units) is characterized by self-governance. "Self-governance" is fine with me, but self-governance taken too far often looks more like "autonomy." Covenant means we each make decisions that are informed by and take seriously the good of the whole. Autonomy means, practically speaking, that each can do whatever they themselves decide to do whether it serves the whole or not. Autonomy is usually expressed in words that amount to, "You can't tell me what to do."

My plea is *not* for an end to covenant, but for a greater sense of responsibility for each other as congregations, regions, and general ministry units. The New Testament frequently uses "body language" to talk about the church. For example, Paul speaks of the church as the body of Christ in I Corinthians 12:12-26. In verse 26, he says, "If one member suffers, all suffer together with it." It is a call for the whole church to take seriously the suffering of any member within the church and so we should. But in this era of individualism, it is at least as important for the individual part of the body (a congregation, a region, a general ministry unit, etc.) to take seriously the needs of the *larger* body. It is not a change of language that is needed so much as a change in attitude, which first asks, "what does the whole body need and how can we here in this part strengthen the whole body?" Yes, each part of the body has the responsibility to take care of itself, but always in the context of taking care of the whole. A related issue is next.

I have often referred to Disciples polity as a "covenantal polity" rather than a "congregational polity." However, I must admit that "covenantal polity" is more aspirational than descriptive for us Disciples.

The Forces of Affiliation That Initially Held Us Together Have Weakened

We Disciples began as part of a movement. As with all social movements, our shared sense of purpose (reuniting the whole church of Jesus Christ) brought us together in the first place and held us together through some difficult times and challenges. But as our unity of purpose began to fragment and we got caught up in arguments about how we should go about fulfilling our purpose, the Movement itself began to fragment (which led to at least two major divisions within our Stone-Campbell Movement during the nineteenth century).

Today, we face cultural challenges that include anti-institutional attitudes prevalent since the 1960s and a loss of community, which is felt throughout American and Canadian culture as people are increasingly drawn to individual expression through social media and other disembodied, non-communal forms of expression. Where there is strong affiliation and community, it is often based on personal political or social agreement rather than on a common commitment to diversity and tolerance. The church is no less subject to these attitudes than other organizations. More than ever, people who are members of a congregation understand themselves to be primarily affiliated *with that congregation* and give little thought to the larger body that likely birthed and shaped that congregation originally (the denomination). It isn't just us. *Every* mainline Protestant denomination reports this same phenomenon.

Most of the members of the Disciples congregation in one town or city don't even know that they are part of a larger tribe which includes the Disciples congregations in surrounding towns and cities. A few of the members of a congregation may remember attending a regional or general assembly at some point in time, but most members have no clue as to what such meetings are about or why in the world they would want to be present for them. If the minister does not continually educate the congregation about the larger body of which they are a part, or worse, if the minister has antipathy toward the larger body, a congregation very quickly begins to think of itself as the church, whole and complete, right here in (name the place).

Here is just one example of how some ministers have become apathetic toward the larger church. Before about 1970, Disciples ministers tended to go to Disciples colleges or, at least, to Disciples seminaries. Some did attend schools such as Chicago, Yale, or Vanderbilt, but there were also communities of Disciples in those places. Thus, Disciples student ministers met other Disciples student ministers, who became friends and colleagues for life. This was part of the "glue" that held our church together. But by the late twentieth century, many serving as Disciples ministers were coming from other traditions or from non-Disciples schools, and thus knew very few other Disciples ministers. This tendency for so many Disciples ministerial students to go to non-Disciples schools was primarily due to needing to attend a college and seminary close to home due to cost or family responsibilities.

None of this is to fault anyone for where they attend college or seminary in preparation for ministry, it is simply to name the fact that ministers who don't know anyone when they come into a denomination that is new to them may not feel the affiliative force that holds things together and may not appreciate the need to help their congregations (as well as themselves) nurture that sense of being a part of a larger body. We Disciples, in all the expressions of our church (congregations, regions, and general ministry units) need to pay attention to this weakening of affiliative forces and help our members and ministers think of themselves as part of a larger body that supports them and provides opportunities to impact the whole world.[3]

Church Organizations Are Deeply Tied to Generational Practices and Characteristics

Another truth that was reinforced for me early on as GMP is that church organizations are deeply tied to generational practices. This is why institutions rooted in and bound to the characteristics and

---

[3] There are certainly exceptions to this example. Some of the finest and most devoted leaders we have are people who came to us from other traditions. But they tend to be the sort of people who *make it a point* to connect with others in the denomination, they *seek* affiliation.

practices of the Builder generation (born between 1915-30) have been so unattractive in some ways to most people born *after* 1950, and why institutions rooted in and bound to the characteristics and practices of younger generations have been unattractive in some ways to most people born *before* 1950. The new "emergent church", as it has been called, is primarily a phenomenon among people born *after* 1980 and is in some ways unattractive to most people born *before* 1980.

Finding ways that we can all move forward together, no matter which generation is home for us, is one of the greatest challenges facing the church of the 21st century it seems to me. We can't just insist that everyone, older or younger, simply yield to one or the other's style. Somehow, we must figure out how to develop institutions that are able to provide a place for all, that meet most of the needs of all, without completely denying the needs of any. However, this is so difficult because we each become attached to our own style of institution, our own styles of music, worship, education, and so forth, and feel threatened when anyone else asserts their right to have a piece of the cultural and religious space. The "natural" tendency (as the Apostle Paul would use the word "natural") is to fear being taken over, so we push back by refusing any quarter whatsoever. The old do this to the young, the young do this to the old, the straight do this to the gay, racial groups do this to each other, nationalities do this to each other....

This is a huge human challenge for the church, but one we Disciples must figure out, congregationally, regionally, and generally.

As I look back on my beginning as GMP in 1993, I think about the General Cabinet, which included the eleven general ministry unit presidents and me. The general ministry unit presidents were almost all Silent generation folks. When I, as a Baby Boomer, convened our first meeting together, I must have appeared to those Silents like a "bull in a china shop."

Such, of course, was not my intention, but I can see now how some might have felt that way. I had been serving in congregations and seeing how our denominational system was failing in so many ways and so badly needed reform. But from their perspective, their ministries were accomplishing good work and stood as a barrier against the chaotic change that was invading the entire culture and society. We were both right, our denominational system was *both* failing and doing some great work at the same time, but we failed to adequately communicate our points of view to each other. I came increasingly to see the Cabinet as an obstacle to needed change and some of them came increasingly to see me as reckless. Much of our misunderstanding of one another was generational—and, I must confess, that by the time I finished my ten years as GMP, *I began to catch myself resisting the insights of the generation after mine!*

Every Institution Needs to Prepare for Change to Overcome Its Own Resistance to Change

I thought I had been elected to change things. Silly me! Institutions always select new leadership amidst *talk* of wanting change. But what institutions really mean is: "We want you to change our *outcomes* but not *us.*" (Yes, this is the definition of insanity: "doing what you've always done but expecting different results.")

What I soon discovered is that the thing every human institution craves more than life itself is homeostasis: the absence of internal change. Institutions will often choose *death* over change![4]

Of course, after the shock of this discovery, and upon further reflection, I realized that institutions need to be "ready" for change before they can really engage in it. As Shakespeare wrote, "The readiness is all." Later, as a consultant, I employed processes to help congregations and other church organizations prepare for change, because I then understood how *much* change is ordinarily resisted, no matter how much it is needed.

John Calvin Is Alive and Well Among Us Disciples

Those who have taken the trouble to understand the history of our tradition know that the Christian Church (Disciples of Christ) is rooted in Scottish Presbyterianism. Thomas and Alexander Campbell, Barton Stone, and Walter Scott were all ordained Presbyterian ministers. They were heavily influenced by the New Light, Anti-Burgher, Seceder, Presbyterian sect – each of these names reflecting a division over doctrine or practice in the Scottish Presbyterian Church. Though Irish, Alexander Campbell spent time as a student in Edinburgh, Scotland, before emigrating to the United States.

Unlike the Presbyterians, we Disciples are a noncreedal church. That is, we don't ascribe to any one creed as a test of faith: Disciples

---

[4] "Homeostasis" as used here is not the biological definition in which homeostasis (avoiding fluctuations of temperature and so forth) is required for an organism to thrive. I use the term in an organizational sense in which unwillingness or inability to change and adapt to a changed environment can be deadly.

may use the Apostles Creed as an affirmation of faith, as did Alexander Campbell in the Disciples Church at Bethany, but we are vehemently opposed to insisting that anyone must agree to every word of that or any other historical creed or confession to demonstrate their orthodoxy or doctrinal worthiness to belong. We treasure the freedom to think for ourselves and to dissent from the majority. To join one of our congregations, one must affirm only that Jesus is the Christ (and we don't have to explain what we mean by *that*). So, it would seem that we left Presbyterianism in the dust as we formed a new movement.

Well, not so much!

You can take the Disciples out of the Presbyterian Church, but you can't so easily take Presbyterian theology out of the Disciples. Theologically, for all our touting of "freedom of thought," we are still firmly in the grip of what scholars call "Reformed theology," which is rooted in the theology of John Calvin.

This gets expressed practically in our life in several ways.

We have a deep commitment to the Bible as revealing the nature and intention of God, while also believing that we must understand it within its own historical context and purpose, lest we read into it our own meanings and understandings. We believe that God reigns and uses us for God's purposes and thus we have a deep-rooted sense that we are all called to be agents of healing and transformation in the world. We are not meant to be merely passive spectators of what God is otherwise doing in the world but are called to be actively engaged in the work of God. This is all good (and not so far from what many Presbyterians currently think).

However, there is that "Calvinistic catch." Because the entire world, including we ourselves, is "fallen," we can't completely trust human motives, actions, or tools. On the one hand, this implies that we should all be subject to "regulation" and accountability. On the other hand, we hate to give anyone or anything the *power* to regulate and hold us accountable.

The government of the United States is, essentially, a presbyterian form: a system of checks and balances to prevent abuses, three branches that watch over each other. We Disciples tend to distrust power, fearing abuse ... but we sometimes overshoot the mark by making it nearly impossible for anyone to lead. This leads to another related truth:

We Disciples Are a Quintessentially American Church

We are also a quintessentially American church and are, in fact, if I may use the word, rather "contaminated" by American culture. We easily confuse democracy and discernment. That is, if we are not sure what the will of God is, we say something like, "Let's vote on it and see." Though a *strict* Calvinist would say everything is up to God, we tend to think it is all up to us and we can do anything if we just try hard enough. This is just true enough, of course, that it continues to function among us.

So here is how I sum up our Calvinistic roots, our Reformed theological underpinnings together with our American perspective: "We are entrusted by God with the transformation of the world, and it is a big job, but we can do it if we just get properly organized!"

Sometimes, this drives us to accomplish things that are, on their face, impossible (like starting 1000 new congregations in 20 years or becoming an anti-racist church). However, sometimes it causes us to misplace our faith in the forms and structures we create rather than in the Spirit of the Living God.

Alongside this American tendency to trust in ourselves and in democracy, there is, as I have noted, a deep Calvinistic suspicion of trust in any human institution or authority. Alexander Campbell didn't trust that the elders of the Presbyterian church on the American frontier were qualified to decide who was fit to take communion or not, that was a matter between individuals and God; *and* as a young man he didn't trust that human organizations beyond the congregation could be trusted.

For *young* Campbell, the congregation was the ultimate expression of church. But he mellowed with age and experience so that by the time he was in his 60s, he was willing to serve as President of the American Christian Missionary Society as an expression of church that was very much beyond a single congregation.

The Independent Christian Churches and the Churches of Christ, our cousins in the Stone-Campbell Movement, still follow Alexander Campbell the younger in this regard, while we Disciples have chosen to follow Alexander Campbell the older.

However, even though Campbell came to appreciate expressions of the church beyond the congregation, he maintained his basic suspicion of institutions. In the end, we Disciples have a love/hate relationship with structure and with leadership, true to both our Presbyterian and American roots.

Disciples Denominational Polity Looks Sort of Episcopal (Hierarchical), But It Is Totally Congregational

There are three basic forms of church polity, three ways in which churches organize themselves: episcopal, presbyterian, and congregational. Episcopal systems feature bishops. But Calvin didn't trust bishops, so his presbyterian polity put a committee in the place of the bishop. But those of us with congregational polity, including us Disciples, don't even trust committees. We tend to put the whole congregation in the position of final authority... just in case some committee or board would try to "slip something by."

Our Disciples polity, which was "born again" in 1968 with Restructure, looks like an episcopal system in some regards. Regional ministers look a lot like bishops and the GMP looks a lot like a presiding bishop. As General Minister and President, I found there were those who wanted me to be a general, those who wanted me to be a minister, and those who wanted me to be a president. I can tell you, however, practically speaking, the system allows only for the GMP to be a minister, that is, a pastor. Although there is huge *responsibility* in the office of GMP, there is practically no *authority* other than the informal authority one can garner by demonstrating humility, service, and caring: exactly as it is with being pastor of a congregation. In an "exit interview," I complained to the General Standing Committee On Renewal and Structural Reform about the vagueness of The Design's job description for the Office of General Minister and President and the ensuing lack of formal power and authority. The Committee did clarify it a bit in the changes to The Design they recommended (and which were passed) in 2005. But much vagueness remains in The Design, and in practice, in regard to the role of General Minister and President.

All Denominations Are Becoming More Congregational

Participating in ecumenical work, rubbing shoulders with people of many different styles and polities, I discovered that nearly *all* denominations have become increasingly congregational. The reasons for this include: 1) there is less and less trust in post-modern culture for leaders of any kind; 2) there is less trust in and appreciation of institutions generally.

I have sometimes heard Disciples say, "Regional ministers are becoming too much like bishops!" I always respond, "On the contrary, bishops are becoming more like regional ministers." That is, people grant less and less formal authority and power to bishops so that their authority and power is becoming more informal, which means it must be earned rather than being bestowed by a formal ceremony of investiture. Some will see this as a good thing, while others will bemoan it. In any case, all church leaders, even those in hierarchical traditions, must understand that this is the new normal in the twenty-first century. Since Disciples have *always* relied on informal power and authority from their leaders, it would seem that we are, in some ways, well-positioned to effectively function in this new era; however, *some* authorization of leadership is essential to institutional health.

Bureaucracies Are Necessary to Do Things We Can't Do Without Them, But They Have Negative Tendencies That Must Be Watched and Corrected from Time to Time

"Bureaucracy" has become a dirty word these days, it seems. But I believe a good word needs to be said for them. There are good things that simply cannot be accomplished without bureaucracies. For example, Social Security makes it possible for millions of Americans to survive. Just try having an effective school system, or financial system, or seminary, or overseas mission program, or any number of other important programs and initiatives without a bureaucracy to nurture them and hold them accountable. Bureaus are always created to serve the mission of the whole body, but the whole body must also keep an eye on their bureaucracies (read the previously mentioned insights of John Calvin regarding the human condition).

The natural tendency of bureaucracies (again, as the Apostle Paul would use the word "natural") is to forget that their purpose is to serve the mission of the whole body and thus begin to be concerned about "life inside the bureau," or "life in the box." Now, you may think I am speaking primarily or simply about denominational bureaucracy. However, remember that every congregation has its own bureaucracy, which requires regular review and attention, just as do regional and general church bureaucracies. But most of us tend to trust our congregational bureaus more easily because they are closer and easier to keep an eye on.

Our general ministry units, and most of our regions, have remarkable records of effectiveness and service. There have been the occasional disasters that should serve as cautionary tales and reminders that no part of any organization should go without regular review and attention. But these have been remarkably few.

No matter which part of the church body we are talking about (general, regional, or congregational), the operative question is always, "Is this bureaucracy, this part of the body, this organizational piece, serving the needs of the whole body or has it become focused on its own needs… 'life in the box'?" This is the question that must be asked constantly by the primary leaders of the bureaucracy and by the larger organization it is designed to serve. This is no reason to *abandon* bureaucracies, it's just a reason to keep an eye on them.

Our Denominational Organization Lacks a Judicial Branch

I drew the similarity between the U.S. government and presbyterian polity before. Also, I have named the fact that we Disciples still bear the marks of our presbyterian roots, both in terms of theology and, to a similar degree, polity (organization). But because we don't really trust leadership enough to provide real formal power and authority to lead, we have a problem: when leadership can't lead, no one can be held accountable to much of anything. When, as GMP, I saw things happening that caused me concern, it was sometimes difficult to raise questions beyond the leadership of the particular expression of the church that was involved. I didn't have the power to *demand* answers unless I already had evidence of malpractice on the part of that expression's leadership.

We lack a "judicial branch" (to use governmental terms); we lack a place where concerns can be formally investigated, with one notable exception. Each region has a commission (or committee) on ministry to which questions or accusations of misconduct can be referred, investigations can be conducted, and binding judgments can be made.

But if there are questions or concerns about individual leaders of regions or general ministry units which involve management practices, for example, there is nowhere to take such concerns except to the board of that region or general ministry unit itself. Very often, those boards will *not* have the wherewithal to follow up on such complaints and the issues will go unaddressed until disaster strikes.

Since we are *unlikely* to authorize the GMP to commence a formal inquiry without the approval of the board responsible for the expression to be investigated, I think we need a body (a committee) that has the authority to conduct such an investigation. I wouldn't call it a "court," but it would be a *sort* of a court, responsible for giving due process to those involved but also able to overrule a particular board for the sake of the larger church. Such a body would likely include a regional minister or two and a general ministry president or two, but the rest of such a body should be made up of perhaps 6 lay members of congregations and 4 ministers of congregations. Such a committee would need to be representative of the whole church and should have the legal right to call on witnesses and to obtain records as needed. Moral concerns about clergy would continue to be directed to the applicable regional or general commission on ministry, but management and leadership issues would be sent to this committee. Some decisions of the committee might require Regional or General Board or Assembly confirmation.

As stated before, this church has been remarkably fortunate in that the number of cases of malfeasance or mismanagement in our regional and general expressions have been remarkably few. But those few have undermined trust and been otherwise devastating to the life and ministries of the church.

God Really Does Work in History, Even When We Can't Easily See It

Sometimes, in the face of the turmoil and trouble we see in the world, we are tempted to think that God has "left the building" or otherwise abandoned the world. But this is not true and one of my favorite examples can be found in our long history of missionary engagement in China. It began in the 19th century and continued right up until the Communist government of Mao Zedong took power after World War II and expelled most missionaries.

The Disciples missionaries were a particularly heroic bunch. They were among those who created a "Safety Zone" in Nanjing in 1937, which protected hundreds of thousands of Chinese citizens from the atrocities of the Imperial Japanese Army. There were an estimated 250,000 – 300,000 Chinese killed in the aptly called "Rape of Nanjing," but hundreds of thousands more were saved because these missionaries "drew a line" around a zone in Nanjing and forbade the Japanese military from crossing it. To this day, these missionaries are honored in China at a special Memorial in Nanjing. Primary among those whose stories are told there are Disciples missionaries, including Searle Bates, Minnie Vautrin, and Lewis Smythe.

When the missionaries were expelled from China in 1950-51, there were perhaps a half-million Chinese Christians, but most Westerners assumed that the church would die. In fact, little was heard from the indigenous church leaders as the church went underground in the face of severe government suppression. For example, during the period of the Cultural Revolution, our Global Ministries executive for East Asia, Xiaoling Zhu, and his mother and his father (who was a Chinese Disciples minister) were forced into labor on a collective farm.

But rumors of the death of the church in China were greatly exaggerated! When Mindy and I, along with United Church of Christ GMP John Thomas and Susan Sanders of UCC Wider Church Ministries, visited China in 2002 as an official delegation (accompanied by Xiaoling Zhu and visiting Jim and Carolyn Higginbotham who were serving as DOM overseas staff in Nanjing at the time), we experienced an indigenous church that had resurfaced with a passion! Today, there is something on the order of forty to sixty million Christians in China (exact numbers are difficult to determine because many congregations are not registered with the government). The Amity Foundation, created to publish Bibles in the various Chinese dialects, produces millions of copies each year. The Nanjing Christian Seminary is educating new church leaders continually. That said, the government has begun a new round of suppression of many religious groups, including Christians. While we do well to be concerned for the safety of Chinese Christians, we should also know that God is still there with them.

I am reminded of that image from Isaiah 11:1-10: "A shoot shall come forth from the stump of Jesse!" It was Isaiah's way of talking about how the seemingly decimated nation of Israel would rise again in God's good time. So has the church of Jesus Christ sprung forth once again in China, stronger than ever. The power of the Gospel is amazing!

Voting Is Not the Best Way to Begin Making a Decision

Processes that work toward developing consensus often achieve a better result than quickly (prematurely) taking votes. This is why I proposed discernment processes instead of so many general assembly resolutions. I have found that *church people are more conservative in principle than they are in practice.* I have seen this time after time. For example, a congregation will often *vote* for a narrow interpretation regarding human sexuality but will embrace people they know personally in the congregation who are gay or lesbian. Thus, intentionally *living* into a new way of being is often better than trying to *vote* into a new way of being.

In Matters of Discernment That Impact the Lives of a Group or Class of Individuals and How They Will Be Treated Officially, It Is Important to Always Have Representatives of That Group or Class at the Table

A related observation is that unless those affected by decisions are at the decision-making table, people tend to reinforce their own comfort zones rather than to push themselves to reflect the "wideness of God's mercy." Thus, white people shouldn't make policy decisions that affect people of color unless people of color are part of the process of discussion and decision-making; straight people shouldn't make policies that affect LGBTQ people unless LGBTQ people are part of the process of discussion and decision-making; men shouldn't be making policy decisions that affect women unless women are part of the process of discussion and decision-making. This may seem obvious (though it is apparently *not* obvious to most of us who are white people), but those of us who have been people of privilege for centuries tend to assume we know what's best for everyone.

Each Denomination Is a Distinct Social System: What Unites Us Is Our Dependence on God's Grace and Our Common Faith in Christ

Each denomination is a distinct social system, a mini culture, which expresses itself in differing practices of worship and organization. Each has its own acronyms, heroes, and versions of history. That which *unites* us is our common faith in Christ ... and we must make that the primary factor in our relationships rather than the differences of practice. By focusing on our common faith, we not only affirm the unity of the body, which Jesus prayed for, but we make it possible to learn from each other .... to see ways in which we can overcome our own excesses. I have learned this repeatedly when worshiping with congregations across North America and the world.

The Stone-Campbell Movement has four major themes at its heart: freedom of the individual; mission; Christian unity; and restoration of the New Testament Church.

Early in the movement, Christian unity and Restorationism were seen to be two sides of the same coin. In our nineteenth-century naiveté, we thought there was a single way of being church to be found in the New Testament and that, if we could identify that way of being church, everyone would have the good sense to join us in living out that single New Testament way.

Over the next century and a half, we finally figured out that there is no <u>one</u> New Testament form for the church, nor even one pure understanding of the life and ministry of Jesus. While we kept trying to reconcile those four Gospel accounts of Jesus, it never seemed to occur to us that we were given all four accounts precisely so we would realize there is NOT just one memory, one perspective, just one way of looking at the ministry of Christ.

There are many practices we inherited from our restorationist strain that I still appreciate: such as communion every week (I miss it when I don't or can't receive it weekly), and believer's baptism by immersion (the person being baptized will certainly remember being dunked under water in front of an audience of fellow believers). And yet, there are limits to how useful restorationism is today, and sometimes, we must allow it to be trumped by our passion for Christian unity. Our restorationist practices have a certain value to us but must not be used to separate us from the rest of Christ's body.

Churches, like *All* Organizations, Need a Clearly Identified Path Forward—A Vision

"Where there is no vision, the people perish" (Proverbs 29:18). Churches and *all* organizations need a clearly identified path forward, a vision (or future story) for what they are to become and do. More than a statement of who they are in their essence currently, it paints a picture of what they will be like in the years ahead if they become and do what they are *called* to become and do.

I realized early on in my service as GMP that the Christian Church (Disciples of Christ) had mostly forgotten what it was called by God to be and do or, in some cases, needed to reconsider what it believed it was called to be and do. And so, beginning with the General Board meeting in 1994, I led a process that ultimately resulted in the General Board and Assembly affirming the "2020 Vision for the Christian Church (Disciples of Christ)". I drew heavily on the language of the prophet Micah (6:8): "What does the Lord require of you but to do justice, love kindness and walk humbly with your God?" The Vision that grew out of this process is, "To be and to share the Good news of Jesus Christ, witnessing, loving, and serving from our doorsteps to the ends of the earth," and "to be a faithful, growing church that demonstrates true community, deep Christian spirituality and a passion for justice." There are also some quantitative benchmarks that were part of the vision: 1) to start 1000 new congregations by the year 2020 (we surpassed that goal by 2020); 2) to revitalize 1000 of our existing congregations by the year 2020; 3) to be a pro-reconciling/anti-racist church; 4) to develop the leadership needed to make these goals possible.

Over these last 20 years or so, the church has reshaped its work in many ways to reflect this vision. Each general ministry unit has sought to find ways to live it out through the lens of their particular mission, regions have done the same, and many congregations have responded in creative and inspired ways.

In the Absence of Vision, Churches Define Themselves in Terms of What They Are *Against*

Much progress has been made simply because the church got some clarity about its calling through this visioning process. Churches and other organizations *need* a clearly identified path forward, a vision of what they are to become and do, what they are *for*. However, the opposite is also true: churches and organizations that do not have a clear vision of what they are to become and do, who do not define themselves in terms of what they are *for*, will often define themselves in terms of what they are *against*. This is what happened when the Disciple Renewal group began in the 1980's. Most of us Disciples spent more time and energy opposing that small group than we did in defining who *we Disciples are and what we are called to be and do*.

Regions Can No Longer Operate Like Pastor-Centered Congregations

In the parlance of church consultants, congregations of about 50 to 150 active members tend to operate in a "pastor-centered" way. That is, the pastor is at the center of everything. This usually works pretty well for a medium-sized congregation, though it can limit growth if the congregation is pushing the 150-member limit. "Pastor-centered" is used descriptively, not judgmentally. It isn't about a pastor's ego but about the organizational form that is most effective in this size range.

Many regional ministers come from having served in pastor-centered size congregations. There is nothing wrong with this per se, but if they consciously or unconsciously carry that pastor-centered style with them into regional ministry, their region will suffer. This is because the affiliative forces have weakened within our denomination, as previously mentioned. Congregations and ministers used to relate to each other more regularly and thus felt strongly connected to one another and to the larger church/denomination. When these affiliative forces were strong, regional staffs were proportionately larger, and there was less conflict in the atmosphere, individual regional ministers and associate regional ministers could spend lots of their time in individual relationships with ministers, lay leaders, and congregations and it was all good.

However, as affiliative forces have diminished, regional staffs have shrunk in size, and conflict is now a daily fact of life in the culture in general and congregations in particular, it is not enough for regional ministers (or bishops, or conferences ministers, as they are called in other traditions) to simply be pastors to individuals. While a pastor-centered approach may seem very effective for a while and generates loyalty to the individual regional minister, it does little to build a sense of loyalty to the larger body. The resulting problem becomes obvious when a pastor-centered-style regional minister leaves that ministry. The new regional minister has to start over building relationships (the same thing that happens when popular pastors leave pastor-centered congregations). The loyalty that is built up for a pastor-centered regional minister vanishes with that regional minister's departure and there is little left to bind the congregations and ministers of the region to each other or to the larger church.

Thus, in this era, regional ministers must not simply be good pastors to individual people and congregations but must work to build up the affiliative forces that hold congregations and denominations together. Rather than simply relating to the (usually) personable and trustworthy regional minister, ministers must be helped to relate to each other, congregations must be helped to relate to each other, and lay leaders must be helped to relate to each other across congregations. Ministers can support ministers, lay leaders can support each other (elders, church treasurers, teachers, youth leaders and so forth can share best practices with each another and otherwise support each other), congregations can engage in mission and education projects together. The fact that most congregations now have access to Zoom makes this all easier (one redemptive outcome of the pandemic). Regional ministers must help initiate such things, but without always putting themselves at the center of the action.

As I have said, regional ministry is one of the most important ministries of the church, but unless it is done in a way that builds affiliation and community between congregations, ministers, and lay leaders, rather than personal loyalty to the regional minister, this ministry (and ultimately the denomination as a whole) will fail.

Adaptive Change Is Needed

Simply tinkering with the current structures will not bring the kind of change needed. Simply working harder won't do it (like trying to fly by flapping your arms harder and harder). Only working smarter will suffice.

Ron Heifetz has written groundbreaking books about change, distinguishing between technical and adaptive change. *Technical* change addresses individual problems with one kind of "fix" or another. If the roof is leaking, technical change means addressing the leaks with roofing tar. *Adaptive* change addresses the whole system and changes the system itself. Using our leaky roof example, adaptive change could mean reconstructing a flat roof so that it is now pitched, thus preventing pools of standing water. It isn't that technical change is bad and adaptive change is good. If the roof is leaking, it is best to do the technical fix of stopping the leak immediately with roofing tar until you can do the adaptive work of reconstructing the roof. Each kind of change, technical and adaptive, has its place. The problem comes when one thinks one is doing profound adaptive change when one is really doing less profound technical change.

I thought I was doing adaptive change as GMP, but it turned out to be mostly technical. It wasn't unimportant work, but we were basically tinkering with structures rather than addressing underlying systemic issues. Resizing General Board section groups to 25 people instead of 50 people solved the technical challenge of enabling people to more easily discuss the board's business. But changing the size of the sections did little to address the underlying systemic issues of the church that have to do with empowering leadership.

We did get started on *some* adaptive change, including becoming an anti-racist, pro-reconciling church. But there is much more adaptive change needed for Disciples congregations and the whole denomination to thrive.

Just "trying harder and harder" will injure more ministers and lay leaders, drive more ministers out of ministry, and bring greater *unhealth* to the church rather than the *healthy* community and individuals God desires. We must break these unhealthy patterns and model true community, Christian spirituality, and justice within our own church's life. Otherwise, we have little to offer a hurting world.

Well, I learned many things as GMP, but there is just one more I want to mention.

One doesn't touch the President of the United States without an invitation to do so.

As previously mentioned, when Bill Clinton was in the White House, I was part of a small delegation of National Council of Churches leaders to lobby the President regarding a matter of justice. We met in the Oval Office, and the President was very generous, giving us nearly half an hour of his time. As we prepared to leave, we decided that we should pray for the President, as we would pray for any President in the face of their overwhelming responsibilities. I happened to be standing closest to the President, and so as we began to pray, in a pastoral gesture, I placed my hand on his shoulder.

Beyond our little delegation and the president, there were only two other people in the room: Clinton's communications director, George Stephanopoulos, and a tall guy with an earpiece who was obviously Secret Service. When I put my hand on the President, their eyes grew wide, and they began to quickly move across the room toward me. The President waved them off (apparently, I didn't look very threatening to him), but I learned that you don't touch the President of the United States unless invited to do so.

I couldn't help but think of the contrast between the President of the United States and Jesus, who, walking through a town, pressed on every side by the curious and by those wanting something from him and by a woman who needed healing and dared touch his garment. To the amazement of his bodyguards (I mean disciples), Jesus sensed her touch, stopped the parade, and ministered to her.

Like any effective local pastor, or regional minister, the General Minister and President, no matter who he or she is, must maintain the capacity to be touched, to notice and to care. Otherwise, he or she cannot effectively lead this bunch of Reformed, restorationist, ecumenical, freedom-loving, mission-driven North American Christians called Disciples of Christ!

Some Personal Advice and Counsel

The following thoughts are the product of my 77 years of living. Perhaps you will find something here that resonates with your own experience and that will be helpful.

1. **Let go of guilt.** Make amends as best you can, apologize in person or in writing, and let it go. Let God have it.
2. **Have grace for others and for yourself.** The toughest challenges I have faced in life have not been difficulties in extending grace to others, but in extending grace to myself.
3. **Know your own strengths and weaknesses.** Then, when in a leadership role, surround yourself with people who have strengths where you have weaknesses. If all your friends and coworkers are just like you, or always agree with you, you'll make the same mistakes over and over because no one on your "team" will see them. Make sure you have someone who sees things differently and will tell you so — and thank God for them.
4. **Recognize your own need for the spiritual disciplines** and make them a regular part of your life.
5. **Ministers, if you are not having any fun in ministry, there is something wrong,** because God doesn't call people to be miserable. It's time to see how much of the problem is the church's and how much of it is yours. Then, change what you can in the church and in yourself.

With Mom in 1949 in Crawfordsville

Chuck and Dick in 1950 in Crawfordsville

The Hamm family at home in St. Petersburg (December 1959)

Dick in 1957 (4th grade in St. Petersburg Pasadena Elementary School)

Hamm's Art and Sign Supply (1960)

High School Yearbook 1966

Mom and Dad Hamm's Art and Sign Supply Store (1965)

Wedding November 21, 1970 at Bluffton, Indiana,
First United Church of Christ (Mindy's home Church)

Son David in 1975

Daughter Laura and Son David in 1979

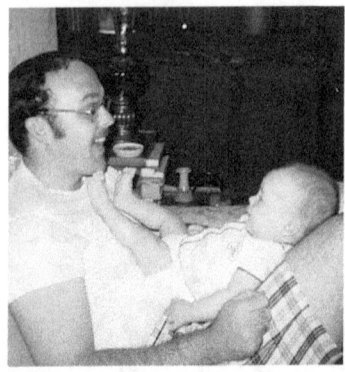

Mindy polishes our beloved N7248J in 1972

1982 as we began in Ft. Wayne

Ordination at Little Eagle Creek Christian Church June 2, 1974

North Oak Christian Church with John Wolfersberger 1979

North Oak Christian Church's first unit arises (1979)

Dick's new office in the Mission's Building in 1993 with
Associates John Foulkes and Don Manworren

Sign Painter
Extraordinaire
(1912-2000)

First Christian Church, Ft. Wayne, Indiana 1982-1990

The Oval Office in 1993

GMP's current and former at 1993 General Assembly
(before Dick was elected)

In NYC with Allen Harris and Jon Lacey on World Aids Day 1995

Dick with Youth at Pacific Southwest event 1995

Jubilee in January 2001 with John Paul II

Preaching through an interpreter at a Church in Beijing

Our UCC/Disciples delegation meets with Bishop Ting in May, 2002 in Nanjing (Mindy, Dick, Bishop Ting, Xiaoling Zhu of Global Ministries, John Thomas, and Susan Sanders

Terri Hord Owens, John Humbert, Dick Hamm in 2022

Epilogue

I am often asked what I now imagine the future of our denomination, the Christian Church (Disciples of Christ) in the US and Canada, holds. It is a mixed picture, obviously. This narrative has been primarily about denominational structures beyond the congregation. But, of course, our congregations are the front line of mission and there is good news and bad news in regard to them.

Nearly 50% of our congregations have perished over the past 25 years. I have written more about congregations than anything else over the course of my ministry, and especially since 2003, because that is where my heart is primarily. The rate of decline in the size and number of congregations, not only among Disciples but among all traditions, has been sometimes stunning. But it is not mysterious. *Any* institution that refuses to engage in needed change can expect to die soon, and so many of our congregations have been stuck in doing things as they have always been done. That's the bad news.

However, there is much good news, too. So many congregations that are continuing to try new things and to "stay light on their feet" are stable, and many are, in fact, thriving. Additionally, many new Disciples of Christ congregations continue to be established, and many of them are receiving a warm welcome from those they seek to serve.

Congregations have always been subject to a "life cycle," short or long, and congregations of all kinds, including Disciples congregations, have died throughout the decades. Some die because the places they serve have died or changed so much that continuing to serve in that location is just too big a stretch for the members remaining. Some die because they resist changing in any meaningful way to address the change in their context. Some die because they become embroiled in conflicts that destroy them. Though always sad, none of this is new. It has been true since the first Disciples congregations were formed in the 19th century. What *has* changed is (1) for the first 150 years of our movement, we started more new congregations than the number that died, *and* (2) the changes in the social contexts in which our existing congregations find themselves have been so fast and furious during the last fifty years that our congregations have tended to allow anxiety to overcome their decision-making processes. This means (1) we need to keep starting new congregations, and (2) existing congregations' members and leaders must resist the urge to make any minor change seem like a life-threatening matter or to make any small mole-hill decision look like a mountain.

Being a leader (clergy or lay) in a congregation has never been easy, and it is more challenging now than usual. I have spoken and written about this for decades. But that is not the primary subject of my writing here. There is much excellent help available to congregations who want to make the needed changes to thrive in their current context. I think I have provided some of that help as a church consultant in the past. But my focus in this writing is our denominational life *beyond* the congregation because I have experience in this arena that most people, frankly, do not have. The dynamics of congregational and denominational life are intertwined and similar in very many ways, but here I am trying to name the challenges faced specifically by denominational structures in this era.

Denominational structures that do not adapt to the new context will collapse (as some have already) and be replaced, if still needed, by more appropriate structures. That said, I am greatly heartened by the adaptive changes I have seen in our structures in recent years. Several regions *have* merged or are working toward that possibility as previously mentioned, and others have restructured their life and ministry to be more responsive to current needs and realities. General ministry units have also adapted in various ways.

The Christian Board of Publication still struggles financially, as the entire publishing industry has come under enormous pressures generated by the rise of online shopping and the shrinking of the church. However, CBP continues to seek to publish books that are relevant to faith and social justice. CBP President Brad Lyons shared with me that after the tragic murder of George Floyd in 2020, Chalice Press (CBP's book imprint) had more books addressing that tragedy in the top 100 than any other publisher. Time will tell whether a denominationally aligned publishing house can thrive, but we have reason to be hopeful.

The Christian Church Foundation was founded in 1961 as church leaders began to see the need for Disciples to invest generational wealth in endowments that could support Disciples mission and ministry perpetually, both by providing a place where money could be safely invested and grown and where help could be found in developing endowment programs for all expressions of the church. Amazingly, today, the Foundation has over $1 Billion in assets under management for the sake of congregations, regions, general ministries, institutions of higher education, and more. These investments provide a lifeline to so many ministries.

The General Ministry unit now called Christian Unity and Interfaith Ministry (CUIM) faces many of the same challenges all ecumenical institutions face. Many state and local councils of churches have disappeared due to diminished financial resources. The National and World Councils of Churches have significantly reduced their size and staff for the same reason. In addition, in a time when people are thinking in very parochial terms, thinking of their own group or nation *first*, it is difficult to penetrate such an anxiety-laden climate with the message of unity. Nevertheless, CUIM and the ecumenical councils continue to convene people for conversation and relationship and to keep the vision of unity alive. How to keep the message before the whole Christian Church (Disciples of Christ) is, however, an ongoing challenge.

The Disciples of Christ Historical Society is in the process of digitalizing resources, making historical materials more easily accessible than ever before. This will help all who seek a deeper understanding of our history, mission, and new challenges as a "movement for wholeness in a fragmented world."

Disciples Church Extension Fund (formerly Board of Church Extension) is focused on both church finances (making loans to Disciples congregations for building, remodeling, and restoration) and on program (providing consulting, education, and counsel for church revitalization and new congregation establishment).

Disciples Home Missions (formerly Division of Homeland Ministries) is another general ministry unit that seeks to enable the faithful ministry and mission of congregations in the areas of children and youth, women and men, ecology, peace, justice, evangelism, and more. On behalf of the whole church, DHM provides for the search and call process, six domestic mission and ministry centers, refugee services, and more.

Division of Overseas Ministries/Global Ministries has focused in two directions: providing collaboration and resources (especially in the form of personnel with specialized expertise) to partners in other nations; and helping North American Christians understand the world better through education and face-to-face contact with Christians from other parts of the world who bring different perspectives than those we constantly hear within our own culture. In a shrinking world, this kind of cross-cultural sharing is perhaps more important than ever.

Higher Education and Leadership Ministries continues to support the higher education institutions of our church (15 undergraduate and 7 graduate schools), providing resources, guidance, and collaboration opportunities between these institutions. HELM also sponsors leadership programs (including Leadership Fellows and the Emerging Clergy Leadership Conference), scholarships, and grants for Disciples students and encourages theological dialogue.

The National Benevolent Association has adapted perhaps more dramatically than all the other general ministries; it has used the approximately $70 million recovered from the 2005 bankruptcy to provide seed money for new ideas and experiments in the areas of health and social service ministries. This has *more* than replaced the work of the Mission Council and Mission Imperative Fund, which were discontinued in 2001 when yet another new mission funding system was implemented.

The Pension Fund continues its excellent record of expressing the church's care for its pastors, teachers, and other employees. Today, the Pension Fund oversees *nineteen* programs under the umbrella of Ministerial Relief and Assistance (its original charge), which focus on the financial, physical, mental, and emotional well-being of pastors and other church employees of all ages, races, ethnicities, and sexual identities.

The Office of General Minister and President is (and I believe has been) well led through the years but continues to face ongoing challenges due to the lack of formal authority and power that is inherent in our "covenantal" polity. Our Disciples love/resist relationship with leadership of any kind makes the work harder.

Nevertheless, this church in all its parts has prospered in many ways since the Restructure of 1968, and GMPs have played a significant role in this. I am grateful to be numbered among these colleagues.

Some of our biggest challenges lie in our governance. I still believe, frankly, that our governance bodies are too big to be able to be as flexible and responsive as they need to be in this century, and that we need some formal authority that makes it possible to call our regional and general expressions to task when needed, whether that authority is granted to the General Minister and President or to a newly created small group equipped and commissioned for the purpose.

Yes, there will continue to be congregations that close, usually because they waited too long to adapt to current needs, but this has been true throughout our history (and the history of the whole church of Jesus Christ, for that matter). So, will we continue to reach out to all kinds of people through both existing and new congregations?

"Evangelism" is a word that people seldom use in mainline circles these days, primarily because of the way the word has been abused in the media and in other parts of the body of Christ. But I make no apology for wanting to see *more* Disciples congregations and *more* Disciples in the U.S. and Canada. We bring a needed corrective to many of the excesses of church history; we stand for justice and the inclusion of all just as Christ includes all of us in his invitation to the Table. When there are more of us, we have more influence in all aspects of life, including moral, ethical, economic, and political spheres. I want to see our influence grow rather than diminish.

I don't believe the Disciples perspective is the only valid perspective, and we certainly have our own excesses and need for correction, which we can find in our ecumenical relationships. Nor do I believe the Christian perspective is the only valid perspective, though I chose, and continue to choose, to be a Christian, because I believe the life and teachings of Jesus are the clearest of all representations of God's *logos*. As a pastor, I know that *everyone* needs to know and benefits from knowing the love of God; *everyone* needs to know how to live abundantly, bless the world out of that abundance, and nurture justice. That's why I share my faith with others and wish to see the Disciples of Christ grow in numbers and influence. For all our challenges around issues of authority and leadership, we are rather well-positioned to be a church of the future in the postmodern world.

When one serves in the general expression of the church, you become easily recognized by leaders in all expressions of the church. You feel you are a part of something much larger and that the work you do is essential, even if *most* people of the church are unaware of your existence or of the exact nature of what you do. This is true of both staff and volunteers. It was expressed well by one general moderator who remarked that at the close of the General Assembly over which he presided, when he walked down the steps off the stage, it was like walking into oblivion! I have had similar feelings sometimes as a former GMP. The image that comes to mind for me is the symphonic piece "Bolero," which mimics the rhythmic motion of a slowly moving caravan through the desert. When you dismount from your camel, the parade keeps moving until you are standing alone there in the desert, watching the caravan pass over the distant hills, the music gradually disappearing, and you are alone there in the desert with only your memories of leading the parade.

Personally, I have received lots of affirmation as a former general minister and president, even though I resigned 21 months before my second six-year term was complete, which was puzzling to many (though many others understood very well). But I think of so many general and regional church staff members and volunteers who served their time faithfully and at great personal sacrifice in many cases, and then sauntered off to a life of relative anonymity. I'm sure many or most employees of corporate America have this same experience, but it seems we should do better in the church. We often lose vast amounts of institutional memory when we summarily dismiss those who have served well. I confess that I was often guilty of the same when I was GMP, sometimes acting as though "nothing of importance happened before I got here." But now I know something of how it feels and what is lost to the church, and I think we can do better in this regard (and I am grateful to my successors who have exhibited much more grace in this regard than did I). I owe apologies to my predecessors and to people who served on my staff for not expressing gratitude often enough, maintaining their visibility and helping the church remember them. I have named a few in this narrative, but there are so many more who deserve to be remembered and celebrated. I am particularly grateful to the

Disciples of Christ Historical Society that seeks to embody and encourage such remembrance.

My final word is one of gratitude. I give thanks to God and to my fellow Disciples for having entrusted me with the privilege of serving this church we all love. I hope, above all else, that I made some contribution toward enhancing the church's faithfulness to God's vision for it and the strengthening of its life and ministry.

Appendix 1

Formal and Informal Power and Authority

I have been teaching Disciples History and Polity for twenty years (usually annually), most of those years in partnership with Dr. Scott Seay, church historian, at Christian Theological Seminary in Indianapolis. Understanding how things work in a Disciples congregation is essential to successful leadership by both ministers and lay leaders. Pastors and other leaders who do not understand how Disciples polity really works are likely to run into trouble early and often. As I like to tell my students, if you don't understand our polity, it will "eat your lunch!"

"Polity" is the fancy word for how a church is organized. More specifically, it refers to how power and authority are distributed in a church system. Every social system has power and authority within it, and the questions are these: How is that power and authority distributed? Who has it? And how does one get it? There are three classic forms of church polity: episcopal, presbyterian, and congregational.

Three Classic Forms of Church Polity

An episcopal system features bishops and church councils. Churches with this form of polity include the Roman Catholic Church, the Episcopal Church, and the United Methodist Church. The Pope is "the Bishop of Rome," and cardinals, archbishops, and local bishops round out the episcopal hierarchy. The Episcopal Church (part of the global Anglican Church, which split with Rome during the Reformation) rejected the power and authority of the Pope but retained most of the hierarchical forms of organization, including bishops. The United Methodist Church, which grew out of the Anglican Church in England, also has bishops, although none is designated "presiding bishop."

The presbyterian system was shaped during the Reformation by John Calvin and his followers and reflects a distrust of bishops (including the Pope and the various other members of the Catholic hierarchy at the time of the Reformation). Thus, presbyterian polity places power in the hands of a group of people, democratically elected, rather than in the hands of a "bishop." Churches that have a presbyterian polity include the Presbyterian Church U.S.A. and the Reformed Church in America. It is worth noting that the government of the United States operates in a way that is parallel to presbyterian polity. Our American founders did not trust the power of a king (pope) and, though a chief office was created by the Constitution of the United States (the presidency), it is held in check by the judicial and legislative branches (a system of checks and balances). Early citizens of this country, including those who immigrated from Western Europe, were suspicious of hierarchy and the potential for abuse of too much power in the hands of too few.

A congregational system takes that distrust of too much power and authority in the hands of too few to an even deeper level than does presbyterian polity. Thus, in a congregational system, the congregation holds ultimate power and authority in matters of policy, budget, and legal matters such as ownership of property and hiring and firing of staff.

What Are Power and Authority?

The definitions I use for power and authority are as follows: Power is the *ability* to do something; authority is the *right* to do something. One can have the power to do something in a system without the authority to do it. But without the authority, such an exercise of power will soon be repudiated by the larger group. On the other hand, if one has the authority to do something, the power (the ability to do something) naturally flows from that authority, that *right* to do something.

To go one step further, there is both *formal* and *informal* power and *formal* and *informal* authority. Formal power and authority are generally written down somewhere: in a constitution and bylaws, in a letter of call, or in a formal statement by a board or other governing body. Informal power and authority are generally unwritten and are based on a people's respect and trust for an individual leader.

In a congregational system (such as that of the Disciples of Christ), informal power and authority reign. That is, as a leader garners the trust and respect of the people, a kind of moral and popular authority grows, and from that grows the power to do things. To put it another way, if a Disciples congregation senses that the pastor is a morally upright person who loves and cares about them as a people, they will allow that pastor to offer effective leadership of the congregation. In the absence of that sense that the pastor is morally upright and cares about the people of the congregation, resistance to that pastor's leadership will quickly grow.

In a congregational system, formal statements of the power and authority of the pastor are essential, but they mean little without the informal power and authority the pastor must develop to underwrite those formal statements. Thus, a new pastor must quickly learn who his or her congregation is and demonstrate that he or she cares about them. In the absence of that demonstration of authentic caring, a congregation can and probably will rapidly turn against the pastor, rendering his or her leadership meaningless.

Our Disciples system is primarily congregational, although we brought a tinge of presbyterian polity into the picture through Restructure in 1968, claiming certain powers for general and regional leadership while holding those leaders accountable to representative groups (the General Board, regional boards, and general and regional assemblies). Thus, for example, the ordination of ministers, which used to be left to individual congregations (when we were purely congregational), is now authorized by regions (through a regional commission or committee on ministry) in consultation with and sponsorship by a congregation or two. The regional minister can intervene in the life of a troubled congregation, but only with the permission of that congregation's lay leadership. The GMP can intervene in the life of a region or of a general ministry unit, but only with the permission of that entity's representative leadership.

In all expressions of the Disciples church (whether a congregation, a region, or the general church), the less well known a new leader is, the harder and faster he or she needs to work to establish informal authority and the power that flows from it. Given our Disciples distrust (which comes, in large measure, from our Calvinistic roots) and our American distrust of formal power and authority (largely shared by Canadian Disciples, as well), informal authority and power are key to effective leadership everywhere in this church.

This is why I counsel *any* pastoral leader of any expression of the church to refuse to accept a call to serve as leader unless he or she receives more than a ninety-percent positive vote by the body confirming their call.[1]

A Final Note About Power and Authority

One of the realities of the current era is that leadership is now distrusted in almost every arena of North American life. This is partly due to many rather spectacular displays and exposures of irresponsible and immoral behavior by public leaders and to the current general distrust and suspicion directed toward institutions of all kinds. This has led to a phenomenon that has been called the "horizontalization" or "flattening" of structures that used to be more hierarchical and that commanded widespread trust from those being led. People now trust what they can *see* (or what they *think* they see ... social media has made confidence in what presents itself as *fact* even more difficult to discern).

From an ecclesiological perspective, this means that *all* forms of church polity require the same demonstration of caring and trustworthiness from leaders, whether popes, cardinals, bishops, regional ministers, presbyters, pastors, or lay leaders. Thus, in a way, *all* forms of polity are becoming more congregational, flatter, and more accountable. This makes leadership more challenging, but it also means that we Disciples are *in our element* when we understand that we are, in many ways, well suited for such a time as this.

---

[1] The only exception might be a congregation that is badly divided over matters that are not directly related to the pastor being considered. But even then, one should proceed to accept such a call with exceptional caution.

Appendix 2

Some Pertinent Statements and Addresses

April 17, 1993

General Board

Nominee's Address to General Board

It is a fearsome time in which to contemplate giving leadership to the church, generally, regionally, or congregationally. I'm reminded of the story of the man who was tarred and feathered and ridden out of town on a rail. Asked how he felt about it, he replied, "Well, if it weren't for the honor of the thing, I'd just as soon have stayed home."

Maybe I don't get the concept here, but I *do* feel very honored for my name to have been brought forward to this point. The words of support and encouragement which Mindy and I have received in these past months have been truly inspiring. I only hope that, if elected, all these well-wishers will feel the same in a couple of years!

We Disciples are at a critical point in our history as a church. (*Every* point is critical, of course, but this is a time I think we *all* recognize as being especially dangerous and full of opportunity.)

The rapid social change of the past thirty years has brought us to a point where we are confused about who we are and what we are supposed to be doing.

The most important question that *any* church can ask at any point in time, whether a congregation or a region or a denomination, is, "Who and what is God calling us to be in this time and in this place?" Unfortunately, the church is often better at answering the question, "Who and what *was* God calling us to do and to be in some *other* time and place?" But the correct question is, "Who and what is God calling us to be in *this* time and in *this* place?" This is our primary task in this day. There are many other issues, of course, but our identity and mission are primary.

There are a number of *secondary* issues facing us, including the issues around human sexuality. These issues are not unimportant: They are *very* important. But in the long haul, such issues are secondary: Within a few decades, these issues, like so many the church has faced through the centuries, will be resolved, and we will wonder what the "big deal" was.

I predict this without predicting where the church will come out on these issues of human sexuality, and without declaring that my own position on these matters is either finished or will rule the day. My point is, simply, that *the primary issue will always be the nature and the mission of the Church.*

Our current crisis is due not to the fact that there are difficult issues facing us, though there are. The fact is that the church has always had to face difficult issues, though they are admittedly coming at us wave after wave in a way that the church has not experienced very often in its history. But our current crisis is primarily due to the fact that we are no longer clear about our nature and purpose, and thus our conversations about issues become argumentative and divide us and lead to the kind of "party spirit" that we as a denomination were created by God to witness against!

Now, of course, the "right" thinks the "left" is the problem, and the "left" thinks the "right" is the problem. But I'll tell you the truth: *We* are the problem! *All* of us! Because we have allowed ourselves to couch our arguments and positions in very personal terms and we have lost our humility. A people without humility is what the Bible calls a "stiff-necked people." And that is what we have become. We must recover our personal sense of dependence on God's grace and extend that grace to one another. We must begin to talk *to* each other instead of *at* each other. And not only talk, we must listen. We must remember that salvation is through faith, not through particular beliefs. There is "One Lord, one faith, one baptism," but there are many, many different beliefs about every matter of the faith. The strength of our church is that we have always celebrated this diversity of gifts and perspectives because it keeps us honest and pushes each of us to a deeper quest for truth.

I began by saying that this is a dangerous time. The danger is that, in the absence of clarity about our nature and mission, we will allow the secondary issues to destroy us as a church. The question now I suppose is, "How do we gain clarity about our nature and mission?"

I see the role of the general minister and president as calling the church together to do exactly this: to gain new clarity about our nature and mission. I don't think the general minister's role is to *give* us a statement of nature and mission. Although I certainly have my own ideas as a leader of this church, and I would draw on them. But I do think this is a whole church task. We need to come together around this question. Also, we need to consult our own history. Churches that fail to learn and appreciate their own history are doomed to repeat their mistakes rather than learning from those mistakes.

You will remember that this church was formed around the desire to reunify Christianity, and we have now divided twice over exactly how we should reunify Christianity. We could divide again if we do not come to understand the forces within us that led to our previous divisions and move to bridle them. I believe it grieved God when we split before and it will grieve God if we split again, because splitting and splintering is exactly the thing we were called to witness against. And when one end of the spectrum or another separates itself from the fellowship, it leaves the rest of the church unbalanced, like tennis shoes in a clothes dryer. The left and the right need each other. The conservative and the liberal need each other. The evangelical and the social activist need each other. All perspectives are necessary to a full, whole understanding of the Christian life and the truth of the gospel.

We are today witnessing the "Balkanization" of the entire planet. Every nation, every society, seems to be coming apart at the seams. The world is threatened with disintegration and tribalism. It is a time when everyone wants to affirm their own position or place by denigrating everyone else's. The left castigates the right, the right castigates the left, and the middle feels very lonely. The most complex of issues are cast in absolute terms. For example, in the struggle between those who are pro-life or pro-choice, there would seem to be no place for those like me who think that abortion is generally bad but that women should have control over their own bodies *and* that a male-dominated legislature should not have the power to make the choice for women. So, I am personally *both* pro-choice and pro-life! Life is full of such ambiguities, and yet we live in a time when everything is reduced to oversimplification and caricature.

Although the church is called to a ministry of reconciliation, of making all things one in Jesus Christ, the church has fallen into the world's habit of division and self-justification. If this is taken to its logical conclusion, then if there are two billion Christians in the world, there will be two billion denominations!

There was a time when the world took its cues from the church, not that I think the church always did such a "hot job" of leading the culture in Godly ways. But that's why churches like ours, the Christian Church (Disciples of Christ), were called mainline, because we influenced the culture so deeply. Today, however, we "mainline" churches have become "sideline" churches, because we no longer influence the culture so much as we seem to take our cues *from* the culture.

Let me take a little side trip here for a moment. When I was first nominated for general minister and president, there was a good deal of interest from the press, but the press's interest was not in what my priorities might be for the church. They did not care much about who I might be personally. What do you suppose they wanted to know? Uh-huh. "What's your position on homosexuality, Dr. Hamm?"

I refused to answer that question for several reasons, including the fact that no matter how I might have responded to questions of such a complex issue, we all know how the headlines would have read. I deserve more than this. You deserve more. The church deserves more.

As it was, and this would be funny if it weren't so sad, from the *Indianapolis Star* to the *New York Times*, to even the *Christian Century*, the articles that appeared about my nomination were more than half by volume about homosexuality, about which I did not comment! Does that strike you as strange? What is going on here? Surely there is something more than journalism occurring! And let's not kid ourselves; if it weren't for the human sexuality issues facing the church, the election of a new GMP would get little or no coverage.

What's my point? My point is that we have to stop trying to do church through the media! The church must take control of its own agenda. We must begin to talk to each other, not at each other!

Who's to blame for the way the press tries to reduce the human condition to a few soundbites? I guess we can't blame the press; they're just trying to sell newspapers.

Besides, maybe we get the press we deserve. It seems most of us would rather hear soundbites than read or listen to substantial reporting.

The media sets the agenda and defines the approach, so we have become much like what we see in the news: divided and alienated from one another. One of the oldest symbols for the church is that of a ship plying the world's waters in the midst of storms. It is one thing to have your ship in the water: That's normal and natural. It's quite another thing to have water in your ship! And the church has been taking on a lot of water lately! In such a condition, the church cannot witness effectively to the world and cannot do its ministry of reconciliation.

We must come together—the left, the right, and the middle; the conservative, the evangelical, and the social activist; the white, the Black, the Asian, and the Hispanic; the male and the female. We must come together to be the church. None of us has a corner on the truth. We must, in humility, work together to be whole.

So, I see the general minister's role in this divisive time above all else, to call the church together to consider again who we are called to be and what God has called us to do together, to hear the wisdom of the general church, the regions, and especially the congregations.

I said that we as a church were called into being to witness *against* the splintering and party-spirit that was ravaging the church in the days of Campbell and Stone. But more than being called to witness against division, we were created and called to witness for Christian unity. And this world in which we live today, this divided world, this severed, segregated, secular world, is dying daily for want of a credible model of how to live together in creative diversity while maintaining personal identity, conviction, and integrity.

When asked what the Disciples of Christ stand for, an increasing number of members are giving answers like one I heard recently: "Being a Disciple means it doesn't matter what you believe so long as you are tolerant." I was appalled. As leaders of this denomination, we should all be appalled at such a statement.

Of *course* it matters what we believe. Of *course,* everyone who joins this church must confess that Jesus is the Christ. Of *course,* we believe that the scripture together with the Holy Spirit are the highest authority for us. But the *genius* of this church is that we understand that the Holy Spirit meets people where they are ... and that we are not all at the same place.

We have always enjoyed using mottos instead of creeds, and one of my favorite mottos has been, "Where the scriptures speak, we speak; where the scriptures are silent, we are silent." But this motto proved to be inadequate to meet the challenges that confronted the church a century ago. So, one Disciples leader declared, "Where the scriptures speak, we speak; where the scriptures are silent, we use sanctified common sense!"

And so, led by the Spirit, and bringing our reason and our experience and the tradition of the church to bear, we arrive at different understandings of the scripture. And appreciating these differences, we fellowship with one another and dialogue with one another so as to learn from each other. Not to prove each other wrong, nor to prove ourselves right, but to add to our understanding of the truth. In the meantime, we must each serve and witness as the Holy Spirit convicts and leads us to do. Tolerance for difference is no virtue in the absence of a sense of personal responsibility for the truth as we understand it so far.

If we are to fulfill this understanding of church, if we are to model this kind of creative diversity, then we must be careful to "test the spirits," as the Letter of John suggests we should. And while "the works of the flesh" (as Paul puts it in Galatians) include anger, dissension, and party spirit, the "fruits of the Holy Spirit" include love, patience, kindness, gentleness, and self-control.

There are many lessons we learned, or should have learned, in Tulsa. I think everyone should have come away recognizing that this is a democratic organization; everyone's vote counts, and there is no conspiracy anywhere to try to disenfranchise anyone.

But perhaps an even more important lesson which needed to be learned by all of us, no matter where we stood on the spectrum of opinion, is that this church is a fragile vessel. We ought not to beat up on the church, or on each other as members of the body

The Christian Church (Disciples of Christ) is such a gift to the world. When we are at our best, I think we are modeling the church of the future. The genius of this church is like a torch which has been entrusted to us, a torch that can give light to a world of division and strife. But the torch has been flickering of late and, if we do not treat it with respect and kindness, the flame could die. This church is a fragile vessel.

As we together seek a renewed understanding of our nature and purpose as a church, let us treat each other with love, patience, kindness, gentleness, and self-control. For that will be pleasing to the Christ in whom we are all one.

A final word. We are not indispensable. God can raise up denominations from stones. But God loves this communion, I am certain, and if we, Disciples of Christ, will be led by the Spirit who gives those good gifts and who, after all, is the true source of any church's life and mission, we will find that this is but our springtime. We were made for a time such as this!

April 19, 1993
Nominee's Acceptance Statement to General Board

There are a number of people I would like to thank. First, a special word of appreciation to Don Zarley and the search committee who provided a very churchly atmosphere throughout the process. Thanks also to Marilyn Moffett and the Administrative Committee; to my friends who have encouraged me; to my family, especially Mindy, for reacting with pride rather than panic; and to all of you, the members of this board, for the trust you are placing in me.

While I was waiting for the results of your deliberations this morning, I took a short walk downstairs in the hotel to the meeting rooms area. One of the signs read, "The Total Employment Interview." Let me assure you that any member of this board could go downstairs and teach that course!

I believe that Jesus is the Christ, sent by the Living God for our salvation.

I am always amazed when I look back on my life and consider how God has worked to bring good things, even during those times when I felt confusion or aloneness ... feelings not unknown to me in recent months. The Spirit does indeed move where it will. Praise God! I feel God's Spirit moving in my life in powerful ways. That's true regardless of what happens in St. Louis.

While I am not taking anything for granted this morning, or in the weeks ahead, you need to know that I feel the call of God in your decision today. I accept your nomination with fear and trembling, but with the utter confidence of one who knows that God is God and that, regardless of what happens in St. Louis, God is with me and my family, and with this church.

Leadership is key for Disciples because, for us, authority does not rest in structures but in one's ability to *lead*. I pledge to you that, if the Christian Church (Disciples of Christ) extends the call through the General Assembly, I will be a leader.

Effective leadership is *pastoral*, demonstrates an *alive faith*, is *passionate*, and *responsive*. Effective leadership consults and listens.

Leaders must help their community maintain its sense of identity, must call the community to focus on real priorities, must be able to hear concerns even when expressed stridently, must have integrity and humility.

I pledge to you that I will seek to be that kind of leader, with the help of God.

I was asked a wonderful question yesterday in one of the section meetings: "What legacy would I like to leave the church upon my departure from office?" There are three accomplishments I hope to see.

First, I would like to leave a church that is clear about its identity and mission.

Second, I would hope that the church would be renewed spiritually, which means it would be truly evangelistic and truly committed to justice. You cannot have one without the other.

Third, I would hope to see a church that is growing.

Again, thank you for your trust and support. Together, with God, you and I can make a difference and build upon the excellent tradition and record of the mission that is the Christian Church (Disciples of Christ). Pray for us. I will pray for you.

July 16, 1993

Nominee's Address to General Assembly

Please pray with me.

> O God, open our hearts and minds in these moments that we may hear your Word. May the words of my mouth and the meditations of my heart be acceptable in your sight, our Maker, Redeemer, and Friend.

"A long and winding road" brings me here today! It is a fearsome time to offer leadership to the church, in any of its expressions, and I feel the weight of that challenge. Nevertheless, whatever your decision Saturday, it means so much to me to stand in this place today. I love this church!

For me, this church is the aroma of warm cherry pies and fried chicken relentlessly drawing a young boy to the kitchen of First Christian Church, Crawfordsville—a foretaste of the feast to come. This church is the awe and wonder of being baptized at the age of ten by Dr. Wayne Drash at Mirror Lake Christian Church in St. Petersburg. It is the excitement and sense of purpose I felt as Mom, Dad, my brother, and I became charter members of Palm Lake Christian Church, worshiping in an old chicken house as though it was the most wonderful sanctuary ever. It is the sense of belonging and importance I felt as a member and Timothy of that loving, caring congregation; the special friendship of Ken Dean, George Farmer, and J. W. Cate.

This church is the joy I felt in CYF Conference at Silver Springs and in committing my life to full-time Christian service on consecration night. It is the challenge I felt every day as a student at Christian Theological Seminary being pushed deeper and deeper into the soil of Christian faith and life. It is the power of professors, elders, and friends laying hands on my head in the act of ordination. It is the pride I felt in bringing my new bride to the parsonage of Little Eagle Creek Christian Church, the pride of seeing a member of my youth group at Central Christian Church in Kansas City choosing ministry, the agony and ecstasy of starting North Oak Christian Church, the indescribable experience of baptizing my own children at First Christian in Ft. Wayne. Many of you have had a similar journey, and others of us have come to the Disciples from other faith traditions and so have all the enthusiasm of "converts": So maybe you understand how I feel in these moments. My heart is so full of gratitude for this church that there is little room for fear.

I *believe* in the Christian Church (Disciples of Christ). I believe we have an important mission. I don't believe this church came to be simply because of historical circumstances or simply because a few people, whom we honor as founders, thought it seemed like a good idea. On the contrary, I believe the Christian Church (Disciples of Christ) was *called* into being by God, and that *we are now being called into an extraordinary future of growth and service to the world that we can hardly imagine.* Most of us are not aware of how important a role this denomination has played, and is playing, in shaping the church of the future.

The modern movement toward Christian unity has made significant progress in bringing scores of Christians closer to one another, in bringing an end to the open hostility that once marked the denominational landscape; and no denomination has had more of an impact on this process than the Christian Church (Disciples of Christ). In my opinion, when we are at our best, we Disciples look significantly like the church of the future.

For example, we have freedom coupled with responsibility; we have an approach to the Bible that takes its historical context seriously; we have an appreciation of the Lord's Supper as a regular part of weekly corporate worship; we have a firm confidence in the priesthood of all believers; our form of organization (or polity) empowers congregations to make decisions about what faithfulness means where they are, and yet recognizes that congregations are connected to each other and to the rest of the church through a covenantal relationship.

It's not that we bear any one of these marks uniquely. *Many* denominations share one or several of these characteristics with us. Rather, it is our unique *combination* of these various characteristics that makes us an important and rich piece of the patchwork quilt that is the whole body of Christ. And until the church of Jesus Christ on earth becomes the seamless garment that it is already, spiritually, we Disciples have an important witness to Christian unity. The history of division within the church is *still* scandalous because it impairs the church's witness to the transforming power of the gospel of Jesus Christ. How can the world believe in the reconciling power of the gospel if there is division between and within denominations?

We Disciples do have our challenges before us. Most pressing, we need a clearer sense of our mission and identity. In the face of thirty years of rapid social change, we have gotten somewhat confused about what it is God is calling us to be and to do in this age. We have tended to "turn in" on ourselves and to forget that the church was made for the world, that we are called to ministries of witness, reconciliation, and justice. Trying to be the church without a clear sense of mission is like trying to run a foot race in galoshes!

It is mission that makes the church go. Among the most profound words of Jesus are these, "Whoever seeks to save his life will lose it, but whoever loses his life for my sake shall surely find it." This is as true for churches as it is for individuals. As a pastor and as a regional minister, I have done a lot of strategic planning in a lot of congregations, and I have learned; dead and dying congregations cannot be revived by merely painting the nursery and adding parking spaces. It is when a congregation takes seriously the needs of the people around it and around the world that the lights go back on, members are energized, and new life is discovered. This denomination will not be revived by rearranging our ecclesiological furniture or even by redoubling our efforts. We're trying! God knows we're trying! But we've been getting bogged down in trying to *save* ourselves! We must refocus our *mission* if we are to live or if we are to be worth saving! Otherwise, we might as well vote now to change the name of our general offices from "the Missions Building" to "the Fissions Building," because we're going to tear ourselves limb from limb.

Along with renewal of our sense of mission and identity, we also need spiritual renewal; we need greater discipline within our life together; we need to get more serious about revitalizing present congregations *and* establishing new congregations; many of our ministers are suffering from burn out and a lack of clarity about their calling and the importance of that calling; Basic Mission Finance contributions have generally not kept up with inflation for the past twenty years; many of our members and congregations are in the "comfort zone."

But because God is with us, none of these problems is insurmountable. In fact, in facing up to these problems, we will be immeasurably blessed as we learn to walk more closely with God. The experience of the Refiner's fire has never been comfortable, and there has been, and will be, *pain* as we are disciplined and refined by the Spirit. But on our way to greater faithfulness as individual Christians and as a church, we will be immeasurably blessed.

I believe that as we look for clues about our mission and identity, and for solutions to our current problems, we need to look back and remember the vision that called us into being. You will remember that in nineteenth-century America, the issue was sectarianism: the tendency of the church to divide itself into a million different pieces over every issue and question of doctrine. Thomas Campbell got into trouble in Pennsylvania because he served communion to New Light Anti-Burgher Seceder Presbyterians when he was an Old Light Anti-Burgher Seceder Presbyterian. So fractured had the church become that Campbell had to use four qualifiers around his denominational identity!

It became apparent to the Campbells, to Stone, Scott, and many others that the church could not be based on particular doctrinal positions, or it would just go on splintering and splintering until, ultimately, there would be as many sects as there were individual Christians. So, they sought a return to the ideal of a church based not on doctrine but simply on faith in Jesus Christ.

Part of the genius of our founders is their recognition that no human being can arrive at a total and complete understanding of God's truth. The truth is much larger than any of us can grasp, and our individual understanding is subject to our own limited perspective and our own peculiar distortions. Therefore, it is essential that Christians of all perspectives remain in fellowship with one another, though we will inevitably disagree on matters of interpretation and action. By remaining in fellowship, we help keep each other honest intellectually and we teach each other, sometimes by surfacing a better idea, sometimes by challenging each other to think through our own positions more carefully.

Whenever the church splits, the truth is again split in significant ways.

But tragically, what was true in the days of our founders is true today: Choosing up sides is energizing. Picking a side to champion and defending it against all the *other* sides, *that's* what makes us feel powerful and important. And some would tell us that to be *faithful* one must not only *choose a side* in the current debates over various issues and doctrines, but one must *attack* those who hold another point of view, as if to say "We have the answers." "We are right and you are wrong." This is and always has been the way of the world. It is what is happening in Bosnia, in Somalia, in the Middle East, in Los Angeles, in every part of the globe. It is that wicked demon which the New Testament calls "party spirit." It can make us feel powerful and important and is particularly tempting and deadly in this era in which everyone feels powerless and unimportant.

The fact is that in all the great moral questions of the day, no matter how we try to oversimplify the issues and to "line up God" on one side or the other, each side has only a piece of the truth. We will just have to live with the complexities of these issues until, through the counsel of the Holy Spirit, we are able to shape new responses—responses that incorporate a greater share of the total truth than any of our sectarian responses presently incorporate. As Robert Frost said it, "We dance around in a ring and suppose, but the Secret sits in the middle and knows." Or as Paul put it, "Now we know in part, then we shall know in full."

In the meantime, we must remember that *the test of our fellowship is not in the accuracy of our belief but in how we manifest the spirit of Christ.* We must maintain the "bond of peace." This is our covenant as Disciples of Christ, to continue to work and live together even when we have grave differences ... yea, *because we have grave differences! This* is creative diversity. This is the vision of our founders, and it is as valid today as it was one hundred and sixty years ago.

No part of this body speaks for the body. But every part of the body has the right to speak to the body. I think some of our problems in recent decades have been due to the fact that some of us have felt that our right to speak to the church, in our own voice, has been somehow denied. I believe there is some validity to this criticism. It is not that wicked leaders have somehow plotted to keep others from being heard. On the contrary, this church has been blessed with very gracious leaders. The problem is more subtle. It is that the systems we have created for ourselves have created their own injustices.

For example, when the General Assembly gathers, it tends to be overly representative of ministers. That is in part because ministers are *expected* to be here, and most of us have some sort of financial assistance from our congregations and institutions to get us here. But most lay people do not get expense money. So, not only do they have to take off time from their work, they also have to take total responsibility for the cost of being here. That means that ministers will inevitably be overrepresented.

Another example. When we vote on resolutions, we report only approval or disapproval. It seems to me that when there is significant division in the house, it would also be helpful to create a minority report. This would help acknowledge the fact that truth cannot be absolutely determined by voting on it!

We can and must find better ways to provide for the *creative* diversity we need.

I want to affirm two efforts currently underway to encourage dialogue in the church. First is the "mission conversations" being offered to congregations by the Church Finance Council and

Regions. This program is right on target. It is an opportunity for every congregation in North America to give direct input into the future shaping of our work together at home and around the world. Second is the program being developed by the Council on Theological Education, which will provide for serious theological conversations across the church around mission and identity. I encourage your personal participation in both of these efforts.

In addition to these two, in consultation with a representative steering committee, I want to develop additional means for regular dialogue around the church. It is not legitimate for some voices to shout down other voices. But it's legitimate for each voice to be heard, and we need to provide ongoing ways for each voice to be heard. We must each listen as well as speak. And our speaking must be done within our covenant to be church together.

When a couple comes for marriage counseling, progress can usually be made if both parties are still committed to the marriage. But if one or the other is no longer committed, no progress will be made no matter how much talking is done. And being committed to the marriage means, in part, that the husband and wife still fulfill their responsibility to take care of each other while the conversation is going on. One does not withhold his or her paycheck until the other gives in. Being faithful to the covenant to be the church together means that individuals who disagree with the rest of the members of a congregation do not withhold their offerings until the other members agree to do it their way. Neither should congregations who disagree with policies or decisions of the wider church withhold BMF monies, holding the wider church hostage to their viewpoint. That's not acting within the covenant of either marriage or church.

Still, as a church, we must do a better job of enabling the voices of those who seem to be speaking to us from the margins (whether theological minorities, ethnic minorities, or others). We must do this not only because it is a matter of justice, but because institutions are almost always renewed from the margins. Not that every word which is spoken from the margins is absolute truth, but when a church stops listening to its margins, it begins to lose its vitality by continually recreating itself in its own image.

Only God has the whole truth, and thus only God—rather than any particular doctrine or interpretation—can serve as the center of our church.

That is why the communion table stood at the center of the church's life for our founders, and why it stands at the center of our life together today, the table, where Christ calls us together around a heavenly feast given to us by him.

It is Christ, and him crucified, who is the center of our fellowship, the center of our creative diversity. You don't need a "token" to come to this table, as you did in the days of the Springfield Presbytery ... Christ has made himself our token. No one will "fence" this table as it was fenced at Cane Ridge, to be certain we are found worthy because we believe the right things. It is only by *God's grace* that *any* of us come to this table. We Disciples, when we are at our best, understand that it is not our particular *beliefs* that save us, or that can make us one, but only our *faith*.

Our tradition has always been "open communion," which means being open to each other, coming to the table together in humility to recognize our common utter dependence upon God's grace. It is around the table that we are called to transcend our differences, to remember our common need, and to celebrate our oneness in Jesus Christ.

A few months ago, I was in a worship service looking at the table ... which can hardly be avoided in a Disciples setting! I found myself meditating on that common inscription found on so many Disciples communion tables. "Do this in remembrance of me." And that word, "remembrance," jumped out at me in a way it never had before.

We come to the table at our Lord's command to "remember" ... to "re-member!" We are the body of Christ, yet the world and church politics would drive us apart, would "*dis*-member" us. And there is *so much* chaos in and around our lives that seeks to dis-member us. But we come together every week around this table to remember that in Him we are one. In Him we are re-membered ... brought back together as the body of Christ.

I think the general minister and president's job is, in part, to continually call us together; to call us to come together not around common belief or common understanding but around common need and common faith—the need for grace and the faith that God provides it. And our experience of that grace will give us our mission. Remember Ezekiel's vision? If we come together around the table in recognition of our poverty of spirit, God will blow the breath of new life into this body as surely as God blew the breath of new life into Israel's dry bones. God will give us new energy for our mission to the world.

Do we really have no clue as to what our mission may be? We are witnessing the Balkanization of the entire planet. The whole world is coming unglued, societies and nations are falling into tribalism and people are being killed, spiritually and physically, through that utter evil which is called by the most abominable euphemism of all time: "ethnic cleansing." The world is *dying* for a model of truly *creative* diversity in which difference is not merely tolerated, but *appreciated*. The world is *dying* for a model of community that is not exclusive but *inclusive*, based not in pride, but in *humility*.

But it is only as we come together in humility to re-member and to be re-membered that we can truly make a difference in a world that is dis-membered and hopeless: the world for which we were created.

I began by saying that I love the Christian Church (Disciples of Christ). I am also certain that God loves this communion, and if we Disciples will be led by the Spirit, who is the true source of any church's life and mission, we will find that this is but our springtime. We were made for such a time as this!

July 17, 1993

Acceptance Statement to General Assembly

There are a number of people I wish to thank, today. First, I want to express a word of gratitude and admiration for two people whose example of graciousness and spiritual maturity has been such a wonderful blessing and witness to us all in these past years. Michael and Kathryn, *you* have blessed us every day.

My deep appreciation to Don Zarley and the search committee, and our excellent Moderator, Marilyn Moffett, who provided a very churchly atmosphere throughout the process. Thanks to the many friends who have given encouragement these past months through their cards and letters, calls and prayers; to our Disciples in Tennessee who have been so supportive and gracious; to our dear family friend and, for these last three years, our pastor, Dan Moseley.

I want to thank the folks of the General Offices who have been so helpful in this time of preparation. I know you join me in special gratitude to two people who, in order to respond to the call of the church they love, interrupted their life plans to move to Indianapolis to work so tirelessly and graciously to bring healing and growth during these last two years. I know I *personally* ran into Bill in airports *twice* in the last six months, and I have heard of many others having the same experience. In the last two years in North America, I'm certain there have been more Bill sightings than Elvis sightings! Thank you, Bill and Claudine Nichols.

There are a number of members of my family present today. I think that they will be recognized on Tuesday, when my parents have arrived, but wherever my aunts and uncles and cousins are seated today, I want you to know how much I appreciate you being here. You've been there for the graduations, the ordination, the installations, and you're here today, and I'm proud of you and I love you.

I'm so thankful for Mindy: for her steadfast support, love and companionship; and to David and Laura, who have taken all of this in stride this year. Especially Laura, who has been most gracious about the prospect of changing high schools. We're so proud of these two.

I think I have been very honest and forthcoming during these past several months in regard to my feelings and beliefs about various issues, and you can expect more of the same frankness and clarity from me in this regard. But I want you to know that I know that the vote this morning is not a referendum on this or that social issue. It is, rather, about your hope for leadership that can help the church get clear about what God is calling us to do and to be. I will continue to express my views on various matters, as I expect you to do, but I will not presume to speak for you. You know that the press will get confused about this from time to time, just as they seem to be unable to grasp the fact that the General Assembly speaks to the church, not for the church. But I can't let the media's confusion about who we are cloud my understanding of who I am.

Don't expect a "peace" maker, if by that you mean peace at any price. Rather, expect me to be a "shalom" maker, a facilitator of the kind of peace that grows out of justice and love for one another.

I must tell you that I've been a little concerned that the "official" biographies have highlighted my role as a mediator in two contract disputes between teachers and school districts. Don't get me wrong: I'm very proud to have been of use in those two very tense situations, but I wouldn't want you to get the impression that I'm "just" a mediator or, worse, that my chief skill is in helping divided camps arrive at a lukewarm, milk-toasty, least common denominator! If you ask people who really know me, I think they will tell you not to expect that from me. If you have elected me because you think I'm just a manager, you aren't going to be very happy. I think I'm a good manager, but while management by objective is helpful, when management *becomes* the objective, it's deadly.

And while I regard myself as being politically astute, I do not regard myself as just a politician. I am a pastor.

I think there is a place for resolutions, an important place. But the church cannot be led by mere resolutions. The church must be led by leaders. Resolutions tend to be impersonal, and no one seems to be responsible for them in a very real way. But a biblical style of leadership is always personal and directly accountable. I pledge to you that I will seek to give the church this kind of leadership and I challenge you to do the same.

Two equally popular musicals take very different approaches to the human condition. Too many of us have been singing, "Somewhere over the rainbow ... why, oh why, can't I?" More of us need to sing, "Climb every mountain ... till you find your dream." Except in this case, it is God's dream we are called to pursue.

What this church needs is fewer resolutions and more resolve. We need less political strategy and more theological centering. We need more talk about God and less talk about ourselves. More dialogue and less debate. More study of the Bible than of budgets. More of the spiritual disciplines and less hand wringing and poor-mouthing.

The church is on the potter's wheel, and we need an outbreak of leadership from every corner of this great denomination.

Most of you here today are leaders of the church. That's why you are here. Let's pledge *together* to give this church the leadership it needs, the leadership it deserves, the leadership God wants it to have.

Thank you for your trust and support. Together, with God, you and I can make a difference and build upon the excellent tradition and record of mission that is the Christian Church (Disciples of Christ). Pray for us. I will pray for you.

December 5, 1993

Council of Ministers

"A Vision for This Council for These Six Years"

I am truly delighted to be here with you in this, my first Council of Ministers meeting as general minister and president. As I prepared my remarks for this hour, it occurred to me how strange it seems to say that I have been looking *forward* to a Council of Ministers meeting ... a meeting which, in years past, I had learned to dread!

But I have been looking forward to this meeting because I have an agenda, and I believe it is an agenda which is important to the future of this church. Let me quickly add that I do not claim to have many answers: I claim only to have an appropriate agenda as we struggle, with the help of the Holy Spirit, to get ourselves out of this present mire and on the road to being a movement again. As the church struggles to understand and live out its mission, I think my role is to help surface the right questions and to call the church together around those questions so that, together, we might discern the will of God for this church in this day and time.

This is exactly what I hope to accomplish in this meeting. During these days together, we will work through a process that has four movements. The first move has to do with the purpose of this Council. The second move has to do with the development of a working mission statement for the Christian Church (Disciples of Christ). The third move will review a proposal regarding resolutions in General Assembly, and the fourth move will look at how we might establish real mission priorities for this church.

Each of these four movements begins with a statement from me to which you will be asked to respond in various ways. While a lot of study, thought, and consultation has gone into what I will say in these presentations, I want you to know that I am not married to any of what I am presenting to you. I want what I offer you to be stronger as a result of having passed through the crucible of this Council. Indeed, we may arrive at conclusions fundamentally different from what I will initially propose. That is fine with me so long as we arrive somewhere together. My heart's desire is for us all to work collegially.

That brings me to the subject of this first movement, which is the purpose of this Council. Let me say that it was both amusing and humbling to hear Bill Miller's presentation of some of the history of the Conference of Regional Ministers and Moderators this week. It pointed out to me that most of my "new" ideas are not new. I was reminded of something Harry Truman, an avid reader of history, once said, "The only thing new under the sun is the history you haven't read!" Much truth here.

Historically, this group was called into being by the first general minister and president, A. Dale Fiers. He established this group, in part, to be a place where regional and general leaders could relate to each other as colleagues. I affirm that purpose.

As a matter of fact, given the cultural context of our life today, I believe this may be a more pressing need than ever before. I have spoken many times in the past year about the phenomenon I have called "the Balkanization of the planet." That is, people are defining their communities in narrower and narrower ways. People are defining themselves more and more as "over against" what others are.

Community is breaking down. As someone recently observed (was it Bill Coffin?): "First there was the magazine called *People*, then the magazine called *Us*, and now there is the magazine called *Self*.

I wish I could say that the church is beyond such dynamics, that community is alive and well in the church of Jesus Christ. But you and I both know that isn't true. The turf wars are about as real in the North American church as they are in Bosnia.

We are in a time of financial distress, which means increased competition for scarce funds, and competition puts pressure on already strained relationships.

Add these dynamics to the fact that the church in all of its manifestations has increasingly become bureaucratized, and the need for a place where we can meet to reaffirm our collegiality is obvious.

My brothers and sisters, as the general, regional, and educational leadership of this church, we meet separately too often! We need to meet together more often. It is by being together that we strengthen our relationships and develop trust and real collegiality. Families cannot hold together if they do not spend quality time together. Neither can the church leadership hold together without quality time together.

I wish to add one aside here that is related. I believe the Conference of Regional Ministers and Moderators should be reconceived. Certainly, it is important to provide training and orientation for regional moderators, so that they see their work connected to the wider church; and it is important to be able to receive the counsel and wisdom of the moderators. But the time required of regional ministers to meet with moderators would be better spent in meeting as a College of Regional Ministers or with this Council of Ministers.

Moderators and regional ministers meeting together is like mixing apples and football helmets. When Bill Miller comes to the part of our history that will reveal why the predecessor of the Conference began with the antecedents of moderators and regional ministers meeting together, I suspect we will find it was for political reasons rather than because it served any real functional purpose. I invite the College of Regional Ministers to rethink the Conference.

In any case, one purpose of this Council must be to provide a place where regional, general, and educational leaders can be together as colleagues.

Another historical purpose of this council is to do biblical and theological reflection on the nature and mission of the church. I affirm this purpose. While I will be proposing the development of a mission statement for this denomination later in this meeting, our understanding of the church's mission must *constantly* be renewed and challenged. This is a place where the general and regional leadership of this church can reflect upon the church's mission and apply that understanding of mission to our common life and program; this is a place where the church's vision can be renewed.

Yet another historical purpose of this Council is to provide for the spiritual nurture of its members. This is certainly a purpose I affirm, and future Council meetings will demonstrate my commitment to this.

The fourth and last historical purpose given this body by Dr. Fiers was to be a consultative body for the GMP. I have already indicated to you that I affirm this purpose. It is my intention to help us surface the right questions and to help us struggle with those questions *together*. Now, in addition to these historical purposes I want to add two other possible purposes.

First, to originate, develop, coordinate, and evaluate programs.

Many of you have heard me say that when I came to regional ministry, people asked me what my biggest surprise was. My answer was, "the disconnectedness of this church." Upon coming to *this* office, people have again asked me, "What is your biggest surprise?" My answer is, "the disconnectedness of this church." I have learned this in a whole new way, and it distresses me greatly. This is nowhere more evident than in the area of programming.

The pattern appears to be that we as regions, units, and institutions generate programs in nearly total isolation from each other, but then we become resentful when our colleagues do not feel ownership in these programs and our colleagues become resentful about the implications of such programs for *their* work.

This Council could be an effective place to conceive program initiatives so that from their very conception they may be grounded in the broad experience and various perspectives of colleagues and may enjoy wide ownership. Likewise, this would be an excellent place for coordination, development in broad terms, and evaluation to occur. I do not mean to suggest that *detailed* program development should be done in this Council. But needs and approaches could certainly be profitably conceived here across manifestation lines.

The second new purpose I wish to suggest is to educate the church through the preparation and dissemination of pastoral letters. These letters could be on any subject we deemed appropriate. Later in this meeting I will suggest how these pastoral letters might be used to replace resolutions in our General Assembly. But I do not want to address that idea now; nor do I wish you to respond to that idea now, For the moment, let us just think in terms of pastoral letters by themselves. There is nothing in The Design that would prohibit us from offering pastoral letters any time we chose to begin doing so. I think it is perfectly appropriate to offer such letters and very much in keeping with Paul's admonition to "equip the saints."

The sad fact is that most of our members get most of their information about issues of the day, and even about the church, through the secular media. We must begin to take our educational responsibilities more seriously as leaders of this church or we don't deserve to be called leaders. Pastors of congregations need to make teaching a priority, as has been pointed out by Clark Williamson and Ron Allen and other writers. But the teaching vocation certainly extends as well to the "bishops" of the church.

Before I give you the opportunity to respond to these ideas, I want to address one more issue: the inclusivity issue.

The reality is that, in significant ways, we have at least four Disciple churches in North America. We have a white church, an African American church, a Hispanic church, and an American Asian church. While The Design would have us believe that these four churches are all served by one regional and general structure, the reality is that cultural barriers interfere with the programmatic wholeness of the church.

Whether one feels comfortable with it or not, the regional and general structures of this church serve mostly white Disciples. Though Black Disciples long ago bought into the wholeness of the church spiritually and theologically and have tried to relate as best they can structurally, the reality remains that Black Disciples still get a large measure of their needs met through the Convocation and informal networks. We who are white leaders simply cannot adequately understand the needs of Black congregations well enough to represent those needs in the absence of African American participation on this Council.

If this is true of African American Disciples, it is doubly true of Hispanic Disciples and three times true of American Asian Disciples. This is truer yet of new immigrants who come to this country and find themselves in Disciples congregations.

Therefore, I believe that there does need to be representation from those three minority groups. I would propose that at all times at least three members of this Council should be African Americans. If there are not enough African Americans who are members through regular provisions, then the Convocation should be invited to select persons who would serve as African American representatives to insure a minimum of three,

Likewise, the National Hispanic pastor should be a regular member to represent our growing Hispanic membership, and the DHM staff person for American Asian ministries should serve to represent our growing American Asian membership.

While females are still a small proportion of this Council's regular membership, it has grown, for which we give thanks. While I am not advocating additional female representative members of this Council, I do believe we need to greatly increase our advocacy of female candidates for various positions of regional and general leadership which would serve simple justice as well as improving the gender balance of this body.

So, in brief, I am proposing that this Council's purpose be (1) to be a place where regional and general leaders can be together as colleagues; (2) to do biblical and theological reflection on the nature and mission of the church; (3) to provide for the spiritual nurture of its members; (4) to be a consultative body for the GMP; (5) to originate, develop, coordinate, and evaluate programs; (6) to educate the church through the preparation and dissemination of pastoral letters.

In carrying out this purpose, I believe that the Council should meet more often, and that care should be given to providing for inclusivity as I have indicated.

If this Council could affirm this purpose, or something like it, I believe we could make a real difference in the life of this church.

One last thought. Let's find a more suitable name for this Council. Pastors of congregations and non-parish ministers should be (and many are) offended to hear of a "Council of Ministers" that includes none of them. I know "Council of Bishops" would be ill-advised, but surely we can come up with a more adequate name than we presently have.

Well, that's my vision for this Council. Think about it, tear it apart, come up with something better. But whatever we end up with, let's arrive together and let's work collegially.

December 6, 1993

Council of Ministers

"Why a Mission Statement?"

My experience as pastor of a congregation and as a regional minister has taught me at least one clear lesson. Any vital institution, any vital community of faith, has a clear sense of what God is calling them to do and to be in the present time and context. This is true of congregations, this is true of regions, this is true of general ministry units and institutions of higher education, and I am convinced that this is just as true for a denomination.

I have been saying that, in the face of the rapid social change of the past thirty years or so, this church has become somewhat confused about what it is God is calling us to do and to be today. We are not alone in this, whatever comfort that may bring us. Every mainline protestant church has been drifting somewhat since the mid-1960s.

The sheer velocity of change during these years is hard to overstate. I remember when I read Toffler's *Future Shock* twenty or so years ago.[1] I thought, "I don't see what the big deal is here." *Now* I understand what the big deal is. If one has doubts about this, one has only to rent one of the "old" James Bond movies. See what kinds of special effects thrilled us just twenty years ago, and then note

---
[1] Alvin Toffler, *Future Shock* (Bantam Books, 1971).

how each has been far surpassed by daily reality. Many of us carry calculators in our briefcase or on our wrists that, not so many years ago, would have filled a room.

But, of course, technological change is merely one aspect of the change. Who, as a pastor doing counseling, has not gotten lost in the maze of a family tree as a parishioner has made reference to their stepbrother who was a product of their mother's third marriage? Nobody wants to invest in a globe or a world map anymore, because national names and borders are changing so rapidly that such maps are obsolete within a few weeks.

I don't need to lecture this group on change. It is everywhere around and within us and it is often overwhelming and confusing.

Another reason the church is confused is because its leadership has not always done a good job of educating the membership about its own life and work. A prime example is our overseas ministry. Most of our members still operate out of a romanticized image of missionary work that we moved away from decades ago, but we have still not effectively communicated the new image nor the mission concept behind it. Responsibility for this anachronistic understanding does not simply or even primarily rest with DOM. It rests with all of us to some degree. But my point is not to fix blame for such confusion; my point is simply that there is much confusion and obsolete self-understanding in the church.

Of course, a large measure of the confusion has to do with the fact that our membership is constantly bombarded from every direction with competing and conflicting images about what it means to be church. Images come from television (including cable), from radio, from print media, from childhood, from coworkers with whom people used to seldom discuss religion.

The fact that denominational loyalty is practically nonexistent anymore for so many people means that we have members and ministers coming into the Christian Church (Disciples of Christ) who have no understanding of our basic ethos. The breakdown of denominational barriers is good on the one hand: It is an indication that we, Disciples, have been doing an effective job of helping people transcend old-style denominationalism. But on the other hand, it means we are challenged to maintain institutional and theological coherence in the face of such an influx of non-Disciple members. We are challenged to provide education and orientation we have not been providing. Thus, we have ministers who are Disciples in name only. They may come from, say, the Baptist tradition (and it's not that there is something inherently bad about Baptist ways, they are just different) and they have brought their Baptist ethos and theology with them. They are essentially Baptists serving Disciples congregations with no commitment to Disciples ways.

Just last week I received a letter from the congregation in Monroe, Tennessee. Now, this church was never a very solidly Disciples church, but most of our congregations are not these days! I felt I had made some inroads with them as their regional minister a couple of years ago. After their "nondenominational" (read "nonaccountable") pastor left, I managed to get a meeting with their search committee chair and with their search committee. After I had made my presentation, everybody seemed to feel very good about my having been there, and we all agreed to work together within the system. I sent names and they began their work. But then, I didn't hear from the chairman for a couple or three weeks, and I began to wonder what was happening. So, I called him. "Oh," he said, "I meant to call you. We have a new minister." "Great!" I said, trying to hide the mounting fear I felt. "Who is it?" "Well, he's a relative of one of our members. He's an independent Baptist ... but we want him to get licensed as a Disciple." My heart sank.

Oh, I sent the papers for this pleasant young pastor to fill out, and we had a pleasant cup of coffee to talk about it all. He was very enthusiastic. But he didn't show up for his appointment with the Commission on Ministry and he wouldn't return phone calls. Last week, he led the church out of the denomination.

Our members and congregations are "sitting ducks," suckers for any line, because we are without a clear sense of who we are and what we are about. This is a serious challenge to the coherence of our institutional life and our ability to work together in an effective worldwide program of mission and ministry.

I could give many other examples, but I think you get my point. This church is confused, like many other churches today, about identity and mission. I recognize that a mission statement is not a magic bullet that will suddenly bring complete coherence to our common life. But I do believe that the development of such a statement would be a great help to us as we seek a new sense of self-understanding.

There are several ways to develop a mission statement. One way would be to involve as many Disciples as possible in gathering ideas and elements of a mission statement. One could imagine "listening conferences" around North America seeking input. Then leaders would seek to bring some order out of that input and thus develop a working statement that would be tested everywhere possible. This approach has validity, but I don't think we have the time or energy to mount such an effort.

An alternative way, which I think is more appropriate to our present situation, is to ask leaders to develop a working statement and then test that statement as widely as possible. I believe this is not only a more efficient method, but a more appropriate method given our church's present state of confusion.

Therefore, I am asking you to begin the task of developing a working mission statement for the Christian Church (Disciples of Christ). What we develop here will then be offered to the church for feedback and further development. It can be presented for comment and suggestion to the Convocation Board meeting next week, to Administrative Committee meeting in February (and to our UCC partners), to regional boards, congregations, and so forth. Hopefully, through such reflection and suggestion, and a process of refining, we will have an effective working mission statement to offer the General Assembly in Pittsburgh.

As we think about the elements of a mission statement, we need to remember that such a statement is effective only if it engages people, only if it captures their imagination and compels them in some sense to own the mission and energizes them to be about it.

I don't want to argue about the difference between "vision" and "mission," or about the difference between an "identity" statement and a "mission" statement. I would simply like us to describe in perhaps a couple of paragraphs what God is calling us to do and to be. What is it to be a Disciple, and what is it God is calling us to do?

December 6, 1993

Council of Ministers

"An Alternative to Resolutions"

I want to begin with a quote from my own address, which I have offered in several places, including a regional assembly; the installation service of a regional minister; and, most recently, the Conference of Regional Ministers and Moderators. "We must reinvent how we approach issues. The resolution process has run its course!"

As it is, the "wild-eyed" can easily "jerk us around," and the politically astute can easily manipulate us. After all, one cannot absolutely determine truth by voting on it! This church must be led to a deeper understanding of the truth by *pastoral leadership*. Therefore, I will be proposing the elimination of resolutions on subjects over which the General Assembly does not have authority. The Assembly would still receive reports and make policy decisions, but there is no point in having votes on complex issues that cannot possibly be reduced to a few paragraphs of resolution in a process that inherently creates "winners and losers" rather than fostering understanding and growth!

I will be asking, instead, for a process whereby our regional ministers and general ministry unit presidents will offer "pastoral letters" to the church on particular issues that face us. Our Disciples scholars, who are terribly underutilized by the church, will be asked to serve as consultants, and any number of other people may be asked to serve as advisors so the group has the benefit of a wide range of representative thinking. In addition, they will receive input from *anyone* in the church who wishes to comment or provide information or viewpoints.

These pastoral letters might be one to ten pages in length, but they may also have a hundred pages of documentation attached so that the whole document can be used for study by congregations and other groups within the life of the church. There would usually be perhaps one of these letters issued per year. Not that *everyone* has agreed with me, I'm sure, but everywhere I have presented this idea, it has been met with spontaneous applause.

Let me make it clear that my motive in offering this "pastoral letter" process has nothing to do with protecting the church from the cutting edge of prophetic issues. On the contrary, I am simply trying to help us find a way to address issues more responsibly, more effectively, in a way that enhances leadership, and in a way that discourages the politicizing of issues. *The basic question is, how shall we offer prophetic leadership to this church?*

While the resolution process has been useful at times in our history (I will admit that I have learned from it myself), I think it has been quite some time since anybody was *saved* by a resolution. The problem is that, in the current politicized environment, most people know what they think about the issues before they arrive at Assembly. And twelve minutes of debate is not likely to bring much new insight!

Some will argue that the General Assembly provides for an expression of democracy within our church, but I think there are some underlying myths that we must confront here. The General Assembly is not democratic by any ordinary use of that term. It is dominated by clergy, many of whom are paid to be there, while relatively few lay people get much help with their expenses. The attendance is always weighted geographically toward the area in which the Assembly happens to be meeting. It tends to be weighted toward the economic class that can afford the time and money to be present. It tends to be weighted toward large churches that can afford to send more ministers. It tends to be weighted racially and culturally. This is not *intended*, and it *is* an open meeting, but these "overrepresentations" are real.

I do value the diversity that is represented by our General Assemblies, and I generally affirm the principle of trying to make our General Assemblies and General Board as representational as we can. But I reject the notion that God's prophetic truth can necessarily be discerned by a secular political process called "democracy." Sometimes the majority is just dead wrong.

I do recognize the need for input from every corner of the church, and I do not wish to move the church toward an elite hierarchy of leadership that simply "hands down" the truth! Leaders are subject to the same temptations as are all members, and so broad input from all parts of the church is an essential counterpoint to cloistered leaders making judgments in isolation from the rest of the church. Nevertheless, while leaders are subject to the same temptations of parochialism as everyone else, we still need leadership and leaders need to lead.

As a regional minister, I found that every effective Disciple organization, whether congregational or regional, has two components present. First, there is the horizontal component, which we could express as "the opportunity for every member of the system to feel that they have the opportunity for input." Second, there is the vertical component, which we could express as "the opportunity for leaders to lead." Using congregational life as an example, some congregations err on the side of the horizontal. Consider the example of the congregation that has to call a congregational meeting in order to get approval of the color of paint that will be used in the repainting of the fellowship hall. In such an organization, leaders cannot or will not lead.

On the other hand, some congregations err on the side of the vertical. This is illustrated by the congregation in which the first time the congregation at large is aware that they will be moving to a new location is when they see a sign on a piece of property at the outskirts of town that reads, "New Home of First Christian Church." (I wish I could tell you that these are both fictional illustrations, but you know better!)

Either extreme is an invitation to terrific conflict. The point is, to be a healthy Disciples organization, there must be an interplay of the vertical and the horizontal. I believe this is as true in our general life as it is of the regional and congregational. The problem has been, in my opinion, that through the resolution process, we have given the General Assembly over to the horizontal entirely—though, curiously, it is greeted by most of our congregations as a completely vertical process! No one seems to be responsible for what the General Assembly votes. Ministers and laypeople alike vote for this or that and then they go home and never say a word about what happened. If someone asks them, their sheepish response suggests they must have been in the lobby when the vote was taken (and perhaps they were). The point is that General Assembly is this nameless, faceless body that everyone blames but for which few will take responsibility. Since no one owns it, no one much owns the decisions it takes either. It represents a peculiar form of moral cowardice for leaders to try to move the church forward while hiding behind the anonymity of the General Assembly crowd.

With a pastoral letter, *real* leaders *sign* the document. No hiding place down here. We are convicted by the Holy Spirit and we reveal our conviction. It is a *pastoral* letter, not an "in your face" letter. But it is honest and forthright.

How would such a letter be prepared to reflect both the horizontal and vertical aspects of good Disciples leadership? Let me sketch a possible scenario.

First, the Council of Ministers, through the facility of a steering committee that would oversee the entire pastoral letter process, would decide three or four years in advance what issues were going to be considered. This allows plenty of lead time so that it would be possible to design General Assembly forums around an issue or issues. In addition to General Assembly forums, I would like to see "off-year" dialogical events held in regions. These might be part of a regional assembly or stand separately, depending on how the individual regions chose to implement it. In some cases, two or more regions might want to come together for a dialogical event. In any case, the theme would be churchwide. Minutes would be taken at these General Assembly forums and regional dialogical events, so that people would not only be heard, but their concerns and ideas would be available to this Council. In addition, the Division of Higher Education is planning dialogical events to be held at our theological institutions beginning, I believe, in 1995. These events would also provide grist for the mill. Other institutions, such as the Commission on Theology, could also be invited to participate. Ecumenical partners could be invited to comment and/or otherwise participate. In addition, any member of the church who wished to do so would be invited to send their concerns and ideas for consideration by the Council.

While these dialogical processes are taking place, those Disciple scholars selected by the Council to be consultants on a particular issue would be putting together their own research papers. Advisors, lay and clergy, would be selected and given assignments.

In the year during and after the dialogues, a committee would meet to pull together these materials and to hammer out the details of a one- to ten-page pastoral letter. The results of this process would be brought before the Council of Ministers, which would digest it, debate it, and make decisions ... finally signing onto a statement.

The resulting document, though one to ten pages in length, might have a hundred or more pages of documentation attached so that people could understand where the assumptions came from. A bibliography could be included. The entire document would then be made available to congregations and other institutions of the church, perhaps with a study guide or, at the least, a "How to use this document" guide.

While such a pastoral letter would not purport to speak for the church any more than does General Assembly, I believe it would certainly speak to the church more forcefully than do resolutions that are two or three paragraphs in length, seldom disclose their underlying assumptions, and receive twelve minutes of debate in a setting where most everybody knows what they think before they arrive or, alternately, don't have a *clue* what to think before they arrive.

When there is an issue arising that cannot be dealt with through the normal two- to three-year process, a provision could be made for a quick response team to advise the general minister and president. This would make it possible for an immediate response should, for example, the president of the United States decide to bomb Cambodia. It would provide for a quicker response, in fact, than would an emergency resolution.

A most interesting possibility I heard from someone yesterday raised the possibility of asking a group within the life of the church to write the essence of a pastoral letter and then standing with them in the presentation of that letter. For example, what if the Convocation were asked to write a letter around the Black experience as it relates to Disciples church life ... the gifts, the pain? Wouldn't it be exciting for this Council of Ministers to stand with the Convocation in such a statement? Other suggestions have been made as to how these pastoral letters might be done, including one that would be patterned on the WCC faith and order model.

This kind of a process would mean that the general and regional leadership would be offering leadership and service to the church around mission instead of *doing* the mission for the church.

What might the subject of our first pastoral letter be? I think an appropriate choice would be "biblical authority." This is one of those issues we have always claimed was at the heart of our identity as Disciples, yet we have nowhere a definitive statement of what we mean by biblical authority. The result? Positively stated, we are open to lots of understandings under this tent. Negatively stated, we are sitting ducks for every imaginable kind of silly and demonic thinking.

If we were to take this on, it would mean we, as a Council, would have to agree to work on a majority principle and each support the final product to the utmost of our ability. If we tried to get complete consensus, we'd never be able to say anything together beyond, "God is great, God is good!"

While I acknowledge that I myself have sometimes learned a great deal from the resolution process over the past twenty-five years, it has been quite a number of years since anyone has learned *much*. In the present cultural context—which is combative, mean spirited, and anxious—it's been quite a while since anyone was saved, or even significantly informed, by a resolution.

Well, that's my case. Work it over. Tear it apart. Start over. Whatever. That's fine with me. But let's seek to get somewhere together that's better than where we are.

May the Holy Spirit guide and enlighten us.

July 23, 1994

St. Louis, Missouri

General Board Address

A personal word: To the saints gathered in St. Louis for General Board meeting. Grace to you and peace from God our Father and the Lord Jesus Christ.

As you may have heard, this is my first General Board meeting as general minister and president! *Most* days, I am delighted to be in this role. As I near the end of my first year, the learning curve continues to be incredibly steep! Every day is a week. The global perspective which is forced upon one in this office is a true challenge. But even more challenging, I think, is remembering what I knew as pastor of a congregation and as a regional minister while incorporating what I am now learning! If I can manage this, then I think I'll be of some use to this church. I pray for that.

I confess that, sometimes, my desire to *do* well interferes with my need to *be* well. You know what I mean. My desire to be productive *for* God sometimes interferes with my need to be receptive *to* God. My need to *create* sometimes undermines my ability to *receive* the spiritual power I must have to be able to give what's needed from me.

For example, last month I was bearing down so hard on preparing for this Board meeting that I was beginning to believe it all depended on me. The more I fell into this trap, perhaps the most Disciples of traps, the less energy and inspiration seemed to come and the more anxious I became.

But a few weeks ago at the Youth Ministry Congress, I heard Bill Thomas speak of how he was trying too hard in auditioning for a role on the Bill Cosby show. Finally, he let go of it and trusted God to help him do his best and to uphold him if he didn't get the part.

He relaxed and the energy and inspiration he needed flowed and he got the part. And just as important, even if he hadn't gotten that part, he would have been okay.

I recognized the truth in Bill's words for me. I had been trying to *single-handedly create* the energy and inspiration that would empower this General Board meeting. After I heard Bill, I gave up trying to *force* something and began to open myself to *receiving* the energy and inspiration that would help me, as *one* leader, help this General Board be empowered! That's when the energy began to flow.

If you came with the notion of *making* this a significant General Board meeting, I invite you to give that up and to open yourself to God's empowerment in these four days we have together.

I have prepared. I trust that *you* are prepared to give yourself to the agenda before us. So, let us trust God for the empowerment we need, the energy we need. And, if the results of our being together are *stunning* or simply preparatory to some yet-to-unfold results, let us give glory to God and trust God's future for us.

Introduction

All around the country, I have been saying the obvious: This is a new day. Things have changed. Some of the changes are good and welcome, and some of the changes are not so good. But ready or not, change is upon us and, as always, the change that has come represents both danger and opportunity. I frequently quote those marvelous words of James Russell Lowell, "New occasions teach new duties, time makes ancient good uncouth; they must upward still and onward, who would keep abreast of truth."[2]

In our fear of the unknown, we human beings naturally tend to greet change with resistance and denial. We Disciples may be even more adept at denial than most. I enjoy telling the story of three preachers who were traveling together in the same automobile when they were hit by a truck and killed outright. Much to their surprise they found themselves in hell. The first preacher, a Methodist, said, "I was saved, I know I was saved. There must be some mistake." The second preacher, a Presbyterian, said, "I know I was among the elect, there must be some mistake." The third preacher, a Disciple, said, "It's not hot and I'm not here!" But, as comforting as denial may be, it is

---

[2] "Once to Every Man and Nation" is a hymn based upon the poem "The Present Crisis" by James Russell Lowell. The original poem was written as a protest against the Mexican–American War. It was put to music by Thomas J. Williams in 1890.

not helpful in the long run. We must face up to the realities of our day and we must, with humility, seek to understand what the future will bring. I say with humility because *any* attempt to see into the future is presumptuous and will be subject to revision as time goes on.

Nevertheless, we must seek to understand our past and our current situation, and we must anticipate the future and plan for it, as presumptuous as this may be and as needful of ongoing revision as our plans will inevitably be. My hope today is to lay out a small perspective on our past and to offer a focus for our work together in the next several years.

The Struggle for a Polity that is True to Our Heritage, and which Reflects Our Learnings and the New Context in which We Find Ourselves

As it began developing in the early 1800s, the Stone-Campbell Movement was described in many ways including, "an experiment in liberty." It was a time when there was a tyranny of denominational structures from which the individual needed rescue. Like most Americans, we *reveled* in individualism, and since, culturally speaking, this amounted to swimming downstream, we grew like wildfire across the frontier.

However, we soon began to see the limits of radical individualism and began seeking cooperative approaches to ministry and mission. In the mid-nineteenth century, the antecedents of regions, the American Christian Missionary Society, and other rudimentary forms began taking shape as ways of fostering cooperative work among Disciples (you will remember that Alexander Campbell was the first president of the American Christian Missionary Society).

If there is anything we have learned, or should have learned, from our "experiment in liberty," it is the importance of connection and relationship. Our restructure in 1968 was an effort to bring about a new "connectedness" within a context of responsible individual freedom.

Today, just twenty-five short years later, we face a radically different social context for our church life than that which we were experiencing in 1968. The individualism of our culture, which we North Americans have always enjoyed and celebrated, is now being lived out in a social context in which value systems and institutions have broken down. We have reached a point where individuals make moral judgments almost entirely on the basis of their internal feelings and perceptions without serious reference to external ethical perspectives.

As Moderator Duane Cummins has described our new reality, "Whereas in the nineteenth century the individual needed saving from the church, now the church needs saving from the individual."

And so, we continue our struggle to find a way of relating the parts and pieces of this church in a way that is freeing yet responsible. Structures beyond the congregation cannot accomplish this alone, and if we try to *impose* an order on this church through regional and general structures, either intentionally or because we forgot who we are as Disciples, we will just recreate the tyranny of structures from which we rebelled originally and we will experience new rebellions! The regional and general manifestations have been authorized to do a number of ministries on behalf of the whole church, and have even been authorized to provide significant means of accountability for the church (especially for the ministry). But we must never forget that we are a volunteer organization in which all of us as individuals and as congregations, regional and general ministry units, and other institutions and organizations within the body *volunteer* to be a part of the whole.

You know, we probably never should have taken "Provisional" out of the title of The Design, or at least we should have found some other title for it that would have reflected a greater measure of humility, that would help us remember that we live "provisionally"! How about "Pilgrims' Progress: The Design"? We Disciples are yet on a pilgrimage, and we need to maintain flexibility in our structures. Our life will be marked by *continual* change and the need for flexibility, just as people on a pilgrimage pitch their tent now here and now there, as they move down the road.

As Duane put it, The Provisional Design gave us the possibility of "more equitable balance between some of our ageless polarities: freedom and community, unity and diversity, congregationalism and catholicity"[3]

Nevertheless, the human tendency is to begin serving the structures rather than to keep the structures as servants. Thus, we must always remember that the primary purpose of the regional

---

[3] D. Duane Cummins, *A Handbook for Today's Disciples* (St. Louis, MO: Chalice Press, 1991), 11.

and general manifestations is not to be ends in themselves, but to enhance the faithfulness and effectiveness of congregations, providing ways and means for congregations to address the world faithfully and effectively.

With the separation of the Churches of Christ in the late 1800s, we effectively said, "No, we aren't giving ourselves to biblical literalism, nor to the worship of restorationism."

With the separation of Independents, we effectively said "no" again to biblical literalism and "no" to absolute congregational autonomy.

So what did we say "yes" to? We said "yes" to the disciplines of biblical and theological scholarship, we said "yes" to ecumenism, and we said "yes" to covenantal relationship. In fact, I propose that we should call our form of organization a "covenantal polity."

The challenge of the nineteenth century was the frontier, where *religious sectarianism* was rampant. The challenge of the twentieth century has been the city, where *secularism* has been rampant. The challenge of the twenty-first century is the social separatism in which people define reality and community in narrower and narrower terms. Our "covenantal polity" is ideal for this kind of a day.

In fact, let me go a step further and say, in the face of the communications age, there may be no viable polity *except* covenantal polity.

Let me go way out on a limb here. There are three kinds of communions and sects in the world today. First, there are those which are ruled by radical individualism, often expressed through a charismatic leader. Some of these churches seem to be thriving at the moment, but they are actually among the "walking dead" who will eventually be disintegrated by the same radical individualism that seems at the moment to be feeding them. Second, there are those churches who are still trying to impose discipline out of a structurally or theologically *hierarchical* approach because they haven't fully grasped what's happening in the world yet. Third, there are those churches who recognize, or are coming to recognize that there is now *only* covenantal polity.

I am not suggesting that we should return to an arrogant or naive congregationalism: I'm warning us against falling into the trap of trying to do general and regional church without *serious* reference to congregational life and individual members' perceptions of what we are doing on their behalf!

The great challenge now, therefore, is to *connect* people across the great schisms of the day, across the lines of social and political and theological balkanization which are little more than expressions of fear and radical individualism.

The Search for an Approach to Mission that Is Relevant to Our Times

In the nineteenth century, we Disciples were *flowing with the tide*, because many were ready to give up the tyranny of hierarchical authority.

In the twentieth century, we have been flowing with the tide as disoriented new city dwellers came in from the farms and small towns of America and established congregations near their new homes. Then, as some of us became more affluent, we took our churches with us to the suburbs.

But today, we find that there are no more geographical frontiers. There are now only the *inner* frontiers, and the frontiers so many of us left behind in the rural areas and towns, and in the urban centers. So, as we approach the twenty-first century, we are swimming *against the tide* because we are now called to confront all the "isms" and "counter-isms" that have been created by the disorientation of migration and mobility and the fear that has been created by recent rapid social change: isms and counter-isms that claim ultimate allegiance, which compete with God. These "isms" are racial, economic, social, theological, political, and intellectual in nature. As we take seriously the calling to confront these social boundaries and dividing walls of hostility that have been created by separatism and what might be called North America's own version of apartheid, we will find that we are now called to a period of mission which is perhaps the most difficult of all! But it is what I believe God is calling us to offer to the world today and for the foreseeable future.

As Disciples of Christ, *when we are at our best*, we have the instincts, the language, and the concepts to model faithful Christian diversity in a world that is threatening to self-destruct in radical individualism and fear. The question is, do we have the *heart*? I believe God has prepared us for such a time as this, but are we up to it? Or will we collapse into a survival mode?

This is the choice that confronts us! A survival mentality or a mission mentality!

It is forever true as Jesus said it, "Whoever seeks to save their life will lose it, but whoever loses their life for my sake shall find it." It's *not* that we are called to commit ecclesiastical suicide, it *is* that we are called to risk our life as a church by giving ourselves freely in mission, for it is in mission that we will find our life. If we do not engage in the mission to which God calls us, we will continue to struggle.

If we fall into a survival mode, it means we will constantly be distracted by side-shows, thinking that each is the most important thing. One reason we experience so much negativism in this church today, so much carping and backbiting, is because in significant ways we have given ourselves to survival ... we have lost our vision of mission ... and without a vision, we perish ... slowly ... excruciatingly ... turning in on ourselves like withering flowers, or trying to recreate a church of the first or nineteenth centuries that *can* never be again and *should* never be again. *With* vision, we may *yet* perish if God so wills it, but we will perish with purpose! There are no guarantees except that God, as always, will be with us ... and God will be pleased with our devotion to mission.

I have been saying that we need a mission statement for this denomination. However, as I began working on such a mission statement, I realized that the mission of the church really does not change from generation to generation. As Clark Williamson said it recently in a Kirkpatrick lecture at the Historical Society (May 1994), "What is the one thing necessary that the church can do that no other institution can do? ... to preach the Gospel of Jesus Christ, to make the Christian witness, to spread abroad in the world the love of God and the love of neighbor."

In simplest terms, then, the mission of the church is the proclamation of the gospel of Jesus Christ. All the pieces of the church's mission (evangelism, nurture, and the pursuit of justice) grow out of this basic gospel mandate.

What we need is a statement that will give us some idea of how and where we should be spending our energy and resources in this generation in order to be faithful to the mission God has given the church. With this in mind, I come to you today bringing a draft of such a statement.

There are four primary sources of information which have informed my work and helped me create this statement. First, there has been my own prayer life and meditation on scripture: especially the Letter to the Ephesians, which I think speaks so directly to the nature and mission of the church. Second, I have been informed by that which I have been hearing around North America as I have been out among the congregations, as I have been reading my mail, and as I have been in conversation with various leaders and groups within the life of the church. By the end of October, I will have been in thirty of our thirty-six regions in some significant way, and I have been in many regions several times. I've not been sitting around in Indianapolis in some tunnel! Third, I have been informed by the clear messages sent to us through the nearly 600 mission conversations, as was reported for us by Robert. What a marvelous gift these Mission Conversations are to us! Fourth, I have been informed by the responses to a letter I sent out in April to every congregation asking for input toward a mission statement and mission imperatives: Though the timeline for response was short, some one hundred and twenty-five responses were received by me from churches of nearly every size and description. The statement I now offer to you comes straight out of these four sources, between which there is astounding agreement.

Statement of Mission Imperatives

"Seeking to be faithful to God's mission for the church, which is the proclamation of the gospel, and "seeking to grow up in every way into Christ," the focus of our life shall be strengthening congregations for ministry and mission by (1) "the equipment of the saints" through the teaching of faith development, the spiritual disciplines (Bible study, prayer, stewardship), and the Disciples ethos; (2) "the work of ministry" to children, youth, and young adults; (3) "building up the body" through evangelism, renewal of existing congregations, and the establishment of new congregations; and (4) "speaking the truth in love" through local and global ministries of compassion, unity, and justice."

Let me unpack this mission imperatives statement for you.

I am calling it a "mission imperatives" statement because it is an attempt to say what is imperative for us to do at this particular point in history. Unfortunately, we have not done much with our "priority" statement since we created it six years ago, though there is much of value in it. (You remember the priority statement, don't you? "To develop vital congregations as dynamic faith communities in prophetic, redemptive and reconciling ministries to the whole world.") In particular, I have picked up what I think is the most helpful part of the priority: its focus on congregational life. Thus, this mission imperative statement says, "the focus of our life shall be strengthening congregations."

For what shall we strengthen congregations? For survival? No, for ministry and mission. "Ministry" refers to that which the church does to nurture and strengthen its own membership in the Good News of Jesus Christ. "Mission" refers to that which the church does to witness to, and to effect change in, the world. Of course, ministry and mission are not completely mutually exclusive. When the world gets into the church, which it does, then mission must also be done within the church.

So, how shall we strengthen the church for ministry and mission? I am suggesting four imperatives, and I do so using phrases from the Letter to the Ephesians.

We shall strengthen the church for ministry and mission, first, by "the equipment of the saints" through teaching faith development, the spiritual disciplines of Bible study, prayer, and stewardship, and the Disciples ethos.

Educational concerns are heard and seen all around this church. We live in a time when *anyone* one can claim *anything* about the message of the Bible and *it is believed* by many because so few of us are actually familiar with the contents and the origins of the Bible. Because so few of us today have an active prayer life, many settle for a second-hand or impersonal relationship with God. Because we have not been effectively teaching stewardship, especially to our younger generations, the ministries of our church, locally and beyond, are not adequately supported. Because we have not taught our Disciples ethos effectively, anyone can claim anything about what it really means to be Disciples.

We need new models for teaching, and new resources. And yet, we are not fully utilizing the resources we do have. Teaching the faith has not been a priority for us as a people in recent decades. For example, our ministers in all three manifestations must again become teachers *and camp counselors*! Our spiritually mature lay leaders must become teachers and mentors. Neither the faith, nor the Disciples ethos and self-understanding can be attained by mere osmosis!

You will remember that education was key in our early days: Some four hundred colleges were founded to educate *laity*! To this day, one finds that much of the central leadership of this church (lay *and* ministerial; congregational, regional, and general) is comprised of people who went to Sunday school regularly, who went to Bible school, who went to camp and conference. Many of them are also graduates of Disciples colleges. As an aside, let me point out that we have relatively few colleges (only fifteen), most of which are rather thinly related to the church. This is neither totally the fault of the church nor of the schools: Rather, both bear responsibility. The point is that church-related higher education has become less influential in the life of the church precisely at the moment in history when there is so much more for all of us to know and the Christian faith is being dramatically challenged.

It must also be said that Christian education is difficult to do today, whether in Sunday school, at evening Bible study, or in college and seminary because it challenges cultural assumptions. This is risky business because none of us like to have our cultural assumptions challenged! All of this means we need to more boldly confront our cultural assumptions in our congregations by spending more time, money and energy in teaching. It means that our colleges need to spend more resources in the teaching of faith and ethics, we need to draw more heavily on the expertise that is present in our colleges and seminaries, and we need to do more recruiting of Disciples students for our colleges and seminaries (our schools need Disciple students more than they need mission dollars).

In summary, we must strengthen education in the church at every level: from preschool years, to youth, to adult education, to education for lay and ministerial leadership.

Second, we will strengthen congregations for ministry and mission through "the work of ministry" to children, youth, and young adults.

One does not have to spend much time in Disciples congregations to realize that there are few children and youth present in most of them, compared to not so long ago. The average age of our members has risen at an alarming rate. I point this up not simply as indication that we will *die* if we do not begin ministering effectively to children, youth, and young adults, though that *may* be true. Rather, I point it out because it is an indication that we have not been effectively meeting the needs of children, youth, and young adults within our congregations or outside them, and thus we have not been completely faithful to our mission.

I recently spent a couple of days with one hundred and sixty of the finest young leaders of our church at the Youth Ministry Congress held at Barton College by the Division of Homeland Ministries. I came away *impressed*! We must not leave this generation to languish in the spiritual and moral chaos of the postmodern world. If ever a generation had need for rootage in the gospel of Jesus Christ, if ever a generation had gifts to give through the church, this is the generation! We *must* reach out *boldly* to this new generation!

Third, we will strengthen our congregations for ministry and mission by "building up the body" through evangelism, renewal of existing congregations, and the establishment of new congregations.

Evangelism is an imperative not because it will save the Christian Church (Disciples of Christ). Evangelism done for the sake of saving the institution is not evangelism but mere institutional self-service. Evangelism is about bringing persons into a saving relationship with God through Jesus Christ *not* about bringing an institution into a saving relationship with more members and money! Evangelism must be done out of a heart full of the good news, a heart so full that it wants to *give* it away! I don't need to preach this sermon do I?

Building up the body also means bringing renewal to those of our existing congregations that are struggling. My experience as pastor of a congregation and as a regional minister convinces me that this is most often, first and foremost, about helping congregations get clear again about *their* mission. We *do* have small, medium, and large congregations that are alive with passion for their mission! We do have rural, suburban, and urban congregations that are alive with passion for their mission! Rather than merely trying to create congregational renewal from Indianapolis or from regional offices, the regional and general manifestations need to *network* the spiritual and programmatic vitality in our strongest congregations to those that have fallen into survival mode or into spiritual and programmatic "ruts." It is a passion for mission that gave the church life and it is that same passion for mission that brings renewal!

Building up the body also means establishing new congregations. This, too, is more than anything else a function of evangelism. It means establishing congregations where the unchurched people are. It means *mission*! As Deborah Thompson says so well, it isn't a matter of *either* new church establishment *or* renewal of existing congregations: It's both!

Fourth, and finally, we will strengthen congregations for ministry and mission by "speaking the truth in love" through local and global ministries of compassion, unity, and justice.

These ministries are needed both within and beyond the church. In regard to ministries of compassion, quoting T. J. Liggett, "the relationship of the Christian community to the world about it must be one of servanthood. The church is not called to seek power or to exercise dominion but to serve the needs of humanity"[4]

Also among the essential elements in the witness of the church is, quoting T.J. again, "Christian community, which transcends in its unity all human barriers and becomes the effective evidence of God's reconciling power in Christ. ... The Christian community thus becomes the 'first fruits' of the new human community that God will create at the end of time."

Yet another key element in the witness of the church is the seeking of justice for all people. Micah said it this way, "What does the Lord require of you but to do justice, and to love kindness, and to walk humbly with your God." Jesus spoke of his mission as being, in part, "to set at liberty those who are oppressed." *His* mission is *our* mission.

Well, this is quite a plateful, I think you will agree. Yet, the statement of mission imperatives may be as important for what it *doesn't* say as for what it *does* say. If we really focus our energy on these imperatives, they will provide organizing centers for our life and work together and we will find the renewal we so desperately want and need. But if we continue to run in every direction—each congregation, region, general ministry unit, and educational institution doing its own thing—we will continue to be in decline.

I lay this statement before you to digest and to work with in sections. It is my hope that you will take what I have presented seriously because it takes the Mission Conversations report and other congregational input seriously. Resist the temptation to "grind your own axe," seeking to make *it* the center of our life together. On the other hand, if you honestly believe this statement points in the wrong direction, or if you feel it needs some adjustment or

---

[4] T .J. Liggett, *Where Tomorrow Struggles to Be Born* (New York: Friendship Press, 1970).

adjustments in order to give the light we need, by all means, express yourself and help make it a stronger statement.

I do not regard this statement as purely pearl; neither do I regard you as swine! But this is at least a starting place, brothers and sisters, as we seek the guidance of the Holy Spirit in the several years ahead!

Implementing the Imperatives Statement after General Board

In seeking to implement the imperatives selected by the General Board, it is essential to remember our history and our "covenantal polity." That is, every congregation, general ministry unit, region, educational institution, and related organization of the church has the right and responsibility to define itself and its own imperatives. Therefore, seeking to implement churchwide mission imperatives is an adventure in cooperation and covenant, *not* a matter of anyone imposing definitions of church or mission on anyone else. It is my earnest hope, however, that every congregation, unit, region, educational institution, and related organization *will* see wisdom in what the General Board concludes is imperative for us Disciples at this point in history and that all will make every effort to cooperate with this representative vision for the next several years.

In this spirit, then, I foresee the following process of implementation of the statement of imperatives.

I. Congregations

A. Immediately after this General Board meeting, the statement will be tested with congregations. A letter will be sent to every congregation offering them the opportunity to participate by returning a response card. Those so indicating a desire to participate will be sent a video in which I will explain the process as it has unfolded so far, presents the General Board's imperative statement, and poses four questions to which members of the congregation are asked to respond as a group:

    (a) Is the "Statement of Mission Imperatives" on target?
    (b) How might you implement these imperatives in your setting?
    (c) What are you already doing in these areas of ministry and mission that you would commend to others?
    (d) To help implement these priorities in your setting, what resources and partnerships would you desire from or with

your region, general ministry units, educational institutions and other congregations?

Participating congregations will receive this video (and a response form with which to report their group's response) by the first week in September. They will be asked to call their group together (this may be a congregational meeting, the board, the elders, or whatever group the congregation's leadership deems appropriate) on Sunday, September 25 or October 2, or at another time if preferable, for a ninety-minute session in which they will see and respond to the video. It will be requested that they mail a report of their response by November 1 so that a composite report can be shared with general, regional, and institutional leaders meeting in December.

B. We already have a great deal of information about what congregations are doing around these imperatives from the reports of the mission conversations.

II. The Visioning Panel

This Panel (authorized by Administrative Committee action in February 1994) will meet for the first time September 1–2, 1994. This group will begin thinking through the implications of the imperatives as well as revisiting the structures of the church. The Panel will offer suggestions to the various regions, general ministry units, institutions, and congregations as to how the imperatives might be implemented.

III. Regions, General Ministry Units, and Educational Institutions

A. In their August and September meetings, the General Cabinet and the College of Regional Ministers will be asked to begin discussing implementation.

B. During the fall, each of the general ministry units, regions, and institutions could begin discussions in their own board meetings or through whatever other devices they might choose or design for the purpose. They will be asked to respond to basically the same four questions as congregations:

(a) Is the "Statement of Mission Imperatives" on target?
(b) How might you implement these imperatives in your setting?
(c) What are you already doing in these areas of ministry and mission that you would commend to others?

(d) To help implement these priorities in your setting, what resources and partnerships would you desire from or with congregations, regions, general ministry units and/or educational institutions?

Reports of these discussions will be sought by November 15, so that they can be shared at the December meeting of general, regional and educational institution leaders.

C. At the December meeting of regional, general and educational institution leaders, the feedback will be discussed and concrete ideas and envisioning of possibilities will begin (time for this purpose will be somewhat limited at this meeting due to a needed discussion of mission funding system matters).

D. A meeting of general, regional, and institutional leadership together with congregational representatives will be called to meet immediately prior to the 1995 General Board meeting (or earlier in the spring) to further develop concrete proposals for implementation.

IV. Administrative Committee and The General Board

A. A report of progress will be prepared by the GMP and shared with the Administrative Committee in its January 1995 meeting for study, reflection and response.

B. A report of progress will be prepared by the GMP and shared with the General Board in its July 1995 meeting. As a body that represents the entire scope of the church's life, the General Board will be asked to respond to the report and to offer further suggestions for implementation of the imperatives to congregations, regions, units and institutions.

V. The General Assembly

In 1995, the General Assembly will receive a report of progress and forums and interest groups will be formed around the imperatives.

The Office of General Minister and President will continue to take responsibility for keeping the process moving and growing. Also, regular reports will be provided to the whole church.

I would remind us that, as important as planning for the implementation of the mission imperatives is, just as important is the discontinuance of obsolete programs and the continual transformation of structures, ways and means (all the while remembering our ethos and our covenantal polity).

Undoubtedly, as we proceed, we will see other possibilities of ways to move the mission imperatives forward. The most important principle is to move forward in a prayerful and collegial way that empowers and renews all manifestations of the church.

As one of four "readers" giving his impressions of the information gathered in the Mission Conversations, Scott Colglazier, pastor of Beargrass Christian Church in Louisville, referred to an essay by Wendell Berry which uses the image of the caretaking of land. He says,

> [C]orporations can't take care of land because they are absentee owners. As in times past, people must "get off their horses and walk on the land so they can know how to take care of it." The Mission Conversations reflect general and regional staff attempts at getting off our horses and walking the locale of the congregational landscape.

Scott goes on to say,

> The priorities stated by these congregations can be summarized as follows. "Please take seriously and supremely the local landscape of our church." With this in mind, every program that is implemented in the future must also signal to congregations "We are walking your landscape and caring for your locale *together* as partners."

Amen!

January 29, 1995

Administrative Committee

Opening Remarks

I give thanks to God for your safe passage to this place and for the gift of your time and talent.

I have now been in this role eighteen months. By now, you may be wondering, "What is Hamm's overall plan?" "Where is he trying to take us, and do we want to go there?" These are fair questions, and I'd like to give you an overview of what I am trying to do.

To begin with, I should share with you my basic philosophy of the office of GMP. I understand there to be three primary roles. First, the office was created to be a sign of the wholeness of the church. In the 1960s, we said that, in a fundamental sense, we were no longer going to be a mere association of individual congregations, agencies, and institutions but we were becoming one church. We changed our name from the Christian *Churches* (Disciples of Christ) to the Christian *Church* (Disciples of Christ). I can tell you friends that there is yet much to be done along these lines, for we remain in many ways a free association with little mutual accountability.

Second, the Office of GMP is called to engage in a ministry of reconciliation. In the face of our divisions, which I will say a bit more about, this, too, is an essential function.

Third, the Office of GMP is called to help the church continually renew its self-understanding: especially its understanding of its mission. This may be the most critical role of all in this time of incredibly rapid social change, for the church has been drifting in its understanding of, and commitment to, mission.

I do *not* believe it is my job to have all the answers, though I think you would like me to have *some* answers, or at least some *ideas*. Rather, my role is to call the church together around the right questions! And this is exactly what I have been trying to do: to call the church together around the right questions.

We have the gifts and graces among our people to arrive at good answers to the questions, but getting the questions right is critical to the future of this communion. So what are the right questions? Presently, I would summarize them as follows:

1. What is our mission?

This is forever the most important question the church can ask in any of its manifestations: congregational, regional, or general. What is it God is calling us to do and to be in this time and in this place? It is much easier for us to answer the question, "What *was* God calling us to do and to be in some *other* time and place?" or "What do *I* want us to do and to be?" But the correct question is, "What does *God* want us to do and to be?"

While a regional minister, I often did "strategic planning processes" with congregations in order to help them get at their particular mission. I led them through a process that includes (a) gathering information about who lives in the church's parish area and what their needs are; (b) gathering information about those who are members of the congregation and what their needs, gifts, and graces are; and (c) identifying the strengths and weaknesses of the congregation as an institution (its financial resources, facilities, location, and so forth). Somewhere within this matrix of external needs and internal gifts lays the mission of a congregation. The task then, having identified the needs and the gifts, is to discern *together* how God wants to put the needs and the gifts together. *There* is the mission exactly: how God wants to put needs and gifts together.

It seems to me that the same basic process is applicable to discerning the mission of the whole denomination: (a) What is the cultural context in which we find ourselves in North America? That is, what are the needs of the people who live here? (b) What are the needs, gifts, and graces of those who are presently members of this denomination? (c) What are our institutional strengths and liabilities? Let's look at these questions a bit more closely.

First, what is our cultural context? That is, what are the social and cultural realities that mark the current time and which will shape the future of the United States and Canada? In the face of these cultural realities, what do people *need* (which is a somewhat different question than "what do people *want*?"). Happily, the Lilly Endowment, and others, have been funding much research into these questions in the past several years. We now have a much better picture of what has been happening to our culture generally and what has been happening to us as a mainline denomination.

- One example of the importance of these questions comes in our understanding the differences in outlooks of baby boomers, babybusters (or generation X): These are people who have world views differing greatly from one another and from the majority of those who currently belong to Disciples congregations (most of whom were born *before* 1945). How can we effectively minister to them if we do not know who they are and how they see things?
- Another example is in our understanding of the "disestablishment" of "mainline" American religion that has been underway most of this century. The result of this disestablishment is that the church's relationship to the culture has changed markedly.
- Another example is in our understanding of the racial and ethnic face of North America. What is our mission in

relationship to the rapidly growing numbers of various racial and ethnic groups?
- Yet another example is in our understanding of the impact of the rapid cultural changes on that majority of our current membership that is white and over sixty. We could cite many other examples of important information we need to understand in order to be able to discern our mission within this cultural context.

Second, what are the needs, gifts and graces of those who are currently members of the Christian Church (Disciples of Christ)? Again, asking about needs is different from asking about wants. Meeting some "wants" could be demonic (for example, many people "want" everyone in their church to see everything as they do, which would result in a condition in which there would be no one to challenge our thinking). But understanding and meeting real *needs* is surely at the heart of the church's mission.

And what are the gifts and graces of our people? Congregations frequently get "down" on themselves because they don't consider what their gifts and graces are and, thus, they conclude they have none. This church is *full* of gifts and graces that have been given to us by God: gifts of talent, vision, reason, compassion, and commitment. We need to identify and employ these.

Third, what are our institutional strengths and liabilities? In our anxiety about the change that is all around us, we have had a tendency to overstate our liabilities and to understate our strengths: a natural response to fear (as opposed to faith). We have tended to be in a "survival mode," which is the surest and quickest way for a church (or any institution) to die (as Jesus said, "Whoever seeks to save their life will lose it, but whoever loses their life for my sake shall find it"). We need a more realistic view of our strengths and liabilities in order to see what we have to bring to the needs that are all about us.

All of these questions are important as we seek to answer the question, "What is our mission in this time and place?" As we have begun to gain clarity in these issues, we have also begun to work on honing statements of identity, mission, and mission imperatives (you have before you a one-page summary of these statements as they currently stand). The mission imperative statement grows directly out of what I think is the right question: "What is God calling us to do and to be in the face of the cultural and institutional context in which we find ourselves?" As our context changes, our mission imperatives will also need to change, as we reconsider from time to time what is most important for us to do in order to be faithful to the real needs around us and within us.

2. How can we best organize ourselves for doing the mission?

In the 1960s, we restructured this church. I believe our leadership did a remarkable job of creating helpful structures that have pulled us together in many ways as a church, confronting the worst aspects of individualism (which have been our weakness), while respecting the best aspects of individualism (which have always been our strength). Nevertheless, that was nearly thirty years ago. The change that has come to North American culture and to the church in these passing years is sometimes mind boggling! It is time for us to ask whether some changes in structure are now needed and appropriate. I believe there *are* changes needed.

However, I am not calling for another "Restructure" like that of the 1960s (which is a relief to many colleagues who experienced that process!). What I am calling for is the kind of ongoing structural adjustment that every organization needs to do if it is to remain effective. We are probably a bit behind in such "ongoing" adjustment, so there may be a disproportionately large amount of it to do in the *immediate* future, but then we should be able to move into a period of more "normal" year to year adjustment to reflect changing needs.

The Vision Panel has been appointed to aid this process of "catch up" and ongoing restructure. Ultimately, given the nature of our polity, units and regions and so forth have to make the changes themselves (each unit and region has the right and responsibility to order its own life), but the Vision Panel can help our institutions change in a way that is coordinated and congruent.

I am delighted that the board of the Church Finance Council has taken the extraordinary step of recommending that CFC be joined into the Office of GMP. Business Item #1430 asks you to approve this. I believe this will strengthen both institutions and that it will set an example for other units, regions, and institutions to follow.

The "sunset rule" that I asked for, and which you affirmed last year, is important symbolically as well as functionally, because it sends a small but powerful message to the whole church that we are not doing business as usual. Likewise, our reduction of the staff of

Christian Church Services (an in-house agency that serves the general offices and units that operate in the missions building) from twenty-seven employees to eight employees sends a powerful message.

The structural issues must not be seen as being about efficiency primarily, though efficiency is certainly to be desired in the name of good stewardship. But the *primary* issues must be seen as "How we can organize in order to most effectively do our *mission*?"! It is mission that must drive our structural efforts.

3. How shall we fund our mission?

This has become a particularly pressing issue for us as Basic Mission Finance dollars have begun to decrease and thus have created financial pressures in every unit, region, and institution (just as many congregations have experienced the same financial pressures). In the face of this press, it is easy and natural for institutional leaders to want to answer this question in a way that smacks of "turf protection." I believe, however, that the ultimate answer to this question of mission funding must come out of the two prior questions: "What is our mission?" and, "How can we best organize ourselves for doing the mission?" The hard fact is that we have some present structures that are more strongly related to history than to current realities.

The issue is not so much an issue of "saving" money, though greater efficiency coupled with greater effectiveness is, again, always to be desired in the name of stewardship. The issue is more about funding *mission* (rather than funding "sacred cows" or anachronisms).

To put it bluntly, for our membership to continue to support Basic Mission Finance (especially those members *under* sixty), our structures will have to be self-evidently dedicated to mission (rather than self-preservation) and will have to be self-evidently effective.

Though it is a natural tendency to focus on how to divide the shrinking resources we have, a question that is just as important is, "How can we better promote and communicate the mission and the ministry that BMF supports?" In addition to what we are already doing through our churchwide promotional strategy, we need a churchwide communication strategy. Our new communication director, Curt Miller, is charged with helping us develop such a strategy. In the face of the communications age and the revolutionary developments in that field, we must find more effective ways to tell the church's story to our own people and to the world.

This also points to the need for effective stewardship education. When responsible foresters harvest trees, they take only the mature trees, while allowing the smaller trees to continue growing and replacing the trees they cut down with seedlings. Irresponsible foresters clear cut. That is, they cut down *all* the trees, large and small, leaving the soil exposed to erosion and making no provision for future crops. The fact is that this church has been clear cutting for about thirty years. That is, we have relied on those who developed their sense of stewardship in the 1930s, 1940s, and 1950s to fund the wider work of the church while doing too little to bring younger people into the church and into relationship with Jesus Christ, and doing too little to educate our younger people to the meaning and joy of Christian stewardship. Restoring demographic balance and a broad-based sense of stewardship will require commitment and will be a long-term process. We can't "fix" this in a couple of years.

As we look at this question of how we fund the church's mission, I want to say a word about the move to new facilities. While I think building a new building may have been a good idea when first conceived, I am now convinced, beyond a doubt, of the wisdom of leasing. We are moving into newly remodeled space that will facilitate closer work and relationships between units and at a cost that is actually less than that required to stay in the Missions Building! We have a lease that gives us the flexibility to obtain more or less space as we need it, which will prevent our decisions from being driven by a building's needs and limitations.

As we shall see, it is essential for us to deal with the residual debt from the original building project, but that is a matter separate from the matter of the new facilities because we have to pay off that debt whether we stay in Missions Building or move downtown. I strongly believe that the new space gives us the productive and flexible facility we need to become more efficient in our work.

4. How can we reconcile the various divisions among us and bring ourselves together in common mission?

The divisions among us are not just conservative/liberal, as much as that division seems to dominate our thinking and the media these days. The deeper divisions which we have never really addressed systemically are the divisions represented by categories such as urban and rural; Anglo, African American, Hispanic, American Asian, and Haitian; large congregations and small congregations; older and younger. It is the fractures between us in these sorts of divisions that are most likely to drive us apart if we do not address them. I believe our differences in theology are more *symptomatic* of our isolation from one another than *causal*.

It is in an effort to begin building bridges, rather than encouraging the church to continue in a style of constantly throwing down the gauntlet, that I have submitted a proposal for a process of discernment. I'm sure that what we end up with will look very different from what I have submitted to this meeting for your review and counsel, but it is clear to me that we must find new and effective ways of doing public witness that help us grow *toward* one another in faithfulness to the gospel mandate for justice rather than merely continuing the violence that we have visited upon each other in recent years. I have sometimes felt battered myself just trying to raise the *question* of whether there might be a better way!

Likewise, we must find ways of bridging the racial and ethnic gaps between us so that, in the proposed words of the Mission Imperative, Business Item #1426, we can truly *share* our gifts and graces. It is in this spirit, for example, that I have called, in consultation with Lucas Torres, a meeting of Hispanic leaders and regional and area ministers, on February 2, to begin identifying issues and possibilities for improving our working relationships.

5. How can we develop and better support faithful and effective leadership for the church?

The matter of "better supporting" becomes key when we look, for example, at the number of women who prepare for ministry only to be cruelly rejected by congregations. But there is also the larger question of, "What kind of leadership do we need for the future?" Specifically, how many lay ministers will we need over the next twenty years, how many part-time ministers, how many bivocational ministers, how many full-time ordained ministers, how many ministers of education and youth? (If you pray for rain, you had better carry an umbrella. And if we are praying for children and youth and making them a mission imperative, we had better begin preparing leaders to meet their needs as they come!)

And what are the implications of these needs for seminaries and for regional commissions on ministry? How do we make the relocation process more humane and helpful? How do we ensure that those who come to us from other denominations are coming for the right reasons and are adequately prepared to be Disciple ministers?

These and a host of other issues are the kind that will be taken up by the new General Commission on Ministry which the General Board authorized in 1993 and which I am now constituting. I have great hopes for this instrumentality, which will make it possible to deal with issues around ministerial leadership *systematically* and with reasonable speed.

In regard to lay leadership in our general life, I have recently been seeking to broaden our leadership pool for general and regional life by asking every pastor for the names of persons who might provide good service. For the first time, included in the profile information we are seeking is the nominees' theological bent. While I do not think it is practical to seek to totally balance the theological make up of our boards and commissions and such, I do believe that the broad spectrum of theological perspectives should be represented. (It is curious to me that, because of this, I have been accused of being a conservative: Actually, I think it makes me something of a liberal!)

In any case, the recruitment, preparation and support of leadership for the next twenty years is, I believe, a crucial matter if we are to move forward.

So, these are the five primary questions I see as key for us at this point in our history:

1. What is our mission?
2. How can we best organize ourselves for doing this mission?
3. How shall we fund our mission?
4. How can we reconcile the various divisions among us and bring ourselves together in common mission?
5. How can we develop and better support faithful and effective leadership for the church?

I have mentioned a number of initiatives on which we have worked in these last eighteen months, including the following: the statement of identity, the Mission Imperatives statement, the Vision Panel, the merger of CFC with the OGMP, the sunset rule, the reduction of staff in CCS (and in the Office of GMP), the churchwide promotional strategy, the development of a churchwide communication strategy, the new facility, a leadership study, the broadening of our leadership pool for regional and general life, the development of a process of discernment to enable a more effective public witness, and the General Commission on Ministry. These initiatives, and some others I have not mentioned, are all designed to help us, and *are* helping us, answer the five questions.

It would be nice if we could take all of these questions one at a time in proper order. At least that would seem nice to my pointed little white male head! But life is seldom linear in its arrangement or in its presentation of challenges (that's why life is so seldom convenient). The fact is that we simply have to address all of these issues at the same time. We must address them simultaneously, but with reference to each other. We are in the midst of a whirling universe of issues.

Negatively stated, we do not have "problems," we have a "mess"!

Positively stated, we have dynamic challenges!

"Systems theory," which I find very helpful, speaks of a life cycle in institutions. Institutions begin as movements and climb to a peak of energy and strength, then they plateau, and then they begin to decline. We are somewhere near a third of the way down the backside of the cycle. Some institutions slip on down to the bottom and either renew themselves, becoming a movement again, or they wink out of existence. It is interesting to note that among the Disciples' primary competition in the mid-1800s was the Shakers: Anybody know a Shaker these days?!

But declining institutions don't *have* to slide all the way to the bottom of the cycle. With an appropriate intervention, they can begin renewing themselves *before* going clear to the bottom. That's what we need! With the Holy Spirit's leadership and wisdom, we need to intervene *now* and begin our revitalization. Even if we do begin the intervention now (and we *have* begun it!), it will take us quite a while to see a quantitative turn around. But whether we see the numbers respond immediately or not, we will be coming back to life in essential ways: and we already see signs of this "coming back to life."

On a personal note, my Myers-Briggs profile indicates I am an ENFP. This means I have at least two serious personality drawbacks as GMP! (Two that I am willing to discuss, anyway!) First, being an extrovert, I have to talk out loud in order to know what I am thinking.

This can be downright inconvenient, as when, for example, I discover what I think as I am in the midst of responding to a question in a public forum where there are two or three hundred people present! I'd kind of like to know what I think *before* they do! This has led me to seek opportunities to "think out loud" with small groups of various kinds.

Second, being intuitive by nature, I often "know" things long before I can clearly articulate them. This sometimes makes it difficult for others to understand how I have arrived at certain conclusions, because I can't always tell them right away!

A third problem lies in the fact that I am a perfectionist. Because I want everything to be perfect before it goes into print, I find it excruciatingly difficult to let go of a manuscript. Preparing major addresses or position papers often sends me into a mild depression and results in near paralysis when it comes time to get anything down on paper. Fortunately, once I actually turn loose of a manuscript, this depressive paralysis is replaced by manic euphoria! (For me, life is more like a roller coaster than a box of chocolates!)

Since people tend to take what a person in this kind of role says too seriously to begin with, these personality characteristics can create problems for me and maybe for the church. However, I have developed a style and strategy that, when I remember to apply it, somewhat offsets these liabilities. This style or strategy is to focus on asking the right *questions* rather than trying to have all the right *answers*. I think this is a strategy which not only suits my personality but which is also an appropriate style for a GMP at this particular moment in our history. It isn't as "clean" and "neat" as having a GMP who always has clear answers to all our church's questions and needs.

It certainly isn't as much *fun* being this kind of GMP, because I am variously accused of being weak-kneed or weak-minded. But it may just be a gift to the church at this point in time as it will facilitate our answering the important questions before us *together*. I *pray* that it can be a gift to the church. I am convinced that the General Board and the Administrative Committee can be places where meaningful dialogue and planning can take place. We proved that in the restructured General Board meeting last summer and we'll prove it with productive work in this Administrative Committee meeting!

I want to thank you all for your commitment to this church and its future, and for the hard work you will be undertaking in this meeting. I thank God for you and for the opportunity to be with you as together we seek to find God's future for this great communion.

July 22, 1995

General Board

GMP Address to General Board

Good afternoon, Church! It is a great privilege to be with you in this my second General Board meeting as general minister and president.

I would like to take this occasion to bring you up to speed on some of the things that are in process as a way of contextualizing your work in these four days God has given us to be together. My staff and I have come to characterize these things in process as "tracks," as in train tracks.

Will Rogers used to say, "Even if y'er on the right track, if you don't move you'll get run over."

Some days I feel like I'm sitting up in the cab of a speeding locomotive with the wind blowing through my ... forehead. Some days I feel like a dispatcher trying to keep all the trains headed in the right direction and from running into each other. Many days I feel like my staff and I are out in front of these speeding trains trying to lay track as fast as the trains are moving so the trains don't get derailed and we don't get run over!

In any case, I'd like to identify ten tracks that are currently carrying trains at one speed or another.

Track #1 is the New Facilities Project.

I am delighted that you all will have the opportunity to see our new facilities. While many of our employees felt trepidation about leaving Missions Building, almost everyone now agrees that this was the right thing to do. We are spending less money for brighter and more efficient space. We are in the heart of a bustling city, which is energizing. Admittedly, it makes some of us uncomfortable when we pass the occasional homeless person or panhandler, but I think this too is good because it reminds us that we are here after all for mission.

This ten-year-long track is about to terminate as soon as we are able to sign over the Missions Building deed to the Retired Housing Foundation, which will be converting it into senior housing ... an appropriate and redemptive use for that structure and one which has been approved by the neighborhood. Hopefully, the deed will be signed over in August.

I want to take just a moment to recognize a person who gave the church such unselfish and excellent service as chair of the New Facilities Committee. Few people know how Lester (Palmer) serves this church in so many ways beyond being president of the Pension Fund. He just finished twenty-seven years of leading the General Board Task Force on Ministry. Lester, would you please stand and be recognized?

Track #2 is the Mission Imperatives.

It has been my conviction that this church, like all mainline churches, has in recent years been drifting in its sense of mission. In the absence of clarity about what it is God is calling us to do and to be in this time, we have subtly gravitated toward the kind of institutional survival mentality that is so deadly. Thus, my first priority as general minister and president has been to help us clarify and renew our sense of mission.

As part of this effort, one year ago you and I worked together to develop a Mission Imperatives Statement, based on listening and conversation with some seven hundred congregations. That document appears on page C-22 of your duplicated document. You'll notice that the form of the Statement has been changed just a bit (to make it "preach" better), but the content is exactly what this Board approved last summer. I hope you will recommend that document as it is now to the General Assembly.

Just last month I convened a Mission Imperatives Strategy Conference to look at how we can get these Mission Imperatives into the *heart* of the life of congregations, regions, general ministry units and other institutions. The report of that Conference is found on page C-70 of your duplicated document, and I think we succeeded in identifying some important core strategies. My primary concern is that the Mission Imperatives become *real* for us and not suffer the fate of the Priority of a few years ago: The Priority never died, it just faded away. I promise you that I plan to "stay in the church's face" about these Mission Imperatives until we make them real.

Someone suggested to me that "there is really nothing new in the Mission Imperatives." That's exactly right. They are as old as the New Testament and the only thing new would be if we began to do them seriously. I am convinced that they are on target and will lead us to greater health as a church if we will take them seriously.

Track #3 is the Vision Panel.

The Vision Panel began meeting almost a year ago and their preliminary report is found on page C-37 of your duplicated document. This report is really two documents: an "ethos statement" and a "structural imperatives" statement. These are not quite final drafts, so if you have suggestions about the language or concepts of either statement, I will be glad to receive them on behalf of the Vision Panel.

I believe these are shaping up to be extremely useful documents as we move toward some fundamental reorganization of our church life. I am most grateful to Kris Culp, David Cole, and Tony Dunnavant, who have given fine leadership to the Vision Panel.

That brings me to Track #4, which is reorganization.

I do not believe we need the kind of massive Restructure that we had in the 1960s because The Design is fundamentally sound. What we need to do might be more accurately defined as "finishing the task of Restructure now that some of the fears, vested interests and other human factors of 1968 have passed."

Of course, this "finishing the task of Restructure" must be done with full awareness that many things have changed in the culture since 1968, and must be set within the context of our mission in this new day. As important as efficiency is, we must reorder our structures around *mission*, *not* declining dollars.

It is also important to remember that in this day, and within this congregational polity, the quickest way to be sure that *no* reorganization would occur would be for us to come up with a big masterplan for the regional and general manifestation and publish it! Whatever change is needed will have to come about in mutual consultation and collegiality. No one can impose anything on any congregation, unit, or region. And yet, this reorganization must come swiftly, for in the midst of our inherited historical structures, we are facing financial and programmatic meltdown. Reorganization is not optional, but neither can it be coerced. I am happy to report that the General Cabinet is engaged in serious conversation about reordering and the College of Regional Ministers have appointed a group to begin that conversation as well.

I will admit that, coming into this office, I did not want to have to spend a lot of energy on organizational things. I wanted to be a pastor, devoting most of my time and energy to being a spiritual leader. But I quickly discovered anew that the church is incarnate, and it's very hard to focus on prayer or mission if your leg is broken and you have appendicitis! This means that as "pastor of the system," if I may use that phrase, it falls to me to give this "reorganization" strong leadership and to invest as much time and energy as it takes to shepherd new organizational forms into being. It also means that our regional and general institutional leaders must be in a creative leadership mode rather than a reactive mode, and this will represent a change for some.

We need fewer general ministry units, regions with more parity in terms of number of congregations and finances, and right sized plenary bodies such as General Board. But we must admit that it is not only the regional and general manifestations which need organizational renewal. There are no more outmoded structures than those found in some of our congregations. So many of our congregations have become so engaged in "church work" that they have no time or energy left to do the work of the church! But that's another subject.

Track #5 is the process of the Church Finance Council moving into the Office of General Minister and President.

While this idea was not mine, I have come to see that it makes great sense both from the standpoint of enhancing the work of each and in terms of dollars. I hope that you will fully endorse this move as it will lead the way in organizational renewal. And I must say that as we have been working more closely together in recent months, it is a real joy to have Robert Welsh working as a colleague within the Office of GMP. The enabling business item is found on page C-86.

Track #6 is the Proposed Mission Funding System.

I believe this proposal must be given a chance. There are some unanswered questions, of course, but I believe we will have to "live into" any system. The proposal now before us is general enough to adjust to the organizational changes that will be developing in the near future, but specific enough that it constitutes a unified system. I do not wish to be overly dramatic, but the failure to develop and to participate within a unified system would mean utter chaos and the end of "whole church."

So, after all these years of conversation and debate, unless someone has a new concept that better serves the wholeness of the church, I say let's get on with it and take the actions recommended on page C-47 of your duplicated docket.

Track #7 is a churchwide communication strategy.

Our new director of communication, Curt Miller, is working collegially with communications people in general ministry units and institutions of higher education, with regional ministers and pastors of congregations, and with communications professionals in and out of the church to develop such a strategy. We are looking at how best we might hook up our congregations with each other and the rest of the church. The technology by which we may establish a practical network among ourselves is now within financial reach. But more challenging than hardware or software, is having something worth transmitting when you have the network in place! This is a great challenge but promises to help us again to tap into such resources as, for example, are represented in our seminary and college faculties. It promises to help us effectively network resources across congregational lines, across *all kinds* of lines and boundaries and barriers.

Track #8 is the development of a coordinated and constructive approach to public witness.

I have called into being a group called the Public Issues Coordinating Council (or PICC). This group is made up of representatives from each of the general ministry units and offices that has traditionally been involved in public issues. Thus, there are representatives from Homeland Ministries, Overseas Ministries, the NBA, the Week of Compassion, the Office of Reconciliation, the Office of GMP, and the National Hispanic Pastor, and the coordinator of American Asian Ministries.

The purpose of the Council is *not* to make public statements. Rather, the group is to provide coordination of efforts between offices and units and advice and counsel as to which issues we might want to address as a church and how. Each participating group retains the right, of course, to make their own statements and actions from time to time, but we want to work together in a spirit of whole church in whatever ways we can. I believe this will help us do public witness in a much more effective and creative way.

The development of the "Process of Discernment" is also a part of this track, and my revised report on this effort is found on page C-1. I have deeply appreciated the comments, suggestions, and encouragement I have received from all around the church in the development of this concept.

While we're on the subject of public witness, there are two policy items, found on pages C-15 and C-26, which reflect different approaches to where and how our public witness will be focused. Section II will have to help us by bringing clear recommendations in this regard.

Track #9 is the General Commission on Ministry.

The General Commission on Ministry was mandated by this board in, I believe, 1993. This is a desperately needed structure that will provide coordination of policies and resourcing of regional commissions on ministry. There are a host of ministerial issues that have needed addressing for so many years, but the old General Board Task Force on Ministry just did not have the time or money to tackle those issues. This new Commission, which is being funded out of the Adjustment Fund until the new mission funding system is in place, has had its first meeting and will be meeting twice a year for three days each time. This will come as especially good news to ministers who have wanted, for example, to see problems with the relocation system addressed.

Track #10 is the development of an effective planning process for the General Board.

The Design charges the General Board with establishing procedures whereby the church may engage in planning its total program of work and witness. Before Restructure, the planning function was fulfilled by the old Home and State Missions Planning Council. But the General Board has never effectively done this. The problem has not been the leadership, or the Board members, but the absence of structures and processes within the Board to enable such planning. With the encouragement I received this morning from the Administrative Committee, and in consultation with the Standing Committee on Renewal and Structural Reform, I will bring a specific proposal to the Administrative Committee in January regarding how this responsibility of the General Board might be more effectively achieved. This coupled with the board's working in ten sections rather than five will greatly enhance our effectiveness.

These then are ten tracks of change for which my office and this board bear heavy responsibility. There are other things in the works, but these are of immediate concern.

There are other important issues to be considered in this board meeting, of course. The COCU action, found on page 236 of the printed docket, and the Mutual Recognition and Reconciliation of Ministries with the United Church of Christ, found on page C-18 of the duplicated document, are important steps forward in our ecumenical journey. The policy item from the National Convocation regarding new African American congregations, found on page C-28, contains information that should be disturbing to all of us and presents us with an important challenge.

We have a lot of very important business before us in this meeting and before us as a church for the next several years. As I wrote to ministers in The Ministers' Bulletin this spring, "The measure of our success in all of this will be whether we are enhancing God's mission: in and through regional, general, and educational institutions, but *especially* in and through congregations."

While we face tremendous pressures and problems in these days, every one of these pressures and problems represent a healthy challenge which, if met in a timely and prayerful fashion, will help lead us toward greater faithfulness as a church.

It is easy to obsess over difficulties, to become depressed and hopeless. But that would be faithlessness. We must know that God is doing new things among us and, as painful as that can be at the points where we need to change, it is also life-giving and renewing! God has not left us alone to struggle with our challenges: God is with us, leading, empowering, encouraging, inspiring! Thus, I say to you, though the challenges that face us have institutional and structural implications, they are not in and of themselves primarily institutional or structural. They are *spiritual*!

We are in a time I like to call The Refiner's Fire, in which we are finding new clarity of mission and identity. As always, our hope is in God, and God is dependable. If we are faithful to what God is calling us to do and to be in this new day, our future will be bright.

Thank you for giving of your time and talent to serve Christ's church in this way. I hope you are as excited as am I about the new day we are entering with all its challenges and possibilities. We really are in the springtime of our life together as the Christian Church (Disciples of Christ).

I began by saying, "Good afternoon, Church." In the light of God's grace and the many new ways we see God moving among us, let me close by saying, "Good morning, Church!"

May 2003

"Mobilizing for Mission"

A Word of Appreciation

I deeply appreciate the opportunity to have served in the role of General Minister and President these ten years. I have met so many interesting people, seen so many wondrous places, participated in so many historic events, and been able to do ministry in so many ways that never would have been possible otherwise. I am truly grateful for God's call to this role and the church's trust in confirming that call twice. I have felt personally supported by so many Disciple friends, colleagues, and strangers, who have held me and my family in prayer and who have extended so many acts of kindness and friendship. This will bless me all my days.

> I will stand at my watch post, and station myself on the rampart; I will keep watch to see what he will say to me, and what he will answer concerning my complaint. Then the Lord answered me and said: "Write the vision; make it plain on tablets, so that a runner may read it. For there is still a vision for the appointed time; it speaks of the end, and does not lie. If it seems to tarry, wait for it; it will surely come, it will not delay!" (Habakkuk 2:1–3)

Around 600 BC, things were pretty much coming unglued in Judah. The rich were oppressing the poor, the nation of Judah was growing weaker every day while the Babylonians were growing stronger. Thus, Judah was faced with the same fate that had befallen Israel at the hands of the Assyrians a hundred years before. The people of God were religiously and morally bewildered.

In the face of this frightening situation, the prophet Habakkuk asks, "How long do we have to cry for help before you actually help?" It is an understandable question. It is a question with which we might identify. "How long will bad things happen to good people?" And in regard to this church we wonder, "When will Disciples start growing again?" "When are mission offerings going to start going up again?" "When will we again be able to speak a prophetic word to this society and be heard?"

God essentially gives three answers to these kinds of questions. The first answer is, "Write the vision: make it plain." That is, discern a clear picture of where you are going, get it clear enough that even those distracted and in a hurry can read and understand it.

The second response is, "God is faithful." That which God has envisioned for us will surely come because God is faithful. Though every human thing does and will fail, God is faithful. Judah's hope was not in the sword, but in the Lord. Our hope for this church is not in our boards ... but in our Lord! Thanks be to God who works *even through our boards*. God is so powerful that the Spirit was able to birth a vision for this church through the efforts of the General Board ... a board that, with two hundred and twenty-five members, is larger than most of our congregations.

Our hope is in the Lord, indeed! God is faithful, and so we dare to hope for a renewed church that is itself a "faithful, growing church that demonstrates true community, deep Christian spirituality, and a passion for justice" ... a church that brings real gifts to the whole world and to the whole body of Jesus Christ, the church universal.

But God gives Habakkuk, and we children of Habakkuk, a third answer. God says, "That which you regard as trouble is actually an instrument of the change I am bringing." This is a hard word. When things go badly for us, and for our church, we want God to take up for us. The last thing we want to hear is that God is inflicting troubles upon us, or allowing our troubles to come upon us ... even if it is in order to help bring about our salvation. This is not the kind of leaven we want in our loaf! But my own life experience has taught me this lesson: I seldom change before I have to change. And so, very often, that which we regard as "trouble" is actually an instrument of the change God is bringing. The harder our hearts, the harder our heads, the more trouble is required to bring about the change God desires.

Those of us who are called to be lay and ordained leaders of this church (generally, regionally, and congregationally) should be among the first to understand what God is seeking to do among us: the first to see it, the first to proclaim it, the first to participate in and to lead the change. Like the faithful prophet Habakkuk, we should be standing in our watch post, stationed on the rampart, craning our necks to see and understand what God is doing.

As leaders we confess that we, too, get distracted by the troubles we see around us. Fear and anxiety creep in when we see the decline in our membership that has continued unabated since 1968. Fear and anxiety set up camp when we see general units and regions cutting back their ministries in the face of decreases in giving to the Disciples Mission Fund and when we see the pool of leadership becoming so shallow. We long for the days when our church, like all mainline churches, grew and our position and influence in the culture were great. We get tired and feel beaten down. All of us who are called to be leaders sometimes fall asleep at our post, or turn on each other seeking places to lay blame, or hide in our organizational fortresses of structure. Thus, we sometimes put our faith in the ramparts themselves rather than in the One who breaks down walls of fear, anxiety, and hostility.

But God is faithful! There is still a Vision for the appointed time, and it does not lie! If the Vision seems to tarry, wait for it ... it will surely come, it will not delay! If we have eyes with which to see and ears with which to hear, we will see that it is beginning to be realized among us even now. Even our troubles are a harbinger of the change God is seeking to work in us Disciples! Thanks be to God.

The vision that God has laid before us is "to be a faithful, growing church that demonstrates true community, deep Christian spirituality and a passion or justice."

Some people think we cannot be both a "faithful church" and a "growing church." In fact, some people think that if a congregation is growing, it probably means it is not faithful, that it has sold out in order to attract people. I hear this especially from people who belong to declining congregations.

In reality, a congregation that demonstrates true community, deep Christian spirituality and a passion for justice is irresistible! This is what people today admit they want most ... they want to be part of a caring community, they want to be in relationship with God, and they want to be part of a community that is making a difference in the world.

This is the *qualitative* challenge of the Vision and, through it, God is nurturing the integrity and growth of this communion, the Christian Church (Disciples of Christ). We have also embraced four *quantitative* challenges out of the Vision and are challenged, by 2020, to start a thousand new congregations, to revitalize a thousand of our existing congregations, to develop the leaders necessary to make this possible, and to become an anti-racist/pro-reconciling church. These goals seemed absurdly large to many Disciples who feel weighted down by the conflict and decline of the past 35 years. There are others who feel that the Vision is not broad enough or that it is otherwise off-target and thus not worthy of support. But there is excellent news to report.

New Congregation Establishment

While we Disciples had been starting five or six new congregations annually, in the first two years of 2020 Vision we started one hundred and sixteen. This says two things: One, setting goals is in itself powerful and, two, the Holy Spirit is indeed in this.

Usually, the Yearbook doesn't count congregations until they are officially chartered, which normally takes a couple of years. But if we count all these new congregations which are now actually meeting and serving, 2002 is the first year since the mid-1960s that we finished the year with more Disciples congregations than we had the year before.

This matters! It matters that there are more Disciples congregations rather than fewer, because this denomination brings value to the whole Church of Jesus Christ. When Disciples are at our best, we bring a unique combination of core values: liberty, Christian unity, restoration, and mission.[5] We hold faith and reason together in a way that is especially important in this postmodern era. We are salt and leaven to the whole body. It matters that we start new congregations that embody the best of our Disciples core values.

Revitalization of Congregations

The reason congregations decline, usually, is because they turn away from mission, turn in on themselves and become more

---

[5] Anthony Dunnavant, *Restructure: Four Historical Ideals in the Campbell-Stone Movement and the Development of the Polity of the Christian Church (Disciples of Christ)* (Peter Lang Publishing, 1993).

concerned about conserving and preserving what they have than about the needs of those in and beyond the congregation. Thus, they become increasingly inflexible, often redoubling their efforts, but "trusting in the ramparts" and becoming "fortresses of the way things were." While people often think of revitalization as a matter of financial grants being made to struggling congregations, my experience has been that grants only hasten their demise. Why? Because an influx of money simply makes it possible for the congregation to avoid needed change for a while longer. This is a hard word, but true.

The life blood of the church (congregationally, regionally, and generally) is forever mission. Jesus said, "Whoever seeks to save their live will lose it, but whoever loses their life for my sake shall find it." These words of Jesus are as true for institutions (including congregations, regions, and whole denominations) as for individuals. Focusing on survival only hastens an institution's demise.

The work of revitalizing congregations (and regions, general units, and denominations) is usually long-term and very challenging. It may be the hardest work in the church. Both inertia and momentum must be overcome. But the Holy Spirit is always present calling the church to mission.

Leadership Development

The third goal is to develop the leadership necessary for a thousand new congregations and a thousand revitalized congregations. Both lay and ordained leadership is crucial.

We are currently ordaining an average of ninety Disciples ministers annually. We need to ordain about two hundred and thirty annually to provide the leadership needed. The good news is that mainline theological institutions have the capacity (though not always the financial means). Many middle-aged people are considering ministry as a second career, and they often bring good and important experience from their previous work lives. Also, from what I see at youth gatherings and at an increasing number of events held for the specific purpose of encouraging young people to consider ministry, the current "crop" of young people is one of the most impressive we have seen for some time. Their first question is most often not, "How can I make the most money?" but, "What can I do with my life that will have meaning and significance?"

There has been a significant increase in the number of events designed to raise the level of interest in ministry as vocation. Fifty years ago, the culture held up ministry as a high status, significant vocation. Today, the culture largely ignores ministry or depicts it as silly. Thus, the church must take responsibility for encouraging people to consider ministry and for helping people prepare.

As a result of a grant made two years ago by the Mission Council from the Mission Imperative Fund, a major consultation is occurring this month to develop a more effective and collaborative approach to recruiting and supporting licensed ministry. This promises to be a signal event.

Anti-Racist/Pro-Reconciling Initiative

The census people tell us that by the year 2030, there will be no single racial/ethnic group that comprises as much as fifty percent of the population of the United States. If we understand that our mission is "from our doorsteps to the ends of the earth," then our congregations must cease to think of themselves as "parishes"[6] and begin to see themselves as mission stations for a mission that is both local and global.[7] Our congregations are on the local "front line" of the mission. This means that, if we are faithful and effective in this mission of outreach, the demographics of our church should begin to mirror the demographics of our home mission field (North America). If this is not the case, then we are not taking seriously all the people who live among us. Currently, this church is composed of people who are nearly ninety-three percent Euro-American. Thus, we have a long way to go to become demographically congruent with our home mission field. But how can we grow in racial/ethnic diversity as a church unless we are an anti-racist/pro-reconciling faith community?

---

[6] A term that refers to the legally established churches of some European nations. A nation was divided into small geographic areas called "parishes" and "parish churches" were established in each. The assumption was that one would be a part of the church of the parish in which he or she was living. Thus, one would be baptized in the parish church, married there, and ultimately buried there. This is very far from the American experience in which people who are church goers will drive past many churches in order to be part of one that they feel meets their needs.

[7] Dale Fiers, first general minister and president and one who is oft regarded as "the father of The Design," says that the test of success for the Restructure of the church is whether "each congregation comes to see itself as a headquarters for global mission."

The good news is that the anti-racism/pro-reconciling initiative is well under way. Most general units and regions now have anti-racism teams that have been trained, and we are now preparing our own "core trainers." The congregational phase will begin this year. In addition, since the General Board's 1999 adoption of an "Open Executive Search Process," we are seeing much greater diversity in regional and general church leadership. For example, there are now four African American regional ministers, while ten years ago there were none. Of eleven general unit presidents, there are now two racial/ethnic persons (an African American and a Hispanic) instead of none. There are now two associate general ministers who are African American instead of one. We have a long way to go, but this represents real progress.

Between 1968 and today, the church has spent a lot of precious energy in conflict and hand-wringing. I believe the "way out" of our anxiety has been and is to commit ourselves to the mission and to the vision that God has laid before us. We Disciples are problem solvers of the first order but, as much as we may want to, we cannot merely organize ourselves into renewal. As with the revitalization of individual congregations, our whole church will be revitalized only as we resist the temptation to become preoccupied with ourselves, our structures, our systems, our "ramparts" and focus instead on our mission and vision.

Recommendations

Therefore, my first recommendation is that the church select a general minister and president who is committed to both the qualitative and quantitative aspects of the vision and who understands the primary task to be nurturing, promoting, and interpreting the vision. There are other issues that need to be addressed, of course, and the day-to-day work of the GMP must be continued. However, there is no more important focus than the vision God has given us and that has been adopted by the General Board and General Assembly. Furthermore, make this work a mandate for the new GMP.

A "mandate" is an important way in which to empower a leader. Without a mandate (a clear, officially approved statement of what the leader is expected to accomplish), a leader is unable to approach delicate matters or to address core issues except by strength of personality or political skill. But personality and political skill are often inadequate in the face of turf and other powerful issues. While a general minister and president can define in large measure how she/he will serve, it is much more difficult to define one's authority: The church must do this. One way to define authority is through a clear mandate.

Of course, this recommendation assumes that the GMP should be a leader and not merely a manager. While leadership always involves management, my experience has been that a large amount of the GMP's time and energy is consumed trying to manage various organizational and political forces that could more effectively and efficiently be addressed by some adjustments (most rather minor) in our governance.

When a regular search committee is appointed to seek a candidate for a full-term GMP, I strongly urge that the search committee create a job description for the GMP. A mandate describes what the GMP is expected to accomplish in the course of his/her term, a job description has more to do with the regular work of the office and describes the kind of day-to-day leadership expected of the GMP. Like the mandate, this is also a way of clarifying authority.

In the face of the urgent matters we need to address within our own life as a church, it would perhaps be tempting to focus the work of the GMP within this communion only. However, I strongly urge that such a job description continue the involvement of the GMP in the church ecumenical. Besides expressing a fundamental core value of who we are as a church, the exposure to the wider church is a constant source of his/her continuing education and inspiration. As Disciples, we share the same cultural context with every other church in North America and we share the same global mission with every other church in the world. I have found my involvements (always in partnership with our ecumenical officer, the president of the Council on Christian Unity) to be essential to understanding this church's own context and mission.

There are governance issues that keep us from moving boldly toward our mission and vision, and these need to be addressed while the primary focus should remain on nurturing the vision. I would not tie up the general minister and president in too much work on governance issues. While his/her ongoing counsel will naturally be helpful (since the GMP lives with the polity daily), this work should be carried out primarily by a group designated for the specific purpose. Whatever group is charged with this responsibility should include some of our finest thinkers/leaders/scholars. This group should be given a mandate to review our governance and to bring solid recommendations that will better enable leadership and that will better position the denomination for mission and the fulfillment of the vision. While a mandate does not mean that their work will automatically be accepted, it does give them authority to engage in the work and implies that some change is truly needed and expected.

Issues to be addressed by a "governance review group" would include (1) bringing our practices, relationships, and structures into congruence with the theology/ecclesiology of The Design, especially in regard to "covenant"; (2) how the accountability of general units and regions to the church's plenary bodies can be satisfactorily lived out so that integrity and ownership remain high; (3) the often apparent lack of congruence between formal and informal authority; (4) the size and function of our plenary bodies (especially the general board); (5) the role and authority of the GMP; (6) the role and composition of the General Cabinet; (7) the role and authority of associate general ministers; and (8) the number and function of regions, general units, and plenary bodies.

In addition, amendment of The Design currently requires a seventy-five-percent vote by the general assembly. It is difficult to get seventy-five percent of Disciples to agree on anything. A motion to amend The Design to require only a two-thirds majority to amend was brought to the 1999 General Assembly (9928), but received only seventy-four percent of the vote. Change is always difficult, but never more so than in a time of universal anxiety such as that which reigns in our culture today. Anxiety always resists change and always supports systemic homeostasis. In order to pave the way for reforms in governance that may be brought by a "governance review group" and the General Board for consideration at the 2005 General Assembly and beyond, I recommend that such an amendment to The Design be proposed again to the 2003 General Assembly.

As stated in my letter of resignation, I am not discouraged. Though I believe it is time for me to move on to other forms of ministry, I remain enthusiastic about the role of general minister and president and will be actively praying and working to support whoever succeeds me. I will also be actively working and praying for general unit colleagues, regional minister colleagues, and the myriad of other leaders, lay and ordained, within all three manifestations with whom it has been my distinct pleasure and privilege to serve. I believe in the work of our general and regional ministries. I believe in higher education institutions that maintain their core values through continued relationship with the church.

I remain unswerving in my conviction that the Christian Church (Disciples of Christ) is a church for just such a time as this. I remain convinced that "strengthening congregations for mission" is a primary role of the regional and general manifestations. I believe this church ought to grow for the sake of God's mission and ministry to the world, and I believe we will because we are being driven more and more by the vision.

May we let go of our grief for the time when we were larger and more prosperous, release ourselves from trying to be the church of thirty-five years ago, and embrace the opportunities for service and mission that God is setting before us now. Let us fully and faithfully live out the vision and thus be a sign of God's presence and grace in today's world.

I've been on the rampart for these ten years, at my watch post, and I've seen the church God wants us to become: It is a wondrous and beautiful thing to behold. As I wrote in *2020 Vision for the Christian Church (Disciples of Christ)*,

> "I see a church that looks a lot like what The Design of the Christian Church (Disciples of Christ) describes. We restructured ourselves in 1968 on the basis of covenant. I believe we still need to develop our understanding of covenant and the realization of a covenant community. We need to move from what often looks like a culture of autonomy to a culture of dependence upon God's Spirit and interdependence with each other.
>
> I see a church that is clear about the Gospel: that God was in Christ reconciling the world to himself, not counting their trespasses against them, and entrusting the message of reconciliation to us.
>
> I see a church that is clear about what it means to be the church: not a club or a mere social organization, but the body of Christ.

I see a church that is faithful to its mission to be and to share the good news of Jesus Christ, witnessing, loving and serving from our doorsteps to the ends of the earth.

I see a church that is less focused on survival and has developed a passion for mission.

I see a church that faithfully and effectively addresses the post-modern world, effectively teaching children and youth, and that has begun reaching Generation X and Y in significant numbers.

I see a church whose ministers have moved the focus of their ministry from management to modeling relationship with God, a church whose ministers are giving authentic Disciples spiritual leadership and who are not burned out or depressed but who are energized, joy filled, and Spirit led.

I see a church that values diversity, welcomes difference, and embraces unity as a sign of God's love for all peoples and cultures and that has recaptured its commitment to the unity of all Christians as a sign and a foretaste of God's good news to a broken and hostile world.

I see a church that has faced up to its bigotry and racism and has begun to live its justice pronouncements with integrity.

I see a church whose general and regional assemblies reinforce our sense of family, resource our congregations' life and mission, and give us joyous encouragement as we worship God together.

I see a church in which we engage in serious biblical, theological, and moral discernment, acting boldly and faithfully on what we discern while maintaining the unity of the Spirit in the bond of peace.

I see a church in which our leadership is forging vibrant new covenantal partnerships across old rigid bureaucratic boundaries that have tied us down and kept us focused on our past rather than on God's possibilities for our future.

And yes, I see a church that is growing spiritually and numerically.

I believe we are exactly the kind of church people of this generation are looking for! No leader today knows exactly what the future holds or exactly how God will get us to it. But I believe we have enough clarity to understand that God has an important place for us in the new world, in the new millennium, and that we will get there if we move with faithfulness and commitment.

How long will it be before we become this vision?
How long? Not long! We can see it unfolding in our midst even now. It does not tarry."[8]

---

[8] Richard L. Hamm, *2020 Vision for the Christian Church (Disciples of Christ)* (Christian Board of Publication, 2001), pp. 134–135.

www.ingramcontent.com/pod-product-compliance
Lightning Source LLC
Chambersburg PA
CBHW052044220426
43663CB00012B/2440